The War in the East

Japan, China and Corea

BATTLE FILED OF PING-YANG

The War in the East
Japan, China and Corea

A complete history of the War: Its causes and results; its campaigns on sea and land; its terrific fights, grand victories and overwhelming defeats.

With a preliminary account of the customs, habits and history of the three peoples involved. Their cities, arts, sciences, amusements and literature.

by

Trumbull White
Late Correspondent of the
"North China Daily News." and the "Kobe Herald."

With an Introduction by
Julius Kumpei Matumoto, A.M. (of Tokio, Japan)

With Illustrations by
Teitoku Morimoto, J.C. Fireman,

First published **1885**

Lancer • New Delhi • Frankfort, IL
www.lancerpublishers.com

LANCER

Published in the United States by

The Lancer International Inc
19558 S. Harlem Ave., Suite 1,
Frankfort, IL. 60423.

First published in India by

Lancer Publishers & Distributors
2/42 (B) Sarvapriya Vihar,
New Delhi-110016

© This edition Lancer 2011

Printed and bound in India.

ISBN-13: 978-1-935501-08-4 • ISBN-10: 1-935501-08-9

Online Military Bookshop
www.lancerpublishers.com

IDR Net Edition
www.indiandefencereview.com

PREFACE

Some striking act in a man's career is necessary to attract general attention to him. The one who moves along through his path in life doing nothing out of the ordinary, will win few glances from the public, and little will the world notice his existence. Worthy of the worthiest he may be, but if he does nothing to demonstrate it, how shall the world know his merit or his strength? But with all this true, it does not follow that it is man's duty to seek an occasion to advertise these qualities. Only when the necessity for action arises, then should he act, and then will the world know what his ability and character are.

The same is true as to the nations of the earth. Those yearn during which they move onward in their national life and history in peace and quietness, however full of latent strength they may be, are not the ones which command the attention of the eyes of the world. It is the year of supreme test, of struggle, moral or physical, that furnishes crucial testimony what the nation really is. War is always a curse unless it be waged to advance justice and assure more worthy peace. But if such a war be necessary, the progress of it, the results, and the lessons they teach are essential to the student of humanity, in whatever quarter of the globe the battles are.

China, Japan and Corea are a strange trinity to most of us in the western world. Separated from us by long distances and by immense differences in race, in language, in religion, and in customs, they have been known here only through the writings of the comparatively few travelers who exchange visits. Of late years, it is true, the hermitages of the Orient have been opening to freer intercourse, trade and treaties have multiplied, and students have come to us for the knowledge we could give them. But there was needed a great movement of some sort to awaken the Orient from its centuries of slumber, and to make known to us the truth of eastern affairs. Nothing could do this as the War in the East has done. We can study its conduct and its results if we will, in a way to teach us more of the characteristics of the three nations than we could learn in any other way.

It has been the object of the author in the present volume, to record the facts of the war and its preliminaries so clearly that every seeker for knowledge might trace the lessons for himself. To justify this effort, it is necessary to say no more than that the conflict involves directly nations whose total population includes more than one-fourth of the human race. And the result will affect the progress of civilization in those countries, as well as the commercial and other interests of all the European and American nations.

Invertebrate China; with scorn of western methods, and complacent rest in the belief that all but her own people are barbarians, had to face an inevitable war with Japan, the sprightly, absorbent, adaptive, western-spirited, whose career in the two score years since her doors were opened to the call of the American Perry has been the marvel of those who knew it. And the conflict was to be on the soil of the Hermit Nation, Corea, "the Land of Morning Calm," for centuries the land of contention between the "Day's Beginning" and "the Middle Kingdom."

It is to record the history and description of these realms and peoples in sufficient detail to make plainer the facts of the war that the preliminary chapters are written. The work must speak for itself. The importance of the subjects included in the volume must be the explanation of any inadequacy of treatment.

TRUMBULL WHITE

TABLE OF CONTENTS

PART IV — THE WAR BETWEEN JAPAN AND CHINA

ILLUSTRATIONS

INTRODUCTION

The unexpected news of war between the Mikado's Empire and the Celestial Kingdom has startled the whole world. Thereby considerable light was thrown upon the Oriental world.

Japan, up to a very short time ago, through the pen and tongue of poets and artists, who have visited this land, has been thought to be merely a country of beautiful flowers, charming mademoiselles, fantastic parasols, fans and screens. Such misrepresentation has long impressed the western mind, and the people hardly imagined Japan as a political power, enlightened by a perfect educational system and developed to a high pitch of excellence in naval and military arts.

The war in the East is certainly interesting from more than one point of view. Viewing it from the humane standpoint, Japan is, indeed, the true standard-bearer of civilization and progress in the far east. Her mission is to enlighten the millions of slumbering souls in the Celestial Kingdom, darkened for generations. Politically, she, with her enterprising genius, youthful courage and alert brain, as well as the art and science of civilization, has lifted herself into the ranks of the most powerful nations of the earth, and compelled the whole of the western powers to reckon her as a "living force," as she has proved her right to a proud place among the chief powers of the world. Commercially, she has demonstrated herself the mistress of the Pacific and Asiatic Seas.

From the outbreak of the war all the civilized nations, except England, have sympathized with Japan, especially the people of America have given a strong moral support to Japan, not because this country is the warmest friend of Japan, but because Japan is, to-day, the propagandist of civilization and humanity in the far east.

At the beginning of the hostilities a majority of the people had an erroneous idea that the overwhelming population and resources of China would soon be able to crush the Island Empire of Japan; but they overlooked the fact that in our day it is science, brains and courage, together with the perfected organization of warfare that grasp the palm of victory. Thousands of sheep could do nothing against a ferocious wolf. So the numerical comparison has but little weight.

Some sagacious writer compared Japan to a lively swordfish and China to a jellyfish, being punctured at every point. Truly Japan has proved it so.

From the sinking of the Kow-shing transport, up to the present time, Japan has an unbroken series of victories over China. At the battle of Asan she gained the first brilliant victories and swept all the Chinese out of Corea, and at Ping-Yang, by both tactics and superb strategy, crushed the best army of China, which Li Hung Chang brought up to the greatest efficiency, by the aid of many European officers, as if it had been all egg shell. Again, at the mouth of the Yalu River, she gained a brilliant naval victory over China, by completely destroying the Ping-Yang squadron. Once more on the land the Japanese army stormed Port Arthur, the strongest naval fort, known as the Gibraltar of China.

All these facts are viewed with amazement by the eyes of the world. For all that the people know about Japan and the Japanese is that the people of Japan are very artistic, as the producers of beautiful porcelain, embroidery, lacquer work and all sorts of artistic fancy goods, and they wonder how it is possible that such an artistic people as the Japanese could fight against sober, calm Chinamen. But such an erroneous notion would soon vanish if they came to learn the true nature and character of the Japanese.

More than once the world has seen that an artistic nation could fight. The Greeks demonstrated this long ago, and the French in the later times have shown a shining example. Japan is reckoned as one of the most artistic people in the world, as the producer of beautiful things, as the lover of fine arts and natural beauties. The Japanese have proved the same as what the ancient Greeks and modern French have shown. The history of Japan reveals the true color of the Japanese as brilliant fighters and a warlike nation. "In no country," says Mr. Rogers, "has military instinct been more pronounced in the best blood of the people. Far back in the past, beyond that shadowy line where legend and history blend, their story has been one of almost continual war, and the straightest path to distinction and honor has, from the earliest times, led across the battle field. The statesmen of Japan saw, as did Cavour, that the surest way to win the respect of nations was by success in war."

The ancestor of the Japanese people, who claim to have descended from high heaven, seems to have been the descendant of the ancient Hittites, the warlike and conquering tribe once settled in the plain of Mesopotamia. The Hittites, so far as our investigation is concerned, extending their sway of conquest towards the north-eastern portion of Asia, must have, at last, brought the Japanese family to the island of Japan. As they settled on the island, they found it inhabited by many different tribes; but they soon vanquished them and established the everlasting foundation of the Mikado's Empire, which they called the "Glorious Kingdom of Military Valour." The first Mikado was Jimmu, whose coronation took place two thousand five hundred and fifty-four years ago, long before Alexander the Great thought he had conquered the world and Julius Caesar entered Gaul. The present Mikado is the one hundred and twenty-second lineal descendant of the first Mikado Jimmu. The unbroken dynasty of the Mikado has continued for twenty-five centuries. The people are brave, adventurous and courageous. Fanatical patriotism for country and strong loyalty towards the Mikado are essential characteristics of the Japanese people. And all these tend to form the peculiar nationality of Japan. Since the establishment of the Mikado's Empire their land has never been defiled by invaders and they have never known how to be subject to a foreign yoke. The history of Japan is the pride of the Japanese people.

The Japanese, in an early time, have displayed their superior courage and distinguished themselves from the rest of the Asiatic nations in the point of military affairs.

In the year A.D. 201 the Empress Jingo, the greatest female character in the Japanese history, undertook a gigantic expedition to the Asiatic continent. She assembled an immense army and built a great navy. Placing herself as the commander-in-chief of the invading army, she sailed for the continent. Her victory was brilliant. Corea was at once subjected without any bloodshed. Long since the Japanese power was established on the Asiatic continent.

Again in the sixteenth century, ambitious Taiko, who is known as the Napoleon of Japan, undertook a great continental expedition, to show the military glory of Japan before the world. He found Japan too small to satisfy his immoderate ambition, and sent word to the emperor of China and the king of Corea that if they would not hear him, he would invade their territory with his invincible army. It was his plan to divide the four hundred provinces of China and eight provinces of Corea among his generals in fiefs, after conquering them. So he assembled his generals and fired their enthusiasm, recounting their exploits mutually achieved. All the generals and soldiers were delighted with the expedition. Fifty thousand samurai were embarked for the continent and sixty thousand reserve was kept ready in Japan as re-enforcement.

The Japanese army was everywhere victorious. After many battles fought and fortresses stormed, the entire kingdom of Corea was subdued. The capitol was taken, the king fled. The emperor of China sent an army forward against the Japanese and a severe battle was fought. The victorious Japanese were on the point of invading China. When in 1598, the death of Taiko was announced and the Japanese government ordered the invading army to return home. Peace was concluded. Thus the conquest of China was frustrated.

The invasion of the Mongolian-Tartars is the most memorable event in Japanese history, which excited the utmost patriotism and valour of the nation. The dangers and glories at this time will never be forgotten by the Japanese.

In the thirteenth century, Genghis Khan, who is now identified as Minamoto Yoshitsune or Gen Gi Kei in Japanese history, who left Japan for Manchilia, began his sway of conquest in Mongolia. The conquest of the whole earth was promised him. He vanquished China, Corea and the whole of Central and Northern Asia, subjected India and overthrew the Caliphate of Bagdad. In Europe, he made subject the entire dominion of Russia and extended the Mongolian Empire as far as the Oder and the Danube. After his death the Empire was divided among his three sons. Kublai Khan received as his share North-eastern Asia He had completely overthrown the Sung dynasty of China and founded the Mongolian dynasty. He placed the whole of Eastern Asia under his yoke, and then sent envoys to Japan, demanding tributes and homage. The nation of Japan was indignant at the insolent demand, for they were never accustomed to such treatment, and dismissed them in disgrace. Six embassies were sent and six times rejected. Again, the haughty Mongolian prince sent nine envoys, who demanded a definite answer from the Japanese sovereign. The Japanese reply was given by cutting off their heads.

At the sight of imminent foreign invasion, the Japanese were in a great hurry to prepare for war. Once more, and for the last time, Chinese envoys came to demand tribute; again the sword gave the answer. Enraged, the great Mongolian prince prepared a gigantic armada to crush the island of Japan, which had refused homage and tribute to the invincible conqueror. The army, consisting of one hundred thousand Chinese and Tartars and seven thousand Coreans, aided by thirty-five hundred of armed navy, that seemed to cover the entire seas, sailed for the invasion in August of 1281. The whole nation of Japan now roused with sword in hand and marched against its formidable foe. Re-enforcements poured in from all quarters to swell the host of defenders. The fierce Mongolian force could not effect their landing, but were driven into the sea as soon as they reached the shore. Aided by a mighty typhoon, before which the Chinese armada was utterly helpless, the Japanese fiercely attacked the invaders and after a bloody struggle, they succeeded in destroying the enemy's war ships, and killing all or driving them into the sea to be drowned. The corpses were piled on the shore or floating on the water so thickly that it seemed almost possible to walk thereon. Only three out of hundreds of thousands of invaders, were sent back to tell their emperor how the brave men of Japan had destroyed their armada.

The courage of the Japanese is fully manifested in these great events. Many ambitious men, seeking for military glory, have expatriated themselves from their won native lands, and gone off to the less warlike countries of Asia, where they found themselves by their distinguished courage and military genius, kings, ministers and generals.

The Japanese seamen have long been renowned for their adventurous spirit and audacity. Trading ships of Japan, in the remotest ancient age, are said to have sailed around the Persian Gulf, beyond the Indian seas. It is said that at the beginning of the fourteenth century a Japanese junk had discovered the American Pacific sea-coast, now known as the regions of Oregon and California. For a long time the Japanese pirates were the mistress of all the eastern seas. China, Siam, Birmah and the southern islands had paid tribute to them. The name of the Japanese was, indeed, the terror of the Oriental world, just as the northmen had been the object of dread to the southern Europeans.

A policy, that was adopted by the Japanese people in the seventeenth century, was an injurious one for its national development. Up to this time, foreign intercourse was free and commerce flourished. Nagasaki, Hirado, Satsuma, and all western seaports were the cosmopolitan cities, where all European and Asiatic tradesmen were found crowded. Unfortunately these foreigners were sources of vice. The avarice and extortion of the foreign traders; bitter sectarian strife between Dominicans Franciscans and the Jesuits; and the most cruel intolerance and persecution by the Catholic people, which were vices unknown to the Japanese mind; political-religious plots of the Christians against the Japanese Government; the slave trade carried on by the foreign merchants, and the like events, disgusted the Japanese authority, and forced them to believe the exclusion of the vicious foreigners was absolutely necessary to the welfare of Japan. Thus the Japanese resolved to expel all foreigners out of the islands. Tokugawa, the founder of Tai Kun shogunate, vigorously enforced this principle and carried it so far that all the Roman Catholics both native and foreign were extinguished and all foreign merchants except a few Dutch, were expelled out of the country. The policy of the Tokugawa Government not only excluded the foreigners but also kept the natives at home. No Foreigners (except the Dutch) were allowed to peep in this forbidden land and no native was permitted to leave his own country. Thus it was cut off from all the rest of the world. Japan furnishes different varieties of productions, which can amply supply all the needs of the nation without any inconvenience; hence commercial intercourse with foreign lands, was not absolutely necessary. In the course of time she had forgotten all about the outside world and so the world neglected her.

The people, however, enjoyed a profound peace by this policy. Ignoring the rise and fall of other nations, the people in this ocean guarded paradise, cultivated arts and learning and developed their own civilization, which is quite different from what we call now the civilization of the nineteenth century. While thus she was enjoying tranquility and cultivating the arts and learning in a secluded corner of the earth, in the western nations, endless struggles and everlasting contests completely revolutionized the old phases of the earth. The peace and culture of two centuries and a half, which Japan has enjoyed, exalted her to the certain state of civilization. But her isolated condition and tranquility lacked the systematic development of army and navy and the arts of international negotiation, which are the weapons vitally important in order to stand on the field of struggle for existence.

Suddenly this tranquility that has continued for two hundred and fifty years, was broken, when in 1853, the war ships of Commodore Perry appeared in the Bay of Yeddo. This event threw into great confusion and panic the whole nation. Japan had no navy and no army to fight with the foreign intruders, nor had she the art of diplomacy, with which to consult regard to the protection of Japan's interest. Japan stood then with her naked civilization against the armed civilization of Europe. She was forced to make a disadvantageous treaty with the European and American states at the cannon's mouth. In this treaty she conceded her sovereign right to the western people who live in the realm.

Thus Japan entered, infamously, the group of the civilized world. She saw at once that the western nations were far in advance of her in the art of war and diplomacy, that they have learned from the constant struggle of the past three centuries, while she was devoted to arts and learning. She perceived that the so-called civilization of the 19th century is but a disguised form of barbarism of iron and fire, covered with comity and humanity, and that to exist in the field of struggle for existence she must adopt the same means by which the European nations stand. Hence the whole nation of Japan, since the intercourse with the western people, has struggled, with the utmost energy, to adopt what is called the 19th century civilization.

In 1868 a revolution took place, from which the New Japan suddenly emanated. The French Revolution did not cause greater changes in France than the Revolution of 1868 in Japan. The old feudal regime, in full force, was cast away. The social system was completely reorganized. New and enlightened criminal and civil codes were enacted; the modes of judicial procedure were utterly revolutionized; the jail system radically improved; the most effective organization of police, of posts, of railways, of telegraphs, telephones and all means of communication were adopted; enlightened methods of national education mere employed; and the Christian religion was welcomed for the sake of social innovation. The most complete national system of navy and army, after the modern European model was achieved. The sound order of the imperial government, financially and politically, were firmly established; the most improved and extended scheme of local government was put into operation, and the central government was organized according to the pattern of the most advanced scale. The imperial constitution was promulgated and the Imperial Diet, consisting of two houses—the House of Lords and House of Commons—elected by popular votes was founded. Freedom of thought, speech and faith was established; the system of an influential press and party rapidly grew up. Now the monarchial absolutism of the Mikado's Empire is replaced by a government by parliament and constitution.

Such is the progress which Japan has achieved in the past twenty-five years. This progress must not, by any means, be taken as strange. The Revolution of 1868 also, must not be imagined as the birthday of the Empire of the Rising Sun. Those who do not know the true condition of the Japanese before the Revolution, and who observe superficially the phases of modern Japan, have

BATTLE OF THE YALU—JAPANESE DRAWING

often said that the Japanese are merely imitating western civilization without any idea of understanding it. This a gross mistake. The Revolution of 1868 is merely a moment of transition when Japan adopted the western system. The Japanese mind was fully developed and enlightened, at the time when they came in contact with foreigners, to fully grasp western civilization. Mentally, the Japanese people were so enlightened as to be able to digest European science and art at one glance. As a clever writer has said: "It must be clearly understood that like a skillful gardener, who grafts a new rose or an apple upon a healthy and well-established stock, so did Japan adopt the scientific and civil government of the west to an eastern root, full of vigorous life and latent force." For these causes we have no reason to wonder at the rapid progress which the Japanese have made in the past twenty-five years. And by all these facts, we have no reason to wonder how the colossal Celestial Empire, that was thought by the Europeans invincible, came to ask the mercy of Japan.

The collision between Japan and China, though it was thought strange to those who are not familiar to eastern affairs, is not a surprising matter to the person well acquainted with Asiatic politics. Japan had predicted, long ago, that the inevitable conflict of the two powers in the Orient must come sooner or later, and the nation has been long prepared for today. She has perceived the weakness and corruption of the Celestial Empire, while the European diplomats were dazzled, in the court of Peking, by an outward appearance of unity, power, and majesty that the huge Middle Kingdom maintained for centuries. She knew quite well that the lack of national spirit and effective system of government, hatred of races, depravity of the officers, ignorance of the people, corruption of naval and military organization and constant maladministration of the Manchoorian government dominated the stupid empire, whose people still proudly style their county the "Flowery Kingdom, in the Enlightened Earth."

The Japanese, as they are polite and artistic, are by no means a blood-thirsty race; nay, far from that. But the present war is in an inevitable chain of circumstances. For a long time the Japanese and Chinese were not good friends, they hated each other, as much, if not more than the French and the Germans do to-day.

Since Japan came in contact with the Europeans, she adopted, with the most marvelous activity, the western methods which have completely revolutionized the nation in a quarter of a century, while China maintained her regime and looked upon all western arts and science with utmost hatred and contempt. So she regarded Japan as the traitor of Asia. Naturally Japan represented the civilization and progress in the far east; and China ultra-conservatism. It was long expected that the collision of these two antagonistic principles must come. And so it has now come.

Moreover, the goal of Japans was, as the leading spirit of Asia, to exalt herself among the first-class powers of the civilized world. But China, up to a very short time ago, pretended to be the mistress of Asia. Thus they envied each other, and conflict of the two powers for supremacy became inevitable. The first collision between Japan and China came in 1874, with the question of the Liu Kiu Islands, which China abandoned for Japan, then the Formosa expedition provoked serious trouble between the two countries. In both cases Japan came off successful in the end.

Again there were collisions in Corea, just as Rome and Carthage met in Sicily. Corea has for a long time, paid tribute both to Japan and China, yet neither had any definite sovereign right over Corea, but mere suzerain powers. In 1875, the Japanese government abandoned all her ancient, traditional suzerain rights in Corea, and concluded a treaty which recognized Corea as an independent State, enjoying the same sovereign powers as Japan. Soon after, the United States, England, France, Germany and Russia followed Japan's example. This friendly act of Japan by which she introduced Corea as an independent State among civilized nations, was a terrible blow to China, who still had the intention of claiming her traditional suzerainty over Corea. It must be remembered that the permanent neutrality of the Hermit Kingdom is of vital importance to the prosperity and safety of the country of the Rising Sun. It is evident from this point of view that Japan can never permit the Chinese claim of suzerainty, nor Russian aggression in Corea.

From the time that Japan recognized Corea as an independent nation, she made great efforts for the progress of Corea. Many Corean students were educated and many Japanese, sent there as instructors and as advisors, assisted the advancement of her civilization. Japan has never failed to show her friendly sympathy towards Corea, for the progress and welfare of Corea as a firm independent state, has great bearing upon Asiatic civilization, and upon the safety of Japan itself.

While Japan was using her best efforts as the sincere friend of Corea, China constantly and secretly intrigued with the Corean government and the conservatives, in order to restore her old suzerainty and to annhilate Japan's influence in Corea. In 1882, an insurrection, instigated by the Chinese officers, broke out in Seoul. It was directed chiefly against the Japanese, as the promoters of foreign intercourse. The mob attacked the Japanese legation and several members were murdered. The Japanese minister and his staff escaped to the palace to find refuge, but found there the gates were shut against them, then they were obliged to cut their way through the mob and run all night to Chemulpo, where they were rescued by an English boat and returned to Japan. The insurrection was suppressed by a Chinese force and a number of the leaders were executed. The Corean government consented to pay a sum of $500,000 as indemnity, but this was subsequently forgiven to Corea in consequence of inability to pay it. There mere already existing in Corea two parties, that is, the progressive and the conservative. The former party represented civilized elements and the spirit of Japan, while the latter represented the majority of the officers and it was supported by the Chinese government. These two parties were bitter enemies and struggled for supremacy.

Since the rebellion of 1882, Chinese influence in Corea rapidly increased, consequently the conservative spirit predominated. Two years later, the leaders of the progressive party undertook a bold attempt when they saw that their party influence was waning. During a dinner party to celebrate the opening of the new post-office, a plan was made to murder all the conservative leaders who had dominant influence in the government. They partly succeeded in the attempt. The revolutionary leaders proceeded to the palace, secured the person and the sympathy of the king, who sent an autograph letter to ask the Japanese minister for the protection of the royal palace. Thereon, the Japanese minister guarded the palace for a few days with his legation guard of one hundred and thirty Japanese soldiers. In the meantime the Chinese force in Seoul, two thousand in number proceeded to the palace, and without any negotiation or explanation fired upon the Japanese guard. The king fled to the Chinese army and the Japanese retired to the palace of their legation which they found surrounded by the Chinese army. They abandoned the spot finding it impossible to maintain the legation without ally provisions, fought their way to Chemulpo, where they found their way to Japan. Many Japanese were killed in this event. The Japanese government demanded satisfaction from China on account of the action of the Chinese soldiers. The convention of Tien-tsin, after long negotiation between Count Ito, the present premier of Japan and Li Hung Chang, the viceroy of China, was concluded. The main points of the Tien-tsin treaty were three: (1) that the king of Corea should provide a sufficient force to maintain order in future, to be trained by officers of some nation other than China or Japan; (2) that certain internal reforms should be made; (3) that if necessary to preserve order and protect their nations either Japan or China should have the right to dispatch troops to Corea, on giving notice each to the other, and that when order was restored both forces should be withdrawn simultaneously.

The event of 1885 completely extinguished the Japanese influence and established the Chinese authority in Corea. The Chinese minister in Seoul got complete possession of the Corean government, entirely crushed the revolutionary party and organized an ultra-conservative government and appointed ministers at his will. Japan's influence in Corea has been almost nill during the past ten years, for she has been very busy with her internal reorganization and has not had much time to look after Corea.

Two prominent leaders of the revolutionary party fled to Japan on account of the failure of the coup d' état of 1885, where they found their asylum. The Chinese and Corean governments dispatched missions to demand the extradition of these unfortunate political reformers, but Japan was firm in her refusal, on the ground of the ethics of international law. The Corean government, sanctioned by that of China, at once began to take measures to effect the removal of these ruined leaders by other processes.

THE FIGHT AT PING-YANG

Official assassins followed their footsteps for ten years in vain. But at last they succeeded in murdering Kim-ok-Kiun, one of those reformers, and most barbarous cruelties were committed by the Chinese and Corean authorities. The murder of Kim-ok-Kiun excited great sympathy from the Japanese public. Many a time China and Corea cast disdain and contempt upon Japan's name. Many a time the political and commercial interest of Japan were impaired by them. Yet Japan forgave their insolence with generous heart.

The progress of the late rebellion in Corea was beyond her power to check. A state of perpetual anarchy seemed to prevail. Insolent China seemed to be using the Corean mobs for her own advantage, and directly against Japan's interests. China, ignoring the treaty of Tien-tsin in 1885, sent troops to Corea. Japan no longer lightly viewed China's insolence and Corean disorder.

Japan's ardent need to take a decided step in Corea, at this moment seemed a more cogent one in the commercial point of view than her political interest. The greater part of the modern trade of Corea has been created by Japan and is in the hands of her merchants; the net value of Corean direct foreign trade for 1892 and 1893 together was $4,240,498 with China; while $8,306,571 with Japan. Hence the interest of Japan is twice that of China. In tonnage of shipping the proportion is vastly greater in favor of Japan. Her tonnage in 1893 was over twenty times that of China, as the exact figures show: tonnage—China, 14,376; Japan, 304, 224. Thus Japan's economic interests in Corea are decidedly greater than any other nation's.

Immediately after China sent troops to Corea, Japan, also, sent her force, to preserve her political as well as economic interests, and determined not to draw back her troops until Corea should restore the sound order of society and wipe out the Chinese claim of Corean suzerainty, for so long as Chinese influence predominates in Corea, any thoughts of her advancement are hopeless. For a long maladministration of the Li government had weakened the Hermit Kingdom. The country is no more than a desert and its people are plunged in the most miserable poverty of any in the poverty-stricken east. The Japanese government proposed to the Chinese government according to the Tien-tsin treaty, a measure of internal reform for Corea, which was rejected with insult by the Chinese authority.

At first Japan had, by no means, any intention to make war with China, but she was forced by her to enter the struggle. She has never infringed the ethics of international law, nor the comity of nations. It was China that provoked the eastern war, now raging in the Orient, but not Japan; the true idea of Japan, in the war, is, by conquest, to put the blame on China for refusing to adhere faithfully to the spirit of her treaties and for trying to keep Corea in barbarism, and for endeavoring to stop the progress of civilization in Eastern Asia. Her mission in the east is to crush the insolent and ignorant self-conceit of the Peking government and to reform the barbarous abuses of the Corean administration. Therefore Japan fights to-day for the sake of civilization and humanity.

After the eastern war was declared, four months had hardly passed, until the fighting power and the economic resources of the Chinese Empire were destroyed and exhausted. China was forced to beg the mercy of Japan. The banner of the "Rising Sun" is now triumphant. Japan dictating the terms of peace, signifies the beginning of a better era for benighted China and the preservation of permanent peace in the Orient.

JULIUS KUMPEI MATUMOTO, A.M.,

Tokio, Japan

CHINA

CHINESE MUSICIAN

HISTORICAL SKETCH OF CHINA FROM THE EARLIEST TIMES TO FIRST CONTACT WITH EUROPEAN CIVILIZATION

Origin of Chinese People—Legends—Golden Age of China—Beginnings of Authentic History—Dynasty of Chow—Cultivation of Literature and Progress—Music, Slavery, Household Habits Three Thousand Years Ago—Confucius and his Work—First Emperor of China—Burning of Books—Han Dynasty—Famous Men of the Period—Paper Money and Printing—Invasions of Tartars and Mongols—Sung Dynasty—Literary Works—Famous Chinese Poet—Literature, Law and Medicine—Kublai Khan—Ming Dynasty—Private Library of a Chinese Emperor—Founding of the Present Dynasty—Connection Between Chinese History and the Best of the World.

Obscurity shrouds the origin of the Chinese race. The Chinese people cannot be proved to have originally come from anywhere beyond the limits of the Chinese empire. At the remotest period to which investigations can satisfactorily go back, without quitting the domain of history for that of legend, we find then already in existence as an organized, and as a more or less civilized nation. Previous to that time, their condition had doubtless been that of nomadic tribes, but whether as immigrants or as true sons of the soil there is scarcely sufficient evidence to show. Conjecture, however, based for the most part upon coincidences of speech, writing or manners and customs, has been busy with their ultimate origin; and they have been variously identified with the Turks, with the Chaldees, with the earliest inhabitants of Ireland, and with the lost tribes of Israel.

The most satisfactory, however, of recent conclusions, based on most careful investigations are as follows: The first records we have of them represent the Chinese as a band of immigrants settling in the north-eastern provinces of the modern empire of China and fighting their way amongst the aborigines much as the Jews of old forced their way into Canaan against the various tribes which they found in possession of the land. It is probable that though they all entered China by the same route they separated into bands almost on the threshold of the empire, one body, those who have left us the records of their history in the ancient Chinese books, apparently following the course of the Yellow river, and turning southward with it from its northernmost bend, settling themselves in the fertile districts of the modern provinces of Shan-hsi and Honan. But as it is believed also that at about the same period a large settlement was made as far south as Anam of which there is no mention in the books of the northern Chinese, we must assume that another body struck directly southward through the southern provinces of China to that country.

Many writers answer the question that arises as to whence these people came, by declaring that research directly points to the land south of the Caspian sea. They find many reasons in the study of languages which furnish philological proof of this assertion. And they affirm that in all probability the outbreak in Susiana of possibly some political disturbance in about the 24th or 23rd century B.C., drove the Chinese from the land of their adoption and that they wandered eastward until they finally settled in China and the country south of it. Such an emigration is by no means unusual in Asia. We know that the Ottoman Turks originally had their home in northern Mongolia, and we have a record of the movement at the end of last century of a body of six hundred thousand Kalmucks from Russia to the confines of China. It would appear also that the Chinese came into China possessed of the resources of western Asian culture. They brought with them a knowledge of writing and astronomy as well as of the arts which primarily minister to the wants and comforts of mankind.

According to one native authority, China, that is, the world was evolved out of chaos exactly 3,276,494 years ago. This evolution was brought about by the action of a First Cause or Force which separated into two principles, active and passive, male and female. Or as some native writers explain it, out of a great egg came a man. Out of the upper half of the egg he created the heavens and out of the lower half he created the earth. He created five elements, earth, water, fire, metal and wood. Out of the vapor from gold he created man and out of vapor from wood he created woman. Traditional pictures of this first man and first woman represent them wearing for dress, girdles of fig leaves. He created the sun to rule the day, the moon to rule the night, and the stars. Those who care to go deeper into these traditions than the limits of this work permit will find ample material for interesting research in the analogies to Christian history.

These principles, male and female, found their material embodiment in heaven and earth and became the father and mother of all things, beginning with man, who was immediately associated with them in a triumvirate of creative powers. Then ensued ten immense periods, the last of which has been made by some Chinese writers on chronology to end where every sober history of China should begin, namely, with the establishment of the Chow dynasty eleven hundred years before the birth of Christ. During this almost immeasurable lapse of time, the process of development was going on, involving such discoveries

CHINESE IDEA OF CREATION

as the production of fire, the construction of houses, boats and wheeled vehicles, the cultivation of grain, and mutual communication by means of writing.

The father of Chinese history chose indeed to carry us back to the court of the Yellow Emperor, B.C. 2697, and to introduce us to his successors Yao and Shun and to the great Yu, who by his engineering skill had drained away a terrible inundation which some have sought to identify with Noah's flood.

This flood was in Shun's reign. The waters we are told rose to so great a height that the people had to betake themselves to the mountains to escape death. Most of the provinces of the existing empire were inundated. The disaster arose, as many similar disasters, though of less magnitude, have

EMPEROR SHUN PLOWING

since arisen, in consequence of the Yellow river bursting its bounds, and the great Yu was appointed to lead the waters back to their channel. With unremitting energy he set about his task, and in nine years succeeded in bringing the river under his control. During this period so absorbed was he in his work, that we are told he took heed neither of food nor clothing, and that thrice he passed the door of his house without once stopping to enter. At the completion of his labors he divided the empire into nine instead of twelve provinces, and tradition represents him as having engraved a record of his toils on a stone tablet on Mount Heng in the province of Hoopih. As a reward for the services he had rendered for the empire, he was invested with the principality of Hea, and after having occupied the throne conjointly with Shun for some years he succeeded that sovereign on his death in 2808 B.C.

But all these things were in China's "golden age," the true record of which is shrouded for us in the obscurity of centuries.

VIEW FROM SUMMER PALACE, PEKING

There were a few laws, but never any occasion to exact the penalties attached to misconduct. It was considered superfluous to close the house door at night, and no one would even pick up any lost property that lay in the high road. All was virtue, happiness and prosperity, the like of which has not since been known. The Emperor Shun was raised from the plow handle to the throne simply because of his filial piety, in recognition of which wild beasts used to come and voluntarily drag his plow for him through the furrowed fields, while birds of the air would hover round and guard his sprouting grain from the depredations of insects.

This of course is not history; and but little more can be said for the accounts given of the two dynasties which ruled China between the "golden age "and the opening reigns of the House of Chow. The historian in question had not many sources of information at command. Beside tradition, of which he largely availed himself, the chief of these was the hundred chapters that had been edited by Confucius from the historical remains of those times, now known as the "Book of History." This contains an unquestionable foundation of facts, pointing to a comparatively advanced state of civilization, even so far back as two thousand years before our era; but the picture is dimly seen and many of its details are of little practical value. This calculation declares that with Yu began the dynasty of Hea which gave place in 1766 B.C. to the Shang dynasty. The last sovereign of the Hea line, Kieh Kwei, is said to have been a monster of iniquity and to have suffered the just punishment for his crimes at the hands of T'ang, the prince of the state of Shang, mlo took his throne from him. In like manner, six hundred and forty years later, Woo Wang, the prince of Chow, overthrew Chow Sin, the last of the Shang dynasty, and established himself as the chief of the sovereign state of the empire.

It is only with the dynasty of the Chows that we begin to feel ourselves on safe ground, though long before that date the Chinese were undoubtedly enjoying a far higher civilization that fell to the share of most western nations until many centuries later. The art of writing had been already fully developed, having passed, if we are to believe native researches from an original system of knotted cords, through successive stages of notches on wood and rude outlines of natural objects down to the phonetic stage in which it exists at the present day. Astronomical observations of a simple kind had been made and recorded and the year divided into months. The rite of marriage had been substituted for capture and although cowries were still employed and remained in use until a much later date, metallic coins of various shapes and sizes began to be recognized as a more practicable medium of exchange. Music, both vocal and instrumental, was widely cultivated; and a kind of solemn posturing filled the place that has been occupied by dancing among nations farther to the west. Painting, charioteering and archery were reckoned among the fine arts the cross bow especially being a favorite weapon either on the battle field or on the chase. The people seem to have lived upon rice and cabbage, pork and fish, much as they do now; they also drank the ardent spirit distilled from rice vulgarly known as "Samshoo" and clad themselves in silk, or their own coarse home stuffs according to the means of each. All this is previous to the dynasty of Chow with which it is now proposed to begin.

The Chows rose to power over the vices of preceding rulers, aided by the genius of a certain duke or chieftain of the Chow state, though he personally never reached the imperial throne. It was his more famous son who in B.C. 1122 routed the forces of the last tyrant of the semi-legendary period and made himself master of China. The China of those days consisted of a number of petty principalities clustering round one central state and thus constituting a federation. The central state managed the common affairs, while each one had its own local laws and administration. It was in some senses a feudal age, somewhat similar to that which prevailed in Europe for many centuries. The various dukes were regarded as vassals owing allegiance to the sovereign at the head of the imperial state, and bound to assist him with money and men in case of need. And in order to keep together this mass, constantly in danger of disintegration from strifes within, the sovereigns of the House of Chow were forever summoning these vassal dukes to the capital and making them renew, with ceremonies of sacrifice and potations of blood, their vows of loyalty and treaties of alliance. At a great feast held by Yu after his accession, there were, it is said, ten thousand princes present with their symbols of rank. But the feudal states were constantly being absorbed by one another. On the rise of the Shang dynasty there were only somewhat over three thousand, which had decreased to thirteen hundred when the sovereignty of the Chows was established.

The senior duke always occupied a position somewhat closer to the sovereign than the others. It was his special business to protect the imperial territory from invasion by any malcontent vassal; and he was often deputed to punish acts of insubordination and contumacy, relying for help on the sworn faith of all the states as a body against any individual recalcitrant. Such was the political condition of things through a long series of reigns for nearly nine centuries, the later history of this long and famous dynasty being simply the record of a struggle against the increasing power and ambitious designs of the vassal state of Ching, until at length the power of the latter not only outgrew that of the sovereign state, but successfully defied the united efforts of all the others combined together in a league. In 403 B.C. the number of states had been reduced to seven great ones, all sooner or later claiming to be "the Kingdom," and contending for the supremacy until Ching put down all the others and in 221 B.C. its king assumed the title of Hwang Ti or emperor and determined that there should be no more feudal principalities, and that as there is but one sun in the sky there should be but one ruler in the nation.

It is interesting to glance backward over these nine hundred years and gather some facts as to the China of those days. The religion of the Chinese was a modification of the older and simpler forms of nature worship practised by their ruder forefathers. The principal objects of veneration were still heaven and earth and the more prominent among the destructive and beneficent powers of nature. But a tide of personification and deification had begun to set in and to the spirits of natural object and influences now rapidly assuming material shape had been added the spirits of departed heroes whose protection was invoked after death by those to whom it had been afforded during life.

The sovereign of the Chow dynasty worshipped in a building which they called "the hall of light," which also served the purpose of an audience and council chamber. It was 112 feet square and surmounted by a dome; typical of heaven above and earth beneath. China has always been remarkably backward in architectural development, never having got

CHINESE TEMPLE

beyond the familiar roof with its turned up corners, in which antiquaries trace a likeness to the tent of their nomad days. Hence it is that the "hall of light" of the Chows is considered by the Chinese to have been a very wonderful structure.

Some have said that the Pentateuch was carried to China in the sixth century B.C., but no definite traces of Judaism are discoverable until several centuries later.

The Chow period was pre-eminently one of ceremonial observances pushed to an extreme limit. Even Confucius was unable to rise above the dead level of an ultra formal etiquette, which occupies in his teachings a place altogether out of proportion to any advantages likely to accrue from the most scrupulous compliance with its rules. During the early centuries this period laws were excessively severe and punishments correspondingly barbarous; mutilation and death by burning or dissection being among the enumerated penalties. From all accounts there speedily occurred a marked degeneracy in the characters of the Chow kings. Among the most conspicuous of the early kings was Muh, who rendered himself notorious for having promulgated a penal code under which the redemption of punishments was made permissible by the payment of fines.

Notwithstanding the spirit of lawlessness that spread far and wide among the princes and nobles, creating misery and unrest throughout the country, that literary instinct which has been a marked characteristic of the Chinese throughout their long history continued as active as ever. At stated intervals officials, we are told, were sent in light carriages into all parts of the empire to collect words from the changing dialects of each district; and at the time of the royal progresses the official music masters and historiographers of each principality presented to the officials appointed for the purpose, collections of the odes and songs of each locality, in order, we are told, that the character of the rule exercised by their princes should be judged by the tone of the poetical and musical productions of their subjects. The odes and songs as found and thus collected were carefully preserved in royal archives, and it was from these materials, as is commonly believed, that Confucius compiled the celebrated "She King" or "Book of Odes."

One hundred years before the close of the Chow dynasty, a great statesman named Wei Yang appeared in the rising state of Ch'in and brought about many valuable reformations. Among other things he introduced a system of tithings, which has endured to the present day. The unit of Chinese social life has always been the family and not the individual; and this statesman caused the family to be divided into groups of ten families to each, upon a basis of mutual protection and responsibility.

The soil of China has always been guarded as the inalienable property of her imperial ruler for the time being, held in trust by him on behalf of a higher and greater power whose vice-regent he is. In the age of the Chows, land appears to have been cultivated upon a system of communal tenure, one-ninth of the total produce being devoted in all cases to the expenses of government and the maintenance of the ruling family in each state. Copper coins of a uniform shape and portable size were first cast, according to Chinese writers, about half way through the sixth century B.C. An irregular form of money, however, had been in circulation long before, one of the early vassal dukes having been advised, in order to replenish his treasury, to break up the hills and make money out of the metal therein; to evaporate sea water and make salt. This, added his advising minister, "will benefit the realm and with the profits you may buy up all kinds of goods cheap and store them until market has risen; establish also three hundred depots of courtesans for the traders, who will thereby be induced to bring all kinds of merchandise to your country. This merchandise you will tax and thus have a sufficiency of funds to meet the expenses of your army." Such were some of the principles of finance and political economy among the Chows, customs duties being apparently even at that early date a recognized part of the revenue.

The art of healing was practised among the Chinese in their prehistoric times, but the first quasi-scientific efforts of which we have any record belong to the period with which we are now dealing. The physicians of the Chow dynasty classify diseases under the four seasons of the year—headaches and neuralgic affections under spring, skin diseases of all kinds under summer, fever and agues under autumn, and bronchial and plumonary complaints under winter. The public at large was warned against rashly swallowing the prescriptions of any physician whose family had not been three generations in the medical profession.

When the Chows went into battle they formed a line with the bowman on the left and the spearmen on the right flank. The centre was occupied by chariots, each drawn by three or four horses harnessed abreast. Swords, daggers, shields, iron headed clubs, huge iron hooks, drums, cymbals, gongs, horns, banners and streamers innumerable were also among the equipment of war. Quarter was rarely if ever given and it was customary to cut the ears from the bodies of the slain.

It was under the Chows, a thousand years before Christ, that the people of China began to possess family names By the time of Confucius the use of surnames had become definitely established for all classes. The Chows founded a university, a shadow of which remains to the present day. They seem to have had theatrical representations of some kind, though it is difficult to say of what nature these actually were. Music must have already reached a stage of considerable development, if we are to believe Confucius himself, who has left it on record that after listening to a certain melody he was so affected as not to be able to taste meat for three months.

Slavery was at this date a regular domestic institution and was not confined—as now to the purchase of women alone; and whereas in still earlier ages it had been usual to bury wooden puppets in the tombs of princes, we now read of slave boys and slave girls barbarously interred alive with the body of every ruler of a state, in order, as was believed, to wait upon the tyrant's spirit after death. But public opinion began during the Confucian era to discountenance this savage rite, and the son of a man who left instructions that he should be buried in a large coffin between two of his concubines, ventured to disobey his father's commands.

We know that the Chows sat on chairs while all other eastern nations were sitting on the ground, and ate their food and drank their wine from tables; that they slept on beds and rode on horseback. They measured the hours with the aid of sun dials; and the invention of the compass is attributed, though on somewhat insufficient grounds, to one of their earliest heroes. They played games of calculation of an abstruce character, and others involving dexterity. They appear to have worn shoes of leather and stockings, and hats, and caps, in addition to robes of silk; and to have possessed such other material luxuries fans, mirrors metal, bath tubs, and flat irons. But it is often difficult to separate truth from falsehood in the statement of Chinese writers with regard to their history. They are fond of exaggerating the civilization of their forefathers, which, as a matter of fact, was sufficiently advanced to command admiration without the undesirable coloring of fiction they have thus been tempted to lay on.

Of the religions of the Chinese we will speak in a succeeding chapter, but it must be said here that during the Chow dynasty was born the most famous of Chinese teachers, Confucius. He was preceded about the middle of the dynasty by Lao-tzu, the founder of an abstruse system of ethical philosophy which was destined to develop into the Taoism of to-day. Closely following, and partially a contemporary, came Confucius, "a teacher who has been equalled in his influence upon masses of the human race by Buddha alone and approached only by Mahomet and Christ." Confucius devoted his life chiefly to the moral amelioration of his fellow men by oral teaching, but he was also, an author of many works. A hundred years later came Mencius, the record of whose teachings also forms an important part modern student in China. His pet theory was that the nature of

IMAGE OF CONFUCIUS

man is good, and that all evil tendencies are necessarily acquired from evil communications either by heredity or association. It was during this same period that the literature of the Chinese language was founded. Of this subject, and some of the famous works, more will be said in a succeeding chapter devoted to literature and education.

In their campaign against the prevailing lawlessness and

MANCHOORIAN MINISTERS

violence, neither Confucius nor Mencius was able to make any headway. Their preachings fell on deaf ears and their peaceful admonitions were passed unheeded by men who held their fiefs by the strength of their right arms, and administered the affairs: of their principalities surrounded by the din of war. The feudal ' system and the dynasty of the Chows were tottering when Confucius died although it was more than two hundred years after when Ch'in acquired the supremacy.

The nine centuries covered by the history of the Chows were full of stirring incidents in other parts of the world. The Trojan war had just been brought to an end and AEneas had taken refuge in Italy from the sack of Troy. Early in the dynasty Zoroaster was founding in Persia the religion of the Magi, the worship of fire which survives in the Parseeism of Bombay. Saul was made king of Israel and Solomon built the temple of Jerusalem. Later on Lycurgus gave laws to the Spartans and Romulus laid the first stone of the Eternal City. Then came the Babylonic captivity, the appearance of Buddha, the conquest of Asia Minor by Cyrus, the rise of the Roman Republic, the defeats of Darius at Marathon and of Xerxes at Salamis, the Peloponnesian War, the retreat of the Ten Thousand, and Roman conquests down to the end of the first Punic war. From a literary point of view the Chow dynasty was the age of the Vedas in India; of Homer, Aechylus, Herodotus, Aristophanes, Thucydides, Aristotle and Demosthenes in Greece; and of the Jewish prophets from Samuel to Daniel; and of the Talmud as originally undertaken by the scribes subsequent to the return from the captivity in Babylon.

It has been stated that the imperial rule of the Chows over the vassal states which made up the China of those early days, was gradually undermined by the growing power and influence of one of the latter, the very name of which was transformed into a byword of reproach, so that to call a person "a man of Ch'in" was equivalent to saying in vulgar parlance, "He is no friend of mine." The struggle between the Ch'ins and the rest of the empire may be likened to the struggle between Athens and the rest of Greece though the end in each case was not the same. The state of Ch'in vanquished its combined opponents, and finally established a dynasty, shortlived indeed, but containing among the few rulers who sat upon the throne, only about fifty years in all, the name of one remarkable man, the first emperor of the united China.

On the ruins of the old feudal system, the landmarks of which his three or four predecessors had succeeded in sweeping away, Hwang Ti laid the foundations of a coherent empire which was to date from himself as its founder. He sent an army of 300,000 men to fight against the Huns. He

GREAT WALL OF CHINA

dispatched a fleet to search for some mysterious islands off the coast of China; and this expedition has since been connected with the colonization of Japan. He built the Great Wall which is nearly fourteen hundred miles in length, forming the most prominent artificial object on the surface of the earth. His copper coinage was so uniformly good that the cowry disappeared altogether from commerce with this reign. According to some, the modern hair pencil employed by the Chinese as a pen was invented about this time, to be used for writing on silk; while the characters themselves underwent certain modifications and orthographical improvements. The first emperor desired above all things to impart a fresh stimulus to literary effort; but he adopted singularly unfortunate means to secure this desirable end. For listening to the insidious flattery of courtiers, he determined that literature should begin anew with his reign. He therefore issued orders for the destruction of all existing books, with the exception of works treating of medicine, agriculture and divination and the annals of his own house; and he actually put to death many hundreds of the literati who refused to comply with these commands. The decree was obeyed as faithfully as was possible in case of so sweeping an ordinance and for many years a night of ignorance rested on the country. Numbers of valuable works thus perished in a general literary conflagration, popularly known as "the burning of the books;" and it is partly to accident and partly to the pious efforts of the scholars of the age, that posterity is indebted for the preservation of the most precious relics of ancient Chinese literature. The death of Hwang Ti was the signal for an outbreak among the dispossessed feudal princes, who, however, after some years of disorder, were again reduced to the rank of citizens by a successful peasant leader who adopted the title of Kaou Ti, and named his dynasty that of Han, with himself its first emperor.

From that day to this, with occasional interregnums, the empire has been ruled on the lines laid down by Hwang Ti. Dynasty has succeeded dynasty but the political tradition has remained unchanged, and though Mongols and Manchoos have at different times wrested the throne from its legitimate heirs, they have been engulfed in a homogeneous mass inhabiting the empire, and instead of impressing their seal upon the country, have become but the reflection of the vanquished. The stately House of Han ruled over China for four hundred years, approximately from 200 B.C. to 200 A.D. During the whole period the empire made vast strides towards a more settled state of prosperity and civilization, although there were constant wars with the Tartar tribes to the north and the various Turkish tribes on the west. The communications with the Huns were particularly close, and even now traces of Hunnish influence are discernible in several of the recognized surnames of the Chinese. This dynasty also witnessed the spectacle, most unusual in the east, of a woman wielding the imperial sceptre; and hers was not a reign calculated to inspire the people of China with much faith either in the virtue or the administrative ability of the sex. In Chinese history however, her place is that of the only female sovereign who ever legitimately occupied the throne.

BUDDHIST PRIEST

It was under the Han dynasty that the religion of Buddha first became known to the Chinese people, and Taoism began to develop from quiet philosophy to foolish superstitions and practices. It was also during this period that the Jews appear to have founded a colony in Honan, but we cannot say what kind of a reception was accorded to the new faith. In the glow of early Buddhism, and in the exciting times of its subsequent persecution, it is probable that Judaism failed to attract much serious attention from the Chinese. In 1850 certain Hebrew rolls were recovered from the few remaining descendants of former Jews; but there was then no one left who could read a word of them, or who possessed any knowledge of the creed of their forefathers, beyond a few traditions of the scantiest possible kind.

But the most remarkable of all events connected with our present period, was the general revival of learning and authorship.

The Confucian texts were rescued from hiding places in which they had been concealed at the risk of death; editing committees were appointed, and immense efforts made to repair the mischief sustained by literature at the hand of the first emperor. Ink and paper were invented and authorship was thus enabled to make a fresh start, the very start indeed, that the first emperor had longed to associate with his own reign, and had attempted to secure by such impracticable means. During the latter portion of the second century B.C., flourished the "Father of Chinese History." His great work, which has been the model for all subsequent histories, is divided into one hundred and thirty books, and deals with a period extending from the reign of the Yellow emperor down to his own times. In another branch of literature, a foremost place among the lexicographers of the world may fairly be claimed for Hsu Shen, the author of a famous dictionary. Many other celebrated writers lived and prospered during the Han dynasty. One man whose name must be mentioned insured for himself, by his virtue and integrity, a more imperishable fame than any mere literary achievement could bestow. Yang Chen was indeed a scholar of no mean attainments, and away in his occidental home he was known as the "Confucius of the west." An officer of government in a high position, with every means of obtaining wealth at his command, lived and died in comparative poverty, his only object of ambition being the reputation of a spotless official. The Yangs of his day grumbled sorely at opportunities thus thrown away; but the Yangs of to-day glory in the fame of their great ancestor and are proud to worship in the ancestral hall to which his uprightness has bequeathed the name. For once when pressed to receive a bribe, with the additional inducement that no one would know of the transaction, he quietly replied—"How so? Heaven would know; earth would know; you would know and I should know." And to, this hour the ancestral shrine of the clan of the Yangs bears as it name "The Hall of the Four Knows."

It was in all probability under the dynasty of the Hans that the drama first took its place among the amusements of the people.

It is unnecessary to linger over the four centuries which connect the Halls with the T'angs. There was not in them that distinctness of character or coherency of aim which leave a great impress upon the times. The three kingdoms passed rapidly away, and other small dynasties succeeded them but their names and dates are not essential to a right comprehension of the state of China then or now. A few points may, however, be briefly mentioned before quitting this period of transition. Diplomatic relations were opened with Japan; and Christianity was introduced by the Nestorians under the title of the "luminous teaching." Tea was not known in China before this date. It was at the close of this transitional period that we first detect traces of the art of printing, still in an embryonic state, and it seems to be quite certain that before the end of the sixth century the Chinese were in possession of a method of reproduction from wooden blocks. One of the last emperors of the period succeeded in adding largely to the empire by annexation toward the west. Embassies reached his court from various nations, including Japan and Cochin China, and helped to add to the lustre of his reign.

The three centuries A.D. 600-900, during which the T'angs sat upon the throne, form a brilliant epoch in Chinese History, and the southern people of China are still proud of the designation which has descended to them as "men of T'ang." Emperor Hsuan Tsung fought against the prevailing extravagance in dress; founded a large dramatic college; and was all enthusiastic patron of literature. Buddhism flourished during this period in spite of edicts against it. Finally, it gained the favor of the emperors and for a time overpowered even Confucianism. It was during the reign of the second emperor of the T'angs and only six years after the Hegira that the religion of Mohomet first reached the shores of China. A maternal uncle of the prophet visited the country and obtained permission to build a mosque at Canton, portions of which may perhaps still be found in the thrice restored structure which now stands upon its site. The use of paper money was first introduced by the government toward the closing years of the dynasty; and it is near to this time that we can trace back the existence of the modern court circular and daily record of edicts, memorials, etc., commonly known as the Peking Gazette.

Another unimportant transition period, sixty years in duration, forms the connecting link between the houses of T'ang and Sung. It is known in Chinese history as the period of the five dynasties, after the five short-lived ones crowded into this space of time. It is remarkable chiefly for the more extended practice of printing from wooden blocks, the standard classical works being now for the first time printed in this way. The discreditable custom of cramping women's feet into the so-called "golden lilies" belongs probably to this date, though referred by some to a period several hundred years later.

It has been said before that the age of the T'angs was the age of Mahomet and his new religion, the propagation of which was destined to meet in the west with a fatal check from the arms of Charles Martel at the battle of Tours. It was the age of Rome independent under her early popes; of Charlemagne as emperor of the west; of Egbert as first king of England; and of Alfred the Great.

The Sung dynasty extended from about A.D. 960 to 1280. The first portion of this dynasty may be considered as on the whole, one of the most prosperous and peaceable periods of the history of China. The nation had already in a great measure settled down to that state of material civilizations and mental culture in which it may be said to have been discovered by Europeans a few centuries later. To the appliances of Chinese ordinary life it is probable that but few additions have been made even since a much earlier date. The national costume has indeed undergone subsequent variations, and at least one striking change has been introduced in later years, that is, the tail, which will be mentioned later. But the plows and hoes, the water wheels and well sweeps, the tools of artisans, mud huts, junks, carts, chairs, tables, chopsticks, etc., which we still see in China, are doubtless approximately those of more than two thousand years ago. Mencius observed that the written language was the same, and axle-trees of the same length all over the empire; and to this day an unaltering uniformity is one of the chief characteristics of the Chinese people in every department of life.

The house of Sung was not however without the usual troubles for any length of time. Periodical revolts are the special features of Chinese history, and the Sungs mere hardly exempt from them in a greater degree than other dynasties. The Tartars too, were forever encroaching upon Chinese territory and finally overran and occupied a large part of northern China. This resulted in an amicable arrangement to divide the empire, the Tartars retaining their conquests in the north. Less than a hundred years later came the invasion of the Mongols under Genghis Khan, with the long struggle which eventuated in a complete overthrow of both the Tartars and the Sungs and the final establishment of the Mongol dynasty under Kublai Khan, whose success was in a great measure due to the military capacity of his famous lieutenant Bayan. From this struggle one name in particular has survived to form a landmark of which the Chinese are justly proud. It is that of the patriot statesman Wen T'ien-hsiang, whose fidelity to the Sungs no defeats could shake, no promises undermine; and who perished miserably in the hands of the enemy rather than abjure the loyalty which had been the pride and almost the object of his existence.

Another name inseparably connected with the history of the Sungs is that of Wang An-shih who has been styled "The Innovator" from the gigantic administrative or innovations he labored ineffectually to introduce the chief of these were a universal system of militia under which the whole body of citizens were liable to military drill and to be called out for service in time of need; and a system of state loans to agriculturists in order to supply capital for more extensive and more remunerative farming operations. His schemes were ultimately set aside through the opposition of a statesman whose name is connected even more closely with literature than with politics. Ssu-ma Kuang spent nineteen years of his life in the compilation of "The Mirror of History," a history of China in two hundred and ninety-four books, the earliest times of the Chow dynasty down to the accession of the house of Sung.

A century later this lengthy production was recast in a greatly condensed form under the superintendence of Chu-Hsi, the latter work   at   once   taking   rank   as   the   standard   history

CHINESE ARCHERS

of China to that date. Chu Hsi himself played in other ways by far the most important part among all the literary giants of the Sungs. Besides holding, during 'a large portion of his life, high official position, with an almost unqualified success, his writings are more extensive and more varied in character than those of any other Chinese author; and the complete collection of his great philosophical works, published in 1713, fills no fewer than sixty-

CHINESE WRITER

six books. He introduced interpretations of the Confucian classics, either wholly or partially at variance with those which had been put forth by the soldiers of the Han dynasty and received as infallible ever since, thus modifying to a certain extent the prevailing standard of political and social morality.

His principle was simply one of consistency. He refused to interpret certain words in a given passage in one sense and the same words occurring elsewhere in another sense. And this principle recommended itself at once to the highly logical mind of the Chinese. Chu Hsi's commentaries were received to the exclusion of all others and still form the only authorized interpretation of the classical books, upon a knowledge of which all success at the great competitive examination for literary degrees may be said to entirely depend.

It would be a lengthy task to merely enumerate the names in the great phalanx of writers who flourished under the Sungs and who formed an Augustan Age of Chinese literature. Exception must however be made in favor of Ou-Yang Hsiu, who besides being an eminent statesman, was a voluminous historian of the immediately preceding dynasties, an essayist of rare ability and a poet; and of Su Tung-p'o whose name next to that of Chu Hsi fills the largest place in Chinese memorials of this period. A vigorous opponent of "The Innovator," he suffered banishment for his opposition; and again, after his rival's fall, he was similarly published for further crossing the imperial will. His exile was shared by the beautiful and accomplished girl "Morning clouds," to whose inspiration we owe many of the elaborate poems and other productions in the composition of which the banished poet beguiled his time; and whose untimely death of consumption, on the banks of their favorite lake, hastened the poet's end, which occurred shortly after his recall from banishment.

Buddhism and Taoisin had by this time made advances toward tacit terms of mutual toleration. They wisely agreed to share rather than to quarrel over the carcass which lay at their feet; and from that date they have flourished together without prejudice.

The system of competitive examinations and literary degrees had been still more fully elaborated, and the famous child's primer, the Three Character Classic," which is even now the first stepping stone to knowledge, had been placed in the hands of school boys. The surnames of the people were collected to the number of four hundred and thirty-eight in all; and although this was admittedly not complete, the great majority of those names which were omitted, once perhaps in common use, have altogether disappeared.

It is comparatively rare nowadays to meet with a person whose family name is not to be found within the limits of this small collection. Administration of justice is said to have flourished under the incorrupt officials of this dynasty. The functions of magistrates were more fully defined; while the study of medical jurisprudence was stimulated by the publication of a volume which, although combining the maximum of superstition with the minimum of scientific research, is still the officially recognized text book on all subjects connected with murder, suicide and accidental death. Medicine and the art of healing came for a considerable share of attention at the hands of the Sungs and many voluminous works on therapeutics have come down to us from this period. Inoculation for small-pox has been known to the Chinese at least since the early years of this dynasty if not earlier.

The irruption of the Mongols under Genghis Khan, and the comparatively short dynasty which was later on actually established under Kublai Khan, may be regarded as the period of transition from the epoch of the Sungs to the epoch of the Migs. For the first eighty years after the nominal accession of Genghilr Khan the empire was more or less in a state of siege and martial law from one end to the other; and then in less than one hundred years afterwards the Mongol dynasty had passed away. The story of Ser Marco Polo and his wonderful travels, familiar to most readers, gives us a valuable insight into this period of brilliant courts, thronged marts, fine cities, and great national wealth.

At this date the literary glory of the Sungs had hardly begun to grow dim. Ma Tuan-lin carried his voluminous work through all the troublous times, and at his death bequeathed to the world "The Antiquarian Researches," in three hundred and forty-eight books, which have made his name famous to every student of Chinese literature. Plane and spherical trigonometry were both known to the Chinese by this time, and mathematics generally began to receive a larger share of the attention of scholars. It was also under the Mongol dynasty that the novel first made its appearance, a fact pointing to a definite social advancement, if only in the direction of luxurious reading. Among other points may be mentioned a great influx of Mohammedans, and consequent spread of their religion about this time.

The Grand Canal was completed by Kublai Khan, and thus, Cambaluc, the Peking of those days, was united by inland water communication with the extreme south of China. The work seems to have been begun by the Emperor Yang Ti seven centuries previously, but the greater part of the undertaking was done in the reign of Kublai Khan. Hardly so successful was the same emperor's huge naval expedition against Japan, which in point of number of ships and men, the insular character of the enemy's country, the chastisement intended, and the total loss of 'the fleet in a storm, aided by the stubborn resistance of the Japanese themselves, suggests a very obvious comparison with the object and fate of the Spanish Armada.

The age of the Sungs carries us from a hundred years previous to the Norman Conquest down to about the death of Edward III. It was the epoch of Venetian commerce and maritime supremacy; and of the first great lights in Italian literature, Dante, Petrarch and Boccacio. English, French, German and Spanish literature had yet to develop, only one or two of the earlier writers, such as Chaucer, having yet appeared on the scene.

The founder of the Ming dynasty rose from starvation and obscurity to occupy the throne of the Chinese empire. In his youth he sought refuge from the pangs of hunger in a Buddhist monastery; later on he became a soldier of fortune, and joined the ranks of the insurgents who were endeavoring to shake off the alien yoke of the Mongols. His own great abilities carried him on. He speedily obtained the leadership of a large army, with which he totally destroyed the power of the Mongols, and finally established a new Chinese dynasty over the thirteen provinces into which the empire was divided. He fixed his capitol at Nanking, where it remained until the accession of the third emperor, the conqueror of Cochin China and Tonquin, who transferred the seat of government back to Peking, the capitol of the Mongols, from which it has never since been removed.

For nearly three hundred years, from 1370 to 1650, the Mings swayed the destinies of China. Their rule was not one of uninterrupted peace, either within or without the empire; but it was

CHINESE CANNONIERS

on the whole a wise and popular rule, and the period which it covers is otherwise notable for immense literary activity and for considerable refinement in manners and material civilization.

From without, the Mings were constantly harrassed by the encroachments of the Tartars; while from within the ceaseless intriguing of the eunuchs was a fertile cause of trouble.

Chief among the literary achievements of this period, is the gigantic

ANCIENT CHINESE ARCH

encyclopedia in over twenty-two thousand books, only one copy of which, and that imperfect, has survived out of the four that were originally made. Allowing fifty octavo pages to a book, the result would be a total of at least one million one hundred thousand pages, the index alone occupying no fewer than three thousand pages. This wonderful work is now probably rotting, if not already rotted beyond hope of preservation, in some damp corner of the imperial palace at Peking. Another important and more accessible production was the so-called "Chinese Herbal." This was a compilation from the writings of no fewer than eight hundred preceding writers on botany, mineralogy, entomology, etc., the whole forming a voluminous but unscientific book of reference on the natural history of China. Shortly after the accession of the third emperor, Yung Lo, the imperial library was estimated to contain written and printed works amounting to a total of about one million in all. A book is a variable quantity in Chinese literature, both as regards number and size of pages; the number of books to a work also vary from one to several hundred. But reckoning fifty pages to a book and twenty or twenty-five books to a work, it will be seen that the collection was not an unworthy private library for any emperor in the early years of the fifteenth century.

The overthrow of the Mings was brought about by a combination of events of the utmost importance to those who would understand the present position of the Tartars as rulers of China. A sudden rebellion had resulted in the capture of Peking by the insurgents, and in the suicide of the emperor who was fated to be the last of his line. The imperial commander-in-chief, Wu Sankuei, at that time away on the frontiers of Manchooria engaged in resisting the incursions of the Manchoo-Tartars, now for a long time in a state of ferment, immediately hurried back to the capitol but was totally defeated by the insurgent leader and once more made his way, this time as a fugitive and suppliant, toward the Tartar camp. Here he obtained promises of assistance chiefly on condition that he would shave his head and grow a tail in accordance with Manchoo custom, and again set off with his new auxilliaries toward Peking, being reinforced on the way by a body of Mongol volunteers. As things turned out, the commander arrived in Peking in advance of these allies, and actually succeeded with the remnant of his own scattered forces in routing the troups of the rebel leader before the Tartars and the Mongols came up. He then started in pursuit of the flying foe. Meanwhile the Tartar contingent arrived and on entering the capitol the young Manchoo prince in command was invited by the people of Peking to ascend the vacant throne. So that by the time Wu San-kuei reappeared, he found a new dynasty already established and his late Manchoo ally at the head of affairs. His first intention had doubtless been to continue the Ming line of emperors; but he seems to have readily fallen in with the arrangement already made and to have tendered his formal allegiance on the four following conditions:

That no Chinese woman should be taken into the imperial seraglio; that the first place at the great triennial examination for the highest literary degrees should never be given to a Tartar; that the people should adopt the national costume of the Tartars in their everyday life; but that they should be allowed to bury their corpses in the dress of the late dynasty; that this condition of costume should not apply to the women of China who were not to be compelled either to wear the hair in a tail before marriage as the Tartar girls do, or to abandon the custom of compressing their feet.

The great Ming dynasty was now at an end, though not destined wholly to pass away. A large part of it may be said to remain in the literary monuments. The dress of the period survives upon the modern Chinese stage; and when occasionally the alien yoke was galled, seditious whispers of "restoration" are not altogether unheard. Secret societies have always been dreaded and prohibited by the government; and of these none more so than the famous "Triad Society," in which heaven, earth, and man are supposed to be associated in close alliance, and whose watchword is believed to embody some secret allusion to the downfall of the present dynasty.

In the latter part of the sixteenth century, the civilization of western Europe began to make itself felt in China by the advent of the Portuguese, and this matter will be returned to in the following chapter.

In other parts of the world, eventful times have set in. In England we are brought from the accession of Richard II. down to the struggle between the king and the commons and the ultimate establishment of the commonwealth. We have Henry IV. in France and Ferdinand and Isabella in Spain. In England, Shakspeare and Bacon; in France, Rabelais and Descartes; in Germany, Luther and Copernicus; in Spain, Cervantes; and in

Italy, Galileo, Machiavelli and Tasso; these names to which should be added those of the great explorers, Columbus and Vasco de Gama, serve to remind one of what was meanwhile passing in the west.

A CHINESE LODGING HOUSE

FROM FIRST CONTACT WITH EUROPEAN
CIVILIZATION TO THE OUTBREAK OF THE WAR

How the Western Nations Formed the Acquaintance of China—First Mention of the Orient by Grecian and Roman Historians—Introduction of Judaism—Nestorian Missionaries Bring Christianity—Marco Polo's Wonderful Journey—Roman Missionaries in the Field—Dissentions among Christians Discredit their Work—Work of the Jesuits—The Dynasty of the Chings—Splendid Literary Labors of Two Emperors—England First Embassy to China—The Opium War—Opening the Ports of China—Treaties with Western Nations—The Tai-Ping Rebellion—The Later Years of Chinese History.

The works of several Greek and Roman historians, principally those of Ptolemy and Arian, who lived in the second century, contain references of a vague character to a country now generally believed to be China. Ptolemy states that his information came from the agents of Macedonian traders, who gave him an account of a journey of seven months from the principal city of eastern Turkestan, in a direction east inclining a little south. It is probable that these agents belonged to some of the Tartar tribes of Central Asia. They represented the name of this most eastern nation to be Serica, and that on the borders of this kingdom they met and traded with its inhabitants, the Seres. Herodotus speaks of the Isadores as a people in the extreme north-east of Asia. Ptolemy also mentions these tribes as a part of Serica and under its sway. Ammianus Marcellinus, a Roman historian of the fourth century, speaks of the land of the Seres as surrounded by a high and continuous wall. This was about six hundred years after the great wall of northern China was built. Virgil, Pliny, Ricitus and Juvenal refer to the Seres in connection with the Seric garments which seem to have been made of fine silk or gauze. This article of dress was much sought after in Rome by the wealthy and luxurious, and as late as the second century, is said to have been worth its weight in gold. From the length and description of the route of the traders, the description of the mountains and rivers which they passed, the character of the people with whom they traded and the articles of traffic, the evidence seems almost conclusive that the nation which the Greeks and Romans designated by the name of Serica is that now known to us as China. The particular countries visited by the caravans which brought the silk to Europe, were probably the dependencies, or territories of China on the west, or possibly cities within the extreme north-west limit of China proper.

The introduction of Judaism into China is evidenced by a Jewish synagogue which existed until quite recently in Kai-fungfoo, a city in the province of Honan. Connected with this synagogue were some Hebrew manuscripts, and a few worshippers who retained some of the forms of their religion, but very little knowledge of its real character and spirit. There is a great deal of uncertainty as to when the Jews came to China, though they have, no doubt, resided there for many centuries.

Nestorian missionaries entered China some time before the seventh century. The principal record which they have left of the success of their missions is the celebrated Nestorian monument in Fen-gan-foo. This monument contains a short history of the sect from the year 630 to 781, and also an abstract of the Christian religion. The missionaries of this sect have left but few records of their labors or of their observations as travelers, but the churches planted by them seem to have existed until a comparatively recent period. The Romish missionaries who entered China in the beginning of the fourteenth century, found them possessed of considerable influence, not only among the people, but also at court, and met with no little opposition from them in their first attempts to introduce the doctrines of their church. It seems to be true that during the period of nearly eight hundred years in which Nestorian Christianity maintained its foothold in China, large numbers of converts were made. But in process of time the Nestorian churches departed widely from their first teachings. After the fall of the Mongolian empire they were cut off from connection with the west, and not having sufficient vitality to resist the adverse influences of heathenism the people by degrees relapsed into idolatry or took up the new faiths that were introduced.

The first western writer, whose works are extant, who has given anything like full and explicit explanation respecting China is Ser Marco Polo. He went to China in the year 1274, in company with his father and uncle, who were Venetian noblemen. At this time, the independent nomad tribes of central Asia being united in one government, it was practicable to reach eastern. Asia by passing through the Mongolian empire. Marco Polo spent twenty-four years in China, and seems to have been treated kindly and hospitably. After his return to Europe he was taken prisoner in a war with the Genoese, and during his confinement wrote an account of his travels. The description he gives of the vast territories of China, its teeming population, and flourishing cities, the refinement and civilization of its people, and their curious customs, seemed to his countrymen more like a fiction of fairyland than sober and authentic narrative. It is said that he was urged when on his death bed to retract these statements and make confession of falsehood, which he refused to do. He was undoubtedly one of the most remarkable travelers of any age.

During the period of the Mongolian empire which comprehended under its sway the greater part of Asia from China on the east to the Mediterranean on the west, an intense desire was kindled in the Roman church to convert this powerful nation to its faith. Among the first and the most noted of the missionaries sent to China at this time, was John of Mount Corvin, who reached Peking in 1293. He was afterward made an archbishop. From time to time bishops and priests were sent out to reenforce this mission, but they met with indifferent success; and when the Mongols were driven from China the enterprise was abandoned as a complete failure. After the fall of the Mongolian empire, direct overland communication with eastern Asia was interrupted, and for about two hundred years China was again almost completely isolated from the western world.

The use of the magnetic needle, and improvements in navigation, made a new era in intercourse with the Orient. It is supposed that the first voyage from Europe to China was made by a Portuguese vessel in 1516. From this period commercial intercourse with China became more frequent, and various embassies were sent to the Chinese court by different nations of Europe. Unfortunately the growing familiarity of the Chinese with western nations did not increase their respect and confidence in them. This was due partly to the servility of most of the embassies to Peking, but principally, no doubt, to the want of honesty and the general lawlessness of most of the traders from the west. The consequence was that the Chinese became desirous of restricting foreign intercourse, and exercising as strict surveillance over their troublesome visitors as possible.

Immediately after connection was established between Europe and the far east by sea, another and a more successful effort was made by the Roman church to propagate its faith in the Chinese empire, this being coincident with the growth of the exchange of business. Francis Xavier, in his attempt to gain an entrance into the country, died on one of the islands of the coast in 1552. Toward the close of the Sixteenth century the Portuguese appeared upon the scene, and from their "concession" at Macao, at one time the residence of Camoens, opened commercial relations between China and the west. They brought the Chinese, among other things, opium, which had previously been imported overland from India. They possibly taught them how to make gunpowder, to the invention of which the Chinese do not seem, upon striking a balance of evidence, to possess an independent claim. About the same time Rome contributed the first installment of those wonderful Jesuit fathers whose names yet echo in the empire, the memory of their scientific labors and the benefits they thus conferred upon China having long survived the wreck and discredit of the faith to which they devoted their lives. At this distance of time it does not appear to be a wild statement, to assert that had the Jesuits, the Franciscans, and the Dominicans been able to resist quarreling among themselves, and had they rather united to persuade papal infallibility to permit the incorporation of ancestor-worship with the rites and ceremonies of the Romish church, China would at this moment be a Catholic country and Buddhism, Taoism, and Confucianism would long since have receded into the past.

Of all these Jesuit missionaries, the name of Matteo Ricci stands by common consent upon the long list. He established himself in Canton in the garb of a Buddhist priest in 1581. He was a man of varied intellectual gifts and extensive learning, united with indomitable energy, zeal and perseverance, and great prudence. In 1601 he reached Peking in the dress of a literary gentleman. He spent many years in China. He associated with the highest personages in the land. He acquired an unrivalled knowledge of the book language, and left behind him several

CHINESE PRIEST

valuable treatises of a metaphysical and theological character, written in such a polished style as to command the recognition and even the admiration of the Chinese. One of his most intimate friends and fellow workers was the well-known scholar and statesman, Hsu Kuang-chi, the author of a voluminous compendium of agriculture, and joint author of the large work which introduced European astronomy to the Chinese. He was appointed by the emperor to co-operate with other Jesuit missionaries in reforming the national calendar, which had gradually reached a stage of hopeless inaccuracy. He wrote independently several small scientific works; also a severe criticism of the Buddhist religion, and

finally, not least in importance, a defense of the Jesuits, addressed to the throne, when their influence at court had begun to excite envy and distrust. Hsu Kuang-chi forms the sole exception the history of China of a scholar and a man of means and position on the side of Christianity.

The age of the Chings is the age in which we live, but it is not so familiar to some persons as it' ought to be that a Tartar and not a Chinese sovereign is now seated on the throne in China. For some time after the accession of the first

MAN OF SWATOW

Manchoo emperor, there was considerable friction between the two races. The subjugation of the empire by the Manchoos was followed by a military occupation of the country, which survived the original necessity, and has remained part of the system of government until the present day. The dynasty thus founded, partly by accident as it seems, as was related in the last chapter, has remained in power through the entire period of intercourse with western nations. The title adopted by the first emperor of the line was Shun-che. It was during the reign of this sovereign that Adam Schaal, a German Jesuit, took up his residence at Peking and that the first Russian embassy, 1656, visited the capital. But in those days the Chinese had not learned to tolerate idea that foreigner should enter the presence of the Son of Heaven unless he were willing to perform the prostration known as the KO-t'ow, and the Russians not being inclined to humor any such presumptuous folly left the capital without opening negotiations.

Of the nine emperors of this line, from the first to the present, the second in every way fills the largest space in Chinese history. Kang Hi, the son of Shun-che, reigned for sixty-one years. This sovereign is renowned in modern Chinese history as a model ruler, a skillful general and an able author. During his reign Thibet was added to the empire, and the Eleuths were successfully subdued. But it is as a just and considerate ruler that he is best remembered among the people. He treated the early Catholic priests with kindness and distinction, and availed himself in many ways of their scientific knowledge. He promulgated sixteen moral maxims collectively known as the "Sacred Edict," forming a complete code of rules for the guidance of every day life, and presented in such terse, yet intelligible terms, that they at once took firm hold of the public mind and have retained their position ever since. Kang Hi was the most successful patron of literature the world has ever seen. He caused to he published under his own personal supervision the four following compilations, known as the four great works of the present dynasty: A huge thesaurus of extracts in one hundred and ten thick volumes; an encyclopedia in four hundred and fifty books, usually bound in one hundred and sixty volumes; an enlarged and improved edition of a herbarium in one hundred books; and a complete collection of the important philosophical writings of Chu Hsi in sixty-six books. In addition to these the emperor designed and gave his name to the great modern lexicon of the Chinese language, which contains over forty thousand characters under separate entries, accompanied in each case by appropriate citations from the works of authors of every age and every style. The monumental encyclopedia contains articles on every known subject, and extracts from all works of authority dating from the twelfth century B.C. to that time. As only one hundred copies of the first imperial edition were printed, all of which were presented to princes of the blood and high officials, it is rapidly becoming extremely rare, and it is not unlikely that before long the copy in the possession of the British museum will be the only complete copy existing. A cold caught on a hunting excursion in Mongolia brought his memorable reign of sixty-one years to a close, and he was succeeded on the throne by his son Yung Ching.

The labors of the missionaries during the years of this last reign have been effective in establishing many churches and bishoprics, and in making many thousands of converts. But the suspicions in the minds of the Chinese rulers that the Christians were leagued with rebels, as well as the controversies between the different sects, antagonized the authorities. Under the third Manchoo emperor, Yung Ching, began that violent persecution of the Catholics which continued almost to the present day, and in the year 1723 an edict was promulgated prohibiting the further propagation of this religion in the empire. From this time the Roman Catholics were subjected to this persecution except for a few alternate periods of comparative toleration. They have retained their position in the face of great difficulties and trials, and since the late treaties with China the number of their converts has rapidly increased.

After a reign of twelve years, Yung Ching was gathered to his fathers, having bequeathed the throne to his son Kien Lung. This fourth emperor of the dynasty enjoyed a long and glorious reign. He possessed many of the great qualities of his grandfather, but he lacked his wisdom and moderation. His generals led a large army into Nepaul and conquered the Goorkhas, reaching a point only some sixty miles distant form British territory. He carried his armies north, south, and west, and converted Kuldja into a Chinese province. But in Burmah, Cochin China, and Formosa his troops suffered discomfiture. During his reign, which extended over sixty years, a full Chinese cycle, the relations of his government with the East India Company were extremely unsatisfactory. The English merchants were compelled to submit to many indignities and wrongs; and for the purpose of establishing a better international understanding Lord Macartney was sent by George III. on a special mission to the court of Peking. The ambassador was received graciously by the emperor, who accepted the presents sent him by the English king, but owing to his

CHINESE PAPER MAKING

ignorance of his own relative position, and of even the rudiments of international law, he declined to give those assurances of a more equitable policy which were demanded of him.

Like his illustrious ancestor, Kien Lung was a generous patron of literature, though only two instead of five great literary monuments remain to mark his sixty years of power. These are a magnificent bibliographical work in two hundred parts, consisting of a catalogue of the books in the imperial library, with valuable historical and critical notices attached to the entries of each; and a huge topography of the whole empire in five hundred books, beyond doubt one of the most comprehensive and exhaustive works of the kind ever published. Kang Hi had been a voluminous poet; but the productions of Kien Lung far outnumber those of any previous or subsequent bard. For more than fifty years this emperor was an industrious poet, finding time in the intervals of state duties to put together no fewer than thirty-three thousand nine hundred and fifty separate pieces. In the estimation however of this apparently impossible contribution to poetic literature, it must always be borne in mind that the stanza of four lines is a favorite length for a poem and that the couplet is not uncommon. Even thus a large balance stands to the credit of a Chinese emperor, whose time is rarely his own, and whose day is divided with wearisome regularity, beginning with councils and audiences long before daylight has appeared. We gain a glimpse into Kien Lung's court from the account of Lord Macartney's embassy in 1796, which was so favorably received by the venerable monarch a short time previous to his abdication, and three years before his death, and forms such a contrast with that of Lord Amherst to his successor in 1816. In 1795, at the age of eighty-five years, Kien Lung abdicated in favor of his fifteenth son who ascended the throne with the title of Kea King.

During the reign of Kea King, a second English embassy was sent to Peking, in 1816, to represent to the emperor the unsatisfactory position of the English merchants in China. The envoy, Lord Amherst, was met at the mouth of the Peiho and conducted to Yuen-ming-yuan or summer palace, where the emperor was residing. On his arrival he was officially warned that only on condition of his performing the Ko-t'ow would he be permitted to behold "the dragon countenance." This of course was impossible, and he

CHINESE PEASANT, PEIHO DISTRICT

consequently left the palace without having slept a night under its roof.

Meanwhile the internal affairs of the country were even more disturbed than the foreign relations. A succession of rebellions broke out in the western and northern provinces and the seaboards were ravaged by pirates. While these disturbing causes were in full play the emperor died, in 1820, and the throne devolved upon Tao Kuang, his second son. It was during the reign of Kea King that Protestant missionaries initiated a systematic attempt to convert the Chinese to Christianity; but the religious toleration of these people, which on the whole has been a marked feature in their civilization of all ages, had been sorely tried by the Catholics and but little progress was made. In another direction some of the early Protestant missionaries did great service to the world at large. They spent much of their time in grappling with the difficulties of the written language; and the publication of Dr. Morrison's famous dictionary and the achievements of Dr. Legge were the culmination of these labors.

Under Tao Kuang both home and foreign affairs went from bad to worse. A secret league known as the Triad Society, which was first formed during the reign of Kang Hi, how assumed a formidable bearing, and in many parts of the country, notably in Honan, Kwang-bei, and Formosa, insurrections broke out at its instigation. At the same time the mandarins continued to persecute the English merchants, and on the expiration of the East India Company's monopoly in 1834 the English government sent Lord Napier to Canton to superintend the foreign trade at that port. Thwarted at every turn by the presumptuous obstinacy of the mandarins, Lord Napier's health gave way under the constant vexations connected with his post, and he died at Macao after but a few months' residence in China.

The opium trade was now the question of the hour, and at the urgent demand of Commissioner Lin, Captain Elliot, the superintendent of trade, agreed that all opium in the hands of English merchants should be given up to the authorities. On the 3rd of April, 1839, twenty thousand two hundred and eighty-three chests of opium were, in accordance with this agreement, handed over to the mandarins, who burnt them to ashes. This demand of Lin's, though agreed to by the superintendent of trade, was considered so unreasonable by the English government that in the following year war was declared against China. The island of Chusan and the Bogue forts on the Canton river soon fell into the English hands, and Commissioner Lin's successor sought to purchase peace by the cession of Hong Kong and the payment of an indemnity of $6,000,000. This convention was, however, repudiated by the Peking government, and it was not until Canton, Amoy, Ninigpo, Shanghai, Chapoo and Chin-keang Foo had been taken by the British troops, that the emperor at last consented to come to terms, now of course far more onerous. By a treaty made by Sir Henry Pottinger in 1842 the cession of Hong Kong was supplemented by the opening of the four ports of Amoy, Foochow Foo, Ningpo, and Shanghai to foreign trade, and the indemnity of $6,000,000 was increased to $21,000,000.

Without noticing the other points at issue and the merits of the dispute concerning them, it is considered by the world at large that one of the blackest pages in the records of the history of civilization is that which tells of the forcing of the opium traffic upon the Chinese by Great Britain. The Chinese people were making most strenuous efforts to abolish the traffic in opium and the habit of its use, which had been introduced from India, and which was rapidly becoming the curse of the nation. But for commercial motives, in this Victorian age of civilization, England sent to force compliance with the demand of her merchants in China that the sale of the drug be legalized. The rapid spread of the use of opium among the hundreds of millions of Chinese, dating from this time, may be charged against England, in the long account which records the oppression and the shame of her dealings with whatever eastern nation she has played the game of war and colonization and annexation.

Death put an end to Tao Kuang's reign in 1850, and his fourth son, Hien Feng, assumed rule over the distracted empire which was bequeathed him by his father. There is a popular belief among the Chinese that two hundred years is the natural life of a dynasty. This is one of those traditions which are apt to bring about their own fulfilment, and in the beginning of the reign of Hien Feng the air was rife with rumors that an effort was to be made to restore the Ming dynasty to tho throne. On

BATTLE OF CRICKETS

such occasions there are always real or pretended scions of the required family forthcoming. And when the flames of rebellion broke out in Kwangshi a claimant suddenly appeared under the title of Teen-tih, heavenly virtue," to head the movement. But he had not the capacity required to play the necessary part, and the affair languished and would have died out altogether had not a leader named Hung Sew-tseuen arose, who combined all the qualities required in a leader of men, energy, enthusiasm, and religious bigotry.

As soon as he was sufficiently powerful he advanced northward into Honan and Hoopih, and captured Woo-chang Foo, the capital of the last named province, and a city of great commercial and strategical importance, situated as it is at the junction of the Han river with the Chiang. Having made this place secure he advanced down the river and made himself master of Gan-ting and the old capital of the

CHINESE MANDARIN

empire, Nanking. Here in 1852 he established his throne, and proclaimed the commencement of Taiping dynasty. For himself he adopted the title of Teen-wang, or "heavenly king." For a time all went well with the new dynasty. The Tai-ping standard was carried northward to the walls of Tien-tsin and floated over the towns of Chin-keang Foo and Soochow Foo.

Meanwhile the imperial authorities had by their stupidity raised another enemy against themselves. The outrage on the English flag perpetrated on board the Chinese lorcha "Arrow," at Canton in 1867, having been left unredressed by the mandarins, led to the proclamation of war by England. Canton fell to the arms of General Straubenzee, and Sir Michael Seymour in December of the same year, and in the following spring the Taku forts at the mouth of the Peiho having been taken, Lord Elgin, who had in the meantime arrived as plenipotentiary minister, advanced up the river to Tien-tsin on his way to the capital. At that city, however, he was met by imperial commissioners, and yielding to their entreaties he concluded a treaty with them which it was arranged should be ratified at Peking in the following year.

But the evil genius of the Chinese still pursuing them, they treacherously fired on the fleet accompanying Sir Frederic Bruce, Lord Elgin's brother, proceeding in 1860 to Peking, in fulfillment of this agreement. This outrage rendered another military expedition necessary, and in conjunction with the French government, the English cabinet sent out a force under the command of Sir Hope Grant, with orders to march to Peking. In the summer of 1861 the allied forces landed at Peh-tang, a village twelve miles north of the Taku forts, and taking these intrenchments in the rear captured them with but a trifling loss. This success was so utterly unexpected by the Chinese, that leaving Tien-bin unprotected they retreated rapidly to the neighborhood of the capital. The allies pushed on after them, and in reply to an invitation sent from the imperial commissioners at Tung-chow, a town twelve miles from Peking, Sir Harry Parkes and Mr. Loch, accompanied by an escort and some few friends, went in advance of the army to make a preliminary convention. While so engaged they were treacherously taken prisoners and carried to Peking.

This act precipitated an engagement in which the Chinese were completely routed, and the allies marched on to Peking. After the usual display of obstinacy the Chinese yielded to the demand for the surrender of the An-ting gate of the city. From this vantage point Lord Elgin opened negotiations, and having secured the release of Sir Harry Parkes and the other prisoners who had survived the tortures to which they had been subjected, and having burnt the summer palace of the emperor as a punishment for their treacherous capture and for the cruelties perpetrated on them, he concluded a treaty with Prince Kung, the representative of the emperor. By this instrument the Chinese agreed to pay a war indemnity of $8,000,000 and to open six other ports in China, one in Formosa, and one in the island of Hainan to foreign trade, and to permit the representatives of the foreign governments to reside at Peking.

GATE AT PEKING

Having thus relieved themselves from the presence of a foreign foe, the authorities were able to devote their attention to the suppression of the Tai-ping rebellion. Fortunately for themselves, the apparent friendliness with which they greeted the arrival of the British legation at Peking enlisted for them the sympathies of Sir Frederic Bruce, the British minister, and inclined him to listen to their request for the services of an English officer in their campaign against the rebels. At the request of Bruce, General Staveley selected Major Gordon, since generally known as Chinese Gordon, who was killed a few years ago at Khartoom, for this duty. A better man or one more peculiarly fit for the work could have been found. A numerous force known as is the ever victorious army," partly officered by foreigners, had for some time been commanded by an American named Ward and after his death by Burgevine, another American. Over this force Gordon was placed, and at the head of it he marched in conjunction with the Chinese generals against the Tai-pings. With masterly strategy he struck a succession of rapid and telling blows against the fortunes of the rebels. City after city fell into his hands, and at length the leaders at Soochow opened the gates of the city to him on condition that he would spare their lives. With cruel treachery, when these men presented themselves before Li Hung Chang to offer their submission to the emperor, they were seized and beheaded. On learning how lightly his word had been treated by the Chinese general, Gordon armed himself, for the first time during the campaign with a revolver, and sought out the Chinese headquarters intending to avenge with his own hand this murder of the Tai-ping leaders. But Li Hung Chang having received timely notice of the righteous anger he had aroused took to flight, and Gordon, thus thwarted in his immediate object, threw up his command feeling that it was impossible to continue to act with so orientally-minded a colleague.

After considerable negotiation however, he was persuaded to return to his command and soon succeeded in so completely crippling the power of the rebels that in July 1864, Nanking, their last stronghold, fell into the hands of the imperialists. Teenwang was then already dead, and his body was found within the walls wrapped in imperial yellow. Thus was crushed out a rebellion which had paralyzed the imperial power in the central provinces of the empire and which had for twelve years seriously threatened the existence of the reigning dynasty.

Meanwhile in the summer following the conclusion of the

OPIUM SMOKERS

treaty of Peking, 1861, the emperor, Hien Beng, breathed his last at Jehol, an event which was in popular belief foretold by the appearance of a comet in the early part of the summer. He was succeeded to the throne by his only son, a mere child, and the offspring of one of the imperial concubines. He adopted the name of Tung Chih. On account of his youth the administration of affairs was placed in the hands the two dowager empresses, the wife of the last emperor and the mother of the new one. These regents were aided by the counsels of the boy emperor's uncle, Prince Kung.

Under the direction of these regents, though the internal affairs of the empire prospered, the foreign relations were disturbed by the display of an increasingly hostile spirit towards the Christian missionaries and their converts, which culminated in 1870 in the Tien-tsin massacre. In some of the central provinces reports had been industriously circulated that the Roman Catholic missionaries were in the habit of kidnapping and murdering children, in order to make medicine from their eyeballs. Ridiculous as the rumor was, it found ready credence among the ignorant people, and several outrages were perpetrated on the missionaries and their converts in Kwang-hsi and Sze-chwan. Through the active interference, however, of the French minister on the spot, the agitation was locally suppressed only to be renewed at Tien-tsin. Here also the same absurd rumors were set afloat, and were especially directed against some sisters of charity who had opened an orphanage in the city.

For some days previous to the massacre on the 21st of June, reports increasing in alarm reached the foreign residents that an outbreak was to be apprehended, and three times the English consul wrote to Chung How, the superintendent of the three northern ports, calling upon him to take measures to subdue the gathering passions of the people which had been further dangerously exasperated by an infamous proclamation issued by the prefects. To these communications the consul did not receive any reply, and on the morning of the 21st, a day which had apparently been deliberately fixed for the massacre, the attack was made. The mob first broke into the French consulate and while the consul, M. Fontanier, was with Chung How endeavoring to persuade him to interfere, two Frenchmen and their wives, and Father Chevrien were there murdered. While returning the consul suffered the same fate. Having thus whetted their taste for blood, the rioters then set fire to the French cathedral, and afterward moved on to the orphanage of the sisters of mercy. In spite of the appeals of these defenseless women for mercy, if not for themselves at least for the orphans under their charge, the mob broke into the hospital, killed and mutilated most shockingly all the sisters, smothered from thirty to forty children in the vault, and carried off a still larger number of older persons to prisons in the city, where they were subjected to tortures of which they bore terrible evidence when their release was at length affected. In addition to these victims, a Russian gentleman with his bride, and a friend, who were unfortunate enough to meet the rioters on their way to the cathedral, were also murdered. No other foreigners were injured, a circumstance due to the fact that the fury of the mob was primarily directed against the French Roman Catholics, and also that the foreign settlement where all but those engaged in missionary work resided, was at a distance of a couple of miles from the city.

When the evil was done, the Chinese authorities professed themselves anxious to make reparation, and Chung How was eventually sent to Paris to offer the apologies of the Peking cabinet to the French government. These were ultimately accepted; and it was further arranged that the Tien-tsin prefect and District magistrate should be removed from their posts and degraded, and that twenty of the active murderers should be executed. By these retributive measures the emperor's government made its peace with the European powers, and the foreign relations again assumed their former friendly footing.

The Chinese had now leisure to devote their efforts to the subjugation of the Panthay rebels. This was a great Mohammedan uprising which dated back as far as 1856 and which had for its object the separation of the province of Yun-nan into an independent state. The visit of the adopted son of the rebel leader, the sultan Suleiman, to England, for the purpose of attempting to enlist the sympathies of the English government in the Panthay cause, no doubt added zest to the action of the mandarins, who after a short but vigorous campaign, marked by scenes of bloodshed and wholesale carnage, suppressed the rebellion and restored the province to the imperial sway.

Peace was thus brought about, and when the empresses handed over the reigns of power to the emperor, on the occasion of his marriage in 1872, tranquility reigned throughout the eighteen provinces. The formal assumption of power proclaimed by this marriage was considered by the foreign ministers a fitting opportunity to insist on the fulfillment of the article in the treaties which provided for their reception by the emperor, and after much negotiation it was finally arranged that the emperor should receive them on the 29th of June, 1873.

Very early therefore on the morning of that day, the ministers were astir and were conducted in their sedan chairs to the park on the west side of the palace, where they were met by some of the ministers of state, who led them to the "Temple of Prayer for Seasonable Weather." Here they were kept waiting for some time while tea and confectionery from the imperial kitchen, by favor of the emperor, were served to them. They were then conducted to an oblong tent made of matting on the west side of the Tsze-kwang pavilion, where they were met by Prince Kung and other ministers. As soon as the emperor reached the pavilion, the Japanese ambassador was introduced into his presence and when he had retired the other foreign ministers entered the audience chamber in a body. The emperor was seated facing southward. On either side of his majesty stood, with Prince Kung, several princes and high officers. When the foreign ministers reached the center aisle they halted and bowed one and all together; they then advanced in line a little further and made a second bow; and when they had nearly reached the yellow table on which their credentials were to be deposited they bowed a third time; after which they remained erect. M. Vlangaly, the Russian minister, then read a congratulatory address in French, which was translated by an interpreter into' Chinese, and the ministers making another reverence respectfully laid their letters of credence upon the yellow table. The emperor was pleased to make a slight inclination of the head towards them, and Prince Kung advancing to the left of the throne and falling upon his knees, had the honor to be informed in Manchoo that his majesty acknowledged the receipt of the letters presented. Prince Kung, with his arms raised according to precedent set by Confucius when in the presence of his sovereign, came down by the steps on the left of the desk, to the foreign ministers, and respectfully repeated this in Chinese. After this he again prostrated himself, and in like manner received and conveyed a message to the effect that his majesty hoped that all foreign questions would be satisfactorily disposed of. The ministers then withdrew, bowing repeatedly, until they reached the entrance.

Thus ended the first instance during the present century of Europeans being received in imperial audience. Whether under more fortunate circumstances the ceremony might have been repeated it is difficult to say, but in the following year the young emperor was stricken down with the small-pox, or "enjoyed the felicity of the heavenly flowers," and finally succumbed to the disease on the twelfth of January, 1875. With great ceremony the funeral obsequies were performed over the body of him who had been Tung Chih, and the coffin was finally laid in the imperial mausoleum among the eastern hills beside the remains of his predecessors. His demise was shortly afterwards followed by the death of the girl empress he had just previously raised to the throne.

For the first time in the annals of the Ching dynasty, the throne was now left without a direct heir. As it is the office of the son and heir to perform regularly the ancestral worship, it is necessary that if there should be no son, the heir should be, if possible, of a later generation than the deceased. In the present instance this was impossible, and it was necessary therefore that the lot should fall on one of the cousins of the late emperor. Tsai-teen, the son of the Prince of Chun, a child not quite four years old, was chosen to fill the vacant throne, and the title conferred upon him was Kuang su or "an inheritance of glory."

Scarcely had the proclamation gone forth of the assumption of the imperial title by Kuang Su, when news reached the English legation at Peking of the murder at Manwyne, in the province of Yun-nan, of Mr. Margary, an officer in the consular service who had been dispatched to meet an expedition sent by the Indian government, under the command of Colonel Horace Browne, to discover a route from Birmah into the south-western provinces of China. In accordance with conventional practice, the Chinese government, on being called to account for this outrage, attempted to lay it to the charge of brigands. But the evidence which Sir Thomas Wade was able to adduce proved too strong to be ignored even by the Peking mandarins, and eventually they signed a convention in which they practically acknowledged their blood guiltiness, under the terms of which some fresh commercial privileges were granted, and an indemnity was paid.

At the same time a Chinese nobleman was sent to England to make apology, and to establish an embassy on a permanent footing at the court of St. James. Since that time the Chinese empire has been at peace with all foreign powers until the eruptions of the recent months. There have been some narrow escapes from war with the European countries holding possessions on the southern Chinese border, but serious results have not followed. Ministers have been maintained in China by the western nations, and by China in the western capitals.

Under the child Kuang Su, who came to the throne in 1875, we have seen the completion Chinese re-conquests in Central Asia and the restoration of Kuldja by the Russians. For many years the progressive party in the nation's councils, under the leadership of Li Hung Chang, Viceroy of Chihli, gradually appeared to gain ground, amply posted as the court of Peking was in the affairs of western countries. Even the old conservative party, of which the successful and the aged general Tso Tsung. tang was the representative, has vastly modified its tone in the last twenty years.

It is true that the short experimental line of railway which had been laid down between Shanghai and Wusung was objected to, and finally got rid of by the Chinese government; but the reason for this apparently retrograde step arose out of the not very scrupulous means employed by the promoters of the scheme, sail out of the very natural dislike of an independent state to be forced into innovations for which it may not be altogether prepared. Since that time several telegraph lines have been constructed, beginning with the first one between Peking and

Shanghai, which formed the final connecting link between the capital of the Chinese empire and the western civilized world. The freedom of residence had been greatly extended to foreigners living in China. Travel has become safer, and popular hatred towards foreigners not as apparent. Slow as it has been to take effect, nevertheless the influence of closer association with western civilization has made its impress on the Chinese nation, and the extreme conservatism in many details has been compelled to waver. The stories of the war which are to follow will indicate much of the characteristics of the later day history of the empire.

THE CHINESE EMPIRE

Origin of the Name of China, and What the Chinese Call their Own Country—Dependencies of the Empire—China and the United States in Comparison—Their Many Physical Similarities—Mountains and Plains— The Fertile Soil—Provinces of China—Rivers and Lakes—Climate—Fauna and Flora—Industries of the People—Commerce with Foreign Nations— The Cities of China—Forms of Government and Administration.

Until recent years the word China was unknown in the empire which we call by that name, but of late it has become more familiar to the Chinese, and in certain regions they are in fact adopting it for their own use, owing to the frequency with which they hear it from the foreigners with whom they are doing business. The name was no doubt introduced in Europe and America from the nations of Central Asia who speak of the Chinese by various names derived from that of the powerful Ching family, who held sway many centuries ago. The names which the Chinese use in speaking of themselves are various. The most common one Chung Kwo, the "Middle Kingdom." This term grew up in the feudal period as a name for the royal domain in the midst of the other states, as a whole in the midst of the uncivilized countries around them. The assumption of universal sovereignty, of being the geographical center of the world, and also the center of light and civilization that have been so injurious to the nation, appear in several of to most ancient names in the oldest classical writings the country is called the Flowery Kingdom, flowery presenting the idea of beautiful, cultivated, and refined. The terms Heavenly Flowery Kingdom, and Heavenly Dynasty are sometimes used, the word heavenly presenting the Chinese idea that the empire is established by the authority of heaven, and that the emperor rules by divine right. This title has given rise to the contemptuous epithet applied to the race by the Europeans, "The Celestials."

The Chinese empire, consisting of China proper and Manchooria, with its dependencies of Mongolia, I-li and Thibet, embraces a vast territory in eastern and central Asia, only inferior in extent to the dominions of Great Britain and Russia. The dependencies are not colonies but subject territories; and China proper itself indeed, has been a subject territory of Manchooria since 1644.

China proper was divided nearly two hundred years ago into eighteen provinces; and since the recent separation of the island of Formosa from Fu-chien, and its constitution into an independent province, we may say that it now consists of nineteen. These form one of the corners of the Asiatic continent, having the Pacific ocean on the south and east. They are somewhat in the shape of an irregular rectangle, and including the island of Hainan he between 18 and 49 degrees north latitude and 98 and 124 degrees east longitude. Their area is about two million square miles, while the whole empire has an area more than twice that large.

In giving a correct general idea of China one cannot perhaps do better than to institute a comparison between it and the United States, to which it bears a striking resemblance. It occupies the same position in the eastern hemisphere that the United States does in the western. Its line of sea coast on the Pacific resembles that of the United States on the Atlantic, not only in length but also in contour. Being found within almost the same parallels of latitude, it embraces almost the same variety of climate and production. A river as grand as the Mississippi, flowing east, divides the empire into nearly two equal parts, which are often designated as "north of the river" and "south of the river." It passes through an immense and fertile valley, and is supplied by numerous tributaries having rise in mountain ranges on either side and also in the Himalayas on the west. The area of China proper is about two-thirds that of the states of the American union.

The resemblance holds also in the artificial divisions. While our country is divided into more than forty states, China is divided into nineteen provinces. As our states are divided into counties, so each province has divisions called fu and each fu is again divided into about an equal number of hien. These divisions and subdivisions of the provinces are generally spoken ken of in English as departments or prefectures, and districts, but they are

CHINESE MINERS

much larger than our corresponding counties and townships. And similarly to our own system of government, each of these divisions slid subdivisions has its own capital or seat of civil power, in which the officers exercising jurisdiction over it reside. The outer dependencies of the Chinese empire are comparatively sparsely populated, and in this work, when China, without specification, is mentioned, it is intended to refer to the eighteen provinces exclusively, which include the vast proportion of the population, intelligence and wealth of the empire.

As to the physical features of China proper, the whole territory may be described as sloping from the mountainous regions of Thibet and Nepaul towards the shores of the Pacific on the east and south. A far extending spur of the Himalayas called the Nanling, or southern range, is the most extensive mountain system. It commences in Yun-nan, and passing completely through the country enters the sea at Ningpo. Except for a few steep passes, it thus forms a continuous barrier that separates the coast regions of south-eastern China from the rest of the country. Numerous spurs are cast off to the south and east of it, which appear in the sea as a belt of rugged islands. On the borders of Thibet to the north and west of this range, the country is mountainous, while to the east and from the great wall on the north to the Po-yang Lake in the south, there is the great plain comprising an area of more than two hundred thousand square miles and supporting in the five provinces contained in it more than one hundred and seventy-five million people.

In the north-western provinces the soil is a brownish colored earth, extremely porous, crumbling easily between the fingers, and carried far and wide in clouds of dust. It covers the sub-soil to an enormous depth and is apt to split perpendicularly in clefts which render traveling difficult. Nevertheless by this cleavage it affords homes to thousands of the people, who live in caves excavated near the bottom of the cliffs. Sometimes whole villages are so formed in terraces of the earth that rise one above another. The most valuable quality of this peculiar soil is its marvelous fertility, as the fields composed of it require scarcely any other dressing than a sprinkling of its own fresh loam. The farmer in this way obtains an assured harvest two and even three times a year. This fertility, provided there be a sufficient rainfall, seems inexhaustible. The province of Shan-hsi has borne the name for thousands of years of the "granary of the nation," and it is, no doubt: due to the distribution of this earth over its surface, that the great plain owes its fruitfulness.

Geographically speaking the arrangement of the provinces of China is as follows: On the north there are four provinces, Chihli, Shan-hsi, Shen-hsi, and Kan-su; on the west two, Szechwan, the largest of all, and Yun-nan; on the south two, Kwag-hsi and Kwang-tung; on the east four, Fu-chien, Chehchang Chiang-su, and Shan.tung. The central area enclosed by these twelve provinces is occupied by Honan, An-hui, Hoopih, Hunan, Chiang-hsi, and Kwei-chau. The latter is a poor province, with parts of it largely occupied by clans or tribes supposed to be the aborigines. The island of Formosa, lying off the coast of Fu-chien, ninety miles west of Amoy, is about two hundred and thirty-five miles in length, fertile and rich in coal, petroleum, and camphor wood. The first settlement of a Chinese population took place only in 1683, and the greater part of it is still occupied by aboriginal tribes of a more than ordinary high type. The population of these provinces is immense, but the various estimates and alleged censuses fluctuate and vary so much that it is impossible to give a definite number as the total. It is a safe estimate however to say that the population of the Chinese empire approximates four Hundred million, or considerably more than one fourth the population of the world, and nearly as much as the total of all Europe and America.

One of the most distinguishing features of China is found in the great rivers. These are called for the most part "ho in the north and chiang "(kiang) in the south. Two of these are famous and conspicuous among the great rivers of the world, the Ho, Hoang-ho, or Yellow River, and the Chiang, generally misnamed the Yang-tsze. The sources of these two rivers are not far from one another. The Ho rises in the plain of Odontala, which is a region of springs and small lakes, and the Chiang from the mountains of Thibet only a few miles distant. The Ho pursues a tortuous course first to the east and north until it crosses the great wall into Mongolia. After flowing a long distance northward of the Mongolian desert, to the northern limit of Shenhsi, it then turns directly south for a distance of five hundred miles. A right angle turns its course again to the eastward and finally north-eastward, when it flows into the Gulf of Pechili in the province of Shan-tung. The Chiang on the contrary turns south where the Ho turns north, and the after a general course to the eastward and northward, roughly paralled with its fellow, flows into the Eastern Sea, not far from Shanghai.

Both rivers are exceedingly tortuous and their courses are only roughly outlined here. Almost the very opening of Chinese history is an account of one of the inundations of the Ho River, which has often in course of time changed its channel. The terrible calamities caused by it so often have procured for it the name of "China's sorrow." As recently as 1887 it burst its southern bank near Chang Chau, and poured its mighty flood with hideous devastation, and the destruction of millions of lives, into the populous province of Honan. Each of these rivers has a course of more than three thousand miles. They are incomparably the greatest in China, but there are many others which would be accounted great elsewhere. In connection with inland navigation must be mentioned the Grand Canal, intended to connect the northern and southern parts of the empire by an easy water communication; and this it did when it was in good order, extending from Peking to Hankow, a distance of more than six hundred miles. Kublai Khan, the first sovereign of the Yuan dynasty, must be credited with the glory of making this canal. Marco Polo described it, and compliments the great ruler for the success of his work. Steam communication all along the eastern seaboard from Canton to Tien-tsin has very much superseded the use of the canal and portions of it are now in bad condition but as a truly imperial achievement it continues to be a grand memorial of Kublai.

The Great Wall was another vast achievement of human labor, constructed more than two thousand gears ago. It has been alleged a myth at some times, but its existence has not been denied since explorations have been made to the north of China Proper. It was not as useful as the canal, and it failed to answer the purpose for which it was intended, a defense against the incursions of the northern tribes. In 214 B.C. the Emperor Che Hwang Ti determined to erect a grand barrier all along the northern limit of his vast empire. The wall commences at the Shan-hsi pass on the north coast of the Gulf of Pechili. From this point it is carried westward till it terminates at the Chia-yu barrier gate, the road through which leads to the "western regions." It is twice interrupted in its course by the Ho River, and has several branch and loop walls to defend certain cities and districts. Its length in a straight line would be one thousand two hundred and fifty-five miles, but if measured along its sinuosities this distance must be increased to one thousand five hundred. It is not built so grandly in its western portions after passing the Ho River, nor should it be supposed that to the east of this point it is all solid masonry. It is formed by two strong retaining walls of brick rising from granite foundations, the space between being filled with stones and earth. The breadth of it at the base is about twenty-five feet, at the top fifteen feet, and the height varies from fifteen to thirty feet. The surface at the top was once covered with bricks but is now overgrown with grass. What travelers go to visit from Peking is merely a loop wall of later formation, enclosing portions of Chihli and Shan-hsi.

China includes many lakes, but they are not so commanding in size as the rivers. There are but three which are essential to mention. These are the Tung-ting Hu, the largest, having a circumference of two hundred and twenty miles, about in the center of the empire; the Po-yang Hu, half way between the former and the sea; and the Tai Hu, not far from Shanghai and the Yang-tsze River. The latter lake is famous for its romantic scenery and numerous islets.

The peculiarities of climate along the Chinese coast are due in great measure to the northern and southern monsoons, the former prevailing with more or less uniformity during the winter, and the latter during the summer months. These winds give a greater degree of heat in summer and of cold in winter than is experienced in the United States in corresponding latitudes. At Ningpo, situated in latitude 30, about that of New Orleans, large quantities office are secured in the winter for summer use. It is, however, very thin measured by what we think proper ice for preservation. In this part of China snow not infrequently falls to the depth of six or eight inches, and the hills are sometimes covered with it for weeks in succession. In the northern provinces the winters are very severe. In the vicinity of Peking, not only are the canals and rivers closed during the winter, but all commerce by sea is suspended during two or three months, while in the summer that part of China is very warm. The period of the change of the monsoon, when the two opposite currents are struggling with each other is marked by a great fall of rain and by the cyclones which are so much dreaded by mariners on the Chinese coast. The southern monsoon gradually loses its force in passing northward: and is not very marked above latitude 82, though its influence is decidedly felt to July and August. With the exception of the summer months the climate of the northern coast of China is remarkably dry; that of the southern coast is damp most of the year, especially during the months of May, June, and July.

In different parts of the country almost every variety of climate can be found, hot or cold, moist or dry, salubrious or malarial. The ports which were at first opened as places of residence for foreigners were unfortunately among the most unhealthful of the empire, not so much from the enervating effects of their southerly latitude as from their local miasmatic influences, being situated in the rice-producing districts and surrounded more or less by stagnant water during the summer months. Under the later treaties which opened new ports in the north, as well as interior cities, foreigners have been permitted to live in regions whose climates will compare favorably with most parts of our own country. The Chinese themselves consider Kwang-tung, Kwanghsi, and Yun-nan to be less healthful than the other provinces; but foreigners using proper precautions may enjoy their lives in every province.

The Chinese are essentially an agricultural people, and from time immemorial they have held agriculture in the highest esteem as being the means by which the soil has been induced to supply the primary wants of the empire, food. Of course the climate and the nature of a district determine the kind of farming appropriate to it. Agriculturally China may be said to be divided into two parts by the Chiang. South of that river, speaking generally, the soil and climate point to rice as the appropriate crop, while to the north he vast plains which as clearly are best designed for growing wheat, barley, oats, Indian corn and other cereals. Culinary or kitchen herbs, mushrooms and aquatic vegetables, with ginger and a variety of other condiments,

CHINESE FARM SCENE

are everywhere produced all widely used. From Formosa there comes sugar, and the cane thrives also in the southern provinces. Oranges, pomegranates, peaches, plantains, pineapples, mangoes, grapes, and many other fruits and nuts are supplied in most markets. The cultivation of opium is constantly in the increase.

Of course the use of tea as a beverage is a national characteristic. The plant does not grow in the north, but is cultivated extensively in the western provinces and in the southern. The infusion of the leaves was little if at all drunk in ancient times, but now its use is universal. Fu-chien, Hoopih, and Hu-nan produce

CHINESE TEA FARM

the greater part of the black teas; the green comes chiefly from Cheh-chiaug and An-hui; both kinds comes from Kwang-tung and Sze-chwan. Next to silk, if not equally with it, tea is China's most valuable export. From rice and millet the Chinese distill alcoholic liquors, but they are very sparingly used and it is a compliment the temperate inclinations the people, that immediately upon the opening of tea houses many years ago, the places for selling liquor found themselves empty of business and were soon compelled to close.

Birds and animals are found in great variety, though the country is too thickly peopled and well cultivated to harbor many wild and dangerous beasts. One occasionally hears of a tiger that has ventured from the forest and been killed or captured, hut the lion was never a denizen of China and is only to be seen rampant in stone in front of temples. The rhinoceros, elephant, and tapir are said still to exist in the forests and swamps of Yun-nan; but the supply of elephants at Peking for the carriage of the emperor when he proceeds to the great sacrificial altars has been decreasing for several reigns. Both the brown and the black bear are found, and several varieties of the deer family, of which the musk deer is highly valued. Among the domestic animals the breed of horses and cattle is dwarfish and no attempts seem to be made to improve them. The ass is a more lively animal in the north than it is in European countries or America, and receives much attention. About Peking one is struck by many beautiful specimens of the mule. Princes are seen riding on mules, or drawn by them in handsome litters, while their attendants accompany them on horseback. The camel is seen only in the north. Many birds of prey abound, including minos, crows, and magpies. The people are fond of songbirds, especially the thrush, the canary, and the lark. The lovely gold and silver pheasants are well known, and also the mandarin duck, the emblem to the Chinese of conjugal fidelity. Many geese too are reared and eaten, while the ducks are artificially hatched. The number of pigs is enormous and fish are a plentiful supply of food.

The people are very fond of flowers and are excellent gardeners, but their favorites are mostly cultivated in pots instead of in beds.

CHINESE STREET SCENE

Silk, linen, and cotton furnish abundant provision for the clothing of the race. China was no doubt the original home of silk. The mulberry tree grows everywhere and silk worms flourish as widely. In all provinces some silk is produced, but the best is furnished from Kwang-tung, Sze-chwan, and Chehchiang. From the twenty-third century B.C. and earlier, the care of the silk worm and the spinning and weaving of its produce have been

CHINESE FARMER

the special work of women. As it is the duty of the sovereign to turn over a few furrows in the spring to stimulate the people to their agricultural tasks, so his consort should perform an analogous ceremony with her silk worms and mulberry trees. The manufactures of silk are not inferior to or less brilliant than any that are produced in Europe, and nothing can exceed the embroidery of the Chinese. The cotton plant appears to have been introduced some eight hundred years ago from Eastern Turkestan and is now cultivated most extensively in the basin of the Chiang River. The well known nankeen is named for Nanking, a center for its manufacture. Of woolen fabrics the production is not large, but there am felt caps, rugs of camels hair and furs of various kinds.

While the Chinese have done justice to most of the natural capabilities of their country, they have greatly failed in developing its mineral resources. The skill which their lapidaries display in cutting the minerals and jewels is well known, but in the development of the utilitarian minerals they have been very negligent. The coal fields of China are enormous, but the majority of then can hardly be said to be more than scratched. Immense deposits of iron ore are still untouched. Copper, lead, tin, silver, and gold are known to exist in many places but little has been done to make the stores of them available. More attention has been directed to their mines since their government and companies began to have steamers of their own and a scheme has been approved by the government for working the gold mines in the valley of the Amoor River. With the government once conscious of its mineral wealth, there is no limit to the results which it may bring, about.

The commerce of China with the western nations has been constantly on the increase for many years. The number of vessels entering and clearing at the various treaty ports is now between thirty thousand and thirty-five thousand annually, and the value of the whole trade, import and export, approximates $300,000,000 annually. Of course the two principal exports are tea and silk. About half of the trade is done by means of vessels under the British flag, and nearly half of the remainder are vessels of foreign type, but owned by Chinese and sailing under the Chinese flag.

The capitals of the different divisions of the empire are all walled cities, and these form a striking feature of the country. There are important distinctions between the cities of the third class, most of which are designated as hien, a few as cheo and others as ting. Though varying considerably in size, these different cities present nearly the uniform appearance. They are surrounded by walls from twenty to thirty-five feet in height, and are entered by large arched gateways which open into the principal streets and are shut and barred at night. These walls are from twenty to twenty-five feet thick at the base and somewhat narrower at the top. The outside is of solid masonry from two to four feet thick, built of hewn stone, or bricks backed with earth, broken tiles, etc. There is generally a lighter stone facing on the inside. The outside is surmounted by a parapet with embrasures generally built of brick.

The circumferences of the provincial cities vary from eight to fifteen miles; those of the fu cities from four to ten miles, and those of the hien cities from two or three to five miles. Some of the larger and more important cities contain a smaller one, with its separate walls, enclosed within the larger outside walls. This is the Tartar or military city. It is occupied exclusively by Tartars with their families, forming a colony or garrison, and numbering generally several thousand soldiers. In times of insurrection and rebellion the emperor depends principally upon these Tartar colonies to hold possession of the cities where they are stationed. In such emergencies the inhabitants of these enclosed Tartar cities, knowing that their lives and the lives of their families are at stake, defend themselves with great desperation.

The provincial capitals contain an average population of nearly one million inhabitants; the fu cities from one hundred thousand to six hundred thousand or even more while the cities of the third class, which are much more numerous, generally contain several tens of thousands. The most of these towns of different classes have outgrown their walls, and frequently one-fourth or even one-third of the inhabitants live in the suburbs, which in some cases extend three or four miles outside the walls in different directions. Property is less valuable in these suburbs, not only because it is removed from the business parts of the city, but also because it is more liable to be destroyed in times of rebellion. All the names to be found on even our largest maps of China, are the names of walled cities, and many of those of the third class are not down for want of space. The total number of these cities is more than one thousand seven hundred. From the number and size of the cities of China it might be inferred that they contain the greater portion of the inhabitants of the empire. This is however by no means the case. The Chinese are mainly an agricultural people and live for the most part in the almost innumerable villages which everywhere dot its fertile plains. A detached or isolated farm house is seldom seen. The country people live in towns or hamlets for the sake of society and mutual protection. Most of the cities, even the smaller ones, have thousands of these villages under their jurisdiction. In the more populous parts of China will frequently be found, within a radius of three or four miles, from one hundred and fifty to two hundred of these villages.

The estimate of population made on a previous page gives an average population of about three hundred persons to the square mile, while that of Belgium and some other European countries is greater. Perhaps no country in the world is more fertile and capable of supporting a dense population than China. Every available spot of ground is brought under cultivation, and nearly all the land is made use of to provide food for man, pasture fields being almost unknown. The masses of China eat very little animal food, and what they do eat is mostly pork and fowls, the raising of which requires little or no waste of ground. The comparatively few horses and cattle and sheep which are found in the country are kept in stables, or graze upon the hill tops, or are tethered by the sides of canals. Taking these facts into consideration, that an extended and exceedingly fertile country under the highest state of cultivation, is taxed to its utmost capacity to supply the wants of a frugal and industrious people, the estimate of population need not excite incredulity.

Nearly all of the cities marked on our maps of the coast of China, are now open ports for traffic and residence of foreigners. The most northerly of these is Niuchwang and the most southern Pak-hoi, while between these familiar names are those of Canton, Swatow, Amoy, Poochow, Ningpo, Shanghai, Tien-tsin and several others. Interior cities have been opened to foreigners include a number on the Chiang River, the one farthest inland being I-chang. Peking is also accessible to foreigners; and several ports on the islands of Hainan and Formosa are opened by treaty. The population of these cities cannot be told with much exactness, as the Chinese census can scarcely claim accuracy. But the largest cities, such as Canton and Peking, are generally credited, in common with several others even smaller, with passing the million mark.

The Chinese government is one of the great wonders of history. It presents to-day the same character which it possessed more

AN IMPERIAL AUDIENCE

than three thousand years ago, and which it has retained ever since, during a period which covers the authentic history of the world. The government may be described as being in theory a patriarchal despotism. The emperor is the father of his people, and just as in a family the father's law is supreme, so the emperor exercises complete control over his subjects, even to the extent of holding, under certain recognized conditions, their lives in his hands. But from time immemorial it has been held by the highest constitutional authorities that the duties existing between the emperor and his people are reciprocal, and that though it is the duty of the people to render a loyal and willing obedience to the emperor, so long as his rule is just and beneficent, it is equally incumbent upon them to resist his authority, to depose him, and even to put him to death, in case he should desert the paths of rectitude and virtue.

As a matter of fact however, it is very difficult to say what extent of power the emperor actually wields. The outside world sees only the imperial bolts, but how they are forged or whose is the hand that shoots them none can tell. The most common titles of the emperor are Hwang-Shang, "The August Lofty One," and Tien-Tsz, "The Son of Heaven." He lives in unapproachable grandeur, and is never seen except by members of his own family and high state officers, save once a year when he gives audience to few foreign diplomats. Nothing is omitted which call add to the dignity and sacredness of his person or character. Almost everything used by him or in his service is tabooed from the common people, and distinguished by some peculiar mark or color so as to keep up the impression of awe with which he is regarded, and which is so powerful an auxiliary to his throne. The outward gate of the palace must always be passed on foot, and the paved entrance walk leading up to it call be used only by him. The vacant throne, or even a screen of yellow silk thrown over a chair, is worshipped equally with his actual presence, and an imperial dispatch is received in the provinces with incense and prostration.

The throne is not strictly and necessarily hereditary, though the son of the emperor generally succeeds to it The emperor appoints his successor, but it is supposed that in doing so he will

PREPARATION OF VERMICELLI

have supreme regard for the best good of his subjects, and will be governed by the will of heaven, indicated by the conferring of regal gifts, and by providential circumstances pointing out the individual whom heaven has chosen. Of course in the case of unusually able men, such as the second and fourth were of the present dynasty, their influence is more felt than that of less energetic rulers; but the throne of China is so hedged in with ceremonials and so padded with official etiquette that unless its occupant be a man of supreme ability he cannot fail to fall under the guidance of his ministers and favorites. In governing so large a realm, of course it is necessary for the emperor to delegate his authority to numerous officers who are regarded as his agents and representatives in carrying out the imperial will. What they do the emperor does through them. The recognized patriarchal character of the government is seen in the familiar expressions of the people, particularly at times when they consider themselves injured or aggrieved by their officers, when they are apt to say, "A strange way for parents to treat their children."

The government of the empire, omitting the regulation of the imperial court and family, or the special Manchoo department, is conducted from the capital, supervising, directing, controlling the different provincial administrations, and exercising the power of removing from his post any official whose conduct may be irregular or dangerous to the state.

There is the Grand Cabinet, the privy council of the emperor in whose presence it meets daily to transact the business of the state, between the hours of 4:00 and 6:00 A.M. Its members are few and hold other offices. There is also the Grand Secretariat, formerly the supreme council, but under the present dynasty very much superseded by the Cabinet. It consists of four grand and two assistant grand secretaries, half of them Manchoos and half Chinese. The business on which the Cabinet deliberates comes before it from the six boards or Luh-pu. These are departments of long standing in the government, having been modeled on much the same plan during the ancient dynasties. At the head of each board are two presidents, called Shang-shu, and four vice-presidents called Shi-lang, alternately a Manchoo and a Chinese. There are three subordinate grades of officers in each board,

Young Lady of Quality

CHINESE LADIES

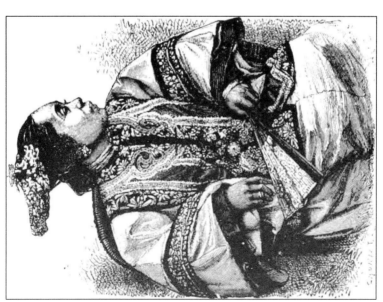

Newly Married

with a great number of minor clerks, and their appropriate departments for conducting the details of the general and peculiar business coming under the cognizance of the board, the whole being arranged in the most business-like style.

The six boards are respectively of Civil Office, of Revenue, of Ceremonies, of War, of Punishments, and of Works. In 1861 the changed relations between the empire and foreign nations led to the formation of what may be called a seventh board styled the Taung-li yamen, or Court of Foreign Affairs. There is also another important department which must be mentioned, the censorate, members of which exercise a supervision over the board, and are entrusted with the duty of exposing errors and crimes in every department of government. Distributed through the provinces they memorialize the emperor on all subjects connected with the welfare oɪ ᴜᴜ people and the conduct of the government. Sometimes they do not shrink even from the dangerous task of criticising the conduct of the emperor himself.

The different boards are all charged with the superintendence of the affairs of the eighteen provinces into which the empire is divided. Fifteen of these provinces are grouped into eight viceroyalties, and the remaining three are administered by a governor. Each province is autonomous, or nearly so, and the supreme authorities, whether viceroys or governors, are practically independent so long as they act in accordance with the very minute regulations laid down for their guidance. The principal function of the Peking government is to see that these regulations are carried out, and in case they should not be to call the offending viceroy or governor to account. Below the governor-general or governor of a province, are the lieutenant-governor, commonly called the treasurer, the provincial judge, the salt-comptroller, and the grain-intendant. The provinces are further divided for the purposes of administration into prefectures, departments, and districts. Each has its officers, magistrates, and a whole host of petty underlings. The rank of the different officials in these provinces is indicated by a knob or button on the top of their caps. In the two highest it is made of red coral; in the third it is clear blue; in the fourth it is lapis lazuli; in the fifth of crystal; in the sixth of an opaque white stone; and in the three lowest it is yellow, of gold or gilt. They also wear insignia or badges embroidered on a square patch in the front or back of their robes, representing birds on the civilians and animals on the military officers.

Each viceroy raises his own army and navy, which he pays, or sometimes unfortunately does not pay, out of the revenues of the government. He levies his own taxes, and except in particular cases is the final court of appeal in all judicial matters within the limits of his rule. But in return for this latitude allowed him, he is held personally responsible for the good government of his territory. If by any chance serious disturbances break out and continue unsuppressed, he is called to account, as having his misconduct contributed to them, and he in his turn looks to his subordinates to maintain order and execute justice within their jurisdiction. Of himself he has no power to remove or punish his subordinate officials, but has to refer all complaints against them to Peking. The personal responsibility resting upon him of maintaining order makes him a severe critic on those who serve under him, and very frequently junior officials are impeached and punished at the instigation their chief. Incapable and unworthy officials, constant opium smokers, those who misappropriate public money, and these who fail to arrest criminals, are those who meet swift punishment. On the whole the conduct of junior officials is carefully watched.

As has been already said, the affairs of each province are administered by the viceroy, or governor, and his subordinates, and speaking generally their rule is as enlightened and as just as could be expected in all oriental country where public opinion finds only a very imperfect utterance. Official purity and justice must be treated as comparative terms in China. The constitution of the civil service renders it next to impossible that any office holder can be clean-handed. The salaries awarded are low, out of all proportion to the necessary expenses pertaining to the offices to which they are apportioned, and the consequence is that in some way or other the officials are compelled to make up the deficiency from the pockets of those subject to them. As a rule. Mandarins seldom enter office with private fortunes, and the wealth therefore, which soothes the declining years of veteran

PALANQUIN OF A HIGH OFFICIAL

officials, may be fairly assumed to be ill-gotten gain. There are laws against these exactions, and very often some magistrate is degraded or executed for levying illegal assessments. The immunity which some mandarins enjoy from the just consequences of their crimes, and

THE GOVERNOR OF A PROVINCE

the severity with which the law is vindicated in the cases of others for much lighter offenses, has a sinister aspect. But in a system of which bribery and corruption practically form a part, one need not expect to find purity in any direction. And it is not too much to say that the whole civil service is, judged by an American standard, corrupt to the core. The people however are ligbtly taxed and they readily submit to

FEMALE TYPES AND CONSTUMES

limited extortion so long as the rule of the mandarin is otherwise just and beneficent.

How rarely does a mandarin earn the respect and affection of the people is obvious from the great parade which is made on the departure from their posts of the very occasional officials who are fortunate enough to-have done so. Archdeacon Gray relates that during his residence of a quarter of a century at Canton he only met one man who had entitled himself to the regret of the people at his departure. When the time came for this man to leave the city, the people rose in multitudes to do him honor and begged for him to return if he could. A somewhat similar scene occurred at Tien-tsin in 1861, on the departure of the most benevolent prefect that the city had ever seen. The people accompanied him beyond the gate on his road to Peking with every token of honor and finally begged from him his boots, which they carried back in triumph and hung up as a memento in the temple of the city god. Going to the opposite extreme, it sometimes happens that the people, goaded into rebellion by a sense of wrong, rise in arms against some particularly obnoxious mandarin and drive him from the district. But the Chinese are essentially unwarlike, and it must be some act of gross oppression to stir their blood to fever heat.

A potent means of protection against oppression is granted to the people by the appointment of imperial censors throughout the empire, whose duty it is to report to the throne all cases of misrule, injustice, or neglect on the part of the mandarins which come to their knowledge. The same tolerance which is shown by the people towards the shortcoming and ill deeds of the officials, is displayed by these men in the discharge of their duties. Only aggravated cases make them take their pens in hand, but when they do, it must be confessed that they show little mercy. Neither are they respectors of persons; their lash fulls alike on all from the emperor on his throne to the policerunners in magisterial courts. Nor is their plain speaking more amazing than the candor with which their memorials affecting the characters of great and small alike are published in the Peking Gazette. The gravest charges, such as of peculation, neglect of duty, injustice, or incompetence, are brought against mandarins of all ranks and are openly published in the official paper.

In the administration of justice the same lax morality as in other branches of government exists, and bribery is largely resorted to by litigants, more especially in civil cases. As rule money in excess of the legal fees has in the first instance to be paid to clerks and secretaries before s case can be put down for hearing, and a decision of the presiding mandarin is too often influenced by the sums of money which find their

PUNISHMENT BY THE GANGUE

way into his purse from the pockets of either suitor. But the greatest blot on Chinese administration the inhumanity shown to both culprits and witnesses in criminal procedure. Tortures of the most painful and revolting kind are used to extort evidence, and punishments scarcely more severely cruel are inflicted on the guilty parties. Flogging with bamboos, beating the jaws with thick pieces of leather, or the ankles with a stick, are some of the preliminary tortures applied to witnesses or culprits who refuse to give the evidence expected of them. Further refinements of cruelty are reserved for hardened offenders by means of which infinite pain and often permanent injury are inflicted.

It follows as a natural consequence that in a country where torture is thus resorted to the punishments inflicted on criminals must be proportionately cruel. Death, the final punishment, can unfortunately be inflicted in various ways, and a sliding scale of capital punishment is used by

FLOGGING A CULPRIT

the Chinese to mark their sense of the varying heinousness of murderous crimes. For parricide, matricide and wholesale murders, the usual sentence is that of Ling-che, or "ignominious and slow death." In the carrying out of this sentence the culprit is fastened to a cross, and cuts varying in number, at the discretion of the judge, from eight to one hundred and twenty are made first on the face and fleshy parts of the body, next the heart is pierced, and finally when death has been thus caused, the limbs are separated from the body and divided. During a recent year ten cases in which this punishment was indicted were reported in the official Peking Gazette. In ordinary cases of capital punishment execution by beheading is the common mode.

This is a speedy and merciful death, the skill gained by frequent experience enabling the executioner in almost every case to perform his task with one blow. Another death which is less horrible to Chinamen, who view any mutilation of the body as an extreme disgrace, is by strangulation. The privilege of so passing out of the world is accorded at times to influential criminals, whose crimes are not of so heinous a nature as to demand their decapitation; and occasionally they are even allowed to be their own executioners.

Asiatics are almost invariably careless about the sufferings of others, and the men of China are no exception to the rule. It is almost impossible to exaggerate the horrors of Chinese prison. The filth and dirt of the rooms, the brutality of the jailers, the miserable diet, and the entire absence of the commonest sanitary arrangements make a picture which is too horrible to draw in detail.

Chinese law-givers have distinguished very markedly between crimes accompanied and unaccompanied with violence. For offenses of the latter description, punishments of a comparatively light nature are inflicted, such as wearing a wooden collar, and piercing the ears with arrows, to the ends of which are attached slips of paper on which are inscribed the crime of which the culprit has been guilty. Frequently the criminals bearing these signs of their disgrace are paraded up and down the street where their offense was committed, and sometimes in more serious cases they are flogged through the leading thoroughfares of the city, preceded by a herald who announces the nature of their misdemeanors. But to give a list of Chinese punishments will be to exhaust the ingenuity of man to torture his fellow creatures. The subject is a horrible one and it is a relief to turn from the dingy prison gates and the halls of so-called justice.

After this review of the impersonal, and the material, and the official character of the Chinese empire as a nation, let us now turn to the more personal consideration of the people themselves, their characteristics, and their manner of life and thought.

OUTSIDE PEKING
FROM A SKETCH

THE CHINESE PEOPLE

Severity of the Judgment of Americans and Chinese Against One Another—Each Sees the Worst Side of the Other—Characteristics of the Chinese, Their Physique, Temperament, and Morals—Tests of Intellectuality—Marriage Customs of the Chinese—The Engagement The Wedding Ceremony—The Position of Women—Concubinage—Divorce—Family Relationship—Dress of Men and Women—Distorted Feet versus Queues—Chinese Houses and Home Life—Children—Education and Schools—National Festivities—Music and Art—Chinese Religions—Language and Literature.

In treating of the personal characteristics and customs of the Chinese people it is the desire of the writer to get away from the hackneyed descriptions of pigtails, shaven heads, thick soled shoes, assumption of dignity and superiority, and great ignorance concerning many subjects with which we are familiar, which usually mark the pages of articles and books concerning this race. The Chinanan is believed by many to be the personification of stupidity, and many writers who wish to make readable matter gladly seize upon and exaggerate anything which can be made to appear grotesque and ridiculous. It would be but a poor answer to these views to say that they correspond remarkably with those which the Chinese entertain of us. They also enjoy a great deal of pleasantry at our expense, finding it almost impossible to regard otherwise than as ludicrous our short cropped hair, tight fitting, ungraceful, and uncomfortable looking clothes, men's thin soled leather shoe, tall stiff hats, gloves in summer time, the wasp-like appearance of ladies with their small waists, our remarkable ignorance of the general rules of propriety, and the strange custom of a man and his wife walking together in public! These views we can afford to laugh at as relating to comparatively trivial matters, but they think they have the evidence that we are also inferior to them in intellectuality, in refinement, in civilization, and especially morals. It is evident that one party or the other has made a serious mistake, and it would be but a natural and reasonable presumption that both may have erred to some extent. We should look at this matter from an impartial standpoint, and take into view not simply facts which are comparatively unimportant and exceptional, but those which are fundamental and of widespread influence, and should construe these facts justly and generously. We should take pains not to form the judgment that because a people or a custom is different from our own it is therefore necessarily worse.

There are many reasons why unfair judgments have been formed by us against the Chinese and by the Chinese against Europeans and Americans. Each nation is apt to see the worst side of the other. It so happens that the Chinese who have come to America are almost all from the southern provinces and from the lower classes of the worst part of the empire. We have formed many of our impressions from our observation of these low class adventurers. They on the other hand have not received the treatment here which would cause them to carry back to China kindly opinions of Americans.

In China the same or similar conditions have existed. In the open ports, where a large foreign commerce has sprung up, an immense number of Chinese congregate from the interior. Many of them are adventurers who come to these places to engage in the general scramble for wealth. The Chinamen of the best class are, as a matter of fact, not the most numerous in the open ports. Moreover foreign ideas and customs prevail to a great extent in these foreign communities, and the natives, whatever they might have been originally, gradually become more or less denationalized, and present a modified type of their race. The Chinese being every day brought into contact with drunken sailors and unscrupulous traders from the west, new lessons are constantly learned from them in the school of duplicity and immorality. The Chinese of this class are no fitting type of the race. It is an accepted fact that the great seaports of the world, where international trade holds sway, are the worst centers of vice, and no estimate of a people formed from these cities call be just.

The Chinese as a race are of a phlegmatic and impassive temperament, and physically less active and energetic than European and American nations. Children are not fond of athletic and vigorous sports, but prefer marbles, kite flying, and quiet games of ball or spinning tops. Men take an easy stroll for recreation, but never a rapid walk for exercise and are seldom in a hurry or excited. They are also characteristically timid and docile. But while the Chinese are deficient in active courage and daring, they are not in passive resistance. They are comparatively apathetic as regards pain and death, and have great powers of physical endurance as well as great persistency and obstinacy. Physical development and strength and longevity vary in different parts of the empire. In and about canton, as well as in most parts of the south, from which we have derived most of our impressions of China, the people are small in stature; but in the province of Shan-tung in the north, men varying height from five feet eight inches to six feet are very common, while some of them are considerably taller. In this part of China too, one frequently finds laborers more than seventy years of age working daily at their trades, and it is not unusual to hear of persons who have reached the age of ninety or more.

The intellectuality of the Chinese is made evident by so many obvious and weighty facts, that it seems strange that persons of ordinary intelligence and information should ever have questioned it. We have before us a system of government and code of laws which will bear favorable comparison with those of European nations, and have elicited a generous tribute of admiration and praise from the most competent students. The practical wisdom and foresight of those who constructed this system are evidenced by the fact that it has stood the test of time, enduring longer than any other which man has devised during the world's history; that it has bound together under one common rule, a population to which the world affords no parallel and given a degree of prosperity and wealth which may well challenge our wonder. It is intelligent thought which has given China such a prominence in the east and also in the eyes of Christendom. She may well point with pride to her authentic history reaching back through more than thirty centuries; to her extensive literature, containing many works of sterling and permanent value; to her thoroughly elaborated language possessed of a remarkable power of expression; to her list of scholars, and her proficiency in belleslettres. If these do not constitute evidences of intellectuality, it would be difficult to say where such evidences could be found, or on what basis we ourselves will rest our claim of intellectual superiority.

China has been so arrogant and extravagant in her assumptions of pre-eminence, that we have perhaps for this very reason been indisposed to accord to her the position to which she is fairly entitled. It should be remembered, that ignorant until recently of western nations, as they have been of her, she has compared herself simply with the nations around her, and a partial excuse for her overweening self conceit may be found in the fact that she only regarded herself as the nations with which she is acquainted have regarded her. She has been for ages the great center of light and civilization in eastern Asia. She has given literature and religion to Japan, to Corea, and to Manchooria, and has been looked up to by these and other smaller nations as their acknowledged teacher. The Japanese have produced no great teachers or sages which they would presume to compare with those of China; and it is clearest evidence of their acknowledgment of the literary superiority of the Chinese that they use Chinese classics as text books in their schools much as we do those of Greece and Rome. It is true that the Chinese know hardly anything of the modern arts and sciences and that there is no word in their language to designate some of them; but how much did our ancestors know two hundred years ago of chemistry, geology, philosophy, anatomy, and other kindred sciences. What did we know fifty years ago of the steamboat, the railroad, and the telegraph? And is our comparative want of knowledge a few years ago and that of our ancestors to be taken as evidence of inferiority of race and intellect? Furthermore, if we go back a few hundred years we are apt to find many things to establish the claims of the Chinese as a superior rather than inferior race. There are excellent grounds to credit the Chinese with the invention or discovery of printing, the use of the magnetic needle, the manufacture and use of gunpowder, of silk fabrics, and of china ware and porcelain, and there seems no doubt that the Chinese discovered America from the westward, long before the discoveries of Europeans.

Intellectual power manifests itself in a variety of ways, and glaring defects are often found associated in the same individual with remarkable powers and capabilities, as particular faculties both of mind and body are often cultivated and developed at the expense of others. Chinese education has very little regard to the improvement of the reasoning powers, and Chinese scholars are deficient in logical acumen and very inferior to the Hindoos in this respect; but in developing and storing the memory they are without a rival. Again their system of training effectually discourages and precludes freedom and originality of thought, while it has the compensating advantages of creating a love of method and order, habitual subjection to authority, and a remarkable uniformity in character and ideas. Perhaps the results which they have realized in fusing such a vast mass of beings into one homogeneous body, could have been reached in no other way.

The morality of the Chinese presents another subject about which there is a wide difference of opinion. It may be a matter of interest and profit to turn for a moment to the views which the Chinese generally entertain of our morality, and their reasons for these views. They are all familiar with the fact that foreigners introduced opium into China, in opposition to the earnest and persistent remonstrances of the Chinese government; that out of the opium trade grew the first war with China; and that when the representatives of Christian England urged the Chinese government to legalize the trade and make it a source of revenue, the Chinese emperor replied that he would not use as a means of revenue that which brought suffering and misery upon his people.

The Chinese form their opinions of western morality to a great extent from the sailors on shore-leave at the open ports, and these men are proverbially vicious under such circumstances. For years foreigners of this class have commanded many of the piratical fleets on the coasts of China, and foreign thieves and robbers have infested many of the inland canals and rivers. In business dealings with strangers from western lands the natives find that duplicity and dishonesty are not confined to their own people. Replying to our criticism of the system of concubinage, the Chinese point to the numerous class of native women in the foreign communities, fostered and patronized by foreigners alone, who appear in the streets with an effrontery which would be regarded as utterly indecent and intolerable in most Chinese cities.

The large importation from Europe of obscene pictures which are offered at every hand, is another fact which the educated Chinese cites in answer to criticisms of his people's morality.

On the general subject of morality and Chinese moral teaching, two quotations from the writings of eminent Englishmen who lived in China for many years are pertinent. Sir John Davis says: "The most commendable feature of the Chinese system is the general diffusion of elementary moral education among the lower orders. It is in the preference of moral to physical instruction that even me might perhaps wisely take a leaf out of the Chinese book, and do something to reform this most mechanical age of ours." The opinion of Thomas Taylor Meadows is thus expressed: "No people whether of ancient or modern times has possessed a sacred literature so completely exempt the Chinese from licentious descriptions and from every offensive expression. There is not a single sentence in the whole of their sacred books and their annotations that may not when translated word for word be read aloud in any family in England."

It must be acknowledged that the Chinese give many evidences, not only in their literature, but also in their paintings and sculpture, of a scrupulous care to avoid all indecent and immoral associations and suggestions. In referring to the above peculiarity of Chinese views and customs, these remarks are not, of course, concerning the private lives and practices of the people, but of their standard of propriety and of what the public taste requires, in objects which are openly represented to be seen and admired by the young and old of both sexes.

The government of the empire is modeled on the government of a household, and at the root of all family ties, says one of the Chinese classics, is the relation of husband and wife, which is as the relation of heaven and earth. Chinese historians record that the rite of marriage was first instituted by the Emperor Fuh-he, who reigned in the twenty-eighth century B.C. But before this period there is abundant evidence to show that as amongst all other peoples the first form of marriage was by capture. At the present day marriage is probably more universal in China than in any other civilized country in the world, for it is regarded as something dispensable and few men pass the age of twenty without taking to themselves a wife. To die without leaving behind a son to perform the burial rites and to offer up the fixed periodical sacrifices at the tomb, is one of the most direful fates that can overtake a Chinaman, and he seeks to avoid it by an early marriage.

Like every other rite in China that of marriage is fenced in with a host of ceremonies. In a vast majority of cases the bridegroom never sees his bride until the wedding night, it being considered a grave breach of etiquette for young men and maidens to associate together or even to see one another. Of course it does occasionally happen that either by stealth or chance a pair become acquainted; but whether they have thus associated, or whether they are perfect strangers, the first formal overture must of necessity be made by a professional go-between, who having received a commission from the parents of a young man, proceeds to the house of the young woman and makes a formal proposal on behalf of the would-be bridegroom's parents. If the young lady's father approves the proposed alliance, the suitor sends the lady some presents as an earnest of his intentions.

The parents next exchange documents which set forth the hour, day, month, and year when the young people were born, and the maiden names of their mothers. Astrologers are then called in to cast the horoscopes, and should these be favorable the engagement is formally entered into, but not so irrevocably that there are not several orthodox ways of breaking it off. But should things go smoothly, the bridegroom's father writes a formal letter of agreement to the lady's father, accompanied by presents, consisting in some cases of sweetmeats and a live pig, and in others of a goose and gander, which are regarded as emblems of conjugal fidelity. Two large cards are also prepared by the bridegroom, and on these are written the particulars of the engagement. One is sent to the lady and the other he keeps. She in return now makes a present to the suitor according to his rank and fortune. Recourse is then again had to astrologers to fix a fortunate day for the final ceremony, on the evening of which the bridegroom's best man proceeds to the house of the lady and conducts her to her future home in a red sedan chair, accompanied by musicians who enliven the procession by wedding airs. At the door of the house the bride alights from her sedan, and is lifted over a pan of burning charcoal laid on the threshold by two "women of luck," whose husbands and children must he living.

In the reception room the bridegroom awaits his bride on a raised dais, at the afoot of which she humbly prostrates herself. He then descends to her level, and removing her veil gazes on her face for the first time. Without exchanging a word they seat themselves side by side, and each tries to sit on a part of the dress of the other, it being considered that the one who succeeds in so doing will hold rule in the household. This trial of skill over, the pair proceed to the hall, and there before the family altar worship heaven and earth and their ancestors. They then go to dinner in their apartment, through the open door of which the guests scrutinize and make their remarks on the appearance and demeanor of the bride. This ordeal is the more trying to her, since etiquette forbids her to eat anything, a prohibition which is not shared by the bridegroom, who enjoys the dainties provided as his appetite may suggest. The attendants next hand to each in turn a cup of wine, and having exchanged pledges, the wedding ceremonies come to an end. In some parts of the country it is customary for the bride to sit up late into the night answering riddles which are propounded to her by the guests; in other parts it is usual for her to show herself for a time in the hall, whither her husband does not accompany her, as it is contrary to etiquette for a husband and wife ever to appear together in public. For the same reason she goes to pay the customary visit to her parents on the third day after the wedding alone, and for the rest of her wedded life she enjoys the society of her husband only in the privacy of her apartments.

The lives of women in China, and especially of married women, are such as to justify the wish often expressed by them that in their next state of existence they may be born men. Even if in their baby days they escape the infanticidal tendencies of their parents, they are regarded as secondary considerations compared with their brothers. The philosophers from Confucius downward have all agreed in assigning them an inferior place to men.

DISCIPLINE ON THE MARCH, IN THE CHINESE ARMY

When the time comes for them to marry, custom requires them in nine cases out of ten, as we have seen, to take a leap in the dark, and that wife is fortunate who finds in her husband a congenial and faithful companion.

There is but one proper wife in the family, but there is no law against a man's having secondary wives or concubines; and such connections are common enough wherever the means of u family are sufficient for their support. The concubine occupies in the family an inferior position to the wife, and her children, if she has any, belong by law to the wife.

There are seven legal grounds for divorcing a wife: disobedience to her husband's parents; not giving birth to a son; Dissolute conduct; jealousy; talkativeness; thieving, and leprosy. These grounds however may be nullified by the three considerations: "If her parents be dead; if she has passed with her husband through the years of mourning for his parents; and if he has become rich from being poor.

So many are the disabilities of married women, that many girls prefer going into nunneries or even committing suicide to trusting their future to men of whom they can know nothing but from the interested reports of the go-between.

The re-marriage of widows is regarded as an impropriety, and in wealthy families is seldom practiced. But among the poorer classes necessity often compels a widow to seek another bread winner. Some, however, having been unfortunate in their first matrimonial venture, refuse to listen to any proposal for a re-marriage, and like the young girls mentioned above seek escape by death from the importunities of relatives who desire to get them off their hands. A reverse view of matrimonial experiences is suggested by the practice of wives refusing to survive their husbands, and putting a voluntary end to their existence rather than live to mourn their loss. Such devotion is regarded by the people with great approbation a deed of suicide is generally — formed in public and with great punctiliousness.

The picture here given of married life in China has been necessarily darkly shaded, since it is, as a rule, only in its unfortu- late phases, that it affords opportunity for remark. Without, doubt there are many hundreds of thousands of families in China which are entirely happy. Happiness is after all a relative term, and Chinese women, knowing no higher status, are as a rule content to run the risk of wrongs which would be unendurable to an American woman, and to find happiness under conditions which are fortunately unknown in western countries.

The family tie in China is strong and the people are clannish. They seldom change their place of residence and most of them live where their ancestors have lived for many generations. One will frequently find the larger portion of a small village bearing the same name, in which case the village often takes its name from the family. Books on filial piety and the domestic relations recommend sons not to leave their parents when married, but to live together lovingly and harmoniously as one family. This theory is carried out in practice to some extent, in most instances. In the division of property some regard is had to primogeniture, but different sons share nearly equally. The eldest simply has somewhat larger portion and certain household relics and valuables.

The position of woman is intermediate between that which she occupies in Christian and in other non-Christian countries. The manner in which they regard their lot may be inferred from the fact related on a previous page, that the most earnest desire and prayer in worshipping in Buddhist temples is, generally, that they may be men in the next state of existence. In many families girls have no individual names, but are simply called No. One, Two, Three, Four, etc. When married they are Mr. So-and so's wife, and when they have sons they are such-and-such a boy's mother. They live in a great measure secluded, take no part in general society, and are expected to retire when a stranger or an acquaintance of the opposite sex enters the house. The claim of one's parents and brothers upon his affections is considered to be paramount to that of his wife. A reason given for this doctrine in a celebrated Chinese work is that the loss of a brother is irreparable but that of a wife is not. Women are treated with more respect and consideration as they advance in years; mothers are regarded with great affection and tenderness, and grandmothers are sometimes almost' worshipped. It must be further said that the Chinese have found the theory of inferiority of women a very difficult one to carry out in practice. There are many families in which the superiority of her will and authority is sufficiently manifest, even though not cheerfully acknowledged.

The rules and conventionalities which regulate social life are exceedingly minute and formal. Politeness is a science, and gracefulness of manners a study and discipline. The people are hospitable and generous to a fault, their desire to appear well in these respects often leading them to expenditures entirely disproportionate to their means.

When under the influence of passion, quarrels arise, the women resort to abuse in violent language, extreme in proportion to the length of time during which the feelings which prompted them have been restrained. Men bluster and threaten in a manner quite frightful to those unaccustomed to it, but seldom come to blows. In cases of deep resentment the injured party often adopts a mode of revenge which is very characteristic. Instead of killing the object of his hate, he kills himself on the doorstep of his enemy, thereby casting obloquy and the stigma of murder on the adversary.

In matters of dress, with one or two exceptions, the Chinese must be acknowledged to have used a wise discretion. They wear nothing that is tight fitting, and make a greater difference between their summer and winter clothing than is customary among ourselves. The usual dress of a coolie in summer is a loose fitting pair of cotton trousers and an equally loose jacket; but the same man in winter will be seen wearing quilted cotton clothes, or if he should be an inhabitant of the northern provinces a sheepskin robe, superadded to an abundance of warm clothing intermediate between it and his shirt. By the wealthier classes silk, satin, and gauze are much worn in the summer, and woolen or handsome fur clothes in the winter. Among such people it is customary except in the seclusion of their homes, to wear both in summer and winter long tunics coming down to the ankles.

In summer non-official Chinamen leave their heads uncovered, but do not seem to suffer any inconvenience from the great heat. On the approach of summer an edict is issued fixing the day upon which the summer costume is to be adopted throughout the empire, and again as winter draws near, the time for putting on winter dress is announced in the same formal manner. Fine straw or bamboo forms the material of the summer hat, the outside of which is covered with fine silk. At this season also the thick silk robes and the heavy padded jackets worn in winter are exchanged for light silk or satin tunics. The winter cap has a turned-up brim and is covered with satin with a black cloth lining, and as in the case of the summer cap a tassel of red silk covers the entire crown.

The wives of mandarins wear the same embroidered insignia on their dresses as their husbands, and their style of dress as well as that of Chinese women generally bears a resemblance to that of the men. They wear a loose fitting tunic which reaches below the knee, and trousers which are drawn in at the ankle after the bloomer fashion. On state occasions they wear a richly embroidered petticoat coming down to the feet, which hangs square both before and behind and is pleated at the sides like a Highlander's kilt. The mode of doing the hair varies in almost every province. At Canton the women plaster their back hair into the shape of a teapot handle, and adorn the sides with pins and ornaments, while the young girls proclaim their unmarried state by setting their hair in fringe across their foreheads after a fashion not unknown among ourselves. In most parts of the country, flowers, natural when obtainable and artificial when not so, are largely used to deck out the head dresses, and considerable taste is shown in the choice of colors and the manner in which they are arranged.

Thus far there is nothing to find fault with in female fashions in China, but the same cannot be said of the way in which they treat their faces and feet. In many countries the secret art of removing traces of the ravages of time with the appliances of the toilet table has been and is practised; but by an extravagant and hideous use of pigments and cosmetics, the Chinese girl not only conceals the fresh complexion of youth, but produces those very disfigurements which furnish the only possible excuse for artificial complexions. Their poets also have declared that a woman's eyebrows should be arched like a rainbow or shaped like a willow leaf, and the consequence is that wishing to act up to the idea thus pictured, China women with the aid of tweezers

A TYPHONN

remove all the hairs of their eyebrows which straggle the least out of the required line, and when the task becomes impossible even with the help of these instruments, the paint brush or a stick of charcoal is brought into requisition. A comparison of one such painted lily with the natural healthy complexion, bright eyes, laughing lips, and dimpled cheeks of a Canton boat girl, for example, is enough to vindicate nature's claim to superiority over art a thousand fold.

But the chief offense of Chinese women is in their treatment of their feet. Various explanations are current as to the origin of the custom of

BANDAGING THE FEET

deforming the women's feet. Some say that it is an attempt to imitate the peculiarly shaped foot of a certain beautiful empress; others that it is a device intended to restrain the gadding-about tendencies of women; but however that may be, the practice is universal except among the Manchoos and the Hakka population at Canton, who have natural feet. The feet are first bound when the child is about five years old and the muscles of locomotion have consequently had time to develop.

A cotton bandage two or three inches wide is wound tightly about the foot in different directions. The four smaller toes are bent under the foot, and the instep is forced upward and backward. The foot therefore assumes the shape of an acute triangle, the big toe forming the acute angle and the other toes, being bent under the foot, becoming almost lost or absorbed. At the same time, the shoes worn having high heels, the foot becomes nothing but a club and loses all elasticity. The consequence is that the women walk as on pegs, and the calf of the leg having no exercise shrivels up. Though the effect of this custom is to produce real deformity and a miserable tottering gait, even foreigners naturally come to associate it with gentility and good breeding, and to estimate the character and position of women much as the Chinese do, by the size of their feet. The degree of severity with which the feet are bound differs widely in the various ranks of society. Country women and the poorer classes have feet about half the natural size, while those of the genteel or fashionable class are only about three inches long.

Women in the humbler walks of life are therefore often able to move about with ease. Most ladies on the other hand are practically debarred from walking at all and are dependent on their sedan chairs for all locomotion beyond they own doors. But even in this case habit becomes a second nature and fashion triumphs over sense. No mother, however keen may be her recollection of her sufferings as a child, or however conscious she may be of the inconveniences and ills arising from her deformed feet, would ever dream of saving her own child from like immediate torture and permanent evil. Further there is probably less excuse for such a practice in China than in any other country, for the hands and feet of both men and women are naturally both small and finely shaped. The Chinese insist upon it that the custom of compressing women's feet is neither in as bad taste nor so injurious to the health as that of foreign women in compressing the waist.

The male analogue of the women's compressed feet in the shaven forepart of the head and the braided queue. The custom of thus treating the hair was imposed on the people by the first emperor of the present dynasty, in 1644. Up to that time the Chinese had allowed the hair to grow long, and were in the habit of drawing it up into a tuft on the top of the head. The introduction of the queue at the bidding of the Manchoorian conqueror was intended as a badge of conquest, and as such was at first unwillingly adopted by the people. For nearly a century the natives of outlying parts of the empire refused to submit their heads to the razor and in many districts the authorities rewarded converts to the new way by presents of money. As the custom spread these bribes were discontinued, and the converse action of treating those who refused to conform with severity, completed the conversion of the empire. At the present day every Chinaman who is not in open rebellion to the throne, shaves his head with the exception of the crown where the hair is allowed to grow to its full length. This hair is carefully braided, and falls down the back forming what is commonly known as the "pig tail." Great pride is taken, especially in the south, in having as long and as thick a queue as possible, and when nature has been niggardly in her supply of natural growth, the deficiency is supplemented by the insertion of silk in the plait.

The staff of life in China is rice. It is eaten and always eaten, from north to south and from east to west, on the tables of the rich and poor, morning, noon, and night, except among the very poor people in some of the northern non-rice producing provinces where millet takes its place. In all other parts the big bowl of boiled rice forms the staple of the meal eaten by the people, and it is accompanied by vegetables, fish and meat, according to the circumstances of the household. Among many people, however, there is a disinclination to eat meat, owing to the influence of Buddhism. The difference in the quality and expense of the food of the rich from that of the poor, consists principally in the concomitants eaten with the rice or millet. The poor have simply a dish of salt vegetables or fish, which costs comparatively little. The rich have pork, fowls, eggs, fish and game prepared in various ways.

Before each chair is placed an empty bowl and two chopsticks, while in the middle of the table stands the dishes of food. Each person fills his basin from the large dishes, or is supplied by the servants, and holding it up to his chi with his left hand he transfers its contents into his mouth with his chop-sticks with the utmost ease. The chop-sticks are held between the first and second, and the second and third fingers, and constant practice enables a Chinaman to lift up and hold the minutest atoms of food, oily and slippery as they often are, with the greatest ease. To most foreigners their skillful use is well nigh impossible. To the view of the Chinese the use of chop-sticks is an evidence of superior culture; and the use of such barbarous instruments as knives and forks, and cutting or tearing the meat from the bones on the table instead of having the food properly prepared and severed into edible morsels in the kitchen, evidences a lower type of civilization.

The meats most commonly eaten are pork, mutton, and goat's flesh, beside ducks, chickens, and pheasants, and in the north deer and hares. Beef is never exposed for sale in the Chinese markets. The meat of the few cattle which are killed is disposed of almost clandestinely. There is a strong and almost universal prejudice against eating beef, and the practice of doing so is declaimed against in some of the moral tracts. Milk is hardly used at all in the eighteen provinces, and in many places our practice of drinking it is regarded with the utmost disgust.

It must be confessed that in some parts of the country less savory viands find their place on the dinner table. In Canton, for example, dried rats have a, recognized place in the poulterers' shops and find a ready market. Horse flesh is also exposed for sale, and there are even to be found dog and cat restaurants. The flesh of black dogs and cats, and especially the former is preferred as being more nutritive. Frogs form a common dish among the poor people and are, it is needless to say, very good eating. In some parts of the country locusts and grasshoppers are eaten. At Tien-tsin men may commonly be seen standing at the corners of the 'streets frying locusts over portable fires, just as among ourselves chestnuts are cooked. Ground-grubs, silkworms and water-snakes are also occasionally treated as food. The sea, lakes, and rivers abound in fish, and as fish forms a staple food of the people the fishermen's art has been brought to a great degree of perfection. The same care as in the production of fish is extended to that of ducks and poultry. Eggs are artificially

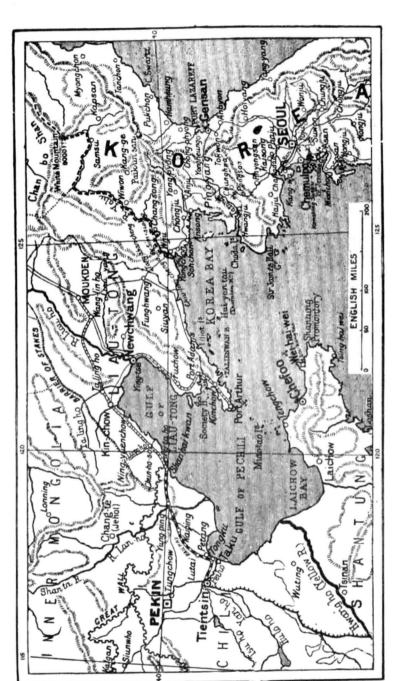

THE SEAT OF THE WAR

hatched in immense numbers, and the poultry markets and boats along the river at Canton are most amazing in their extent.

The funerals of grown persons, and especially of parents, are as remarkable for burdensome ceremonies, extravagant manifestations of grief and lavish expense, as those of children are for their coldness and neglect. Candles, incense and offerings of food are placed before the corpse, and a company of priests is engaged to chant prayers for the departed spirit. An abundance of clothing is deposited with the body in the coffin and various ceremonies are performed during several days immediately after that, and on every subsequent seventh day, closing with the seventh seven. When the coffin is carried out for burial, men and women follow in the procession clothed in coarse white garments, white being used for mourning.

Inasmuch as the coffin must remain in the hall for forty-nine days, naturally hey are prepared with a great deal of care. Very thick planks are used in its construction, cut from the hardest trees, caulked on the outside and cemented on the inside, and finally varnished or lacquered. Sometimes a coffin containing. a body is kept in the house for a considerable length of time after the forty-nine days have expired, while arrangements are being made for a burying place and other preliminaries are attended to. The lids being nailed down in cement they are perfectly air-tight.

The notions which Chinamen entertain concerning the future life rob death of half its terrors and lead them to regard their funeral ceremonies and the due performance the proper rites by their descendants as the chief factors of their future well being. Among other things the importance of securing a coffin according to the approved fashion is duly recognized, and as men approach old age they not infrequently buy their own coffins, which they keep carefully by them. The present of a coffin is considered a dutiful attention from a son to an aged father.

The choice of a site for the grave is determined by a professor of the "Fung Shuy" superstition, who, compass in hand, explores the entire district to find a spot which combines all the qualities necessary for the quiet repose of the dead. When such a favored spot has been discovered a priest is called in to determine a lucky day for the burial. This is by no means an easy matter and it often happens that the dead remain unburied for months or even years on account of the difficulties in the way of choosing either fortunate graves or lucky days.

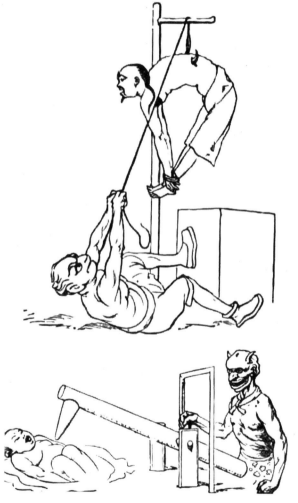

THE PUNISHMENTS OF HELL.—FROM CHINESE DRAWINGS

The ceremonies of the interment itself and of mourning that follows are most elaborate in character, and too much involved for detailed description here.

But universal as the practice of burying may be said to be in China there are exceptions to it. The Buddhist priests as a rule prefer cremation, and this custom, which came with the religion they profess from India, has at times found imitators among the laity. In Formosa the dead are exposed and dried in the air; and some of the Meaou-tsze tribes of central and southern China bury their dead, it is true, but after an interval of a year or more, having chosen a lucky day, they disinter them. On such occasions they go accompanied by their friends to the grave, and having opened the tomb they take out the bones and having brushed and washed them clean they put them back wrapped in cloth.

The necessity in the Chinese mind that their bones must rest in the soil of their native land with their ancestors, has made to exist some peculiar practices among the colonizing Chinese in the United States and other countries. The bones of those who die thus far away from home are carefully preserved by their countrymen and shipped back, sometimes after many years, to find a resting place in the Middle Kingdom.

It is a curious circumstance that in China where there exists such a profound veneration for everything old, there should not be found any ancient buildings or old ruins. That there is an abundant supply of durable materials for building is certain, and for many centuries the Chinese have been acquainted with the art of brick making, yet they have reared no building possessing enduring stability. Not only does the ephemeral nature of the tent, which would indicate their original nomadic origin and recollection of old tent homes, appear in the slender construction of Chinese houses, but even in shape they assume a tent-like form. Etiquette provides that in houses of the better class a high wall shall surround the building, and that no window shall look out ward. Consequently streets in the fashionable parts of cities have a dreary aspect. The only breaks in the long line of dismal wall are the front doors, which are generally closed, or if not, movable screens bar the sight of all beyond the door. Passing around one such screen one finds himself in a court-yard which is laid out as a garden or paved with stone. From this court yard one reaches, on either side, rooms occupied by servants, or

directly in front, another building. Through this latter another court-yard
is reached, in the rooms surrounding which the family live, and behind
this again are the women's apartments, which not infrequently give exit to
a garden at the back.

Wooden pillars support the roofs of the buildings, and the intervals
between these are filled up with brick work. The window-frames are
wooden, over which is pasted either paper or calico, or sometimes pieces of
talc to transmit the light. The doors are almost invariably folding doors; the
floors either stone or cement; and ceilings are not often used, the roof being
the only covering to the rooms. Carpets are seldom used, more especially
in southern China, where also stoves for warming purposes are known.
In the north, where in the winter the cold is very great, portable charcoal
stoves are employed and small chaffing dishes are carried about from room
to room. Delicate little hand-stoves, which gentlemen and ladies carry
in their sleeves, are very much in vogue. In the colder latitudes a raised
platform or dais is built in the room, of brick and stone, under which a fire
is kindled with a chimney to carry off the smoke. The whole substance of
this dais becomes heated and retains its warmth for several hours. This is
the almost universal bed of the north of China. But the main dependence
of the Chinese for personal warmth is on clothes. As the winter approaches
garment is added to garment and furs to quilted vestments, until the wearer
assumes an unwieldy and exaggerated shape. Well-to-do Chinamen seldom
take strong exercise, and they are therefore able to bear clothes which to a
European would be unendurable.

Of the personal comfort obtainable in a house, Chinamen
are strangely ignorant. Their furniture is of the hardest and most
uncompromising nature. Chairs made of a hard black wood, angular in
shape, and equally unyielding divans, are the only seats known to them.
Their beds are scarcely more comfortable, and their pillows are oblong
cubes of bamboo or other hard material. For the maintenance of the
existing fashions of female head dressing, this kind of pillow is essential
to women at least, as their hair, which is only dressed at intervals of
days, and which is kept in its shape by the abundant use of bandoline,
would be crushed and disfigured if lain upon for a moment. Women,

therefore, who make any pretension of following the fashion, are obliged to sleep at night on their backs, resting the nape of the neck on the pillow and thus keeping the head and hair free from contact with anything.

The ornaments in the houses of the well-to-do are frequently elaborate and beautiful. Their wood carvings, cabinets, and ornamental pieces of furniture, and the rare beauty of their bronzes and porcelain, are of late years well known and much sought for in our own country. Tables are nearly uniform in size, furnishing a sent for one person on each of the four sides, and tables are multiplied sufficiently to accommodate whatever number requires to be served. When guests are entertained, the two sexes eat separately in different rooms, but in ordinary meals the members of the family of both sexes sit down together with much less formality.

The streets in the towns differ widely in construction in the northern and southern portions of the empire. In the south they are narrow and paved, in the north they are wide and unpaved, both constructions being suited to the local wants of the people. The absence of wheel traffic in the southern provinces makes wide streets unnecessary, while by contracting their width the sun's rays have less chance of beating down on the heads of passers and it is possible to stretch awnings from roof to roof. It is true that this is done at the expense of fresh air, but even to do this is a gain. Shops are all open in front, the counters forming the only barrier. The streets are crowded in the extreme, and passage is necessarily slow.

This inconvenience is avoided in the wide streets of the cities of the north, but these streets are so in kept that in wet weather they are mud and in dry they are covered inches deep in dust. Of the large cities of the north and south Peking and Canton may be taken as typical examples and certainly, with the exception of the palace, the walls, and certain imperial temples, the streets of Peking compare very unfavorably with those of Canton. The walls surrounding Peking are probably the finest and best kept in the empire. In height they are about forty feet and the same in width. The top, which is defended by massive battlements, is well paved and is kept in excellent order, Over each gate is built a fortified tower between eighty and ninety feet high.

The power of a Chinese father over his children is complete except that it stops short with life. The practice of selling children is common, and though the law makes it a punishable offense, should the sale be effected against the will of the children, the prohibition is practically ignored. In the same way a law exists making infanticide a crime, but as a matter of fact it is never acted upon; and in some parts of the country,

CHINESE CART

more especially in the provinces of Chiang-hsi and Fu-chien, this most unnatural offense prevails among the poorer classes to an alarming extent. Not only do the people acknowledge the existence of the practice, but they even go the length of defending it. It is only however abject poverty which drives parents to this dreadful expedient, and in the more prosperous and wealthy districts the crime is almost unknown. Periodically the mandarins inveigh against the inhumanity of the offense and appeal to the better instincts of the people to put a stop to it; but a stone which stands near a pool outside the city of Foochow bearing the inscription, "Girls may not be drowned here," testifies with terrible emphasis to the futility of their endeavors.

The large number of cast-a-way bodies of dead infants seen in many parts of China is often regarded, though unjustly, as evidence of the prevalence of this crime. In most instances, however, it really indicates only the denial of burial to infants. This is due, at least in many places, to the following superstition: When they die it is supposed that their bodies have been inhabited by the spirit of a deceased creditor of a previous state of existence. The child during its sickness may be cared for with the greatest tenderness, but if it dies parental love is turned to hate and resentment. It is regarded as an enemy and intruder in the family who has been exacting satisfaction for the old unpaid debt; and having occasioned a great ideal of anxiety, trouble, and expense, has left nothing to show for it but disappointment. The uncared for and uncoffined little body is cast away anywhere; and as it is carried out of the door the house is swept, crackers are fired, and gongs beaten to frighten the spirit so that it may never dare

SCHOOL BOY

enter the house again. Thus do superstitions dry up the fountains of natural affection.

The complete subjection of children to their parents is so firmly imbued in the minds of every Chinese youth, that resistance to the infliction of cruel and even unmerited punishment is seldom if ever offered, and full-grown men submit meekly to be flogged without raising their hands. The law steps in on every occasion in support of parental authority. Filial piety is the leading principle in Chinese ethics.

School life begins at the age of six, and among the wealthier classes great care is shown in the choice of master. The stars having indicated a propitious day for beginning work, the boy presents himself at school, bringing with him two small candles, some sticks of incense, and some paper money, which are burnt at the shrine of Confucius, before which also the little fellow prostrates himself three times. There being no alphabet in Chinese the pupil has to plunge at once into the middle of things and

CHINESE SCHOOL

begins by learning to read. Having mastered two elementary books, the next step is to the "Four Books." Then follow the "Five Classics," the final desire of Chinese learning. A full comprehension of these Four Books and Five Classics, together with the commentaries upon them, and the power of turning this knowledge to account in the shape of essays and poems, is all that is required at the highest examination in the empire. This course of instruction has been exactly followed out in every school in the empire for many centuries.

The choice of a future calling, which is often so perplexing in our own country, is simplified in China by the fact of there being but two pursuits which a man of respectability and education can follow, namely the mandarinate and trades. The liberal professions as we understand them are unknown in China. The

JAPANESE ENGINEERS LAYING A MILITARY TELEGRAPH

judicial system forbids the existence of the legal profession except in the case of official secretaries attached to the mandarins' courts; and medicine is represented by charlatans who prey on the follies of their fellowmen and dispense ground tiger's teeth, snake's skins, etc., in lieu of drugs. A lad, or his parents for him, has therefore practically to consider whether he should attempt to compete at the general competitive examinations to qualify him for office, or whether he should embark in one of the numerous mercantile concerns which abound among the money making and thrifty Chinese.

The succession of examinations leading up to the various honorary degrees and official positions, are complicated and exacting. The successful candidates have great honor attached to them, and are the prominent and successful people of the empire. These examinations are open to every man in the empire of whatever grade, unless he belong to one of the following four classes, or be the descendant of one such within three generations; actors, prostitutes, jailers, and executioners and servants of mandarins. The theory with regard to these people is that actors and prostitutes being

SCHOOL GIRL

devoid of all shame, and executioners and jailers having become hardened by the cruel nature of their offices, are unfit in their own persons or as represented by their sons to win posts of honor by means of the examinations.

The military examinations are held separately, and though the literary calibre of the candidates is treated much in the same way as at the civil examinations, the same high standard of knowledge is not required; but in addition skill in archery and in the use of warlike weapons is essential. It is illustrative of the backwardness of the Chinese in warlike methods, that though they have been acquainted with the use of gunpowder for some centuries, they revert in the examination of military candidates to the weapons of the ancients, and that while theoretically they are great strategists, strength and skill in the use of these weapons are the only tests required for commissions.

Persons of almost every class and in almost every station of life make an effort to send their boys to school, with the hope that they may distinguish

themselves, be advanced to high positions in the state, and reflect honor upon their families. Of those who compete for literary honors a very small proportion are successful in attaining even the first degree, though some strive for it for a lifetime. These unsuccessful candidates and the graduates of the first and second degrees, form the important class of literary men scattered throughout the empire the large proportion of this class are comparatively poor, and their services may be obtained for a very

CHINESE ARTIST

small remuneration. They are employed to teach the village schools. Rich families in different neighborhoods often assist in keeping up the school for the credit of the village, and opportunities for obtaining an education are thus brought within the reach of all. Graduates of the first and second degrees, generally have the charge of more advanced pupils, and many are engaged as tutors in private families, commanding higher wages. They are also employed as scribes or copyists, and to write letters, family histories, genealogies, etc. In the larger cities schools are established by the government, and in many places free schools are supported by wealthy men, but these institutions do not seem to be popular and are not flourishing.

Though trade practically holds its place as next in estimation to the mandarinate, in theory it should follow both the careers of husbandry and of the mechanical arts. All land is held in free-hold from the government, and principally by clans or families, who pay an annual tax to the crown, amounting to about one-tenth of the produce. As long as this tax is paid regularly the owners are never dispossessed, and properties thus remain in the hands of clans and families for many generations. In order that farming operations shall be properly conducted, there are established in almost every district agricultural boards, consisting of old men learned in

CHINESE BARBER

husbandry. By these veterans a careful watch is kept over the work done by the neighboring farmers, and in the case of any dereliction of duty or neglect of the prescribed modes of farming, the offender is summoned before the district magistrate, who inflicts the punishment which he considers proportionate to the offense. The appliances of the Chinese for irrigating the fields and winnowing the grain are excellent, but those for getting the largest crops out of the land are of a rude and primitive kind.

Among their artisans the Chinese number carpenters, masons, tailors, shoemakers, workers in iron and brass, and silversmiths and goldsmiths, who can imitate almost any article of foreign manufacture; also workmen in bamboo, carvers, idol makers, needle manufacturers, barbers, hair-dressers, etc. Business men sell almost every kind of goods and commodities wholesale and retail. Large fortunes are amassed very much in the same way and by the same means as are now in our own country. The wealth of the rich is invested in lands or houses, or employed as capital in trade or banking, or is lent out on good security, and often at a high rate of interest.

Traveling in China is slow and leisurely, and the modes of it vary greatly in different parts of the empire. In many of the provinces, especially along the coast and in the south, canals take the place, for the most part, of roads. In the vicinity of Ningpo the country is supplied with a complete network of them, often intersecting each other at distances of one or two miles or less. Farmers frequently have short branch canals running off to their houses, and the farm boat takes the place of the farm wagon. Heavy loaded passage or freight boats ply in every direction. The ordinary charge for passage is less than one-half a cent per mile. The boats are admirably adapted to the people and circumstances,' being built for comfort rather than for speed. These water courses then, with the rivers which are so numerous, furnish the most general way of traveling throughout the empire.

In the north, where the country is level and open, the existence of broad roads enables the people to use rude carts for the conveyance of passengers and freight. Mules are used for riding purposes, and palanquins borne by two horses, or sedan chairs carried by two coolies, are popular ways of traveling. The seagoing junks are very much larger than the river craft, and different in construction. The best ones are divided into water tight compartments and are capable of carrying several thousand tons of cargo. They are generally three-masted and carry huge sails made of matting.

Although the Chinese have the compass, they are without the knowledge necessary for taking nautical observations, so they either hug the land or steer straight by them copass until they reach some coast with which they are familiar. In these circumstances it is easy to understand why the loss of junks and lives on the Chinese coast every year is so great. The immense number of people who live in boats on the rivers in southern China, render the terrible typhoons which sweep the sea and land especially

PORTER'S CHAIR

destructive. For the most part these boat-people are not of Chinese origin but are remnants of the aborigines of the country. That the race has ever survived is a constant wonder, seeing the hourly and almost momentary danger of drowning in which the children live on board their boats. The only precaution that is ever taken, even in the case of infants, is to tie an empty gourd between their shoulders, so that should they fall into the water they may be kept afloat until help comes. They are born in their boats, they marry in their boats, and die in their boats.

The Chinese calendar and the festivities that accompany different seasons and anniversaries, are peculiarly interesting and different from our own, but space forbids any detailed account of them. The four seasons correspond to ours, and in addition to the four seasons the year is divided into eight parts called "joints," or divisions, and these are again subdivided into sixteen more called "breaths," or sources of life. There are forty festivals of China which are celebrated with observances generally throughout the empire and are considered to be important. They do not occur at regular intervals, and there is no periodical day of rest and recreation corresponding at all to our Sunday. The festivities of the new year exceed all others in their prominence and continuance, and in the universality and enthusiasm with which they are observed. "The Feast of Lanterns" and "The Festival of the Tombs" are two of the most interesting of Chinese festivals. The ninth day of the ninth month is a great time for flying kites. On that day thousands of men enjoy the sport and immense kites of all grotesque shapes fill the air. Theaters are very common in China, but the character and associations of the stage are very different from those of western lands and are very much less respected. Actors are regarded as an inferior class. Females do not appear upon the stage, but men act the part of female characters. Gambling is very common in China and is practiced in a variety of ways. Its in effects are acknowledged, and there are laws prohibiting it, but they are a dead letter. There are many kinds of stringed and reed instruments used by the musicians of China. Bells, also, are very numerous, and excellent sweet toned bells are made. A careful watch is kept over the efforts of composers by the imperial board of music, whose duty it is to keep alive the music of the ancients and to suppress all compositions which are not in harmony with it. It is difficult for western ears to find anything truly beautiful in Chinese music.

The medical art of China is not of a sort to win much admiration from us. The Chinese know nothing of physiology or anatomy. The functions of the heart, lungs, liver, kidneys, and brain are sealed books to them and they recognize no distinction between veins and arteries and between nerves and tendons. Their deeply rooted repugnance to the use of a knife in surgery or to post-mortem examinations prevents the possibility of their acquiring any accurate knowledge of the position of the various organs. They consider that from the heart and pit of the stomach all ideas and delights proceed, and that the gall bladder is the, seat of courage. Man's body is believed to be composed of the five elements, fire, water, metal, wood, earth. The medical profession in China is an open one, for there are no medical colleges and no examination tests to worry the minds of would-be practitioners. Some doctors have prescriptions as valuable and of the same sort as those prepared from herbs and vegetables by many an old woman in our own country settlements. On the other hand, some of the most ridiculous remedies are given, such as tiger's teeth, gold and silver leaf, and shavings of rhinoceros horns, or ivory. Fortunately for the people inflammatory diseases are almost unknown in China, but small-pox, consumption, and dysentery rage almost unchecked by medical help; skin diseases are very prevalent, and cancer is by no means uncommon. Of late the practice of vaccination has begun to make its way among the people.

There are hosts of superstitions among the Chinese people, and their beliefs regarding spirits and the influence of the dead, of sorcerers, and of devils, are myriad. These superstitions pervade every rank of society, from the highest to the lowest. The general term applied to the whole system of superstition and luck is fung-shwuy, and the practitioners and learned men in this science are called upon to determine what action shall be taken in all sorts of circumstances.

There are benevolent societies in China corresponding in variety and almost in number to those of Christian lands. There are orphan asylums, institutions for the relief of widows, and for the aged and infirm, public hospitals and free schools, together with other kindred institutions more peculiarly Chinese in their character. In some parts of China schools for girls exist, taught by female teachers. In most places, however females are seldom taught letters, and schools for their benefit are not known. Foreigners in establishing them invariably give a small sum of money or some rice for each day's attendance, and it is thought that these schools could not be kept together in any other way.

The Chinese describe themselves as possessing three religions, or more accurately three sects, namely, Joo keaou, the sect of scholars. Fuh keaou, the sect of Buddha; and Tao keaou, the sect of Tao. Both as regards age and origin, the sect of scholars, or as it is generally called, Confucianism, represents pre-eminently the religion of China. It has its root in the worship of Shang-te, a deity associated with the earliest traditions of the Chinese race. This deity was a personal god, who ruled the affairs of men, rewarding and punishing as appeared just. But during the troublous times which followed the first sovereigns of the Chow dynasty, the belief in a personal deity grew dim, until when Confucius began his career there appeared nothing strange in his atheistic teachings. His concern was with a man as a member of society, and the object of his teachings as to lead him into those paths of rectitude which might best coil tribute to the happiness of the man, and to the well-being of the community of which he formed a part. Man, he held, was born good and was endowed with qualities, which when cultivated and improved by watchfulness and self-restraint, might enable him to acquire godlike wisdom. In the system of Confucius there is no place for a personal god. Man has his destiny in his own hands to make or mar. Neither had Confucius any inducement to offer to encourage men in the practice of virtue, except virtue itself. He was a matter of-fact, unimaginative man, who was quite content to occupy himself with the study of his fellow men, was disinclined to grope into the future. Succeeding ages, recognizing the loftiness of his aims, eliminated all that mas impracticable and unreal in his system, and held fast to that part of it that was true and good. They clung to the doctrines of filial piety, brotherly love, and virtuous living. It was admiration for the emphasis which he laid on these and other virtues, which has drawn so many millions of men unto him and has adorned every city of the empire with temples built in his honor.

Side by side with the revival of the Joo keaou, under the influence of Confucius, grew up a system of a totally different nature, which when divested of its esoteric doctrines and reduced by the practically minded Chinamen to a code of morals, was destined in future ages to become affiliated with the teachings of the sage. This wits Taoism, which was founded by Lao-tzu, who was a contemporary of Confucius. The object of his teaching was to induce men, by the practice of self-abnegation, to reach

CHINESE EMPEROR, KING OF COREA, AND CHINESE OFFICIALS

absorption in something which he called Tao, and which bears a certain resemblance to the Nirvana of the Buddhists. The primary meaning of Tao is "the way," "the path," but in Lao-tzu philosophy it was more than the way, it was the way-goer as well. It was an eternal road; along it all beings and things walked; it was everything and nothing, and the cause and effect of all. All things originated from Tao, conformed to Tao, and to at last returned. It was absorption into this "mother of all things" that Lao-tzu aimed at. But these subtilties, to the common people were foolishness, and before long the philosophical doctrine of the identity of existence and non-existence assumed in their eyes a warrant for the old Epicurean motto, "Let us eat and drink, for to-morrow we die." The pleasures of sense were substituted for the delights of virtue, and to prolong life the votaries began a search for elixirs of immortality, and charms. Taoism quickly degenerated into a system of magic. To-day the monopoly which Taoist priests enjoy as the exponents of the mysteries of nature, inherited from the time when they sought for natural charms, makes them indispensably necessary to all classes, and the most confirmed Confucianist does not hesitate to consult the shaven followers of Lao-tzu on the choice of the site for his house, the position of his family graveyard, or a fortunate day for undertaking an enterprise. Apart from the practice of these magical arts, Taoisn has become assimilated with modern Confucianism and is scarcely distinguishable from it.

The teachings of Lao-tzu bore a sufficient resemblance to the musings of Indian sages, that they served to prepare the way for the introduction of Buddhism. A deputation of Buddhists arrived in China in the year 216 B.C., but were harshly treated, and returned to their homes without leaving any impress of their religion. It was not until some sixty years after Christ, in the reign of the Emperor Ming Ti, that Buddhism was actually introduced. One night the emperor dreamed that a monster golden image appeared and said, "Buddha bids you to send to the western countries to search for him and to get books and images." The emperor obeyed, and sent an embassy to India which returned after an absence of eleven years bringing back images, the red writings, and missionaries who could translate these scriptures into Chinese. Thus was introduced into China the knowledge of that system which in purity and loftiness of aim takes its place next to Christianity among the religions of the world. From this time Buddhism grew and prevailed in the land.

The Buddhism of China is not, however, exactly that of India. The Chinese believe in a material paradise, which is obviously inconsistent with

BUDDHIST TEMPLE

the orthodox belief in Nirvana. Like the other faiths of China, orthodox Buddhism could not entirely satisfy the people. Like the Jews of old they were eager after signs, and self interest made their spiritual rulers nothing loth to grant them their desire. From the mountains and monasteries came men who claimed to possess the elixir of immortality, and proclaimed themselves adepts in witchcraft and sorcery. By magic incarnations they exorcised evil spirit and dissipated famine, pestilence, and disease. By the exercise of their supernatural powers they rescued souls from hell, and arrested pain and death. In the services of the church they added ritual to ritual such means they won their way among the people, and even sternly orthodox Confucianists make use of their services to chant the liturgies of the dead. But while superstition compels even the wise and the learned to pay homage to this faith, there is scarcely an educated man who would not repudiate a suggestion that he is a follower of Buddha; and though the common people throng the temples to buy charms and consult astrologers, they yet despise both the priests and the religion they profess. But Buddhism has after all been a blessing rather than a curse in China. It has to a certain extent lifted the mind of the people from the too exclusive consideration of mundane affairs, to the contemplation of a future state. It has taught them to value purity of life more highly; to exercise self-constraint and to forget self; and to practise charity towards their neighbors.

It will be seen that no clearly defined line of demarcation separates the three great sects of China. Each in its turn has borrowed from the others, until at the present day it may be doubted whether there are to be found any pure Confucianists, pure Buddhists, or pure Taoists. Confucianism has provided the moral basis on which the national character of the Chinese rests, and Buddhism and Taoism have supplied the supernatural element wanting in that system. Speaking generally then, the religion of China is a medley of the three great sects which are now so closely interlaced that it is impossible either to classify or enumerate the members of each creed. The only other religion of importance in China is Mohammedanism, which is confined to the south-western and north-western provinces of the empire. In this faith also the process of absorption in a national mixture of beliefs is making headway. And since the suppreesion of the Panthay rebellion in Yun-nan, there has been a gradual decline in the number of the followers of the prophet.

The speech and the written composition of the Chinese differ more than those of any other people. The former addresses it self, like all other languages, to the mind through the ear: the latter speaks to the mind through the eye, not as words but as symbols of ideas. All Chinese literature might be understood and translated though the student of it could not name a single character. The colloquial speech is not difficult of acquisition, but the written composition is slow of learning by foreigners. "Pidgin English" is a mixed Chinese, Portuguese and English language, which is a creation of the necessities of communication between Chinese and foreigners at the open ports, while neither party had the time or means or wish to acquire an accurate knowledge of the language of the other. "Pidgin" is a Chinese attempt to pronounce our word business, and the materials of the lingo are nearly all English words similarly represented or misrepresented. The idiom on the other hand is entirely that of colloquial Chinese. Foreigners master it in a short time so as to carry on long conversations by means of it, and to transact important affairs of business. This jargon is passing away. Chinese who know English and English who know Chinese are increasing in number from year to year.

In the first two chapters, containing a sketch of Chinese history, mention has been made of the greater literary works produced in the early centuries of the empire; and the calamity of the burning of the books has been described. Of the famous classics which are yet cherished we will not speak again here. After the revival of literature, and the encouragement given to it by the successors of the emperor who destroyed the libraries of the empire, the tide has flowed onward in an ever-increasing volume, checked only at times by one of those signal calamities often overtaking the imperial libraries of China. It is noteworthy that however ruthlessly the libraries and intellectual centers have been destroyed, one of the first acts of the successful founders of succeeding dynasties has been to restore them to their former completeness and efficiency.

The Chinese divide their literature into four departments, classical, philosophical, historical and belles lettres. The "nine classics," of which we have already spoken as being the books studied by every Chinese student, form but the nucleus of the immense mass of literature which has gathered around them.

The historical literature of China is the most important branch of the national literature. There are works which record the purely political events of each reign, as well as those on chronology, rites and music, jurisprudence, political economy, state sacrifices, astronomy, geography, and records of the neighboring countries. On drawing, painting, and medicine much has

TEMPLE OF FIVE HUNDRED GODS, AT CANTON

been written. Poems, novels, and romances, dramas, and books written in the colloquial style, are frequent in the Chinese literature. There is no more pleasant reading than some of their historical romances, and some of the best novels have been translated into European languages. There is, however, considerable poverty of imagination, little analysis of character, and no inter-weaving of plot in the fiction.

The glance that we have taken at the habits and customs of life among the Chinese people, shows that while they lack many of the things that we have been taught to believe essential to civilization, they nevertheless are equipped with many good things. They have the same human instincts, and are ready and able to absorb learning with great rapidity, when once they become convinced of the value of it. It is their conservatism and their belief that they are the only truly civilized people in the world, while all others are barbarians, that has made them so slow to adopt any of the better things of western civilization. The war which this work records may prove to be the most effective means that could possibly have been devised to awaken China from the sleep of centuries, and convince her of the value and efficacy of western methods. If this prove true, a description of China written a generation in the future may have to describe the things here related as existing conditions, to be historical facts after twenty years.

JAPAN

JAPANESE MUSICIAN

THE MIKADO AND HIS PRINCIPAL OFFICERS

HISTORICAL SKETCH OF JAPAN FROM THE EARLIEST TIMES TO FIRST CONTACT WITH EUROPEAN CIVILIZATION

The Oldest Dynasty in the World and its Records—The First Emperor of Japan—Some of the Famous Early Rulers—Invasion and Conquest of Corea by the Empress Jingo—How Civilization Came from Corea to Japan—The Rise of the Dual System of Government—Mikado and Shogun—Expulsion the Hojo Dynasty of Shoguns—The Invasion of the Mongol Tartars—Annihilation of the Armada—Corruption of the Shogun Rule—Growth of the Feudal System—Another Conquest of Corea—Founding of the Last Dynasty of Shoguns—Advance of Japan in the Age of Hideyoshi.

In a historical sketch of the life of a nation which counts twenty-five centuries of recorded history, but the briefest outline can be given. The scope of such a work as this does not admit of minute historical details. When it is said that traditions exist carrying back the history for a number of years which requires several hundred ciphers to measure, the effort to relate even an outline becomes almost appalling. Until the twelfth century of our era, Europe did not know even of the existence of Japan and the reports which were then brought by Marco Polo, who had learned of the island empire of Zipangu from the Chinese were as vague as they were enticing. The successes of the Jesuit missionaries led by Xavier, and the commercial intercourse established by the Portuguese in the latter part of the 16th century, and by the Dutch somewhat later, promised to disclose the mysteries of the far Pacific empire; but within few generations these were more hopelessly than ever sealed against foreign intrusion. Only forty years ago the United States of America knocked at the door of Japan, met a welcome under protest, and the country began to open to western civilization. Even yet the great mass of the people of our own country have far from a right conception of the ancient civilization which has for ages prevailed in these islands of the Pacific.

The Japanese imperial dynasty is the oldest in the world. Two thousand five hundred and fifty-four gears ago in 660 B.C., the sacred histories relate that Jimmu Tenno commenced to reign as the first Mikado, or Emperor of Japan. The sources of Japanese history are rich and solid, historical writings forming the largest and most important divisions of their voluminous literature. The period from about the ninth century until the present time is treated very fully, while the real history of the period prior to the eighth century of the Christian era is very meagre. It is nearly certain that the Japanese possessed no writing until sixth century A.D. Their oldest extant composition is the "Kojiki," or "Book of Ancient Traditions." It may be called the Bible of the Japanese. It comprises three volumes, composed A.D. 711-712, and is said to have been preceded by two similar works about one hundred years earlier, but neither of these have been preserved. The first volume treats of the creation of the heavens and earth, the gods and goddesses, and the events of the holy age or mythological period. The second and third give the history of the mikados from the year I (660 B. C.) to the year 1280 of the Japanese era. It was first printed in the years A. D. 1624-1642. The "Nihongi" completed A.D. 720 also contains a Japanese record of the mythological period, and brings down the annals of the mikados to A.D. 699. These are the oldest books in the language. They contain so much that is fabulous, mythical or exaggerated, that their statements especially in respect of dates cannot be accepted as true history. A succession of historical works of apparent reliability illustrate the period between the eighth and the eleventh centuries, and still better ones treat of the mediaeval period from the eleventh to the sixteenth century. The period from 1600 to 1853 is less known than others in earlier times, because of mandates that existed forbidding the production of contemporary histories.

Whatever may be the actual fact, Jimmu Tenno is popularly believed to have been a real person and the first emperor of Japan. He is deified in the Shinto religion, and in thousands of shrines dedicated to him the people worship his spirit. In one official list of mikados he is named as the first. The reigning Emperor refers to him as his ancestor, from whom he claims unbroken descent as the 123rd member of this dynasty. The seventh day of April is fixed as the anniversary of his accession to the throne and that day is a national holiday on which the birth, the accession and death of this national hero are still annually celebrated. Then one may see flags flying from both public and private buildings, and hear the reverberations of a royal salute fired by the ironclad navy of modern Japan from Krupp guns, and by the military in French uniforms from Remington rifles. The era of Jimmu is the starting point of Japanese chronology, and the year of the Japanese era is that upon which he ascended the throne at Kashiwavara.

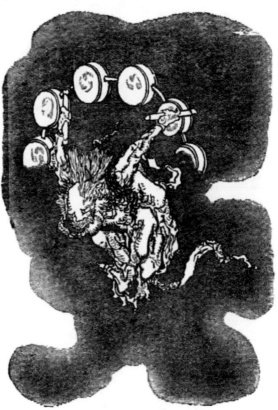

JAPANESE GOD OF THUNDER

In the beginning there existed, according to one interpretation of the somewhat perplexing Shinto mythology, chaos, which contained the germs of all things. From this was evolved a race of heavenly beings and celestial "Kami" of whom Izanagi, a male, and Izanami, e female, were the litst iadividusls. Other authorities on Shinto maintain that infinite space and not chaos existed in the beginning; others argue that in the beginning there was one god. However, all agree as to the appearance on the scene of Izanagi and Izanami, and it is with these we are here concerned; for by their union were produced the islands of Japan, and among their children were Amaterasu, the sun goddess, and, her younger brother, Susanoo, afterward appointed god of the sea. On account of her bright beauty the former mas made queen of the sun, and had given to her a share on the government of the earth. To Ninigi-no-mikoto, her grandson, she afterward consigned absolute rule over the earth, sending him down by the floating bridge of heaven upon the summit of the mountain Kirishima-yama. He took with him the three Japanese mirror, now in one of the Shinto shrines of Ise; the sword, now treasured in the temple of Atsuta, near Nagoya; and the ball of rock crystal in possession of the emperor. On the accomplishment of the descent, the sun and the earth receded from

JAPANESE GOD OF RIDING

one another, and communication by means of the floating bridge ceased. Jimmu Tenno, the first historic emperor of Japan, was the great grandson of Ninigi-no-mikoto.

According to the indigenous religion of Japan, therefore, a religion which even since the adoption of western civilization has

JAPANESE PEASANTRY

been patronized by the state, the mikados are directly descended from the sun goddess, the principal Shinto divinity. Having received from her the three sacred treasures, they are invested with authority to rule over Japan as long as the sun and moon shall endure. Their minds are in perfect harmony with hers; therefore they cannot err and must receive implicit obedience. Such is the traditional theory as to the position of the Japanese emperors, a theory which was advanced in its most elaborate form, as recently as the last century, by Motoori, a writer on Shinto, which of late years has no doubt been much modified or even utterly discarded by many of the more enlightened among the people. Even yet, however, it is far from having been abandoned by the masses.

The mikados being thus regarded as semidivinities, it is not surprising that the very excess of veneration showed them tended more and more to weaken their actual power. They were too sacred to be brought much into contact with ordinary mortals, too sacred even to have their divine countenances looked upon by any but a select few. Latterly it was only the nobles immediately around him that ever saw the mikado's face; others might be admitted to the imperial presence, but it was only to get a glimpse from behind a curtain of a portion of the imperial form, less or more according to their rank. When the mikado went out into the grounds of his palace in Kioto, matting was spread for him to walk upon; when he left the palace precincts he was borne in a sedan chair, the blinds of which were carefully drawn down. The populace prostrated themselves as the procession passed, but none of them ever saw the imperial form. In short, the mikados ultimately became virtual prisoners. Theoretically gifted with all political knowledge and power, they were less the masters of their own actions than many of the humblest of their subjects. Although nominally the repositories of all authority, they had practically no share in the management of the national affairs. The isolation in which it was deemed proper that they should be kept, prevented them from acquiring the knowledge requisite for governing, and even had that knowledge been obtained, gave no opportunity for its manifestation.

From the death of Jimmu Tenno to that of Kimmei, in whose

reign Buddhism was introduced, A.D. 571, there were thirty mikados. During this period of one thousand three hundred and thirty-six years, believed to be historic by most Japanese, the most interesting subjects are the reforms of Sujin Tenno, the military expeditions to eastern Japan by Yamato-Dake, the invasion of Corea by the Empress Jingo Kogo, and the introduction of Chinese civilization and Buddhism.

Sujin or Shujin, B.C. 97-30, was a man of intense earnestness and piety. His prayers to the gods for the abatement of a plague were answered, and a revival of religious feeling and worship ensued. He introduced many forms in the practices of religion and the manners of life. He appointed his own daughter priestess of the shrine and custodian of the symbols of the three holy regalia, which had hitherto been kept in the palace of the mikado. This custom has continued to the present time, and the shrines of Uji iu Ise, which now hold the sacred mirror, are always in charge of a virgin princess of imperial blood.

The whole life of Sujin was one long effort to civilize his half savage subjects. He regulated taxes, established a periodical census, and encouraged the building of boats. He may also be called the father of Japanese agriculture, since he encouraged it by edict and example, ordering canals to be dug, water courses provided, and irrigation to be extensively carried on.

The energies of this pious mikado were further exerted in devising a national military system whereby his peacably disposed subjects could be protected, and the extremities of his realm extended. The eastern and northern frontiers were exposed to the assaults of the mild tribes of Ainos, who were yet unsubdued. Between the peaceful agricultural inhabitants and the untamed savages a continual border war existed. A military division of the empire into four departments was made, and a shogun or general appointed over each. The half subdued inhabitants in the extremes of the realm needed constant watching, and seem to have been as restless and treacherous as the Indians on our own frontiers.

The whole history of the extension and development of the mikado's empire is one of war and blood, rivalling that of our own country in its early struggles with the Indians. This constant military action and life in a camp resulted, in the course of time, in the creation of a powerful and numerous military class, who made war professional and hereditary. It developed that military genius and character which so distinguish the modern Japanese and mark them in such strong contrast with other nations of eastern Asia.

Towards the end of the first century A.D., Yamato-Dake, son of the emperor Keiko, reduced most of the Ainos of the north to submission. These savages fought much after the manner of the North American Indian, using their knowledge of woodcraft most effectually, but the young prince with a well equipped army embarked on a fleet of ships and reaching their portion of the island, fought them until they were glad to surrender.

It was in the third century that the Empress Jingo invaded and conquered Corea. In all Japanese tradition or history, there is no greater female character than this empress. She was equally renowned for her beauty, piety, intelligence, energy and martial valor. To this woman belongs the glory of the conquest of Corea, whence came letters, religion and civilization to Japan. Tradition is that it was directly commanded her by the gods to cross the water and attack Corea. Her husband, the emperor, doubting the veracity of this message from the gods, was forbidden by them any share in the enterprise.

Jingo ordered her generals and captains to collect troops, build ships, and be ready to embark. She disguised herself as a man, proceeded with the recruiting of soldiers and the building of ships, and in the year 201 A.D. was ready to start. Before starting, Jingo issued these orders for her soldiers: "No loot. Neither despise a few enemies nor fear many. Give mercy to those who yield but no quarter to the stubborn. Rewards shall be apportioned to the victors, punishments shall be meted to the deserters."

It was not very clear in the minds of these ancient filibusters where Corea was, or for what particular point of their horizon they were to steer. They had no chart or compass. The sun, stars and the flight of birds were their guide. None of them before had ever known of the existence of such a country as Corea, but the same gods that had commanded the invasion protected the invaders, and in due time they landed in southern Corea.

The king of this part of the country had heard from his messengers of the coming of a strange fleet from the east, and terrified exclaimed, "We never knew there was any county outside of us. Have our gods forsaken us?"

It was a bloodless invasion, for there was no fighting to do. The Coreans came holding white flags and surrendered, offering to give up

their treasures. They took an oath to become hostages and be tributary to Japan. Eighty ships well laden with gold and silver articles of wealth, silks and precious goods of all kinds, and eighty hostages, men of high families, were given to the conquerors. The stay of the Japanese army in Corea was very brief, and the troops returned in two months. Jingo was, on her arrival, delivered of a son, who in the popular estimation; of gods and mortals holds even a higher place of honor than his mother, who is believed to have conquered southern Corea through the power of her yet unborn

JAPANESE GOD OF WAR

illustrious offspring. The motive which induced the invasion into Corea seems to have been mere love of war and conquest, and the Japanese still refer with great pride to this, their initial exploit on foreign soil.

The son Ojin, who became the emperor, was, after his death,

TOKIO—TYPES AND COSTUMES

deified and worshipped as the god of war, Hachiman, and down through the centuries he has been worshiped by all classes of people, especially by soldiers, who offer their prayers and pay their vows to him. Ojin was also a man of literary tastes, and it was during his reign that Japan began to

JAPANESE MUSICIAN

profit from the learning of the Coreans, who introduced the study of the Chinese language, and indeed the art of writing itself. During the immediately succeeding centuries various emperors and empresses were eminent for their zeal in encouraging the arts of peace. Architects, painters, physicians, musicians, dancers, chronologists, artisans and fortune tellers were brought over from Corea to instruct the people, but not all of these came at once. Immigration was gradual, but the coming of so many immigrants brought new blood, ideas, methods and improvements. Japan received from China, through Corea, what she has been receiving from America

JAPANESE SILK SPINNER

and Europe for the last forty years—a new civilization. The records report the arrival of tailors in 283 and horses in 284 from Corea to Japan. In 285 a Corean scholar came to Japan, and residing at the court, instructed the mikado's son in writing. In 462 mulberry trees were planted, together with the silk worm, for whose sustenance they were implanted, from China or Corea. And this marks the beginning of silk culture in Japan. When in 552 the company of doctors, astronomers and mathematicians live at the Japanese court, they brought with them Buddhist missionaries, and this may be called the introduction of continental civilization. Beginning with Jingo, there seems to have poured into the island empire a stream of immigrants, skilled artisans, scholars and teachers, bringing arts, literature and religion. This was the first of three great waves of foreign civilization in Japan. The first was from China, through Corea, in the sixth; the second from western Europe in the fifteenth century; the third was from America, Europe and the world, in the decade following the advent of Commodore Perry.

In the eighth century, during the greater part of which the capital of the country was the city of Nara, about thirty miles from Kioto, Japan had largely under the government of empresses reached a most creditable stage of progress in the arts of peace. Near the close of the eighth century the emperor Kuwammu took up his residence at Kioto, which until 1868 remained the capital of the country, and is even now dignified with the name of Saikiyo, or "Western Calital." Here he built a palace very unlike the simple dwelling in which his predecessors had been content to live. It had a dozen gates, and around it was reared a city with twelve hundred streets. The palace he named "the Castle of Peace," but for years it proved the very centre of the feuds which soon began to distract the country. This did not happen however until some centuries after the death of Kuwammu. But even after his time there were not wanting indications that the control of affairs was destined to slip into the hands of certain powerful families at the imperial court.

The first family to rise into eminence was that of Fujiwara, a member of which it was that got Kuwammu placed upon the throne. For centuries the Fujiwaras controlled the civil affairs of the empire, but a more important factor in bringing about the reduction of the mikado's power and the establishment of that strange system of government which was destined to be so characteristic of Japan, was the rise into power of the rival houses of Taira and Minamoto, otherwise called respectfully Hei and Gen. This system of government has almost always been misunderstood in America and Europe. Two rulers in two capitals gave to foreigners the impression that there were two emperors in Japan, an idea that has been incorporated into most of the text books, and encyclopedias of Christendom. Let it be clearly understood however that there never was but one emperor in Japan, the mikado, who is and always was the only sovereign, though his measure of power has been very different at different times. Until the rise and domination of the military classes, he was in fact, as well as by law, supreme.

With the feuds of Hei and Gen commences an entirely new era in the history of the country, an era replete with tales alike of bloodshed, intrigue and chivalry. We see the growth of a feudal system at least as elaborate as that of Europe, and strangely enough, assuming almost identical forms, and that during the same period.

The respective founders of the Taira and Miuamoto families were Taira Takamochi and Minamoto Tsunemoto, two warriors of the tenth century. Their descendants were for generations military vassals of the mikado, and were distinguished by red and white flags, colors which suggest the red and white roses of the rival English houses of Lancaster and York. For years the two houses served the emperor faithfully; but even before any quarrel had arisen between them, the popularity of the head of the Minamoto clan, with the soldiers with whom he had been placed, so alarmed the emperor Toba (1108-1124, A.D.) that he issued an edict forbidding the Samurai, the military class, of any of the provinces, from constituting themselves the retainers of either of these two families.

It was in the year 1156 that the feuds between the two houses broke out, and it arose in this way. At the accession of Go-Shirakawa to the throne in that year, there were living two ex-emperors who would seem to have voluntarily abdicated; one of them, however, Shutoku, was averse to the accension of the heir, being himself anxious to resume the imperial power. His cause was espoused by Tameyoshi, the head of the Milamoto house, while among the supporters of Go-Shirakawa was Kiyomori, of the house of Taira. In the conflict which followed, Go-Shirakawa was successful, and immediately thereafter we find Taira Kiyomori appointed Daijo-Daijin, or prime minister, with practically all political power in his hands. On the abdication within a few years of the mikado, the prime minister was able to put whatever member of the imperial house he willed upon the throne; and being himself allied by marriage to the imperial family, he at length saw the accession of his own grandson, a mere babe. Thus, to use the term connected with European feudalism of the same period, the mayor of the palace virtually, though not nominally, usurped the imperial functions. The emperor had the name of power but Kiyomori had the reality.

But this state of matters was not destined to last long. The Minamotos were far from being finally quieted. The story of the revival of their power is a romantic one, but we cannot dwell upon. It was in the battle of Atiji that Kiyomori seemed at length to have quelled his rivals. Yoshitomo, the head of the Minamoto clan was slain in the fight, but his beautiful wife Tokiwa succeeded in escaping with her three little sons. Tokiwa's mother, however, was arrested. This roused the daughter to make an appeal to Kiyomori for pardon. She did so, presenting herself and children to the conqueror, upon whom her beauty so wrought that he granted her petition. He made her his concubine, and not withstanding the remonstrances of his retainers, also spared the children who were sent to a nionastery, there to be trained for the priesthood. Two of these children became famous in the history of Japan. The eldest was Yoritomo the founder of the Kamakura dynasty of shoguns, and the babe at the mother's breast was Yoshitsune, one of the flowers of Japanese chivalry, a hero whose name even yet awakens the enthusiasm of the youth of Japan and who so impressed the Ainos of the north whom he had been sent to subdue, that to this day he is worshiped as their chief god. A Japanese has even lately written a book in which he seeks to identify Yoshitsune with Genghis Khan.

It is unnecessary to dwell on the circumstances which brought Yoritomo and Yoshitsune into note; how the two brothers raised the men of the eastern provinces, and after a temporary check at the pass of Hakone, succeeded in utterly routing the Taira forces in a dreadful battle, half by land and half by sea, at the straits of Shimonoseki. Suffice it to say, that Yoshitsune having been slain soon after a famous victory, through the treachery of his brother Yoritomo, who was jealous of his fame and popularity, that warrior was left without a rival. Yoritomo received from the emperor the highest title which could be conferred upon him, that of Sei-i-tai-shogun, literally "Baibarian-subjugating great general." This title is generally contracted to shogun, which means simply general. Thus appointed generalissimo of all the imperial forces, he looked about for a city which he might make the center of his power. This he found in Kamakura about fifteen miles westward of the site of the modern Yokohama.

Thus before the close of the twelfth century was founded that system of dual government which lasted with little change until the year 1868. The Mikado reigned in Kioto with the authority of his sacred person undisputed; but the shogun in his eastern city had really all the public business of the country in his own hands. It was he who appointed governors over the different provinces and was the real master of the country; but every act was done in the name of the emperor whose nominal power thus remained intact.

Yoritomo virtually founded an independent dynasty at Kamakura, but it was not destined to be a lasting one. His son Yoriye succeeded him in 1199, but was shortly afterwards deposed and assassinated; and the power though not the title of shogun passed to the family of Yoritomo's wife, that of Hojo, different members of which swayed the state for more than a century.

After a cheokered career of various shoguns of the Hojo family, their tyranny became supreme. None of the family ever seized the office of shogun, but in reality they wielded all and more of the power attaching to the office. The political history of these years is but that of a monotonous recurrence of the exaltation of boys and babies of noble blood to whom was given the semblance of power, who were sprinkled with titles and deposed as soon as they were old enough to be troublesome. In an effort made by the ex-emperor Gotoba to drive the usurping Hojo from power the chains were riveted tighter than ever. The imperial troops were massacred by the conquering Hojo. The estates of all who fought on the emperor's side were confiscated and distributed among the minions of the usurpers. The exiled emperor died of a broken heart. The nominal Mikado of Kioto and the nominal shogun at Kamakura were set up, but the Hojo were the keepers of both. The oppression, the neglect of public business and the carousals of the usurpers became intolerable. Armies were raised spontaneously to support the emperor and the Ashikaga leader in their revolt against the existing evils. All over the empire the people rose against their oppressors and massacred them. The Hojo domination which had been paramount for nearly one hundred and fifty years was utterly broken.

The Hojo have never been forgiven for their arbitrary treatment of the Mikallos. Every obloquy is cast upon them by Japanese historians, dramatists, poets and novelists, and yet there is another side to the story. It must be conceded that the Hojos were able rulers and kept order and peace in the empire for more than a century. They encouraged literature and the cultivation of the arts and sciences. During their period the resources of the county were developed, and some branches of useful handicraft and fine arts were brought to a perfection never since surpassed. To this time belongs the famous image carver, sculptor and architect, Unkei, and the lacquer artists who are the "old masters" in this bratlch of art. The military spirit of the people was kept alive, tactics were improved, and the methods of governmental administration simplified. During this period of splendid temples monasteries, pagodas, colossal images and other monuments of holy zeal,

COLOSSAL JAPANESE IMAGE FIFTY FEET HIGH

Hojo Sadatoki erected a monument over the grave of Kiyomori at Hiogo. Hojo Tokimune raised and kept in readiness a permanent war fund so that the military expenses might not interfere with the revenue reserved for ordinary government expenses. To his invincible courage, patriotic pride, and indomitable energy are due the vindication indication of the national honor and the repulse of the Tartar invasion.

During the early centuries of the Christian era, Japan and Chitla kept up friendly intercourse, exchanging embassies on various missions, but chiefly with the mutual object of bearing congratulations to an emperor upon his accession to the throne. The civil disorders in both countries interrupted these friendly relation in the twelfth century, and communication ceased. When the acquaintance was renewed in the time of the Hojo it was not on so friendly a footing.

In China the Mongol Tartars had overthrown the Sung dynasty and had conquered the adjacent country. Through the Coreans the Mongol emperor, Kublai Khan, at whose court Marco Polo and his uncles were then visiting, sent letters demanding tribute and homage from Japan. Chinese envoys came to Kamakura, but Hojo Tokimune, enraged at the insolent demands, dismissed them in disgrace. Six embassies were sent, and six times rejected. An expedition from China consisting of ten thousand men was then sent against Japan. They landed, were attacked, their commander was slain, and they returned, having accomplished nothing. The Chinese emperor now sent nine envoys to announce their purpose to remain until a definite answer was returned to their master. They were called to Kamakura, and the Japanese reply was given by cutting off their heads. The Japanese now began to prepare for war on land and sea. Once more Chinese envoys came to demand tribute. These were decapitated. Meanwhile the armada was preparing. Great China was coming to crush the little strip of land that refused homage to the invincible conqueror. The army numbered one hundred thousand Chinese and Tartars, and seven thousand C'oreans in ships that whitened the sea. They numbered three thousand five hundred in all. It was in July, 1281, that the sight of the Chinese junks greeted the watchers on the hills of Daizaifu. Many of the junks were of immense proportion, larger than the natives of Japan had ever seen, and armed with the engines of European warfare which their Venetian guests had taught the Mongols to construct and work. The naval battle that ensued was a terrible one. The Japanese had small chance of success in the water, owing to the smallness of their boats, but in personal valor they were much superior, and some of their deeds of bravery are inspiringly interesting. Nevertheless the Chinese were unable to effect a landing, owing to the heavy fortifications along the shore.

The whole nation was now roused. Re-enforcements poured in from all quarters to swell the hosts of defenders. From the monasteries and temples all over the country well up unceasing

JAPANESE FEMALE TYPES

prayer to the gods to ruin their enemies and save the land of Japan. The emperor and ex-emperor went in solemn state to the

SHINTO TEMPLE

chief priest of Shinto, and writing out their petitions to the gods sent him as a meesenger to the shrines of Ise. It is recorded as a miraculous fact that at the hour of noon as the sacred envoy arrived at the shrine and offered a prayer, the day being perfectly clear, a streak of cloud appeared in the sky that soon overspread the heavens, until the dense masses portended a storm of awful violence. One of those cyclones called by the Japanese tai-fu, of appalling velocity and resistless force, such as whirl along the coast of Japan and China during late summer and early fall of every year, burst upon the Chinese fleet. Nothing can withstand these maelstorms of the air. We call them typhoons. Iron steamships of thousands of horse power are almost unmanageable in them. The helpless Chinese junks were crushed together, impaled on the rocks, dashed against the cliffs or tossed on land like corks on the spray. Hundreds of the vessels sank. The corpses were piled on the shore or floating on the water so thickly that it seemed almost possible to walk thereon. The vessels of the survivors in large numbers drifted or were wrecked upon Taka island, where they established themselves and cutting down trees began building boats to reach Corea. Here they were attacked by the Japanese, and after a bloody struggle, all the fiercer for the despair on the one side and the exultation on the other, were all slain or driven to the sea to be drowned except three, who were sent back to tell their emperor how the gods of Japan had destroyed their armada.

This was the last time that China ever attempted to conquer Japan, whose people boast that their land has never been defiled by an invading army. They have ever ascribed the glory of the destruction of the Tartar fleet to the interpositioi of the gods of Ise, who thereafter received special and grateful adoration as the guardian of the seas and the winds. Great credit and praise were given to the Lord of Kamakura, Hojo Tokimune, for his energy, ability and valor. The author of one native history says, "The repulse of the Tartar barbarians by Tokimue and his preserving the dominions of our Son of Heaven were sufficient to atone for the crimes of his ancestors."

Nearly six centuries afterward when "the barbarian" Perry anchored his fleet in the bay of Yeddo, in the words of the native annalist, "Orders were sent by the imperial court to the Shinto priest at Ise to offer up prayers for the sweeping away of the barbarians."

Millions of earnest hearts put up the same prayers their fathers had offered fully expecting the same result.

To this day the Japanese mother hushes her fretful infant by the question, "Do you think the Mongols are coming?" This the only serious attempt at invasion ever made by any nation upon the shores of Japan.

The internal history of Japan during the period of time covered by the actual or nominal rule of the Ashikaga family, from 1336 until 1573, except the very laat yeam of it, is not very attractive to a foreign reader. It is a confused picture of intestinal war. It was by foul means that Ashikaga Takugi, one of the generals who overthrew the Hojos, attained the dignity of shogun, and a

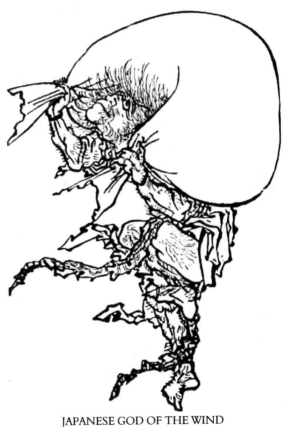

JAPANESE GOD OF THE WIND

period of more than two centuries, during which his descendants held sway at Kamakura, was characterized by treachery, bloodshed and almost perpetual warfare. The founder of this line secured the favor of the mikado Go-Daigo, after he was recalled from exile, upon the overthrow of the military usurpation. Ashikaga soon seized the reins in his own hands. The mikado fled in terror, and a new mikado way declared in the person of another of the royal family. Of course this man was willing to confer upon Ashikaga, his supporter the title of shogun. Kamakura again became a military capital. The duarchy was restored, and the war of the northern and southern dynasties began, to last fifty-six years.

The act by which more than any other the Ashikagas earned the curses of posterity, was the sending of an embassy to China in 1401, bearing presents, acknowledging in a measure the authority of China, and accepting

DAIMIOS OF JAPAN

in return. In the title of Nippon 0, or king of Japan. This which was done by Ashikaga Yoshimitsu, the third of the line, was an insult to the national dignity for which he has never been forgiven. It was a needless humiliation of Japan to her arrogant neighbor and done only to exalt the vanity and glory of the usurper, who, not content with adopting the style and equipage of the mikado, wished to be called a king and yet dared not usurp the imperial throne. Japan of all the Asiatic nations to have brought the feudal system to the highest state of perfection. While in Europe the nations were engaged in throwing off the feudal yoke and inaugurating modern government, Japan was riveting the fetters which stood intact until 1871. The daimios were practically independent chieftains, who ruled their own provinces as they willed; and the more arlbitioiansd powerful did not hesitate to make war upon the neighboring clans. There were on all sides struggles for pre-eminence in which the fittest survived, annexing to their own territories those of the weaker class which they had subdued. Nor was it merely rival clans that were disturbing the country. The Buddhist clergy

SKETCH SHOWING DEVELOPMENT OF THE JAPANESE ARMY
FROM 1867 TO THE PRESENT.

had acquired immense political influence, which they were far from scrupulous in using. Their monasteries were in many cases castles, from which themselves living and every kind of luxury,

BUDDHIST PRIESTS

they tyrannized over the surrounding country. The history of these often reads strikingly like that of the corresponding institutions in Europe during the middle ages; indeed the hierarchical as well as the feudal development of Europe and Japan have, been wonderfully alike.

Probably the three names most renowned in Japan are Nobunaga, Hideyoshi aid Iyeyasu. The second and third of these were generals subordinate to the first, who deposed the Ashikaga shoguns, persecuted the Buddhists, encouraged the Jesuits, and restored to a great extent the supremacy of the mikado. The Buddhists look on this leader as an incarnate demon sent to destroy their faith. He was a Shintoist, with bitter hatred for the Buddhists, and never lost an opportunity to burn property of his enemies or butcher priests, women, and children of that faith. These who have just been named, by their prowess and the strength of their armies, rose to highest positions among the daimios.

When these three great men appeared, the was in a most critical state. The later Ashikaga shoguns had become as powerless as the mikado himself in the manngement of affairs. Nobunaga first rose into note. By successive victories, he became ruler of additional provinces, and his fame became so great that the emperor committed to him the task of tranquilizing country. He deposed first one usurping shogun and then another, and thus came an end to the domination the Ashikagas. Nobunaga was now the most powerful man in the country, and was virtually discharging the duties of shogun though he never obtained the title. Hideyoshi became virtual lord of the empire, after the assassination of Nobunaga. He rose from the ranks of the peasants to the highest position in Japan under the emperor. Having in connection with Nobunaga and Iyeyasu reduced all the Japanese clans into subjection, he looked abroad for some foreign power to subdue.

The immoderate ambition of Hideyoshi's life was to conquer Corea, and even China. Under the declining power of Ashikaga, all tribute from Corea had ceased and the pirates who ranged the coasts scarcely allowed any trade to exist. We have seen how it was from Corea that Japan received Chinese learning and the arts of civilization, and Coreans swelled the number of Mongol 'Tartars who invaded Japan with the armada. On the other hand Corea was more than once overrun by Japanese armies, even partly governed by Japanese officials, and on different occasions had to pay tribute to Japan in token of submission. Japanese pirates too were for six hundred years as much the terror of the Chinese and Corean costs as were the Danes and Norsemen of the shores of the North Sea. The discontinuance of the embassies and tribute from Corea, thus afforded the ambitious general a pretext for disturbing the friendly relations with Corea, by the dispatch of an ambassador to complain this neglect. The behavior of this ambassador only too clearly reflected the swagger of his overbearing lord, and the consequence was an invasion of Corea.

Hideyoshi promised to march his generals and army to Peking, and divide the soil of China among them. He also scorned the suggestion that scholars versed in Chinese should accompany the expedition. Said he, "This expedition will make the Chinese use our literature." Corea was completely overrun by Hideyoshi'e forces, although the commander himself was unable to accompany the expedition, owing to his age and the grief of his mother. Further details of this invasion will be found later in the historical sketch of Corea. It may be said here however, that the conquest terminated ingloriously, and reflects no honor on Japan. The responsibility of the outrage upon a peaceful nation rests wholly upon Hideyoshi. The Coreans were a mild and peaceable people, wholly unprepared for war. There was scarcely a shadow of provocation for the invasion, which was nothing less than a huge filibustering scheme. It was not popular with the people or the rulers, and was only carried through by the will of the military leader. The sacrifice of life on either side must have been great, and all for the ambition of one man. Nevertheless, a party in Japan has long held that Corea was by the conquests of the third and sixteenth centuries a part of the Japanese empire, and the reader will see how 1772 and again in 1775 the cry of "On to Corea" shook the nation like an earthquake.

After the deaths of Nobunanga and Hideyoshi, Tokugawa Iyeyasu was left the virtual ruler of Japan. At first he governed the county as regent, but his increasing popularity awoke the jealousy of the partisans of Hideyori, the son of Hideyoshi, who was nominated as his successor, as well as of Nobunaga's family.

These combined to overthrow him, and the consequence was the great battle of Sekigahara, fought in 1600, in which Iyeyasu came off completely victorious. Three years later, he was appointed by the emperor shogun. Like Yorotomo he resolved to select a city as the center of his power, and that which seemed to him most suitable was not Kamakura, which had lost much of its glory, but the little castle town of Yeddo, about thirty-five miles farther north. Here he and his successors, and the dynasty he founded, swayed the destinies of Japan from 1608 until the restoration in 1868.

JAPANESE JUNK

It is not difficult to account for the tone of admiration and pride with which a modern Japanese speaks of "The age of Taiko." There are many who hold that Hideyoshi, or Taiko, was the real unifier of the empire. Certain it is that he originated many of the most striking forms of national administration. In his time the arts and sciences were not only in a very flourishing condition, but gave promise of rich development. The spirit of military enterprise and internal national improvement was at its height. Contact with the foreigners of many nations awoke a spirit of inquiry and intellectual activity; but it was on

OLD TIME JAPANESE FERRY

the seas that genius and restless activity found their most congenial field.

This era is marked by the highest production in marine architecture, and the extent and variety of commercial enterprise. The ships built in this century were twice the size and vastly the superior in model of the junks that now hug the Japanese shores or ply between China

SCENES OF INDUSTRIAL LIFE (FROM A JAPANESE ALBUM)

and Japan. The pictures of them preserved to the present day, show that they were superior in size to the vessels of Columbus, and nearly equal in sailing qualities to the contemporary Dutch and Portuguese galleons. They were provided with ordnance, and a model of a Japanese breech-loading cannon is still preserved in Kioto. Ever a brave and adventurous people, the Japanese then roamed the seas with a freedom that one who knows only of the modern bound people would scarcely credit. Voyages of trade, discovery or piracy have been made to India, Siam, Birmah, the Philippine Ialands, Southern China, the Malay Archipelago and the Kuriles, even in the fifteenth century, but were more numerous in the sixteenth. The Japanese literature contains many references to these adventurous sailors, and when the records of the far east are thoroughly investigated, and this subject fully studied, very interesting results are apt to be obtained showing the widespread influence of Japan at a time when she was scarcely known by the European world to have existence.

HISTORICAL SKETCH FROM THE COMING OF THE FIRST
EUROPEAN TRAVELERS TO THE PRESENT TIME

A New Dynasty of Shoguns—Mendez Pinto's Visit—Arrival of the Jesuit Missionaries—Kind Reception of Christianity—Quarrels between the Sects—Beginning of Christian Persecution—Expulsion of the Missionaries—Torture and Martyrdom—The Massacre of Shimgunate— Arrival of Commodore Perry's Fleet—The Knock at the Door of Japan— An Era of Treaty Making—Rapid Advance of Western Manners and Ideas in Japan—Attack on Foreigners—The Abolition of the Shogunate Japan's Last Quarter Century.

Hitherto we have seen two readily distinguishable periods in the history of Japan, the period during which the mikados were the actual as well as the nominal rules of the empire; and the period during which the imperial power more and more passed into the hands of usurping mayors of the palace, and the country was kept in an almost constant ferment with the feuds of rival noble families which coveted this honor. Successively the power, although not always the title, of shogun, had been held by members of the Minamoto, Hojo, Ashikaga, Ota and Toyotomi families. With Iyeyasu we pass into a third period, like the second in that the dual system of feudal government still prevailed, but unlike it in that it was a period of peace. Much strife had accompanied the erection of the fabric of feudalism, but it now stood complete. The mikado in Kioto and the diamios in their different provinces, alike ceased to protest against the dual administration. Within certain limits they had the regulation of their own affairs; the mikado was ever recognized as the source of all authority, and the daimios in their own provinces were petty kings; but it was the shogun in Yeddo who, undisputed, at least in practice, whatever some of the more powerful daimios may have said, swayed the destinies of the empire.

Let us now note the policy which the Shoguns adopted towards the foreigners who as missionaries or merchants had found their way to Japan, and the course of settlement and trade of foreigners.

It seems now certain that when Columbus set sail from Spain to discover a new continent, it was not America he was seeking, but the land of Japan.' Marco Polo, the Venetian traveler, had spent seventeen years, 1275-1292, at the court of the Tartar emperor Kublai Khan, and while in Peking had heard of a land lying to the eastward, called in the language of the Chinese, Zipangu, from which our modern name Japan has been corrupted. Columbus was an ardent student of Polo's book, which had been published in 1298. He sailed westward across the Atlantic to find this kingdom. He discovered not Japan, but an archipelago in America on whose shores he eagerly inquired concerning Zipangy. Following this voyage, Vasco de Gama and n host of other brave Portuguese navigators sailed into the Orient and came back to tell of densely populated empires enriched with the wealth that makes civilization possible, and of which Europe had scarcely heard. Their accounts fired the hearts of the zealous who longed to convert the heathen, aroused the cupidity of traders who thirsted for gold, and kindled the desire of monarchs to found empires in Asia.

Mendez Pinto, a Portuguese adventurer, seems to have been the first European who landed on Japanese soil. On his return to Europe he told so many wonderful stories that by a pun on his Christian name he was dubbed "the mendacious." His narrative was, however, as we now know, substantially correct. Pinto while in China had got on board a Chinese junk, commanded by a pirate. They were attacked by another corsair, their pilot was killed, and the vessel was driven off the coast by a storm. They made for the Liu Kiu Islands, but unable to find a harbor, put to sea again. After twenty-three days' beating about, they sighted the islands of Tanegashima and landed. The name of the island, "Island of the seed," was significant. The arrival of these foreigners was a seed of troubles innumerable. The crop was priestcraft of the worst type, political intrigue, religious persecution, the inquisition, the slave trade, the propagation of Christianity by the sword, sedition, rebellion, and civil war. Its harvest was garnered in the blood of sixty-thousand Japanese.

The native histories recount the first arrival of Europeans in 1542, atid note that year as the one in which fire-arms were first introduced. The pirate trader who brought Pinto to Japan cleared twelve hundred per cent. on his cargo, and the three Portuguese returned to China loaded with presents. The new market attracted hundreds of Portuguese adventurers to Japan, who found a ready welcome. The missionary followed the merchant. Already the Portuguese priests and Franciscan friars were numerous in India. Two Jesuits and two Japanese who had been converted at Goa, headed by Xavier, landed at Kagoshima in 1549. Ravier did not have great success, and in a short time left Japan disheartened. He had, however, inspired others who followed him, and their success was amazingly great.

The success of the Jesuit missionaries soon attracted the attention of the authorities. Organtin, a Jesuit missionary in Kioto, writing of his experiences, says that he was asked his name and why he had come to Japan. He replied that he was the Padre Organtin and had come to spread religion. He was told that he could not be allowed at once to spread his religion, but would be informed later on. Nobunaga accordingly took counsel with his retainers as to whether he would allow Christianity to be preached or not. One of these strongly advised not to do so, on the ground that there were already enough religions in the country, but Nobunaga replied that Buddhism had been introduced from abroad and had done good in the country, and he therefore did not see why Christianity should not be granted a trial. Organtin was consequently allowed to erect a church and to send for others of his order, who, when they came, were found to be like him in appearance. Their plan of action was to care for the sick, and so prepare the way for the reception of Christianity, and then to convert every one and make the thirty-six provinces of Japan subject to Portugal. In this last clause we have an explanation of the policy which the Japanese government ultimately adopted towards Christianity and all foreign innovations. Within five years after Xavier visited Kioto, seven churches were established in the vicinity of the city itself, while scores of Christian communities had sprung up in the south-west.

In 1581 there were two hundred churches and one hundred and fifty thousand native Christians.

In 1583 an embassy of four young noblemen was dispatched by the Christian daimios to the pope to declare themselves vassals of the Holy See. They returned after eight years, having had audience of Phillip II of Spain, and kissed the feet of the pope at Rome. They brought with them seventeen Jesuit missionaries, an important addition to the list of religious instructors. Spanish mendicant friars from the Philippine Islands, with Dominicans and Augustinians, also flocked into the country, teaching and zealously proselyting. The number of "Christians" at the time of the highest success of the missionaries in Japan was, according to their own figures six hundred thousand, a number that seems to be no exaggeration if quantity and not quality are considered. The Japanese less accurately set down a total of two million nominal adherents to the Christian sects. Among the converts were several princes, large numbers of lords, and gentlemen in high official positions, and beside generals of the army and admirals of the navy. Churches and chapels were numbered by the thousand, and in some provinces crosses and Christian shrines were as numerous as the kindred evidences of Buddhism had been before. The methods of the Jesuits appealed to the Japanese, as did the forms and symbols of the faith, but the Jesuits began to attack most violently the character of the native priests, and to incite their converts to insult their gods, burn the idols and desecrate the old shrines.

As the different orders, Jesuits, Franciscans and Augustinians increased, they began to clash. Political and religious war was almost universal in Europe at the same time, and the quarrels of the various nationalities followed the buccaneers, pirates, traders and missionaries to the distant seas of Japan. All the foreigners, but especially Portuguese, then were slave traders, and thousands of Japanese were bought and sold and shipped to China and the Philippines. The sea ports of Hirado and Nagasaki were the resorts of the lowest class of adventurers of all European nations, and the result was a continuous series of uproars, broils and murders among the foreigners. Such a picture of foreign influence and of Christianity as the Japanese saw it was not calculated to make a permanently favorable impression on the Japanese mind.

Latterly Nobunaga had somewhat repented of the favor he had shown to the new religion, though his death occurred before his dissatisfaction had manifested itself in any active repression. Hideyoshi had never been well disposed to Christianity, but other matters prevented him from at once meddling with the policy of his predecessors. In 1588 he ventured to issue an edict commanding the missionaries to assemble at Hirado, an island off the west come of Kiushiu and prepared to leave Japan, and the missionaries obeyed, but as the edict was not enforced they again returned to the work of evangelization in private as vigorously as ever, averaging ten thousand converts a year. The Spanish mendicant friars pouring in from the Philippines, openly defied Japanese laws. This aroused Hideyoshi's attention and his decree of expulsion was renewed. Some of the churches were burned. In 1596 six Franciscan and three Jesuit priests with seventeen Japanese converts were taken to Nagasaki and there burned.

When Hideyoshi died, affairs seemed to take a more favorable turn, but only for a few years. Iyeyasu was as much opposed to Christianity as Hideyoshi, and his hatred of the new religion was intensified by his partiality for Buddhism. The new daimios, carrying the policy of their predecessors as taught them by the Jesuits, but reversing its direction, began to persecute their Christian subjects, and to compel them to renounce their faith. The native converts resisted, even to blood and the taking up of arms. The idea of armed rebellion among the farmers was something so wholly new that Iyeyasu suspected foreign instigation. He became more vigilant as his suspicions increased, and resolving to crush this spirit of independence and intimidate the foreign emissaries, met every outbreak with bloody reprisals.

Iyeyasu issued a decree of expulsion against the missionaries in 1600, but the decree was not at once carried into effect. The date of the first arrival in Japan of Dutch merchants was also 1600. They settled in the island of Hirado. In 1606 an edict from Yeddo forbade the exercise of the Christian religion, but an outward show of obedience warded off active persecution. Four years later the Spanish friars again aroused the wrath of the government by defying its commands and exhorting the native converts to do likewise. In 1611 Iyeyasu obtained documentary proof of what he had long suspected, the existence of a plot on the part of the native converts and the foreign emissaries to reduce Japan to the position of a subject state. Fresh edicts were issued, and in 1614 twenty-two Franciscan, Dominican and Augustinian friars, one hundred and seventeen Jesuits and hundreds of native priests were embarked by force on board junks and sent out of the country. The next year the shogun pushed matters to an extreme with Hideyori, who was entertaining some Jesuit priests, and laid siege to the castle of Ozaka. A battle of unusual ferocity and bloody slaughter raged, ending in the burning of the citadel and the total defeat and death of Hideyori and thousands of his followers. The Jesuit fathers say that one hundred thousand men perished in this brief war.

The exiled foreign friars kept secretly returning, and the shogun pronounced sentence of death against any foreign priest found in the country. Iyemitsu, the next shogun, restricted all foreign commerce in Nagasaki and Hirado; all Japanese were forbidden to leave the country on pain of death. Any European vessel approaching the coast was at once to be referred to Nagasaki, whence it was to be sent home; the whole crew of any junk in which a missionary should reach Japanese shores were to be put to death; and the better to remove all temptation to go abroad, it was decreed that no ships should be constructed above a certain size and with other than the open sterns of coasting vessels.

Fire and sword were used to extirpate Christianity and to paganize the same people who in their youth were Christianized by the same means. Thousands of the native converts fled to China, Formosa and the Philippines. The Christians suffered all sorts of persecutions and tortures that savage ingenuity could devise. Yet few of the natives quailed or renounced their faith. They calmly let the fire of wood, cleft from the crosses before which they once prayed consurne, them. Mothers carried their babes to the fire or the edge of the precipice rather than leave them behind to be educated in pagan faith. If any one doubt the sincerity and fervor of the Christian converts of to-day, or the ability of the Japanese to accept a higher form of faith, or their willingness

JAPANESE BELL TOWERS

to suffer for what they believe, he has but to read the accounts of various witnesses to the fortitude of the Japanese Christians of the seventeenth century.

The persecution reached its climax in the tragedy of Shimabara in 1637. The Christians arose in arms by tens of thousands, seized an old castle, repaired it and fortified it, and raised the flag of rebellion. The armies of veterans sent to besiege it expected an easy victory, and sneered at the idea of having any difficulty in subduing these farmers and peasants. It took two months by land and water, however, of constant attack before the fort was reduced, and the victory was finally gained only with the aid of Dutch cannon furnished under compulsion by the traders of Deshima. After great slaughter the intrepid garrison surrendered, and then began the massacre of thirty-seven thousand Christians. Many of them were buried into the sea from the top of the island rock of Takaboko-shima, by the Dutch named Pappenberg, in the harbor of Nagasaki.

The result of this series of events was that the favorable policy adopted by Iyeyasu in regard to foreign trade was completly reversed. No foreigners were allowed to set foot on the soil of Japan, except Chinese and a few Dutch merchants. The Dutch gained the privilege of residing in confinement on the little island of Deshima, a piece of made land in the harbor of Nagasaki. Here under degrading restrictions and constant surveillance lived less than a score of Hollanders, who were required every year to send a representative to Yeddo to do homage to the shogun. They were allowed one ship per annum to come from the Dutch East Indies for the exchange of the conlmodities of Japan for those of Holland.

Says Doctor Griffis in his study of this era of Japanese history, "After nearly a hundred years of Christianity and foreign intercourse, the only apparent results of this contact with another religion and civilization were the adoption of gunpowder and fire-arms as weapons, the use of tobacco and the habit of smoking, the making of sponge cake, the naturalization into the language of a few foreign words, the introduction of new and strange forms of disease, among which the Japanese count the scourge of the venereal virus, and the permanent addition to that catalogue of terrors which priest and magistrate in Asiatic countries ever hold as welcome, to overawe the herd. For centuries the mention of that name would bate the breath, blanch the cheek and smite with fear as with an earthquake shock. It was the synomyn of sorcery, sedition, and all that was hostile to the purity of the home and the peace of society. All over the empire, in every city, town, village and hamlet; by the roadside,

IMAGE OF BUDDHA

ferry or moutain pass; at every entrance to the capitol, stood the public notice boards on which with prohibitions against the great crimes that disturbed the relations of society's government was one tablet written with a deeper brand of guilt, with a more hideous memory of blood, with a more awful terror of torture, than when the like superscription as affixed at the top of a cross that stood between two thieves on a little hill outside Jerusalem. Its daily and familiar sight startled ever and anon the peasants who clasped hands and uttered a fresh prayer; the Bonze, or Buddhist priest, to add new venom to his maledictions; the magistrate to shake his head; and to the mother a ready word to hush the crying of her fretful babe. That name was Christ. So thoroughly was Christianity or the "corrupt sect" supposed to be eradicated before the end of the seventeenth century, that its existence was historical, remembered only as an awful scar on the national memory. No vestiges were supposed to be left of it, and no knowledge of its tenets was held save by a very few scholars in Yeddo, trained experts who were kept as a sort of spiritual blood hounds to scent out the adherents of the accursed creed. It was left to our day since the recent opening of Japan, for them to discover that a mighty fire had been smoldering for over two centuries beneath the ashes of persecutions. As late as 1829 seven persons, six men and an old woman, were crucified in Ozaka on suspicion of being Christians and communicating with foreigners. When the French brethren of the Mission Apostolique of Paris came to Nagasaki in 1860, they found in the villages around them over ten thousand people who held the faith of their fathers of the seventeenth century.

JAPANESE SAMURAI OR WARRIOR OF
THE OLD TIME

The Portuguese were not the only race to attempt to open a permanent trade with Japan. Captain John Saris, with three ships, left England in April, 1611, with letters from King James I to the "Emperor" (shogun) of Japan. Landing at Hirardo he was well received, and established a factory charge of Richard Cocks. The captain and a number of the party visited Yeddo and other cities and obtained from the shogun a treaty defining the privileges of trade, and signed minamoto Iyeyasu. After a tour of three months Saris arrived at Hirado again, having visited Kioto, where he saw the splendid Christian churches and Jesuit palaces. After discouraging attempts to open a trade with Siam, Corea and China, and hostilities having broken out between them and the Dutch, the English abandoned the pact of permanent trade with Japan, and all subsequent attempts to reopen it failed.

Will Adams, who was an English pilot, and the first of his nation in Japan,

JAPANESE GENERAL OF THE OLD TIME (FROM A NATIVE DRAWING)

arrived in 1607 and lived in Yeddo till he died thirteen years later. He rose into favor with the shoguns and the people by the sheer force of a manly, honest character. His knowledge of shipbuilding, mathematics, and foreign affairs made him a very useful man. Although treated with kindness and honor, he was not allowed to leave Japan. He had a wife and daughter in England. Adams had a son and daughter born to him in Japan, and there are still living Japanese who A claim descent from him. One of the streets of Yeddo was named after him, and the people of that street still hold an annual celebration on the fifteenth of June in his honor.

The history of the two centuries and a half that followed the triumphs of Iyeyasu is that of profound peace and stern isolation. We must pass rapidly in review of them. This great shogun took pains to arrange the empire after the appointment to the office, in such a way that the shoguns of the Tokugawa family, the dynasty which he founded, should have strictest power and most certain descent. His sons and daughters were married where they would be most powerful in influence with the great families of daimios. It must not be forgotten that Iyeyasu and his succeesor were both in theory and in reality vassals of the emperor, though they assumed protection of the imperial person. Neither the shogun nor the daimios were acknowledged at Kioto as nobles of the empire. The loweat kuge, or noble, was above the shogun in rank. The shogun could obtain his appointment only from the mikado. He was simply the most powerful among the daimios, who had won that pre-eminence by

JAPANESE BRIDGE.

the sword, and who by wealth and power and a skillfully wrought plan of division of land among the other daimios was able to rule.

In 1600 and the years following, Iyeyasu employed an army of three hundred thousand laborers in Yeddo improving and building the city. Before the end of the century, Yeddo had a population of more than half a million, but it never did have, as the Hollanders guessed and the old text books told us, two million five hundred thousand souls. Outside of Yeddo the strength of the great unifier was spent on public roads and highways, post stations, bridges, castles and mines. He spent the last years of his life engaged in erasing the scars of war by his policy of conciliation, securing the triumphs of peace, perfecting his plans for fixing in stability a system of government, and in collecting books and manuscripts. He bequeathed his code of laws to his chief retainers, and advised his sons to govern in the spirit of kindness. He died on the eighth of March, 1616.

The grandson of Iyeyasu, Iyemitsu, was another great shogun, and it was he who established the rule that all the daimios should visit and reside in Yeddo during half the year. Gradually these rules became more and more restrictive, until the guests became mere vassals. Their wives and children were kept as hostages in Yeddo. During his rule the Christian insurrection and massacre at Shimabara took place. Yeddo was vastly improved, with aqueducts, fire watch towers, the establishment of mints, weights and measures. A general survey of the empire was executed; maps of various provinces and plans of the daimios' castles were made; the councils called Hiojo-sho (discussion and decision), and Wakadoshiyori (assembly of elders), were established and Corean envoys received. The height of pride and ambition which this shogun had already reached, is seen in the fact that in a letter of reply to Corea he is referred to as Tai Kun, ("Tycoon"), a title never conferred by the mikado on any one, nor had Iyemitsu any legal right to it. It was assumed in a sense honorary or meaningless to any Japanese, unless highly jealous of the mikado's sovereignty, and was intended to overawe the Coreans. The approximate interpretation of it is "great ruler."

Under the strong rule of the Tokugawa shoguns, therefore, the long distracted Japanese empire at length enjoyed two-and-a-half centuries of peace and prosperity. The innate love of art, literature, and education, which almost constant warfare had prevented from duly developing among the people, had now an opportunity of producing fruit. And as it had shown itself in former intervals of rest, so was it now. Under the patronage of Iyeyasu was conposed the Dai Nihon Shi, the first detailed history of Japan. Tsunayoshi, his successor, 1681 to 1709, founded Seido a Confucian university, and was such an enthusiast for literature that he used to assemble the princes and high officials about him and expound to them passages from the Chinese classics. Yoshimune, another shogun, was much interested in astronomy and other branches of science, beside doing much to improve agriculture. Legal matters also engaged his attention; he altered Iyeyasu's policy so far as to publish a revised criminal code, and improved the administration of the law, forbidding the use of torture except in cases where there was flagrant proof of guilt. He built an astronomical observatory at Kanda and established at his court a professorship of Chinese literature.

Iyenori, shogun from 1787 to 1838, threw the classes of the Confucian university open to the public. Every body from the nobility down to the masses of the people began to appreciate literary studies. Maritime commerce within the limits of the four seas was encouraged by the shogun's government, regular service of junks being established between the principal ports. Nor must it be forgotten that to the Tokugawas is due the foundation of the great modern city of Yeddo with its vast fortifications and its triumphs of art in the shrines of Shiba and Uyeno. It was at this period too that the matchless shrines of Nikko were reared in memory of the greatness of Iyeyasu and Iyemitsu. The successors of the former, the shoguns of the Tokugawa dynasty, fourteen in all, were with one exception buried alternately in the cemeteries of Zozoji and Toyeizan, in the city districts of Shiba and Uyeno.

But throughout all this period of peace and progress the light of the outer world was excluded. The people made the best use of the light they had, but after all it was but dim. The learning by rote of thousands of Chinese characters, and the acquisition of skill in the composition of Chinese and Japanese verse, were little worthy to be the highest literary attainments possible to the most aspiring of the youth of Japan. In the domain of art there was more that was inviting, but scientific knowledge was tantalizingly meagre and that little was overlaid with Chinese absurdities. When we consider that the isolation of the country was due to no spirit of exclusiveness in the national character, that indeed it was the result of a policy that actually went against the grain of the people, how many restless spirits must there have been during these long years, who kept longing for more light. Fortunately there was one little chink at Deshima, in the harbor at Nagasaki, and of this some of the more earnest were able to take advantage. Many instances are recorded and there must be many more of which we can know nothing, of Japanese students displaying the truest heroism in surmounting the difficulties that lay in the way of their acquiring foreign knowledge. Let us now see how there came at length an unsettled dawn, and after the clouds of this had cleared, a dazzling inpouring of the light.

It was the American Union which opened the door of Japan to western civilization. It had been desired by all of the European nations, as well as by the United States, to obtain access to Japanese ports. Supplies were frequently needed, particularly water and coal, but no distress wan ever considered a sufficient excuse for the Japanese to permit the landing of a foreign vessel's crew. Shipwrecked sailors frequently passed through seasons of great trial and danger, before they were restored to their own people. Even Japanese sailors who were shipwrecked on other shores, or carried out to sea, were refused re-admission to their own country when rescued by foreigners.

Commodore Matthew Calbraith Perry of the American navy, urged upon President Millard Fillmore the necessity and possibility of making some sort of a treaty with the exclusive empire. It was decided that the most effective way to advance this desire was to sail into the bay of Yeddo with a squadron sufficient to command respect. A fleet was assigned to the undertaking, under the command of Perry, and the American vessels sailed away to the Orient to rendezvous at the chief city of the Liu Kiu islands, Napha. From Napha the fleet sailed for Japan, the Susquehanna, the flagship, the advance of the line of the ships of seventeen nations.

It was on the seventh day of July, 1853, under a sky and over a sea of perfect calm, that the four American warships appeared off Uraga in the Bay of Yeddo. Without delay the officials of Uraga emphatically notified the "barbarian" envoy that he must go to Nagasaki, where all business with foreigners had to be done. The barbarian refused to go. He informed the messengers

BAPTISM OF BUDDHA

that he was the bearer of a letter from the President of the United States to the Emperor of Japan; that he had sailed as near as possible to the destination of the letter and would now deliver it and continue it on its way by land, but he would not retrace his path until the letter was delivered. The shogun Iyeyoshi on receiving information of such decision, was exceedingly troubled and called his officials to a council. Alarm was wide spread, and it was ordered that strict watch should be kept along the shore to prevent the barbarian vessels from committing acts of violence. During the eight days while Commodore Perry's fleet was waiting in the Bay of Yeddo, the boats of his ships were busily engaged in taking soundings and surveying the shores and the anchorage. No sailors were permitted to land, and no natives were molested. Every effort was made to indicate to the Japanese the desire for a peaceful friendship.

A learned Chinese scholar was sent by the shogun to Uraga, who acted as an official and eminent interpreter in an interview with the American envoy. Continued councils were called by the shogun, not only of his chief officers but of the daimios, the nobles, and the retired nobles of Yeddo. The citizens of Yeddo and the surrounding villages were in great tumult, fearing that there would be a war, for which the country was totally unprepared. Meanwhile the envoy was impatiently demanding an answer. At last, after eight days, the patience and the impatience, combined with the demonstrations made by the vessels of the fleet, which were highly impressive to the Japanese who had never seen a steamboat, won success for Commodore Perry's message. A high Japanese commissioner came to Uraga, prepared a magnificent pavilion for the ceremonies, and announced himself ready to receive the letter to the emperor. With great pomp and ceremony the Americans landed and in this pavilion with proper formalities, delivered the letter and presents from the president. Then having, for the first time in history, gained several important points of etiquette in a country where etiquette was more than law or morals, the splendid diplomat and warrior Perry sailed away with his fleet July 17, 1853.

It was in response to a temporizing policy on the part of Japan, and to the good judgment and careful decision of Commodore

Perry, that the fleet sailed away without demanding an immediate reply to his letter. The American envoy was informed that in a matter of so much importance a decision could not be at once reached, and that if he now left, he would on his return get a definite answer. No wonder there was commotion. The nineteenth century had come suddenly into contact with the fourteenth. The spirit of commerce and the spirit of feudalism, two great but conflicting forces, met in their full development, and the result was necessarily a convulsion. We are hardly surprised to hear that the shogun died before Commodore Perry's return, or that during the next few years the land was harassed by earthquakes and pestilences.

Perry's second appearance was in February, 1854, this time with a much larger fleet. A hot debate took place in the shogun's council as to the answer that should be given. The old daimio of Mito, the head of one of the three families, which, forming the Tokugawa clan, furnished the occupants of the shogunate, wanted to fight and settle the question once for all. "At first," he said, "they will give us philosophical instruments, machinery and other curiosities; will take ignorant people in; and trade being their chief object they will manage to impoverish the country, after which they will treat us just as they like, perhaps behave with the greatest rudeness and insult us, and end by swallowing up Japan. If we do not drive them away now we shall never have another opportunity."

Others gave contrary advice, saying, If we try to drive them away they will immediately commence hostilities, and then we shall be obliged to fight. If we once get into a dispute we shall have an enemy to fight who will not be easily disposed of. He does not care how long he will have to spend over it, but he will come with myriads of men-of-war and surround our shores completely; however large a number of ships we might destroy, he is so accustomed to that sort of thing that he would not care in the least. In time the country would be put to an immense expense and the people plunged into misery. Rather than allow this, as we are not the equals of foreigners in the mechanical arts, let us have intercourse with foreign countries, learn their drill and tactics, and when we have made the nation as united as one family, we shall be able to go abroad and give lands in foreign countries to those who have distinguished themselves in battle."

The latter view carried and a treaty with the United States was signed on the thirty-first of March, 1854. Now be it observed that the shogun did this without the sanction of the mikado, whom indeed he had never yet consulted on the matter, and that he subscribed himself Tai Kun, ('Tycoon,") or great ruler, a title to which he had no right and which if it meant anything at all involved an assumption of the authority of supreme ruler in the empire. This was the view naturally taken by Perry and by the ambassador from European countries who a few years later obtained treaties with Japan. They were under the impression that they were dealing with the emperor; and hearing of the existence of another potentate living in an inland city, surrounded with a halo of national veneration, they conceived the plausible but erroneous theory that the tycoon was the temporal sovereign, and this mysterious mikado the spiritual sovereign of the country. They little dreamed that the so-called tycoon was no sovereign at all, and that consequently the treaties which he signed had no legal validity.

The shogun could ill afford thus to lay himself open to the charge of treason. From the fire there had been a certain class of daimios who had never heartily submitted to the Tokugawa administration. The principal clans which thus submitted to the regime under protest against what they considered a usurpation, an encroachment on the authority of the mikado, whom alone they recognized as the divinely appointed ruler of Japan, were those of Satsuma, Choshiu, and Tosa. As the years of peace cast their spell over the nation, making the people forgetful of war and transforming the descendants of Iyeyasu into luxurious idlers, much more like impotent mikados than successors of the energetic soldier and law-giver, their hopes more and more arose that an opportunity would be given them to overthrow the shogunate and bring about the unification of the empire at the hands of the mikado. Their time had now come. The shogun was enervated and he had so far forgotten himself as to open the country to foreign trade, without the sanction of the "Son of Heaven." It was this illegal act of the shogun that precipitated the confusion, violence and disaster of the next few years, reaching ultimately in 1868 to the complete overthrow of his own power and the restoration of the mikado to his rightful position as actual as well as nominal ruler of the empire.

Fearing the consequences of the illegal act into which he had been driven, the shogun lost no time in sending messengers Kioto to inform the mikado of what had happened and seek his sanction to the policy adopted. It was plead in excuse for the course of conduct, that affairs had reached such a condition that the shogun was driven to sign the treaty. The emperor in great agitation summoned a council. The decision was unanimous against the shogun's action, and the messengers were informed that no sanction could be given to the treaty. The next important step was not taken until July, 1858, when Lord Elgin arrived with propositions on the part of Great Britain for a treaty of amity and commerce. He was unaccompanied by any armed force, and brought a steam yacht as a present from Queen Victoria to the tycoon of Japan.

A few months later treaties were entered into with all the leading powers of Europe, but if there was a political lull between 1854 and 1858, the poor Japanese had distractions of a very different kind from a violent earthquake and consequent conflagration, one hundred and four thousand of the inhabitants of Yeddo lost their lives. A terrific storm swept away one hundred thousand more, and in a visitation of cholera thirty thousand persons perished in Yeddo alone. Moreover, just when the treaties were being signed, the shogun Iyesada died, "as if," says Sir R. Alcock, "a further victim was required for immolation on the altar of the outraged gods of Japan."

The political tempest that had been gathering now swept over the nation. For the next ten years there was so much disorder, intrigue, and bloodshed, that Japan became among the western nations s byword for treachery and assassination. Defenseless foreigners were cut down in the streets of Yeddo and Yokohama and even in the legations. Twice was the British legation attacked, on one of the occasions being taken by storm and held for a time by a band of free-lances. No foreigners life was safe. Even when out on the most trivial errand, every foreign resident was accompanied by an armed escort furnished by the shogun's government. It is needless to give an account of all the different assassinations, successful or attempted, which darkened the period. The secretary to the American legation was cut down near Shiba, Yeddo, when returning from the Prussian legation with an armed escort; a Japanese interpreter attached to the British legation was fatally stabbed in broad daylight while standing at the legation flagstaff; one of the guard at the same legation murdered two Englishmen in the garden and then committed suicide; an Englishman was cut down on the highway between Yokohama and Yeddo by certain retainers of the daimio of Satsuma, whose procession he had unwittingly crossed on horseback; and these were not all.

It is not a satisfactory answer to say that hatred of foreigners was the leading motive that inspired all these acts of violence. This was no doubt more or less involved, but the true explanation is to be found in the hostility of the mikado's partisans to the shogun's government. All possible means were taken to thwart the shogun and bring him into complications with the ambassadors at his court. Every attack on a foreigner brought fresh trouble upon the Yeddo government and hastened its collapce. Long before foreigners arrived, the seeds of revolution had sprouted and their growth was showing above the soil. It is to the state of political parties and of feudalism at this epoch in Japanese history, and not to mere ill will against foreigners, that this policy of intrigue and assassination must be ascribed.

It would take too long to discuss all the complications of this period and to inquire, for instance, how far when the Japanese government failed to arrest and execute the murderer of Mr. Richardson, the British were justified in demanding an indemnity of $500,000 from the shogun and $125,000 from the daimio of Satsuma, or in enforcing their demands with a threatened bombardment of Yeddo and an actual bombardment of Kagoshima. It is out of our scope here to inquire into the shelling of the batteries of the daimio of Choshiu, at Shimonoseki, in turn by the Americans, British, French and Dutch, the men of Choshiu having fired upon some Dutch, American, and French vessels that had entered the straits against the prohibition of the Japanese.

Aa irldenoifty $3,000,000 wars also exacted and distributed among these nations.

Such stern measures doubtless appeared to the foreign ambassadors necessary to prevent the expulsion or even the utter extermination of foreigners. Whether their policy was mistaken or not, certain it is that they can have had no adequate conception of the difficulties with which the shogun had to contend. The position of that ruler was one of such distraction as might well evoke for him the pity of every disinterested onlooker. Do as he would, he could not escape trouble; on the one side were the mikado's partisans ever growing in power and in determination to crush him, and on the other were the equally irresistible foreigners with their impatient demands and their alarming threats. He was as helpless as a man between a wall of rock and an advancing tide.

The internal difficulties of the country were increased by dissensions which broke out in the imperial court. The clans of Satsuma and Choshiu had been summoned to Kioto to preserve order. For some reason the former were relieved of this duty, or rather privilege, and it therefore devolved exclusively upon the Choshiu men. Taking advantage of their position, the Choshiu men persuaded the mikado to undertake a progress to the province of Yamato, there to proclaim his intention of taking the field against foreigners; but this proposal roused the jealousy of the other clans at the imperial court, as they feared that the men of Choshiu were planning to obtain possession of the mikado's person and thus acquire pre-eminence. The intended expedition was abandoned, and the men of Choshiu, accompanied by Sanjo, afterward prime minister of the reformed government, and six other nobles who had supported them, were banished from Kioto.

The ill feeling thus occasioned between Choshiu and Satsuma, was fomented by an unfortunate incident which occurred at Shimonoseki early in 1864. The former clan recklessly fired upon a vessel, which being of European build they mistook for a foreign one, but which really belonged to Satsuma. Thus Choshiu was in disfavor both with the shogun and with the mikado, and in this year we have the strange spectacle of these two rulers leaguing their forces together for its punishment.

August 20, 1864, the Choshiu men advanced upon Kioto, but were repulsed with much slaughter, only however after the greater part of the city had been destroyed by fire. The rebellion was not at once quelled; indeed the Choshiu samurai were proving themselves more than a match for the troops which the shogun had sent against them, when at length the imperial court ordered the fighting to be abandoned. Simultaneously with the Choshiu rebellion the shogun had to meet an insurrection by the daimio of Mito, in the east. His troubles no doubt hastened his death, which took place at Osaka in September, 1866, shortly before the war against Choshiu terminated. Then there succeeded Keiki, the last of the shoguns.

It should be noted, however, that before this the mikado's sanction had been obtained to the foreign treaties. In November, 1865, British, French, and Dutch squadrons came to anchor off Hiogo, of which the foreign settlement of Kobe is now a suburb, and sent letters to Kioto demanding the imperial consent. The nearness of such an armed force was too great an argument to be withstood, and the demand was granted. Little more than a year after his accession to the shogunate Keiki resigned. In doing so he proved himself capable of duly appreciating the national situation. Now that foreigners had been admitted, it was more necessary than ever that the government should be strong, and this, it was seen, was impossible without the abolition of the old dual system. He had secured the mikado's consent to the treaties, on the condition that they should be revised, and that Hiogo should never be opened as a port of foreign commerce.

But the end had not yet come. On the same day when the shogunate was abolished, January 3, 1868, the forces friendly to the Tokagawas were dismissed from Kioto, and the guardianship of the imperial palace was committed to the clans of Satsuma, Tosa, and Geishiu. This measure gave Keiki great offense, and availing himself of a former order of the court which directed him to continue the conduct of affairs, he marched with his retainers and friends to Ozaka and sent a request to the mikado that all Satsuma men who had any share in the government should be dismissed. To this the court would not consent, and

Keiki marched against Kioto with a force of thirty thousand men, his declared object being to remove from the mikado his bad counselors. A desperate engagement took place at Pushimi, in which the victory was with the loyalists. But this was only the beginning of a short but sharp civil war, of which the principal fighting was in the regions between Yeddo and Nikko.

The restoration was at last complete. Proclamation was made "to sovereigns of all foreign nations and their subjects, that permission had been granted to the shogun Yoshinobu, or Keiki, to return the governing power in accordance with his own request;" and the manifesto continued: "henceforward we shall exercise supreme authority both in the internal and external affairs of the country. Consequently the title of emperor should be substituted for that of tycoon which had been hitherto employed in the treaties." Appended were the seal of Dai Nippon, and the signature of Mutsuhito, this being the first occasion in Japanese history on which the name of an emperor had appeared during his lifetime.

With the triumph of the imperial party one might have expected a return to the old policy of isolation. There can be no doubt that when the Satsuma, Choshiu, and other southern clans commenced their agitation for the abolition of the shogunate, their ideas with regard to foreign intercourse were decidedly retrogreesive. But after all, the leading motive which inspired them was dissatisfaction with the semi-imperial position occupied by the upstart Tokugawas; to this their opposition to foreigners was quite secondary. It so happened that the Tokugawa shoguns got involved with foreigners, and it was so much the worse for the foreigners. To go deeper, what was at the bottom of this desire was the overthrow of the shogunate. Doubtless their patriotism, what they had at heart, was the highest welfare of their country, and this they believed impossible without its unification. Their primary motive then, being patriotism, we need not be surprised that they were willing to entertain the notion that perhaps after all the prosperity of their country might best be insured by the adoption of a policy of free foreign intercourse. This idea more and more commended itself, until it became a conviction; and when they got into power they astonished the

WOMAN OF COURT OF KIOTO

world by the thoroughness with which they broke loose from tho old traditions and entered upon a policy of enlightened reformation. To the political and social revolution which accompanied the restoration of the mikado in 1868, there has been no parallel in the history of mankind.

One of the first acts of the mikado after the restoration, was to assemble the kuges and daimios and make oath before them "that a deliberative assembly should be formed, and all measures be decided upon by public opinion; that impartiality and justice should form the basis of his action; and that intellect and learning should be sought for throughout the world in order to establish the foundations of the empire." In the mid-summer of 1868, the mikado, recognizing Yeddo as really the center of the nation's life, made it the capital of the empire and transferred his court thither; but the name Yeddo, being distasteful on account of its associations with the shogunate, was abolished, and the city renamed Tokio, or "Eastern Capital." At the same time the ancient capital Kioto, received the new name of Saikio or "Western Capital." For the creation of a central administration, however, more was necessary than the abolition of the shogunate and the establishment of the mikado's authority. The great fabric of feudalism still remained intact. Within his own territory each daimio was practically an independent sovereign, taxing his subjects as he saw fit, often issuing his own currency, and sometimes even granting passports so as to control intercourse with neighboring provinces. Here was a formidable barrier to the consolidation of the empire. But the reformers had the courage and the tact necessary to remove it.

The first step towards the above revolution was taken in 1869, when the daimios of Satsuma, Choshiu, Hizen, and Tosa addressed a memorial to the mikado requesting his authorization for the resignation of their fiefs into his hands. Other nobles followed their example, and the consequence was the acceptance by the mikado of control over the land and revenues of the different provinces, the names of the clans however being still preserved, and the daimios allowed to remain over them as governors, each with one-tenth of the former assessment of his territory as rental. By this arrangement the evil of too suddenly terminating the relation between the clans and their lords was sought to be avoided, but it was only temporary in 1871 the clan system was totally abolished, and the country redivided for administrative purposes, with officers chosen irrespectively of hereditary rank or clan connection.

But the payment of hereditary pensions and allowances of the ex-daimios and ex-samurai proved such a drain upon the national resources that in 1876 the reformed government found it necessary to compulsorily convert them into capital sums. The rate of commutation varied from five years' purchase in the case of the largest pensions, to fourteen years' in that of the smallest. The number of the pensioners with whom they had thus to deal was three hundred and eighteen thousand four hundred and twenty-eight. The act of the daimios in thus suppressing themselves looks at first sight like a grand act of self-sacrifice, as we are not accustomed to see landed proprietors manifesting such disinterestedness for the patriotic object of advancing their country's good. But the vast majority of daimios had come to be mere idlers, as the greater mikado had been. Their territories were governed by the more able and energetic of their retainers, and it was a number of these men that had most influence in bringing about the restoration of the mikado's authority. Intense patriots, they saw that the advancement of their country could not be realized without its unification, and at the same time they cannot but have preferred a larger scope for their talents, which service immediately under the mikado would give them. From being ministers of their provincial governments, they aspired to be ministers of the imperial government. They were successful; and their lords, who had all along been accustomed to yield to their advice quite cheerfully, acquiesced when asked for the good of the empire to give up their fiefs to the mikado. One result of this is that while most of the ex-daimios have retired into private life, the country is now governed almost exclusively by ex-samurai. Such sweeping changes were not to be accomplished without rousing opposition and even rebellion. The government incurred much risk in interfering with the ancient privileges of the samurai. It is not surprising that several rebellions had to be put down during the years immediately succeeding 1868.

Dr. William Elliot Griffis, in his exhaustive and interesting work, "The Mikado's Empire," discusses at length the change of Japan from feudalism to its present condition, the abolition of the shogunate, and the rebellions that followed that event. He declares that popular impression to be wrong which suggests that the immediate cause of the fall of the shogun's government, the restoration of the mikado to supreme power, and the abolition of the dual and feudal systems, was the presence of foreigners on the soil of Japan. The foreigners and their ideas were the occasion, not the cause, of the destruction of the dual system of government. Their presence served merely to hasten what was already inevitable.

The history of Japan from the abolition of feudalism in 1871 up to the present time is a record of advance in all the arts of western civilization. The mikado, Mutsuhito, has shown himself to be much more than a petty divinity, a real man. He has taken a firm stand in advocacy of the introduction of western customs, wherever they were improvements. The imperial navy, dockyards, and machine shops have been a pride to him. He has withdrawn himself from mediaeval seclusion and assumed divinity, and has made himself accessible and visible to his subjects. He has placed the empress in a position like to that occupied by the consorts of European monarchs, and with her he has adopted European attire. In the latter part of June, 1872, the mikado left Tokio in the flagship of Admiral Akamatsu, and made a tour throughout the south and west of his empire. For the first time in twelve centuries the emperor of Japan moved freely and unveiled among his subjects.

Again in the same year Japan challenged the admiration of Christendom. The coolie trade, carried on by Portuguese at Macao, in China, between the local kidnappers and Peru and Cuba, had long existed in defiance of the Chinese government. Thousands of ignorant Chinese were yearly decoyed from Macao and shipped in sweltering shipholds, under the name of "passengers." In Cuba and Peru their contracts mere often broken, they were cruelly treated, and only a small portion of them returned alive to tell their wrongs. The Japanese government had with a fierce jealousy watched the beginning of such a

traffic on their own shores. In the last days of the shogunate, ooolie traders
came to Japan to ship irresponsible hordes of Japanese coolies and women
to the United States. To their everlasting shame, be it said some were
Americans. Among the first things done by the mikado's government after

CHINESE COOLIE

the restoration, was the sending
of an official who effected the
joyful delivery of these people
and their return to their homes.
So the Japanese set to work to
destroy this nefarious traffic. The
Peruvian ship Maria Luz, loaded
with Chinese, entered the port
of Yokohama. Two fugitive
coolies in succession swim to
the English war ship - Iron
Duke. Hearing the piteous story
of their wrongs, Mr. Watson,
the British charge affairs, called
the attention of the Japanese
authorities to these illegal acts in
their waters. A protracted enquiry
was instituted and the coolies
landed. The Japanese refused
to force them on board against
their will, and later shipped
them to China, a favor which
was gratefully acknowledged by
the Chinese government. The
act of a pagan nation achieved
a grand moral victory for the
world and humanity. Within

four years the coolie traffic, which was but another name for the slave
trade, was abolished from the face of the earth, and the coolie prisons of
Macao were in ruins, Yet the act of freeing the Chinese coolies in 1872
was done in the face of clamor and opposition, and a rain of protests from

JAPANESE GYMNASTS—KIOTO

the foreign consuls, ministers, and a part of the press. Abuse and threats and diplomatic pressure were in vain. The Japanese never wavered, but marched straight to the duty before them, the liberation of the slaves. The British charge and the American consul, Colonel Charles O. Shepherd, alone gave hearty support and unwavering sympathy to the right side.

During the same year, 1872, two legations and three consulates were established abroad, and from that time forward the number has been increasing until the representatives of Japan's government are found all over the world. Scores of daily newspapers and hundreds of weeklies have been furnishing the country with information and awakening thought. The editors are often men of culture or students returned from abroad.

The Corean war project had, in 1872, become popular in the cabinet and was the absorbing theme of the army and navy. During the Tokugawa period Corea had regularly sent embassies of homage and congratulation to Japan; but not relishing the change of affairs in 1868, disgusted at the foreignizing tendencies of the mikado's government, incensed at Japan's departure from Turanian ideals, and emboldened by the failure of the French and American expeditions, Corea sent insulting letters taunting Japan with slavish truckling to the foreign barbarians, declared herself an enemy, and challenged Japan to fight. About this time a Liu Kiu junk was wrecked on eastern Formosa. The crew was killed by the savages, and, it is said, eaten. The Liu Kiuans appealed to their tributary lords at Satsuma, who referred the matter to Tokio. English, Dutch, American, German, and Chinese ships have from time to time been wrecked on this cannibal coast, the terror of the commerce of Christendom. Their war ships vainly attempted to chastise the savages. Soyejima, with other, conceived the idea of occupying the coast, to rule the wild tribes, and of erecting light houses in the interests of commerce. China laid no claim to eastern Formosa, all trace of which was omitted from the maps of the "Middle Kingdom." In the spring of 1873, Soyejima went to Peking and there, among other things granted him, was an audience with the Chinese emperor. He thus reaped the results of the diplomatic labors of half a century. The Japanese ambassador stood upright before the "Dragon Face" and the "Dragon Throne," robed in the tight black dress-coat, trousers, and linen of western civilization, bearing the congratulations of the young mikado of the "Sunrise Kingdom" to the youthful emperor of the "Middle Kingdom." In the Tsung-li Yamen, Chinese responsibility over eastern Formosa was disavowed, and the right of Japan to chastise the savages granted. A Japanese junk was wrecked on Formosa, and its crew stripped and plundered while Soyejima was absent in China. This event piled fresh fuel on the flames of the war feeling now popular even among the unarmed classes.

FORMOSAN TYPE

Japan at this time had to struggle with opposition within and without, to every move in the direction of advancement in civilization. Says Griffis, "At home were the stolidly conservative peasantry backed by ignorance, superstition, priestcraft, and political hostility. On their own soil they were fronted by aggressive foreigners who studied all Japanese questions through the spectacles of dollars and cents and trade, and whose diplomatists too often made the principles of Shylock their system. Outside the Asiatic nations beheld with contempt, jealousy and alarm the departure of one of their number from Turanian ideas, principles, and civilization. China with ill-concealed anger, Corea with open defiance taunted Japan with servile submission to the 'foreign devils.'

"For the first time the nation was represented to the world by an embassy at once august and plenipotentiary. It was not a squad of petty officials or local nobles going forth to kiss a toe, to play the part of figure-heads, or 'stool-pigeons, to beg the aliens to get out of Japan, to keep the scales on foreign eyes, to buy gun-boats, or to hire employees. A noble of highest rank, and blood of Immemorial antiquity, with four cabinet ministers, set out to visit the courts of the fifteen nations having treaties with Dai Nippon. They were ncconpanied by commissioners representing every government department, sent to study and report upon the methods and resources of foreign civilizations. They arrived in Washington February 29, 1872, and for the first time in history a letter signed by the mikado was seen outside of Asia. It was presented by the ambassadors, robed in their ancient Yamato costume, to the President of the United States on the 4th of March, Mr. Arinori Mori acting as interpreter. The first president of the free republic, and the men who had elevated the eta to citizenship stood face to face in fraternal accord. The one hundred and twenty-third sovereign of an empire in its twenty-sixth centennial saluted the citizen ruler of a nation whose century aloe had not yet bloomed. On the 6th of March they were welcomed on the floor of Congress. This day marked the formal entrance of Japan upon the theater of universal history."

In its subordinate objects the embassy was a signal success. Much was learned of Christendom. The results at home were the splendid series of reforms which mark the rear 1872 as epochal. But in its prime object the embassy was an entire failure. One constant and supreme object was ever present, beyond amuseneut or thirst for knowledge. It was to ask that in the revision of the treaties the extra-territoriality clause be stricken out, that foreigners be made subject to the laws of Japan. The failure of the mission was predicted by all who knew the facts. From Washington to St. Petersburg point-blank refusal was made. No Christian governments would for a moment trust their people to pagan edicts and prisons. While Japan slandered Christianity by proclamations., imprisoned men for their beliefs, knew nothing of trial by jury, of the habeas corpus writ, or of modern jurisprudence; in short while Japan maintained the institutions of barbarism, they refused to recognize her as a peer among nations.

At home the watchword was progress. Public persecution for conscience' sake vanished. All the Christians torn from their homes and exiled and imprisoned in 1868 were set free and restored to their native villages. Education advanced rapidly, public decency was improved, and the standards of Christedom attempted.

While in Europe Iwakura and his companions in the embassy kelt cognizant of home affairs. With eyes opened by all that they had seen abroad, mighty results, but of slow growth, they saw their country going too fast. Behind the war project lay an abyss of ruin. On their return the war scheme brought up in a cabinet meeting was rejected. The disappointment of the army was keen and that of expectant foreign contractors pitiable. The advocates of war among the cabinet ministers resigned and retired to private life. Assassins attacked Iwakura, but his injuries did not result fatally. The spirit of feudalism was against him.

On the 17th of January, the ministers who had resigned sent in a memorial praying for the establishment of a representative assembly in which the popular wish might be discussed. Their request was declined. It was officially declared that Japan was not ready for such institutions. Hizen, the home of one of the great clans of the coalition of 1868 was the chief seat of disaffection. With perhaps no evil intent, Eto, who had been the head of the department of justice, had returned to his home there and was followed by many of his clansmen. Scores of officials and men assembled with traitorous intent, and raised the cry of "On to Corea." The rebellion was annihilated in ten days. A dozen ringleaders were sent to kneel before the blood pit. The national government was vindicated and sectionalism crushed.

The Formosan affair mas also brought to a conclusion. Thirteen hundred Japanese soldiers occupied the island for six months, conquering the savages wherever they met, building roads and fortifications. At last the Chinese government in shame began to urge their claims on Formosa and to declare the Japanese intruders. For a time war seemed irevitable. The

ENTRANCE TO NAGASAKI HARBOR

man for the crisis wee Okubo, a leader in the cabinet, the master spirit in crushing the rebellion, and now an ambassador at Peking. The result was that the Chinese paid in solid silver an indemnity of $700,000 and the Japanese disembarked. Japan single-handed, with no foreign sympathy, but with positive opposition, had in the interests of humanity rescued a coast from terror and placed it in a condition of safety. In the face of threatened war a nation having but one tenth the population, area, or resources of China, had abated not a jot of its just demands nor flinched from battle. The righteousness of her cause was vindicated.

The Corean affair ended happily. In 1875 Kuroda Kiyotaka with men of war entered Corean waters. Patience, skill, and tact were crowned with success. On behalf of Japan a treaty of peace, friendship, and commerce was made between the two countries February 27,1876. Japan thus peacefully opened this last of the hermit nations to the world.

The rebellions which we have mentioned were of a mild type compared with that which in 1877 shook the government to its foundations. In the limits of our space it is impossible to enter deeply into the causes of the Satsuma rebellion. Its leader, Saigo 'Takamori, was one of the most powerful members of the reformed government until 1878 when he resigned as some of his predecessors had done, indignant at the peace policy which was pursued. A veritable Cincinnatus, he seems to have won the hearts of all classes around him by the Spartan simplicity of his life and the affability of his manner, and there was none more able or more willing to come to the front when duty to his country called him. It is a thousand pities that such a genuine patriot should have sacrificed himself through a mistaken notion of duty. Ambition to maintain and extend the military fame of his country seems to have blinded him to all other more practical considerations. The policy of Okubo and the rest of the majority in the cabinet, with its regard for peace and material prosperity, was in his eyes unworthy of the warlike traditions of old Japan. But we cannot follow out the story of this famous rebellion-how Saigo established a private school in his native city of Kagoshima for the training of young Shizoku in military tactics, how the reports of the policy of the government more and more dissatisfied him, until a rumor that Okubo had sent policemen to Kagoshima to assassinate him precipitated the storm that had been brewing. This report was not supported by satisfactory evidence, although the Kagoshima authorities extorted a so-called confession from a policeman. Okubo was too noble to be guilty of such an act. It was only after eight months of hard fighting, during which victory swayed from one side to another, and the death of Saigo and his leading generals when surrounded at last like rats in a trap, and the expenditure of over forty million yen, that the much tried government could freely draw breath again. The people of Satsuma believe that Saigo's spirit has taken up its abode in the planet Mars, and that his figure may be seen there when that star is in the ascendant.

By this time railways, telegraphs, lighthouse service, and a navy were well under construction in native works. Two national exhibitions were had, one in 1877 and the second in 1881; the latter particularly was a pretentious one and a great success. In 1879 Japan annexed the Liu Kiu islands, bringing their king to Tokio, there to live as a vassal, and reducing the islands to the position of a prefecture in spite of the warlike threats of China. In the same year occurred the visit to Japan of General Grant while he was on his tour around the world. The famous American was entertained most enthusiastically by the citizens of Tokio for some two weeks in July. The enthusiasm awakened by his visit among the citizens was remarkable. Arches and illuminations were on every hand for miles. The entertainment provided by the Japanese for their distinguished guests at any time is so unique when seen by western eyes that it is always impressive and delightful.

LIMITS AND POSSESSIONS OF THE JAPANESE EMPIRE

The Islands and their Situation—The Famous Mountain Fuji-yama—Rivers and Canals—Ocean Currents and Their Effect on the Japanese Climate—Japan not a Tropical country—Flora and Fauna—The Important Cities—Strange History of Yokobama—Commerce—Mining—Agricultural Products—Ceramic Art—Government of the Realm.

The empire of Japan is a collection of islands of various dimensions, numbering nearly four thousand, and situated to the east of the Asiatic continent. Only four of these however, are of size sufficient to entitle them to considerable fame, and around these a sort of belt of defense is formed by the thousands of islets. Dai Nippon is the name given by the natives to their beautiful land, and from this expression, which means Great Japan, our own name for the empire has been taken. Foreign writers have very often blundered in calling the largest island Nippon or Niphon. This more properly applies to the entire empire, while the main island is named in the military geography of Japan, Hondo. This word itself means main land. The other three important islands are Kiushiu, the lost southeasterly of all; Shikoku, which lies between the latter and Hondo; and Yesso, which is the most northerly of the chain.

Japan occupies an important position on the surface of the globe, measured by political and commercial possibilities. Its position is such that its people may not unreasonably hope to form a natural link between the Occident and the Orient. Lying in the Pacific Ocean, in the temperate zone and not in the torrid, as many have the thought, it bends like a crescent off the continent of Asia. In the extreme north, near the islalnd Saghalien, the distance from the main land of Asia is so short that it is little more than a day's sail in a junk. At the southern extremity, where Kiouhiu draws nearest to the Corean peninsula, the distance to the main land is even less. Between this crescent of islands and the Asiatic main land is enclosed the Sea of Japan. For more than four thousand miles eastward stretches the Pacific Ocean with no stopping point for steamers voyaging to San

Francisco unless they diverge far from their course for a call at Honolulu.

The island connections of Japan are numerous. To the south are the Liu Kiu islands, which have been annexed to Japan, and still farther the great island of Formosa. To the north are the Kurile islands, which extend far above Yesso and were ceded to Japan by Russia in return for Saghalien, over which rule was formerly disputed. The chain is almost continuous, although broken and irregular, to Kamtchatka, and thence prolonged by the Aleutian islands in an enormous semicircle to Alaska and our own continent.

The configuration of the land is that resulting from the combined effects of volcanic action and wave erosion. The area of the Japanese islands is about one hundred and fifty thousand square miles, or nearly as great as the New England and Middle States. But of this surface nearly two-thirds consists of mountain land, much of it still lying waste and uncultivated though apparently capable of tillage. On the main island a solid backbone of mountainous elevations runs through a great portion of its length, with subordinate chains extending at right angles and rising again in the other islands. The mountains decrease in height towards the south and there are few highlands along the sea coast. The range is reached by a gradual rise from the sea, until the backbone of the great island chain is reached. Japan rises abruptly from the sea, and deep water begins very close to the shore, indicating that the entire range of islands may be properly characterized as an immense mountain chain thrown up from the bottom of the ocean. The highest peak is Fuji-yama, which rises to a height of more than twelve thousand feet above the sea. It is a wonderfully beautiful mountain, and is the first glimpse that one has of land in approaching Yokohama from the Pacific Ocean. Of the position which this mountain occupies in the affections and traditions of the Japanese, mention will be made in a later chapter.

The islands forming the empire of Japan are comprehended in these limits; between twenty-four degrees and fifty-one degrees north latitude, and one hundred and twenty-four degrees and one hundred and fifty-seven degrees east longitude. That is, speaking roughly, it lies diagonally in and north of the subtropical belt, and has northern points corresponding with Paris and Newfoundland, and southern ones corresponding with Cairo and the Bermuda islands; or coming nearer home, it corresponds pretty nearly in latitude with the eastern coast line of the United States, added to Nova Scotia and Newfoundland, and the contrasts of climate in the latter island and in Florida are probably not more remarkable than those which are observed in the extreme northern and southern regions of Japan.

The most striking geographical feature of Japan is the Inland Sea, which

FUJI-YAMA

is one of the beauties of the world. It is a long, irregularly shaped arm of the sea, with tides and rapid currents, of variable width and no great depth, studded with innumerable thickly wooded islands. It is the water area which separates Hondo from Shikoku and Kiushiu, and is often spoken of as the Japanese Mediterranean.

One or two of the rivers of Japan, such as the Sumida, on the banks of which Tokio, the capital, lies, and which is about as broad as the East River between New York and Brooklyn, are worthy of note. Here at the present time are situated several ship yards, and many modern craft built in the American fashion may be seen along the shore. Here it may be mentioned that any particular appellation given to a river in Japan holds good only for a limited part of its course, so that it changes its name perhaps four or five times in flowing a few hundred miles. Indeed the river which passes through the city of Ozaka changes its name four times within the city limits. Most of the larger rivers in the main land run a course tending almost north and south. The general contour of the land is such that they must be short, but this direction gives them the greatest length possible. There are brief periods of excessively heavy rain, and they are often then in fierce flood, carrying everything before them and leaving great plains of water-worn stones and gravel around their mouths. There are many picturesque waterfalls which attract travelers and command the admiration of native artists and poets. The rivers at a short distance from their outlets are rendered navigable chiefly by the courage and expertness of the boatmen,—who are among the most daring and skillful in the world.

Till recently little has been done to deepen river channels or protect their banks, except in the interest of agriculture. In the lower courses, where broad alluvial plains of great fertility have been formed, they are frequently intersected by numerous shallow canals, for the most part of comparatively recent excavation, but some of them are many centuries old and these have been of immense service in keeping up communication throughout the country. In spite of their shallowness and rapid silting, some of the rivers of Japan are capable of being improved so as to admit of the passage of steam vessels of the largest size, and there are fine natural inlets and spacious bays which form harbors of great excellence.

The Japanese coast is usually steep and even precipitous. Its chief natural features, such as sunken rocks, capes, straits, entrances to bays and harbors and the mouths of rivers are now well marked with beacons or lighthouses of modern construction. The tides are not great, and in Yeddo bay the rise is only about four feet on an average. In spring tides it rarely exceeds six feet, and in general the height of the flood tide is never very great.

Navigation in summer is somewhat dangerous and difficult. owing to the mists and fogs which are deemed by its sailors to be the great scourge of Japan. Indeed these malarious cloud banks are probably as dangerous to the health of the landsmen as they are to the safety of the mariner. While a large area of land lying under shallow water, during rice cultivation, may have some share in the formation of these dangerous mists, there is the more general cause which is readily to be found in the ocean currents.

Japan occupies a striking position in these currents which flow northward from the Indian ocean and the Malay peninsula. That branch of the great Pacific equatorial current called the Kuro Shiwo, or dark tide or current, on account of its color, flows in a westerly direction past Formosa and the Liu Kiu islands, striking the south point of Kiushiu and sometimes in summer sending a branch up the Sea of Japan. With great velocity it scours the east coast of Kiushiu and the south of Shikoku; thence with diminished rapidity it envelopes the group of islands south of the Bay of Yeddo; and at a point a little north of Tokio it leaves the coast of Japan and flows northeast towards the shores of America, ultimately giving to our own Pacific coast states a far milder climate than the corresponding latitudes on the Atlantic coast.

The yearly evaporation at the tropics, of fully fourteen or fifteen feet of ocean water, causes the great equatorial current of the Pacific to begin its flow. When the warm water reaches the colder waters to the northward, condensation of the water-laden air takes place, with the resulting formation of great cloud banks. The water appears to be of a deep, almost indigo-blue color, whence the name given to the current by the Japanese. Fish occur in great numbers where the Arctic current of fresher, lighter, and cooler water meets the warm salt stream from the south, amidst great commotion. The analogy of this great current to the Gulf stream of the Atlantic is apparent, and there can be no doubt as to its great influence on the climate of Japan. A difference of from twelve to sixteen degrees may be observed in passing from its waters to the cold currents from the north, and the effect of this on the atmosphere is very marked. The sudden and severe changes of temperature are often noticed on the southern coast of Japan and even in Yeddo bay. They are evidently due to eddies or branch currents from the great streams of cold and warm water which interweave themselves in the neighborhood.

In the island of Yesso, the most northerly of the large ones, the extremes of temperature are nearly as great as in New England. In the vicinity of Tokio the winter is usually clear and mild, with occasional sharp frosts and heavy falls of snow. In summer the heat is oppressive for nearly three months. Even at night the heat remains so high that sleep becomes almost-impossible, the air being oppressive and no breeze stirring. The greateat heat is usually from the middle of June to early in September. The cold in winter is much more severe on the northwestern coast, and the roads across the main island are often blocked with snow for many months. In Yokohama the snow fall is light, not often exceeding two or three inches. The ice seldom exceeds an inch in thickness. Earthquake shocks are frequent, averaging more than one a month, but of late years there have been none of great severity.

The winds of Japan are at all seasons exceedingly irregular, frequently violent, and subject to sudden changes. The northeast and easterly winds are generally accompanied by rain, and are not violent. The southwest and westerly winds are generally high, often violcnt, and accompanied with a low barometer. It is from the southwest that the cyclones or typhoons almost invariably come. On clear and pleasant days, which in the neighborhood of Yokohama prevail in excess of foggy ones, there is a regular land and sea breeze at all seasons. The rainfall is above the average of most countries, and about two-thirds of the rainfalls during the six months from April to October.

The flora of Japan is exceedingly interesting, not only to botanists and specialists, but to casual travelers and readers. The useful bamboo flourishes in all parts of the land; sugar cane and the cotton plant grow in the southern part; tea is grown almost everywhere. The tobacco plant, hemp, corn, mulberry For silk. worm food, rice, wheat, barley, millet, buckwheat, potatoes, and yams are all cultivated. The beech, the oak, maples, and pine

JAPANESE IDOLS

trees in rich variety; azaleas, camelias, etc., grow in the forests. Some of the more characteristic plants are wisteria, cryptomeria, calceolaria and chrysanthemums. Various varieties of evergreens are grown, and the Japanese gardeners are peculiarly expert in cultivating these trees in dwarf forms of great beauty. Many familiar wild flowers can be gathered, such as violets, blue-bells, forget-me-nots, thyme, dandelions, and others. The woods are rich in ferns, among which the royal fern is conspicuous, and in orchids, ivies, lichens, mosses and fungi. The beautiful locusts, though imported, may now fairly be considered as naturalized. There are marly water lilies, reeds and rustles, some of which are of great beauty at others of utility.

The mammalia of Japan are not numerous. In ancient times, before the dawn of history, two species of dwarf elephants existed in the plains around Tokio. There are many monkeys in some parts, even in the extreme northern latitudes. Foxes about and are regarded with reverence. Wolves and bears are destructive in the north. There are wild antelopes, red deer, wild boars, dogs, raccoons, badgers, otters, ferrets, bats, moles, and rats; while the sea is specially rich in seals, sea-otters, and whales. The country has been found quite unsuitable for sheep, but goats thrive well, although they are not much favored by the people. Oxen are used for draught purposes. Horses are small but are fair quality, and the breed is being improved. The cats are nearly tailless. The dogs are of a low, half-wolfish breed. There are some three hundred varieties of birds known in Japan. Few of them are what we call song-birds, but the lark is one brilliant exception. Game birds are plentiful, but are now protected.

Insects are very numerous, as no traveler will dispute, and Japan is a great field for investigation by entomologists. Locusts are often destructive, and mosquitoes are a great pest. Bees, the silk worm and the wax-insect are highly appreciated.

There are several kinds of lizards, a great variety of frogs, seven or eight snakes, including one deadly species, and two or three kinds of tortoise. The crustaceans are numerous and interesting, and of fish there is extraordinary variety, especially those found in salt water. Oysters and clams are excellent and plentiful.

Let us now turn to the temporal affairs of the people who dwell in this island empire, their cities, their industries, and to their government.

Japan like its oriental companion, China, is a country of great cities, although the smaller empire has not so many famous for their size as has China. With scarcely an exception these greater cities are situated at the heads of bays, most of them good harbors and accessible for commerce. The largest of these cities, of course, is the capital Tokio, which doubtless passes a million inhabitants, although it is impossible that it should justify the American tradition of not many years ago, that its numbers mere twice a million. Tokio, or the old city of Yeddo, is situated near the head of Yeddo Bay, but a few miles from Yokohama, and but little farther from Uraga where the first reception to Commodore Perry was given. Among the other more important cities on the sea coast are Nagasaki, Yokohama, Hakodate, Hiogo, Ozaka, Hiroshima, and Kanagawa.

Nagasaki is situated on the southwest coast of the island of Kiushiu, and is built in the form of an amphitheater. The European quarter in the east, stands upon land reclaimed from the sea at considerable labor and expense. Desima, the ancient Dutch factory, lies at the foot, and behind it is the native part of the town. The whole is sheltered by high wooden mountains. The city of Nagasaki was almost the first which attracted the attention of foreigners, partly from its being already known by name from the Dutch colony established there; partly because it was the nearest point to China and a port of great beauty; and also because before the political revolution which overthrew the power of the shogunate, the daimios of the south were there enabled, owing to its distance from Yeddo, to transact foreign affairs in their own way unmolested. This comparative importance did not last long, for affairs soon began to be concentrated in Yokohama, and the opening of the ports of Hiogo and Ozaka further reduced it to a secondary rank among commercial towns. It is still, however, a busy place and a great portion of the navigation of the Japanese seas passes by its beautiful port. But it is not a town of the future, and will be supplanted in prosperity to considerable extent by the more northern cities.

'Yokohama, situated on the Gulf of Yeddo, owes its rise and importance to the merchants who came to seek their fortunes in the empire of the rising sun immediately after the signature of the treaties which threw open the coasts of Japan to adveturous foreigners. When Perry, with his augmented fleet, returned to Japan in February, 1854, the Japanese found him as inflexibly firm as ever. Instead of making the treaty at Uraga he must take it nearer Yeddo. Yokohamn was the chosen spot, and there on the 8th of March, 1854, were exchanged the formal articles of convention between the United States and Japan.

By the treaty of Yokohama, Shimoda was one of the ports opened to Americans. Before it began to be of much service the place was visited by an earthquake and tidal wave, which overwhelmed the town and ruined the harbor. The ruin of Shimoda was the rise of Yokohams. By a new treaty Kanagawa, three miles across the bay from Yokohama, was substituted for Shimoda. The Japanese government decided to make Yokohama the future port. Their reasons for this were many. Kanagawa was on the line of the great highway of the empire, along which the proud Daimios and their trains of retainers were continually passing. With the antipathy to foreigners that existed, had Kanagawa been made a foreign settlement, its history would doubtless have had many more pages of assassination and incendiarism than did Yokohams. Foreseeing this, even though considered by the foreign ministers a violation of treaty agreements, the Japanese government immediately set to work to render Yokohama as convenient as possible for trade, residence and espionage.

They built a causeway nearly two miles long across the lagoons and marshes to make it of easy access. They built granite piers, custom house and officers quarters, and dwellings and store houses for the foreign merchants. After a long quarrel over which should be the city, the straggling colony of diplomats, missionaries, and merchants of Kanagawa finally pulled up their stakes and joined the settlement of Yokohama. Yokohama was settled in a squatter-like and irregular manner, and the ill effects of it are seen to this day. When compared with Shanghai, the foreign metropolis of China, it is vastly inferior.

The town grew slowly at first. Murders and assassinations of foreigners were frequent during the first few years. Diplomatic quarrels were constant, and threats of bombardment from some foreign vessel in the harbor of frequent occurrence. A fire which destroyed nearly the whole foreign town seemed to purify the place municipally, commercially, and morally. The settlement was rebuilt in a more substantial and regular manner. As the foreign population grew, banks, newspaper offices, hospitals, postoffices, and consulate buildings reappeared in a new dignity. Fire and police protection were organized. Steamers began to come from European ports and from San Francisco. Social life began as ladies and children came, and houses became homes. Then came the rapid growth of society and the finer things. Churches, theaters, clubs, schools were organized in rapid succession. Telegraph connection with Tokio, and thence around the globe, was accomplished, and the railway system increased rapidly. Within the thirty-five years of the life of Yokohama, it has grown from a fishing village of a few hundred to a city of fifty thousand people. Its streets are lighted with gas and electricity; its stores are piled full of rare silks, bronzes and curios. At present the foreign population of Yokohama numbers about two thousand residents. In addition to these the foreign transient population, made up of tourists and officers and sailors of the navy, and the merchant marine, numbers between three thousand and six thousand. Several daily newspapers, beside weeklies and monthlies, printed in English, furnish mediums of communication and news. Yokohama has become and will remain the great mercantile center of American and European trade in Japan.

Hiogo, or rather Kobe, as the foreign part has been called since the concession, is near Ozaka, both towns being situated on the inland Sea of Japan, near the south end of the Island of Niphon. Kobe is a considerable foreign settlement, with many fine houses and spacious warehouses. Ozaka, which contains more than half a million inhabitants, is one of the chief trading cities of Japan, and an immense proportion of the merchandise imported into the empire passes through it.

The commerce between Japan and western nations, European and American, increases year by year. England enjoys the profits from more than half of the total interchange, the United

JAPANESE JUGGLERS

States is second, with a large portion of the remainder, and the rest of the commerce is divided among Germany, France, Holland, Norway, and Sweden. It is impossible to obtain figures recent enough to be a satisfactory index of the total volume of commerce annually, but it is now very many millions of dollars a year. Japan exports tobacco, rice, wax, tea, silks, and manufactured goods, such as curios, bronzes, lacquer ware, etc. The principal imports of Japan are cotton goods, manufactures of iron, machinery of all sorts, woolen fabrics, flour, etc.

Mining in Japan is seldom carried on by modern methods, and the mineral wealth has not been developed as it will be within a few years. In almost every portion of Japan are found ores of some kind and there is scarcely a district in which there are not traces of mines having been worked. No mines can be worked without special license of the government, and foreigners are excluded from ownership in any mining industry. Japan seem to be fairly well, though not richly, provided with mineral wealth. The mines include those for gold, silver, copper, lead, iron, tin, plumbago, antimony, arsenic, marble, sulphur, alum, salt, coal, petroleum, and other minerals.

The annual export of tea amounts to nearly thirty million pounds, of which considerably more than half is shipped from Yokohania. All Japanese tea is green and the United States is the chief customer for it.

The exact area of Japan is not known, though it is computed at nearly one hundred and fifty thousand square miles, with a population of more than two hundred persons to a square mile. The number of acres under cultivation is about nine million, or one-tenth of the entire area. Not one-fourth of the fertile portion of Japan is yet under cultivation. Immense portions of good land await the farmers' plow and seed to return rich harvests. For centuries the agricultural art has been at a standstill. Population and acreage have increased, but the crop in bulk and quantity remains the same. The true wealth of Japan consists in her agricultural and not in her mineral and manufacturing resources. The government and intelligent classes seem to be awakening to this fact. The islands are capable of yielding good crops and adapted to support the finest breeds of cattle. With these branches of industry increased to the extent that they deserve, the prosperity of the empire will show constant increase.

The ceramic art of Japan and the art of the lacquer worker are two that have helped to make Japanese wares famous in the western world. The various wares of porcelain faience are made in Japan in quality and art inferior to none in the world.

Since the restoration to power of the mikado in 1868, the government of Japan has been growing nearer and nearer into the forms of western monarchical governments. In a prior chapter the promise of the young mikado to advance the freedom of his people, and ultimately to adopt constitutional forms of rule, has been quoted. In the later years he has been aiming for the fulfillment of this promise. Supporting him, the party of progressionists, largely influenced by contact with European and American civilization, urge on every reform. The present government is simply the modernized form of the system established more than a thousand years ago, when centralized monarchy succeeded simple feudalism. After the emperor conies the Dai Jo Kuan, which is practically a supreme cabinet, and following this, three other cabinets of varying powers and duties. The council of ministers is made up of the, heads of departments, the foreign office, home office, treasury, army, navy, education, religion, public works, judiciary, imperial household, and colonization. The Dai Jo Kuan directs the three imperial cities and the sixty-eight ken or prefectures. The provinces are now merely geographical divisions.

In the course of the efforts to bring the Japanese forms of government more into harmony with those of Europe and America, many important changes have been made. A system of nobility was devised, and titles were granted to those who were considered to be entitled to then, whether by birth or achievement. The four or five ranks included in this system closely follow the English models.

The judiciary, too, has been remodeled in many details to make it approach the western system. The methods of procedure are gradually conforming nearer and nearer to our own, as well as the names and jurisdiction of the courts. The Japanese people have been exceedingly anxious of late years to expunge the extra territoriality clause which appears in the treaties with all western nations. It provides, in effect, that offenses by a foreigner against a Japanese shall be judged in a consular court presided over by the consul of that country whence the foreigner comes. In other words, Japanese courts have no jurisdiction over the doings of foreigners having consuls in that country.

JAPANESE COURT DRESS, OLD STYLE

This provision has become very obnoxious to the Japanese people, placing them on a level, as it does, with barbaric and semi-barbaric countries, where like provisions hold. This has been one of the potent factors in influencing Japan to adopt western legal methods. Recent treaties which have been drawn with the United States and with England provide that this clause shall be expunged, and if they are finally agreed upon we may soon see Japan more absolutely independent than she has yet been.

In 1890 a constitution wan granted to Japan by the emperor, and a few months later legislative bodies for the first time began deliberation in Tokio. The powers of this parliament are constantly increasing. The war between China and Japan has been a strong influence to weld the people of opposing political faiths into harmony, and in parliament conservatives and radicals alike have risen in patriotism, and have been glad to cast votes for every measure that would hold up the hands of those who were bearing the battles. With a government drawing for itself lines parallel with those of enlightened western nations, increasing the freedom of its people, the power of the people's legislators, and the honesty of the people's courts, Japan has every right to name herself as worthy of a place in full brotherhood with the family of civilized nations.

COUNCIL OF WAR ON A JAPANESE BATTLE SHIP
(Form A Drawing By A Japanese Artist)

PERSONAL CHARACTERISTICS OF THE JAPANESE PEOPLE

Difference of Opinion as to the True Significance of Their Rapid Adoption of Western Civilization—Physique of Man and Woman—Two Great Classes of the Population—The Samurai—The Agricultural Laborer—Wedding Ceremonies—Elopements—Japanese Babies—Sports of Childhood and of Age—Dress of Man and Woman—Food—Homes of the People—Family Life—Art, Science, Medicine, Music—Language and Literature—Religion.

In such a state of transition are the Japanese people themselves, as truly the government, that it is difficult to describe their personal characteristics. Different observers reach different conclusions as to their personality. One affirms that great quickness of imitation and judgment in discovering what is worth imitating, seem to be the prominent characteristics of the Japanese. They want originality and independence of thought, and character which accompanies it. The Japanese are not slow in adopting the inventions of modern civilization, and even in modifying them em to suit their own convenience, but, says another observer, that they will ever add anything of importance to them may be doubted. The same is true in a political point of view. The more enlightened of the Japanese are already beginning to recognize the superiority of the European forms of government. The upper classes are all sedulously imitating Paris and London fashions of dress. In our own country we have seen the prevalence of an offensive Anglomania among certain classes of society in the larger cities, but in Japan a corresponding mania for the forms of western civilization has become almost universal, and is reaching the real bulk of the nation. Such extraordinary capacity for change may mark a versatile but unreliable race; for it seems hard to believe that a people who are parting with their ancestral notions with such a total absence of any pangs of sorrow, will be likely to adhere with much steadfastness to a new order of things. On the other hand, other students of this movement take it to be only a most gratifying indication that Japan was a nation which had outgrown its narrow limits of thought and learning, ready to adopt whatever was good, and yearning for it when the opportunity came, with a strength that made rapid assimilation of ideas entirely proper, and no sign of instability. It is to be hoped that the latter interpretation is the right one.

In moral character the average Japanese is frank, honest, faithful, kind, gentle, courteous, confiding, affectionate, filial, and loyal. Love of truth for its own sake, chastity, and temperance are not characteristic virtues. A high sense of honor is cultivated by the Samurai. In spirit the average artisan and farmer is lamblike. In intellectual capacity the a actual merchant is mean, and his moral character low. He is beneath the Chinaman in this respect. The male Japanese is far less overbearing and more chivalrous to woman than any other Asiatic. In political knowledge, or gregarious ability, the countryman is a baby and the city artisan a boy. The peasant is a pronounced pagan, with superstition ingrained into his inmost nature. In reverence to elders and to antiquity, obedience to parents, gentle manners, universal courtesy, and generous impulses the Japanese are the peers of any and superior to many peoples of Christendom. The idea of filial obedience has been developed into fanaticism and is the main blot of paganism and superstition.

The Japanese in physique are much of the same type as the Spaniards, and inhabitants of the south of France. They are of middle or low stature. The men are about five feet six inches in height or a trifle less on an average, while the women rarely exceed five feet. When dressed the Japanese look strong, well proportioned men, but when in the exceedingly slight costumes which they very often are pleased to adopt, it is then apparent that though their bodies are robust their legs are short and slight. Their heads are somewhat out of proportion to their bodies, being generally large and sunk a little between the shoulders, but they have small feet and delicate hands. The resemblance the Japanese bear to the Chinese is not nearly as marked as popular opinion would have it. The faces of the former are longer and more regular, their noses more prominent, and their eyes less sloped. The men are naturally very hirsute, but they never wear beards. Their hair is glossy, thick, and always black. Their eyes are black, their teeth white and slightly prominent. The shade of their skin is totally unlike the yellow complexions of the

Chinese; in some cases it is very swarthy or copper colored, but the most usual tint is an olive brown. Children and young people have usually quite pink complexions.

The women follow the Chinese type a little closer. The eyes are narrower and sloped upward, and the head is small. Like the men their hair is glossy and very black, but it never reaches the length of American women's hair. They have clear, sometimes even perfectly white skin, especially among the aristocracy, oval faces, and slender, graceful forms. Their manners are peculiarly artless and simple. But the harmony of the whole is spoiled in many instances by an ugly depression of the chest, which is sometimes observed in those who are otherwise handsomest and best formed.

DRESSING THE HAIR

About the end of the eighth century a reform was instituted in the military system of the empire, which had become unsatisfactory and defective. The court decided that all those among the rich peasants who had capacity and were skilled in archery and horsemanship, should, compose the military class, and that the remainder, the weak and feeble, should continue to till the soil and apply themselves to agriculture. This was one of the most significant of all the changes in the history of Japan. Its fruits are seen to-day in the social constitution of the Japanese people. Though there are many classes, there are but two great divisions of the Japanese, the military and the agricultural.

This change wrought a complete severance of the soldier and the farmer. It lifted up one part of the people to a plane of life on which travel, adventure, the profession and pursuit of arms, letters, and the cultivation of honor and chivalry were possible and by which that brightest type of Japanese men, the Samurai was produced. This is the class which for centuries has moriopolized arms, polite learning, patriotism, and intellect of Japan. They are the men whose minds have been open to learn, from whom sprung the ideas that once made and later overthrew the feudal system, which wrought the mighty reforms that swept away the shogunate in 1868, and restored the mikado to ancient power, who introduced those ideas that now rule Japan, and sent their sons abroad to study the civilization of the west. To the Samurai Japan looks today for safety in war and progress in peace. The Samurai is the soul of the nation. In other lands the priestly and the military castes were formed, in Japan one and the same class held the sword and the pen; the other class, the agricultural, remained unchanged.

Left to the soil to till it, to live and die upon it, the Japanese farmer has remained the same today that he was then. Like the wheat, that for successive ages is planted as wheat, sprouts, beards and fills as wheat, the peasant with his horizon bounded by his rice fields and water courses or the timbered hills, his intellect laid away for safe keeping in the priest's hands, is the son of the soil. He cares little who rules him unless he is taxed beyond the power of flesh and blood to bear, or an overmeddlesome official policy touches his land to transfer, sell or divide it. Then he rises to rebel. In time of war he is a disinterested and a passive spectator and he does not fight. He changes masters with apparent unconcern. Amidst all the ferment of ideas induced by the contact of western civilization with Asiatic within the last four decades, the farmer stolidly remains conservative. He knows not nor cares to hear of it and hates it because of the heavier taxes it imposes upon him.

The domestic solemnities of the Japanese, marriage especially, are made the subjects of deep and careful meditation. In the upper classes marriage is arranged between two young people when the bridegroom has reached his twentieth and the bride her sixteenth year. The will of the parents is almost without exception the dominating power in the matrimonial arrangements, which are carried out according to agreement among the relatives, but love affairs of a spontaneous kind form a large element in the romantic literature of Japan. The wedding is preceded by a betrothal, which ceremony offers an occasion for the members of both families to meet one another; and it not unfrequently pens that the future couple then learn for the first time the wishes of their parents respecting their union. If perchance the bridegroom elect is not satisfied with the choice, the young woman returns home again. With the introduction of other western ideas, this inconvenient custom is little by little falling into disuse. Nowadays, if a young man wishes to marry into a family of good position or one which it would be advantageous to his prospects to enter, he endeavors first to see the young lady, and then if she pleases him he sends a mediator, chosen usually from amongst his married friends, and the betrothal is arranged without any further obstacle. Even more American-like than this, however, there are many instances, and the number is constantly increasing, in which the match is the result of mutual affection, and sometimes elopements are known to occur among the best families.

When things are carried through conventionally, the betrothal and wedding are usually solemnized on the same day and without the assistance of any minister of worship. The customary ceremonies are all of a homely nature, but at the same time are extremely complicated and numerous. Upon the day fixed, the trousseau of the young bride and all the presents she has received, are brought to the home of the bridegroom, where the ceremony is to be performed, and arranged in the apartments set apart for the affair. The bride arrives soon afterward, dressed in white and escorted by her parents. The groom, arrayed in gala costume, receives her at the entrance of the house, and conducts her into the hall where the betrothal takes place. Here grand preparations have been made. The altar of the domestic gods has been decorated with images of the patron saints of the family and with different plants, each having its symbolical meaning.

When all have taken their places according to the recognized form of precedence, the ceremony is begun by two young girls, who hand around unlimited quantities of saki to the guests. These two damsels are surnamed the male and female butterfly, the emblems of conjugal felicity, because according to popular notion butterflies always fly about in couples. The decisive ceremony is tinged with a symbolism which has a considerable touch of poetry in it. The two butterflies, holding between them a two necked bottle, approach and offer it to the engaged couple' to drink together from the two mouths of the bottle till it is emptied, which signifies that husband and wife must drain together the cup of life whether it contain nectar or gall; they must share equally the joys and sorrows of existence.

The Japanese is the husband of one wife only, but he is at liberty to introduce several concubines under the family roof. This is done in all classes of society, especially amongst the daimios. It is asserted that in many of the noble families the legitimate wife not only evinces no jealousy, but has even a certain pleasure in seeing the number of her household thus augmented, as it supplies her with so many additional servants. In the middle classes, however, the custom is often the cause of bitter family dissentions.

The heavy expenses of the marriage ceremonies often occasion considerable domestic strife and misery, at least if they are celebrated according to all the established conventionalities. Debts are then incurred which perhaps the young couple are unable to meet, so that when other expenses grow, and trouble or misfortune overtake them, they are speedily plunged into the deepest distress and indigence. The natural consequence of these arbitrary customs is the increase of runaway matches. The elopement, however, is usually wisely winked at by the parents, who feign great lamentation and anger, then finally assemble their neighbors, pardon their recreant children, and circulate the inevitable saki, and the marriage is considered as satisfactory as if performed with all the requisite formalities.

The birth of a child is another occasion for the meeting of the whole circle of relations, and the consumption of a great many more bumpers of saki. The baptism of the young Japanese citizen takes place thirty days later, when the infant is taken to the temple of the family divinity to receive its first name. The father has previously written three different names upon three separate slips of paper, which are handed over to the officiating bonze or priest. The latter throws them into the air, and the piece of paper which in falling first touches the ground contains the name which is to be given to the child. There are no godparents, but several friends of the family declare themselves the infant's protectors and make it several presents, among which is a fan if it be a boy, or a pot of rouge if a girl.

The Japanese child is early taught to endure hardships, and is subjected from its infancy to all the small miseries of life, so far as may be thought wise for its training. The mother nurses it till it is two years of age, and carries it continually about with her attached to her back for convenience. The children are daintily pretty, chubby, rosy, sparkling-eyed. The children's heads are shaved in all curious fashions, some with little topknots, and others with bald spots. The way the babies are carried is an improvement upon the Indian fashion. He is lugged on the back of his mother or his sister, maybe scarcely older than himself, either strapped loosely but safely, with his head just peering above the shoulder of the bearer, or else enclosed in a fold of the garment she wears. It is a popular belief among travelers that Japanese babies are the best in the world and never cry, but the Japanese themselves claim no such

CHILD CARRYING BABY

distinction for the little ones, very proud of them though they are, and affirm that they have their fits of temper as well as American babies.

Education is not forced too early upon the children, but nature is allowed its own way during the first years of childhood. Toys, pleasures, fetes of all kinds, are liberally indulged in. One writer has said that Japan is the paradise of babies; not only is this true but it is also a very delightful abode for all who love play. The contrast between the Japanese and Chinese character in this respect is radical. The whole character, manners, and even the dress of the sedate and dignified Chinaman, seems to be in keeping with that aversion to rational amusement and athletic exercises which characterize that adult population. In Japan, on the contrary, one sees that children of the larger growth enjoy with equal zest, games which are the same or nearly the same as those of the little ones. Certain it is that the adults do all in their power to provide for the children their full quota of play and harmless sports.

A very noticeable change has passed over the Japanese people since the recent influx of foreigners, in respect of their love of amusements. Their sports are by no means as numerous or elaborate as formerly, and they do not enter into them with the enthusiasm that formerly characterized them. The children's festivals and sports are rapidly losing their importance, and some are rarely seen. There is no country in the world in which there are so many toy shops for the sale of the things which delight children. Street theatrical shows are common. Sweet meats of a dozen strange sorts are carried by men who do tricks in gymnastics to please the little ones. In every Japanese city there are scores if not hundreds of men and women who obtain a livelihood by amusing the children. There are indoor games and outdoor games, games for the day time and games for the evening. Japanese kite flying and top spinning are famous the world over, and experts in these sports come to exhibit their adeptness in our own country. In the northern provinces, where the winters are severe, Japanese boys have the same sports with snow and ice, coasting, sliding, fighting mimic battles with snowballs, that are known to our own American boys. Dinners, tea parties, and weddings, keeping store, and playing doctor, are imitated in Japanese children's games.

On the third day of the third month is held the wonderful "Feast of Dolls" which is the day especially devoted to the girls, and to them it is the greatest day in the year. The greatest day in the year for the boys is on the fifth day of the fifth month, when they celebrate what is known as the "Feast of Flags."

A Japanese attains his majority at fifteen years of age. As soon as this time has arrived he takes a new name, and quietly discards the pleasures of infancy for the duties of a practical life. His first care, if he belong to the middle classes, is the choice of

THE CHINESE FLEET AT WEI-HAI-WEI

a trade or profession. The opportunities for this choice are much greater than in China, just as the scope of Japanese learning and life has increased in the last quarter century. Practically all of the businesses and trades that we know in our own country are to-day known in Japan, those which were not there before, having crept in with the advent of the foreigners. The Japanese young man, if he is to be a merchant or to learn a trade, serves an apprenticeship for a period sufficient to fit him for the mastery of his work, and then it is he provides himself with a wife.

The dress of the Japanese is changing in harmony with the introduction of other foreign habits. Custom has always obliged married women to shave their eyebrows and blacken their teeth, but of late years the practice has been decreasing and now it does not prevail among the better classes and in the larger cities. They have also made a most immoderate use of paint, covering their brow, cheeks, and neck with thick coats of rouge and white. Some have even gone so far as to gild their lips, but the more modest have been content to color them with carmine, and the excessive use of paints is diminishing.

The kirimon, a kind of long, open dressing gown, is worn by every one, men and women alike. It is a little longer and of better quality for the women, who cross it in front and confine it by a long wide piece of silk, or other material tied in a quaint fashion at the back. The men keep theirs in its place by tying a long straight scarf around them. The Japanese use no linen, the women alone wearing a chemise of silk crepe, but it must be remembered that they bathe daily or even oftener, and that simplicity of dress is affected by all.

The middle classes wear in addition to the kirimon, a doublet and pantaloons. These are also worn in winter by men of the lower orders, the pantaloons fitting tightly, and made of checked cotton. The peasants and porters usually wear a loose overall in summer, made of some light paper material, and in winter not unfrequently consisting of coarse straw. The women also envelop themselves in one or several thickly wadded mantles. Linen gloves with one division for the thumb are very generally worn. Sandals are made of plaited straw, and in bad weather are disoarded for wooden logs, raised from the ground by means of two bits of wood under the toe and heel. As might naturally be expected, locomotion under such circumstances is performed with difficulty, and the hobbling gate which these Drops necessitate has often been commented on. This peculiarity is most noticeable among the women, whose naturally easy gait is almost as much diverted from its normal movement by these small stilts as that of their sisters in the west by their high heeled shoes. The costume of the country is exactly alike for both the lower and higher classes, with the difference that the latter always wear silk material. The costumes worn by officials, and those of the nobility, are distinguished by the amplitude of the folds and the richness of the texture. Wide flowing pantaloons are often substituted

JAPANESE BATH

for the kirimon, which trail on the ground, completely concealing the feet, and give the wearer the appearance of walking on his knees, which indeed is the delusion it is intended to produce. A kind of overcoat with wide sleeves reaching to the hips completes the costume.

The dwelling houses of the Japanese are well adapted to their manners of life, except that they are not always sufficient protection against severe cold. Rich and poor live side by side, although in Tokio there are still traces of the castes of the feudal age, and there are also growing tendencies in the rising mercantile and moneyed classes to separate themselves from the common mass. There are now great portions of the capital densely populated by the working classes only, and quite destitute of any open spaces of practical value for health and recreation.

The proverb "Every man's house is his castle," might very readily be appropriated by the Japanese, whose home, however humble it may be in all other respects, is always guarded by a moat. In a feudal mansion the moat was usually deep enough to prove a genuine obstacle. While it is still almost universally retained, the muddy water is hidden in summer time by the leaves of the lotus, and the bridges are not drawn. The smaller gentry imitate the grandeur of those above them, and when at last we come down to the lowest level we still find a miniature moat which is often dry, of a foot or so in breadth, and at most about two inches deep.

In houses of some pretensions there is an enbankment behind the moat, with a hedge growing above it. Behind this there is either a wall or fence of bamboo, tiles, or plaster. As the name of the street is not to be found at the street corner as with us, it is repeated on every doorway. The towns are divided into wards and blocks, and the numbers of the houses are often confused and misleading. A slip of white wood is nailed on one of the posh of the gate, and is inscribed with the name of the street or block, the number, name of house holder, numbers and sexes of household. The gates of the larger houses are heavy, adorned with copper or brass mountings, and often studded with large nails.

When one enters by the gate there is generally found a court, from the sides of which the open verandas of the building may be reached. The verandas are high and there is a special entrance by heavy wooden stairs. The court is sometimes paved with large stones, and sometimes it is left bare or covered with turf. The gardens even of somewhat humble mansions are graced with carved stone lanterns. The well placed near the kitchen often has a rim of stone around it, and the bucket is raised by a beam, or a long bamboo.

In front of the doorway there is a small space unfloored call the doma, where one takes off his shoes after announcing himself by calling, or by striking a gong suspended by the door post. There is often only one story in Japanese houses, and very rarely more than two. Almost all of them are built of wood; the ground floor is raised about four feet above the ground, the walls are made of planks covered with coarse mats; and the roof is supported by four pillars. In a two-storied house the second story is generally built more solidly than the first; experience having shown that the edifice can thus better resist the shock of an earthquake. Sometimes the walls are plastered with a coating of soft clay or varnish, and are decorated with gildings and paintings. The stair to the second story is very steep. The ceilings are composed of very thin, broad planks, and are lower than we are accustomed, but it must be remembered that the people do not sit on chairs and have no high beds or tables. Doorways, or rather the grooved lintels in which the screen doors slide, are very low and the Japanese, who are always bowing, seem to enjoy having an unusual number of them to pass through in extensive houses. No room is completely walled in, but each one opens on one or more sides completely into the garden, the street, or the adjoining room. Sliding shutters, with tissue paper windows, the carpentry of which is careful and exact, move in wooden grooves almost on a level with the floor, which is covered with padded woven mats of rushes. As a protection against the severities of the weather rain shutters are also used.

All Japanese dwellings have a cheerful, well-cared-for appearance, which in a great measure is the result of two causes; first, that every one is bound constantly to renew the paper coverings of the outside panels, and next that the frequent fires which each time make immense ravages often render it necessary to reconstruct an entire district. In the interior the houses are generally divided into two suites of apartments, the one side being apportioned to the women as private rooms, and the other side being used for the reception rooms. These apartments are all separated from one another by partitions made of slight wooden frames, upon which small square bits of white paper are pasted, or else a kind of screen is used which can be moved at pleasure and the room enlarged or contracted according as the occasion requires. Towards nightfall these screens are usually folded up so as to allow a free passage of air throughout the house.

The mats of rushes or rice straw which carpet the floors are about three inches thick, and are soft to the touch. They are of uniform size, about six feet by three, and this fact dominates all architecture in Japan. Estimates for building houses and the cutting of wood rest upon this traditional custom. The inhabitants never soil them with their boots but always walk barefooted about the house. The mat in Japan answers the purpose of all ordinary furniture, a takes the place of our chairs, tables, and beds. For writing purposes only do they use a low round table about a foot high, which is kept in a cupboard and only brought out when n letter has to be written. This they do kneeling before the table, which they carefully

JAPANESE COUCH

put away again when the letter is finished. The meals are laid upon square tables of very slender dimensions, around which the whole family gather, sitting on their heels.

In the walls are recesses with sliding doors into which the bedding is thrust in the daytime. At bedtime out of these recesses are taken the soft cotton stuffed mattresses and the thick coverlets of silk or cotton which have been rolled up all day, and these are spread upon the mats. The Japanese pillows are of wood, with the upper portions stuffed or padded, and in form something like a large flat iron. Sometimes each one contains a little drawer in which the ladies put their hairpins. When a Japanese has taken off his day garments he rests his head on this wooden pillow and composes himself to sleep. Everything is put away in the morning, all the partitions are opened to give air, the mats are carefully swept, and the now completely empty chamber in transformed during the day into an office, sitting room, or dining room, to become again the sleeping apartment the following night.

Clothes are kept in plaited bamboo boxes usually covered with black or dark green waterproof paper. The furniture is very simple, and there are often in the best houses no chairs, no tables, no bedsteads. There may be some low, short-legged side tables of characteristic Japanese pattern and one or two costly vases or other ornaments, a few pictures which are changed in deference to guests and seasons, some flowers or dwarf trees in vases and a lamp or two. There are, however, two pieces of furniture which are to be found in the houses of every class. These are the brazier and the pipe box, for the Japanese is a great tea drinker and a constant smoker. Every hour in the day this hot water must be ready for him, and the brazier kept burning both day and night both in summer and winter.

The principal meal takes place about the middle of the day, and after it the family indulge themselves with several hours' sleep, so that at this time the streets are almost deserted. In the evening they have another meal, and then devote the rest of the time till bedtime to all kinds of amusements. In the highest Japanese circles the dinner hour is sometimes enlivened by music from an orchestra stationed in an adjoining room.

In summer a well-planned Japanese house is the very ideal of coolness, grace and comfort. In winter it is the extreme of misery. There are no fire-places and there is unmitigated ventilation. People keep themselves warm by holding themselves close over some morsels of red hot charcoal in a brazier, and frost bite is very common. At night, when cold winds blow, a heating apparatus is put beneath the heavy cotton coverlets. It often gets overturned; a waterman from his ladder-like tower sees afar off a dull red glow, bells begin to clang, and soon the city is in an uproar of excitement over another conflagration. In a few hours a great fainthearted gap has appeared in the city. One goes at day-break to find the scene of destruction, but it has already almost disappeared. Crowds of carpenters have rushed in, and have already done much to erect on the hot and smoking ruins wooden houses nearly as good as those swept away by the fire of the night before.

The yashikis or palaces in which the people of rank reside, are nothing more than ordinary houses grouped together and surrounded by whitewashed outhouses, with latticed windows of black wood. These outhouses serve a two-fold purpose, as habitations for the domestics, and as a wall of the enclosure. Always low, and usually rectangular, they look very much like warehouses or barracks. The palace of the sovereign has, however, a certain character of its own. It is a perfect labyrinth of courts and streets formed by the many separate houses, pavilions, and corridors or simple wooden partitions. The roofs are supported by horizontal beams varnished white, or gilded at the extremities, and decorated with small pieces of sculpture, many of which are very beautiful works of art. The ancient palace of the Tycoons is remarkable for boldness and richness of outline. Everything breathes a spirit of the times when the power and prosperity of the shogunate was at its height. Upon the ceilings of gold, sculptured beams cross each other in squares, the angles where they meet being marked by a plate of gilt bronze of very elegant design.

The greatest novelties in the eyes of foreigners are the gardens attached to every house. The smallest tradesman has his own little plot of ground where he may enjoy the delights of solitude, take his siesta, or devote himself to copious potations of tea and saki. These gardens are often of exceedingly small size. They consist of a quaint collection of dwarf shrubs, miniature lakes full of gold fish, lilliputian walks in the middle of diminutive flower beds, tiny streams over which are little green arches to imitate bridges, and finally arbors or bowers beneath which a rabbit might scarcely find room to nestle.

The Japanese are as strict in the observance of etiquette at a funeral as at their marriage ceremonies. The rites take place both at the time of the actual interment, and afterwards at the festivals celebrated in honor of the gods on these occasions. There are two kinds of funerals, interment and cremation. Most of the Japanese make known during life either to the heir or to some intimate friend their wishes respecting the mode of the disposal of their remains. When the father or mother in a family is seized with a mortal illness and all hope of recovery is past and the end approaching, the soiled garments worn by the dying person are removed and exchanged for perfectly clean ones. The last wishes of the dying one are then recorded on paper. As soon as life has departed all the relations give way to lamentations; the body is carried into another room, covered with a curtain and surrounded by screens. In the higher classes the body is watched for two days, but in the lower it is buried a day after death.

Contrary to the customs at marriage ceremonies, the bonzes or priests preside over all the funeral rites. It is they who watch beside the dead until the time for interment. This is usually carried out by men who make it their profession. The corpse is placed in a coffin, somewhat of the shape of a round tub, in a squatting position, with the head bowed, the legs bent under, and the arms crossed; the lid of the coffin is then fastened down by wooden pegs. The funeral procession proceeds to the temple, the bonzes marching first, some carrying flags, others different symbols, such as little white boxes full of flowers, others wringing small hand-bells. Then follows the corpse, preceded by a long tablet upon which is inscribed the new name given to the deceased. The eldest son follows, and then the family, intimate friends, and domestics. The nearest relations are dressed in white which is the color worn for mourning.

When the procession arrives at the temple the coffin is placed before the image of the god and then various ceremonies commence, the length of which is regulated by the rank of the deceased, as with us. After that all the friends and acquaintances return home, whilst the relations turn to the place where the body is to be laid. If the deceased has expressed the desire that his body should be burned, the coffin is carried from the temple to a small crematory a short distance away. It is there placed upon a kind of stone scaffold, at the base of which a fire is kept burning until the body is consumed. The men employed in this

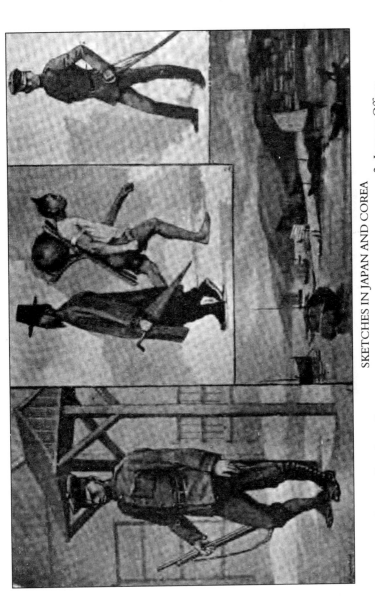

SKETCHES IN JAPAN AND COREA

1. Japanese Private on Guard over Stores.
2. Japanese Officer.
3. Corean Farmer and Coolie.
4. Landing Place at Chemulpo.

work draw out the bones from the ashes by means of sticks, the remaining ashes are placed in an urn, and carried to the tomb by the relations. The burials of the poor outcasts from society are very simple. The body is interred at once without entering in the temple, or else it is burnt in some waste spot.

Japanese cemeteries are most carefully cherished spots, and are always bright with vendure and flowers. Each family has its own little enclosure, where several simple commemorative stones stand. Once a year a festival for the dead is held. It is celebrated at night. The cemetery is illuminated by thousands of colored fires, and the whole population resort there, and eat, drink, and enjoy themselves in honor of their dead ancestors.

Their incapacity for conceiving sorrow is one of the most characteristic features of the Japanese. Perhaps this psychological phenomenons due to the influences amidst which this happy people have the privilege of living. It is an indisputable fact that where nature is bright and beautiful the inhabitants themselves of that particular spot, like the scenery, seem to expand under its sweet influence and to become bright and happy. Such is the case with the Japanese, who while yielding almost unconsciously to these influences, deepen them by their eager pursuit of all things gay and beautiful.

Japan is progressive enough that it has a compulsory system of education, which is sure to be ultimately fatal to idolatrous religions. There are more than three million children in the elementary schools, not to mention those in the higher institutions. The ability to read and write is almost universal among the people. Steady improvement is observed from year to year, in the attendance and quality of the government schools. The various schools in connection with the protestant and Roman missions, which are numerous and influential are also well attended and constantly growing. A large number also of the wealthier classes have their children taught privately at home. The average attendance of the Japanese children at the schools is nearly one-half the total number of school age. Education is very highly esteemed by every class, and all are willing to make genuine sacrifices to obtain it for their children.

Penmanship is laid great stress upon, and there are many

different styles in use. The blackboard is used in all schools now, and the artistic tendencies of the people are often well displayed on it. The Arabic numerals are fast displacing the old Chinese system. A great many of the methods of European and American teaching have been introduced into Japan, and their use is constantly on the increase.

Universities and academies supported by the government have been chiefly under the direction of American and European professors, and the western languages are taught everywhere. In addition to this educational element introduced into the country, there is that brought in by the large number of Japanese young men who have been sent to the universities of the United States, Germany, France, and England to complete their education. In our own colleges these young men have ranked with the highest as linguists, scientists, and orators. The influence that they have exerted in Japan, where they have invariably taken a high position, either officially or educationally, has been most beneficial to the advance of learning in the island empire.

The excessive cleanliness of the Japanese, the simplicity of their apparel, which allows their bodies to be so much exposed to the open air, added to the salubrity of their country, might reasonably lead one to imagine that they enjoy excellent health. Such however is not the case. Diseases of the skin, and chronic and incurable complaints are very prevalent. The hot baths are the great remedies for everything, but in certain cases the aid of the physicians is enlisted. These form a class of society which has existed from a very early date, and enjoy certain privileges. They are divided into three classes, the court physicians, who are not permitted to practice elsewhere, the army physicians, and lastly the common physicians, not employed by the government, who attend all classes of the community. As no formalities used to be required for the practice of medicine, each member entered on the career at his pleasure and practiced according to his own theories on the subject. It is a profession often handed down from father to son, but it is not a lucrative one, and is looked upon as an office of little importance or consideration.

Medical men nevertheless abound in Japan, and in addition to recognized practitioners, there is a class of quacks exactly answering to those of our own country. Their science principally partakes of the nature of sorcery. Where hot baths fail to produce the desired effect, they have recourse to acupuncture and cauterisation. Acupuncture consists in pricking with a needle the part affected, a mode of healing which has been practiced from time immemorial in the east. After the skill has been stretched sufficiently tight, the needle is thrust in perpendicularly either by rolling between the fingers or by a direct gentle pressure, or else by striking it lightly with a small hammer made for the purpose.

Cauterisation is performed with little cones called moxas, formed of

GEISHA GIRLS PLAYING JAPANESE MUSICAL INSTRUMENTS

dried wormwood leaves, and prepared in such a manner as to consume slowly. One or more of these is applied to the diseased part and set alight. The mode of cauterising wounds has frequently the effect of strongly exciting the nervous system, but does not seem to improve the general health of the patient materially. The national university of Tokio has a medical department in connection with it, which teaches medical science according to our own western methods. Hospitals exist in the large cities of Japan which are similarly equipped to those of our own country, and are under the direction of physicians and surgeons, most of whom are either Europeans and Americans, or Japanese who have been educated in medical colleges abroad. Many young women of Japan have come to America to take courses in nursing in our great hospitals and training schools, and on their return to Japan are spreading the knowledge they have thus gained.

Music is one of the most cultivated of the fine arts of Japan, and Japanese tradition accords it a divine origin. The Japanese have many stringed, wind, and percussion instruments, but the general favorite is the sam-sin or guitar

JAPANESE ALPHABET, NEW

with three strings. There are also the lutes, several kinds of drums and tambourines, fifes, clarioneta, and flageolets. The Japanese have no idea of harmony. A number of them will often perform together, but they are never in tune. They are not more advanced in melody; their airs recall neither the savage strains of the forest nor the scientific music of the west. In spite of this their music has the power of charming them for hours together, and it is only among the utterly uneducated classes that a young girl is to be found unable to accompany herself in a song on the sam-sin.

In the department of jurisprudence great progress has been made. Scarcely any nation on earth can show a more revolting list of horrible methods of punishment and torture in the past, and none on show greater improvement in so short a time. The cruel and blood-thirsty code was mostly borrowed from China. Since the restoration, revised statutes and regulations have greatly decreased the list of capital punishments, reformed the condition of prisons, and made legal processes more in harmony with mercy and justice. The use of torture to obtain testimony is now entirely abolished. Law schools have also been established and lawyers are allowed to plead, thus giving the accused the assistance of counsel for his defense.

The Japanese tongue has for a long time been regarded merely as

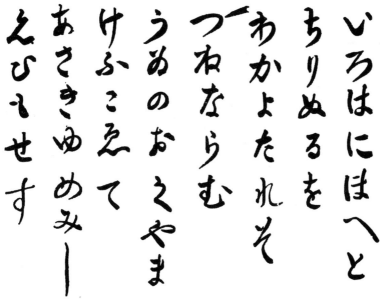

いろはにほへと
ちりぬるを
わかよたれそ
つねならむ
うゐのおくやま
けふこえて
あさきゆめみ
ゑひもせす

JAPANESE ALPHABET, OLD

an offshoot of the Chinese language, or at any rate as being very nearly connected with it. Study however, and the comparison of the two languages has rectified this error. Japanese understand Chinese writing because the Chinese characters form part of the numerous kinds in use in Japan. This is easily understood when it is remembered that Chinese characters represent neither letters nor meaningless sounds, which are only the constituent parts of a word, but are words themselves, or rather the ideas that these words express; consequently the same idea can be communicated although expressed by different words to any one who is acquainted with the signification of the characters. The Japanese language is very soft and agreeable to the ear, but travelers declare that no one born out of the country could possibly pronounce some of the words. They have a system of forty-eight syllabic signs, which can be doubled by means of signs added to the consonants, which modify the sound, and render it harder or softer. This system, it is said, dates from the eighth century and can be written in four different series of characters.

Japanese literature comprises books on science, biography, geography, travels, philosophy, and natural history, as well as poetry, dramatic works, romances, and encyclopedias. The latter seem to be little more than picture books, with explanatory notes, arranged like other Japanese dictionaries, sometimes alphabetically, but more often quite fancifully and without any attempt at scientific classification. The poets of Japan strive to express the most comprehensive ideas in the fewest possible words, and to employ words with double meanings for the-sake of typical allusions. They also delight in descriptions or similes furnished by the scenery, or the rich variety of natural productions with which they are surrounded.

Of their older books on science none are of any value but those which treat of astronomy. The proof of their progress in this science is afforded by the fact that almanacs, which mere at first brought from China, have now become very general and are composed in Japan. The Japanese, until western education began to have its influence over them, had only a slight knowledge of mathematics, trigonometry, mechanics, or engineering. History and geography are very fairly cultivated. Reading is the favorite recreation of both sexes in Japan. The women confine themselves to the perusal of romances, and those works on etiquette and kindred subjects prepared for them. Every young girl who can afford it has her subscription to a library, which for the sum of a few copper coins per month furnishes her with as many books, ancient and modern, as she can devour. Except for their titles, these productions seem all formed on one pattern. In the choice of their characters and their subjects the authors seem by no means desirous of breaking through the narrow limits within which prejudice and custom have confined them.

The ancient religion of the Japanese is called "Kami no michi," way, or doctrine of the gods. The Chinese form of the same is Shinto, and from this foreigners have called it Shintoism. In its purity the chief characteristic of this religion is the worship of ancestors and the deification of emperors, heroes, and scholars. The adoration of the personified, forces of nature enters largely into it. It employs no idols, images, or effigies in its worship, and teaches no doctrine of the immortality of the soul. Shinto has no moral code, and no accurately defined system of ethics or belief. Tho leading principle of its adherents is imitation of the illustrious deeds of their ancestors, and they are to prove themselves worthy of their descent by the purity of their lives. The priests of Shinto are designated according to their rank. Sometimes they receive titles from the emperor, and the higher ranks of the priesthood are court nobles. Ordinarily they

SHINTO PRIEST

dress like other people, but are robed in white when officiating, or in court dress when in court. They marry, rear families, and do not shave their heads. The office is usually hereditary.

After all the research of foreign scholars, many hesitate to decide whether Shinto is a native Japanese product or whether it is not closely allied with the ancient religion of China which existed before the period of Confucius. The weight of opinion inclines to the latter belief. The Kojiki is the Bible of Shintoism. It is full of narrations, but it lays down no precepts, teaches no morals or doctrines prescribes no ritual. Shinto has very few of the characteristics of a religion as understood by us. The most learned native commentators and exponents of the faith expressly maintain the view that Shinto has no moral code. Motoori, the great modern revivalist of Shinto, teaches with emphasis that morals were invented by the Chinese because they were an immoral people, but in Japan there was no necessity for any system of morals, as every Japanese acted aright if he only consulted his own heart. The duty of a good Japanese, he says, consists in obeying the commands of the mikado without questioning whether these commands are right or wrong. It was only immoral people like the Chinese who presumed to discuss the character of their sovereign. The opinion of most scholars from America and Europe, studying Shinto on its own soil, has been that the faith was little more than an influence for reducing the people to a condition of mental slavery. Its influence is weakening every year.

The outlines of Buddhism in its Chinese forms have been indicated in a foregoing chapter. It is well, however, to take another glance at it here in connection with its Japanese significance. This religion reached the Japanese empire about the middle of the sixth century after Christ, twelve centuries after its establishment. Buddhism originated as a pure atheistic humanitarianism, with a lofty philosophy and a code of morals higher perhaps than any heathen religion had reached before or has since attained. First preached in India, a land accursed by secular and spiritual oppression, it acknowledged no caste and declared all men equally sinful and miserable, and all equally capable of being freed from sin and misery through knowledge. It taught that the souls of all men had lived in a previous state of existence and that all the sorrows of this life are punishments for sins committed in a previous state. After death the soul must migrate for ages through stages of life inferior or superior,

JAPANESE TROOPS LANDING AT CHEMULPO. SEPTEMBER 9TH

until perchance it arrived at last in Nirvana or absorption in Buddha. The true estate of the human soul, according to the Buddhist, was blissful annihilation.

The morals of Buddhism are superior to its metaphysics. Its commandments are the dictates of the most refined morality. Such was Buddhism in its early purity. Beside its moral code and philosophical doctrines it had almost nothing. But in the twelve centuries which passed while it swept through India, Birmah, Siam, China, Thibet, Manchooria, Corea, and Siberia, it acquired the apparel with which Asiatic imagination priestly necessity had clothed and adorned the original trines of Buddha. The ideas of Buddha had been expanded into a complete theological system, with all the appurtenances of a stock religion. Japan was ready for the introduction of any religion as attractive as Buddhism, for prior to that time nothing existed except Shinto, of which there was little but the dogma of the divinity of the mikado, the duty of all Japanese to obey him implicitly, and some Confucian morals.

Buddhism came to touch the heart, to fire the imagination, to feed the intellect, to offer a code of lofty morals, to point out a pure life through self-denial, to awe the ignorant, and to terrify the doubting. With this explanation of the field which Buddhism found and what it offered, it is sufficient to say that the faith spread with marvelous rapidity until the Japanese empire was a Buddhist land. This did not necessarily exclude Shinto from the minds of the same people, and the two faiths have existed side by side in harmony. Of late years, however, the Japanese have not only been losing faith in their own religions but in all others, and to-day they are said by many to form a nation of atheists. This does not apply to the common people so truly as to the educated ones, and of course is not nearly as general a truth as has been often assumed. In no country of Asia has Christianity made such rapid and permanent advance as in Japan. It is the only oriental country having a government of its own in which there is absolute freedom in religious belief and practice, and- in which there is no state religion and no state support.

It has been for years the prophetic declaration of missionaries in the east that the first nation to extend full liberty of conscience in religion would be the dominant power of Asia. That Japan has fulfilled this condition is not more remarkable than are her rapid strides to political power since that country opened its doors to Christianity. That Japan is sincere in its treatment of an alien religion is attested by the fact that native Christian chaplains accompany her armies in their marches against China, and these are representative men of the Methodist, Congregational, and

STREET SCENES—FROM A JAPANESE ALBUM

Presbyterian churches in Japan There is no doubt that the whole Christian element in Japan, foreign and native, has been loyal to the country and in thorough sympathy with the aggressive movement made by Japan. The sympathy between Corea and Japan has been greatly strengthened by the active support rendered Presbyterian missionaries in Corea by the whole Christian body in Japan. The work of Mr. Johnson, a Presbyterian missionary in Corea, made him an adviser of the king, and this assisted in leading the latter rather towards Japan than towards China. The corner stone of Japan's position to-day is religious toleration. All that the Christian missionaries have asked in Asia is equal privilege with other religions, and these they have had in Japan. History is only repeating itself, and the results of religious toleration in Europe centuries ago are being duplicated in Asia in 1895.

The student of Asiatic life, on coming to Japan, is cheered and pleased on contrasting the position of women in Japan with that in other countries. He sees them treated with respect and consideration far above that observed in other quarters of the Orient. They are allowed greater freedom, and hence have more dignity and self-confidence. The daughters are better educated and the national annals will show probably as large a number of illustrious women as those of any other country in Asia. In these last days of enlightenment public and private schools for girls are being opened and attended. Furthermore, some of the leaders of new Japan, braving public scandal, and learning to bestow that measure of honor upon their wives which they see is enthusiastically awarded by foreigners to theirs, and are not ashamed to be seen in public with them. No women excel the Japanese in that innate love of beauty, order, neatness, household adornment and management, and the amenities of dress and etiquette as prescribed by their own standard. in maternal affection, tenderness, anxiety, patience, and long suffering, the Japanese mothers need fear no comparison with those in other climes. ' As educators of their children, the Japanese women are peers to the mothers of any civilization in the care and minuteness of their training, and their affectionate tenderness and self-sacrificing devotion within the limits of their knowledge. The Japanese maiden is bright, intelligent, interesting, modest, ladylike, and self-reliant. What the American girl is in Europe the Japanese maiden is among Asiatics.

So far our attention has been devoted exclusively to the Japanese proper, that is, to those people inhabiting Hondo and the other islands to the south of it. But a few words remain to be said about a people, who, while forming part of the empire of

Japan, yet differ essentially from the great majority of the population. They are the Ainos, or the original inhabitants of the Japanese archipelago, now only to be found in the island of Yesso. These people are decreasing in numbers year by year, and will soon be named with those extinct races of whom it is only known that they have once existed. The Ainos, however, have had their day of glory. In olden times, several centuries before our era, they were masters of all the north part of the island of Hondo, and their power equalled that of the Japanese; but little by little their influence diminished, and they were driven before the Japanese, and finally confined to the island of Yesso. There the Japanese pursued them and a long war ensued, but finally reduced them to complete submission about the fourteenth century. Since then the state of servitude in which their conquerors have held them has been such as to stifle even the instinct of progress within them, so that in the nineteenth century they offer the image of a people hardly past its first infancy.

The origin of the Ainos is unknown. They themselves are perfectly ignorant of their own history, and they have no written documents existing which could throw light upon their past. It is most probable that they originally came from the far interior of the Asiatic continent, for they bear not the slightest resemblance to any of their neighbors in the tribes scattered along the eastern coasts of the north of Asia. The Ainos are generally small, thick-set, and awkwardly formed; they have wide foreheads and black eyes, not sloping; their skin is fair but sunburnt. Their distinguishing feature is their hairiness, and they never dress their heads or trim their beards. The little children have a bright, intelligent look, which, however, gradually wears away as they grow older. The dwellings are of the simplest construction, and only contain a few implements for hunting and fishing, and some cooking utensils. They are built in small groups or hamlets, never containing more than a hundred individuals. They are a gentle, kindly, hospitable, and even timid people. Fishing is their chief occupation, and hunting is another profitable pursuit. There is no sign of agriculture, nor is any breed of cattle to be found among these people. Dogs are utilized to draw their sledges in winter. Their organization is quite patriarchal.

GROUP OF AINOS

They have neither king, princes nor lords, but in every hamlet the affairs of the community vested in the hands of the oldest and most influential member. Although the intelligence of the Ainos is very little developed, they evince great aptitude for knowledge and eagerly seize every opportunity for acquainting themselves with Japanese laws and customs.

The London Times, in 1859, predicted that "The Chinaman, would still be navigating the canals of his country in the crazy

RATS AS RICE MERCHANTS.—FROM A JAPANESE ALBUM

education of the higher kind is telling upon the people, and many works are now undertaken from which the authorities would have shrunk a few years ago as being impossible for them to grapple with. Original investigation in many lines has been pursued, and particularly in the study of earthquake phenomena has Japan given to the world results of extreme value. The influence of the modern scientific spirit is immense and ever growing. Western influence in its better nature is constantly on the increase. It appears to-day as if Japan were to be the civilizing influence in the east of Asia.

COREA

COREAN LANDSCAPE

RAW LEVIES FOR THE CHINESE ARMY

HISTORICAL SKETCH OF COREA,
THE HERMIT NATION

Aboriginal Inhabitants of the Land—Founding the Kingdom of Cho-sen— The Eva of the three Kingdoms—Dependence on China and Japan—Period of Peace and Prosperity—Invasion of Corea by the Japanese in the sixteenth century—Introduction of Christianity—The Modern history of Corea— Breaking down the walls of isolation—The French expedition—American relations with Corea—Ports opened to Japanese commerce—The year of the Treaties—A hermit nation no longer.

Until recent years our knowledge of the remarkable country of Corea, known indeed to the general public by little more than its name, has been limited to the meagre and scanty information imparted to us by Chinese and Japanese sources. After having been for several thousands of years the scene of sanguinary and murderous feuds between the various races and tribes who peopled the peninsula, and of the intrigues and wars of conquest of its rapacious neighbors, Corea succeeded after its final union under the sway of one ruler, but with considerable loss of territory, in driving back the invaders behind its present frontiers, enforcing since that time with an iron rule, that policy of exclusion which effectually separated it from the whole outer world. Corea, though unknown even by name in Europe until the sixteenth century, was the subject of description by Arab geographers of the middle ages. The Arab merchants trading to Chinese ports crossed the Yellow Sea, visited the peninsula, and even settled there. The youths of Shinra, one the Corean states, sent by their sovereign to study the arts of war and peace at Nanking, the mediaeval capital of China, may often have seen and talked with the merchants of Bagdad and Damascus.

As has been said, nearly all that the western world was able to learn about Corea until recent years, has been collected from Chinese and Japanese sources, which confine themselves mainly to the historical and political connection with these countries, The meagre early accounts owed to Europeans on this interesting subject, originate either from shipwrecked mariners who have been cast upon the inhospitable shores of Corea and there been kept imprisoned for some time, or from navigators who have extended their voyages of discovery to these distant seas and who have touched a few prominent points of the coast.

Like almost every country on earth, Corea is inhabited by a race that is not aboriginal. The present occupiers of the land drove out or conquered the people whom they found upon it. They are the descendants of a stock who came from beyond the northern frontier. It may not be a wrong conjecture, which is corroborated by many outward signs, to look for the origin of the people in Mongolia, in a tribe which finally settled down in Corea after roaming about and fighting its way through China. We may also take those who bear the unmistakable stamp of the Caucasian race to have come from Western Asia whence they had been driven by feuds and revolutions. At the conclusion of the long wars which have at last led to the union of the different states founded by various tribes, a partial fusion had taken place, which, though it has not succeeded in eradicating the outer signs of a different descent, at least caused the adoption of one language and of the same manners and customs.

Most of the Coreans claim to be in complete darkness and ignorance of their own origin; some declare quite seriously that their ancestors have sprung from a black cow on the shores of the Japan sea, while others ascribe their origin to a mysterious and supernatural cause.

The first mention of the inhabitants of Corea we find in old Chinese chronicles about 2350 B.C., at which period some of the northern tribes are reported to have entered into a tributary connection with China. The first really reliable accounts, however, commence only with the twelfth century B.C., at which time the north-westerly part of the peninsula first stands out from the dark.

The last Chinese emperor of the Shang dynasty was Chow Sin, who died B.C. 1122. He was an unscrupulous tyrant, and one of his nobles, Ki Tsze, rebuked and remonstrated with his sovereign. His efforts were hopeless, and the nobles who joined him in protest were executed. Ki Tsze was cast into prison. A revolt immediately ensued against the tyrant; he was defeated and killed, and the conqueror Wu Wang released the prisoner and appointed him prime minister. Ki Tsze however refused to serve one whom he believed to be an usurper and exiled himself to the regions lying to the north-east. With him went several thousand Chinese immigrants, most the remnant of the defeated army, who made him their king. Ki Tsze reigned many years and left the newly founded state in peace and prosperity to his successors. He policed the borders, gave laws to his subjects, and gradually introduced the principles and practices of Chinese etiquette and polity throughout his domain. Previous to his time the people lived in caves and holes in the ground, dressed in leaves, and were destitute of manners, morals, agriculture and cooking. The Japanese pronounce the founder's name Kishi, and the Coreans Kei-tsa or Kysse. The name conferred by the civilizer upon his new domain was that now in use by the modern Coreans, "Cho-sen," or "Morning Calm."

The descendants of Ki Tsze are said to have ruled the country until the fourth century before the Christian era. Their names and deeds are alike unknown, but it is stated that there were forty-one generations, making a blood line of eleven hundred and thirty-one years. The line came to an end in 9 A.D., though they had lost power long before that time.

This early portion of Cho-sen did not contain all of the territory of the modern Corea, but only the north-western portion of it. While the petty kingdoms of China were warring among one another, the nearest to Cho-sen encroached upon it and finally seized the colony. This was not to be permanent however, and there ensued a series of wars, each force becoming alternately successful. The territory of Cho-sen grew in area and the kingdom increased in wealth, power and intelligence under the rule of King Wie-man, who assumed the authority 194 B.C. Thousands of Chinese gentry fleeing before the conquering arms of the Han usurpers settled within the limits of the new kingdom, adding greatly to its prosperity. In 107 B.C. after a war that had lasted one year, a Chinese invading army finally conquered the kingdom of Cho-sen and annexed it to the Chinese empire. The conquered territory included the north half of the present kingdom of Corea.

Things remained in this condition until about 30 B. C., at which time a part of Cho-sen taking advantage of the disorders which had broken out afresh in China, separated itself from the empire and again formed a state by itself, but still remained tributary; while the other portions of the old kingdom for some time longer remained under Chinese rule, until they also joined the portion that had been freed. Up to this period Cho-sen forming the north-west of the present Corea, had been the only part of that country that had become more closely connected with China. The tracts to the north-east, south-west and south were occupied by different independent tribes, and little more is known of them than that they were ruled by chiefs of their own clan. In course of time three kingdoms, Korai, Hiaksai, and Shinra, were formed out of these various elements, subsisting by the side of Cho-sen, at a later date fighting either beside or against China, and almost incessantly at feud with each other, until Shinra gained the predominance about the middle of the eighth century A.D. and kept the same up to the sixteenth century. It was then supplanted in the leading position by Korai, which united under its supremacy all those parts of Corea which had hitherto been separate, and constituted the whole into a single state. Like the three kingdoms of England, Scotland and Wales, these Corean states were distinct in origin, were conquered by a race from without, received a rich infusion of alien blood, struggled in rivalry for centuries, and were finally united under one nation with one flag and one sovereign.

Hiaksai was for a while the leading state in the peninsula. Buddhism was introduced from Thibet in 384 A.D. And to this state more than any other part of Corea, Japan owes her first impulses towards the civilization of the west. The kingdom prospered until the decade from 660 to 670, when it was overrun and practically annihilated by an army of Chinese, despite the aid of four hundred junks and a large body of soldiers sent from Japan to the aid of Corea.

Korai of course took its turn in struggling with the Dragon of China. Early in the seventh century China had been defeated, and for a generation peace prevailed. But the Chinese coveted Koraian territory and again an invading fleet attacked the country.

It took years to complete the conquest, but finally all Korai with its five provinces, its one and seventy-six cities and its four or five millions of people, was annexed to the Chinese empire.

Shinra, in the south-west of the peninsula, was probably the most advanced of all of the states. It was from this kingdom that the tradition reached Japan which tempted the Amazonian queen of Japan, Jingo, to her invasion and conquest. The king of Shinra submitted and became a declared vassal of Japan, but in all probability Shinra was far superior to the Japan of that early day in everything except strength. From this kingdom came a stream of immigrants which passed into Japan carrying all sorts of knowledge and an improved civilization. It is well to remember from this point that the Japanese always laid claim to the Corean peninsula and to Shinra especially as a tributary nation. They supported that claim not only whenever embassies from the two nations met at the court of China, but they made it a more or less active part of their national policy.

During this period Buddhism was being steadily propagated, learning and literary progress increased, while art, science, architecture were all favored and improved. Kion-chiu, the capital of Shinra, mas looked upon as a holy city, even after the decay of Shinra's power. Her noble temples, halls and towers stood in honor and repair, enshrining the treasures of India, Persia, and China, until the ruthless Japanese torch laid them in ashes in 1596.

From the year 755 A.D. up to the beginning of the tenth century, Shinra maintained its undisputed rule over the other countries of the peninsula, but about this time successive revolts occurred, Shinra was conquered, and the three kingdoms now united were called Korai, a name which was retained to the end of the fourteenth century. The kingdoms now thoroughly subdued, never recovered their old position and independence, and composed from that time forward the undivided kingdom of Corea, such as it has been maintained until the present it day. In 1218 A.D. the king of Corea promised allegiance to the Chinese emperor Taitsou who was the Mongol Genghis Khan.

Here we find explanation for some features of the war now in progress between China and Japan. Corea has at various times acknowledged its dependence upon both of these countless. Tho Japanese laid claim to Corea from the second century until the 27th of February, 1876. On that day the mikado's minister plenipotentiary signed the treaty recognizing Cho-sen as an independent nation. Through all the seventeen centuries, which according to their annals elapsed since their armies first completed the vassalage of their neighbor, the Japanese regarded the states of Corea as tributaries. Time and again they enforced their claim with bloody invasion, and when through a more enlightened policy the rulers voluntarily acknowledged their former enemy as an equal, the decision cost Japan almost immediately afterward seven months of civil war, twenty thousand lives, and $50,000,000 in treasury. The mainspring of the "Satsuma rebellion" of 1877 was the official act of friendship by treaty, and the refusal of the Tokio government to make war on Corea. It seemed until 1877 almost impossible to eradicate from the military mind of Japan the conviction that to surrender Corea was cowardice and a stain upon the national honor.

From the ninth century onward to the sixteenth century, the relations of the two countries seem to be unimportant. Japan was engaged in conquering northward her own barbarians. Her intercourse, both political and religious, grew to be so direct with the court of China, that Corea in the Japanese annals sinks out of sight except at rare intervals. Nihon increased in wealth and civilization, while Cho-sen remained stationary or retrograded. In the nineteenth century the awakened "Suurise Kingdom" has seen her former self in the "Land of Morning Calm," and has stretched forth willing hands to do for her neighbor now what Corea did for Japan in centuries long gone by. It must never be forgotten that Corea was the bridge on which civilization crossed from China to the archipelago.

About 1368 the reigning King of Corea refused vassalage to China. His troops refused to repel the invasion that threatened, and under their General Ni Taijo, deposed the king. Taijo himself was nominated king. He paid homage to the Chinese emperor and revived the ancient name of Cho-sen. The dynasty thus established is still the reigning family in Corea, though the direct line came to an end in 1864. The Coreans in their treaty with Japan in 1876, dated the document according to the four hundred and eighty-fourth year of Cho-sen, reckoning from the accession of Ni Taijo to the throne. One of the first acts of the new dynasty was to change the location of the national capital to the city of Han Yang, situated on the Han river about fifty miles from its mouth. The king enlarged the fortifications, enclosed the city with a wall of masonry, and built bridges, renaming the city Seoul or "capital." He also redivided the kingdom into eight provinces which still remain. An era of peace and flourishing prosperity ensued, and in everything the influence of the Chinese emperors is most manifest. Buddhism, which had penetrated into every part of the country,

PAGODA AT SEOUL

and had become in a measure at least the religion of the state, was now set aside and disestablished. The Confucian ethics were dilligently studied and were incorporated into the religion of the state. From the early part of the fifteenth century, Confucianism flourished, until it reached the point of bigotry and intolerance, so that when Christianity was discovered to be existing among the people, it was put under the ban of extirpation, and its followers thought worthy of death.

At first the new dynasty sent tribute regularly to the shogun of Japan, but as intestinal war troubled the Island Empire and the shoguns became effeminate, the Coreans stopped their tribute and it was almost forgotten. The last embassy from Seoul was sent in 1460. After that they were never summoned, so they never came. Under the idea that peace was to last forever, the nation relaxed all vigilance; the army was disorganized and the castles were fallen into ruin. It was while the country was in such a condition that the summons of Japan's great conqueror came to them, and the Coreans learned for the first time of the fall of Ashikaga and the temper of their new master.

As the Mongol conquerors issuing from China had used Corea as their

COREAN SOLDIERS

point of departure to invade Japan, so Hideyoshi resolved to make the peninsula the road for his armies into China. He sent an, envoy to Seoul to demand tribute, and then, angered at the utter failure of his mission, commanded the envoy and all his family to be put to death. A second ambassador was sent with more success, and presents and envoys were exchanged. Hideyoshi, however, became enraged at the indifference of the Corens to assist him in his dealings with China, and resolved to humble the peninsular kingdom, and China, her overlord.

The invasion of Corea was made as related in the earlier chapters on Japan. The Coreans were poorly prepared for war, both as to leaders, soldiers, equipments and fortifications. The Japanese swept everything like s whirlwind before them, and entered the capital within eighteen days after their landing at Fusan. The accounts of the war are preserved in detail, and are exceedingly interesting, but the limits of this volume compel their omission to provide space for the war of 1894-5. At first Chinese armies coming to reinforce the Coreans were defeated and turned back, but another effort of the allies was more effective and the Japanese troops found advance turned to retreat. The Japanese armies concentrated at Seoul to receive the

FIGHTING BEFORE THE GATE OF SEOUL

advance of the allies numbering some two hundred thousand. The capital was burned by the Japanese, nearly every house being destroyed, and hundreds of men, women, and children, sick and well, living quietly there, were massacred. The allied troops were beaten back in a ferocious battle, but hunger reached both armies, pestilence entered the Japanese camp, and both sides were utterly tired of war and ready to consider terms of peace.

Konishi, the general of the Japanese army, had been converted to Christianity by the Portuguese Jesuits. During this period of tiresome waiting he sent to the superior of the missions in Japan asking for a priest. In response to this request came Father Gregorio de Cespedes and a Japanese convert. These two holy men began their labors among the Japanese armies, preaching from camp to camp, and administering the right of baptism to thousands of converts, but their work was stopped by the jealousy of the Buddhist power. The Jesuits in Japan were then being expelled for their political machinations, and

OLD MAN IN COREA

the chaplains in Corea were brought under the same ban. Konishi was called back to Japan with the priest and was unable to convince the shogun of his innocence. A few Corean converts were made during this time, and one of them a lad of rank, was afterward educated in the Jesuit seminary at Kioto. He endeavored to return to Cores as a missionary, but the condition of affairs in Japan interrupted his intentions and in 1625 he was martyred during the prosecutions of the Christians. Of the large number of Corean prisoners sent over to Japan, many became Christians. Hundreds of others were sold as slaves to the Portuguese. Others rose to positions of honor under the government or in the households of the daimios. Many Corean lads were adopted by the returned soldiers or kept as servants. When the bloody persecution broke out, by which many thousand Japanese found death, the Corean converts remained steadfast to their Christian faith, and suffered martyrdom with fortitude equal to that of their Japanese brethren. But by the army in Corea, or by the Christian chaplain Cespedes, no trace of Christianity was left in the land of Morning Calm, and it was two centuries later before that faith was really introduced.

The fortunes of the war alternated, and finally, after deeds of heroism on both sides, a period of inaction ensued, the result of exhaustion. At this time Hideyoshi fell sick and died, September 9, 1598, at the age of sixty-three years. Almost his last words were, 66 Recall all my troop from Cho-sen." The orders to embark for home were everywhere gladly heard. It is probable that the loss of life in the campaigns of this war was nearly a third of a million. Thus ended one of the most needless, unprovoked, cruel, and desolating wars that ever cursed Corea. More than two hundred thousand human bodies were decapitated to furnish the ghastly material for the "ear-tomb" mound in Kioto. More than one hundred and eighty-five thousand Corean heads were gathered for mutilation, and thirty thousand Chinese, all of which were despoiled of ears and noses. It is probable that fifty thousand Japanese left their bones in Corea.

Since the invasion the town of Fusan, as before, had been held and garrisoned by the retainers of the Daimio of Tsushima. At this port all the commerce between the two nations took place. From an American point of view, there was little trade done between the two countries, but on the strength of even this small amount Earl Russell in 1862 tried to get Great Britain included as a co-trader between Japan and Corea. He was not, however, successful. A house was built at Nagasaki by the Japanese government which was intended as a refuge for Coreans who might be wrecked on Japanese shores. Wherever the waifs were picked up, they were sent to Nagasaki and 'sheltered until a junk could be dispatched to Fusan.

The possession of Fusan by the Japanese was, until 1876, a perpetual witness of the humiliating defeat of the Coreans in the war of 1592-1597, and a constant irritation to their national pride. Yet with all the miseries inflicted on her, the humble nation learned rich lessons, and gained many an advantage even from her enemy. The embassies which were yearly dispatched to yield homage to their late invaders were at the expense of the latter. The Japanese pride purchased the empty bubble of homage by paying all the bills.

The home of the Manchoos was on the north side of the Everwhite mountains. From beyond these mountains was to roll upon China and Corea another avalanche of invasion. By the sixteenth century the Manchoos had become so strong that they openly defied the Chinese. Formidable expeditions previous to the Japanese invasion of Corea kept them at bay for a time, but the immense expenditure of life and treasure required to fight the Japanese drained the resources of the Ming emperors, while their attention being drawn away from the north, the Manchoo hordes massed their forces and grew daily in strength. To repress the rising power in the north, and to smother the life of the young nation, the Peking government resorted to barbarous cruelties and stern coercion. Unable to protect the eastern border of Liao Tuug the entire population of three hundred thousand souls, dwelling in four cities and many villages, were removed westward and resettled on new lands. Fortresses were planned in the deserted land to keep back the restless cavalry raiders from the north. Thus the foundation of the neutral strip of fifty miles was unconsciously laid, and ten thousand square miles of fair and fertile land west of the Yalu were abandoned to the wolf and tiger. What it soon became it remained until yesterday- a howling wilderness.

In 1615 the king of the Manchoo tribes was assassinated as the result of a plot by the Ming emperor. This exasperated the tribes to vengeance and they began hostilities. China now had to face another great invasion. Calling on her vassal, Corea, to send an army of twenty thousand men, she ordered them to join the imperial army about seventy miles west of the Yalu River. In the battle which ensued the Coreans were the first to face the Manchoos. The imperial legions were beaten, and the Coreans seeing which way the victory would turn, deserted from the Chinese side to that of their enemy. This was in 1619. Enraged by alternate treachery to both sides from the Coreans, the Manchoos invaded Corea in 1627, to which time the war had been prolonged. They crossed the frozen Yalu in February, and at once attacked and defeated the Chinese army. They then began the march to Seoul. Town after town was taken as they pressed onward to the capital, the Coreans everywhere flying before them. Thousands of dwellings and stores of provisions were given to the flames and their trail was one of blood and ashes. After the siege of Seoul began, the king sent tribute offerings to the invaders, and concluded a treaty of peace, by which Corea again exchanged masters, this time confessing subjection to the Manchoo sovereign. As soon as the invading army had withdrawn, the Corean king, confident that the Chinese would be ultimately successful over the Manchoos, annulled the treaty. No sooner were the Manchoos able to spare their forces for the purpose than they again marched into Corea and overran the peninsula.

The king now came to terms, and in February, 1637, utterly renounced his allegiance to the Ming emperor, gave his two sons as hostages, and promised to send an annual embassy with tribute to the Manchoo court. After the evacuation of Corea the victors marched into China, where bloody civil war was raging. The imperial army of China had been beaten by the rebels. The Manchoos joined their forces with the imperialists and defeated the rebels, and then demanded the price of their victory. Entering Peking they proclaimed the downfall of the house of Ming. The son of the late king was set upon the dragon throne, and as we have seen in a foregoing chapter the royal house of China came to be a Manchoo family.

When, as it happened the very next year, the shogun of Japan demanded an increase of tribute to be paid in Yeddo, the court of Seoul plead in excuse their wasted resources, consequent upon the war with the Manchoos, and their heavy burdens newly laid

COAST NEAR CHEMULPO

upon them in the way of tribute to their conqueror. Their excuse was accepted. Twice within a single generation had the little peninsula been devasted by mighty invasion that laid waste the country.

In 1650 a captive Corean maid, taken prisoner in their first invasion, became sixth lady in rank in the imperial Manchoo household. Through her influence her father, the ambassador, obtained a considerable reduction of the annual tribute that had been fixed by treaty. Other portions of the tribute had been remitted before, so that by this time the tax upon Corean loyalty became very slight, and the embassy became one of ceremony rather than tribute bringing.

In the seventeenth century some information about Corea began to reach Europe, first from the Jesuits in Peking, who sent home a map of the peninsula. There is also a map of Corea in a work by the Jesuit Martini, published in 1649 in Amsterdam. The Cossacks who overran northern Asia brought reports of Corea to Russia, and it was from Russian sources that Sir John Campbell obtained the substance of his history of Corea. In 1645 a party of Japanese crossed the peninsula, and one of them on his return wrote a book descriptive of their journey. In 1707 the Jesuits in Peking began their great geographical enterprise, the survey of the Chinese empire, including the outlying vassal kingdoms. A map of Corea was obtained from the king's palace at Seoul and sent to Europe to be engraved and printed. From this original most of the maps and supposed Corean names in books published since that time have been copied.

The first known entrance of any number of Europeans into Corea was that of Hollanders belonging to the crew of the Dutch ship Hollaiidra which was driven ashore in 1627. Coasting along the Corean shores, John Wetterree and some companions went ashore to get water, and were captured by the natives. The magnates of Seoul probably desired to have a barbarian from the west, as useful to them as was the Englishman Will Adams to the Japanese in Yeddo, where the Corean ambassadors had often seen him. This explains why Wetterree was treated with kindness and comparative honor, though kept as a prisoner. When the Manchoos invaded Corea in 1635, his two companions were killed in the war, and Wetterree was left alone. Having no one with whom he could converse he had almost forgotten his native speech, when after twenty-seven years of exile, in the fifty-ninth year of his age, he met some of his fellow Hollanders, and acted as interpreter to the Coreans.

In the summer of 1653 the Dutch ship Sparwehr was cast on shore on Quelpaert island, off the southwest coast of Corea. The local magistrate did what he could for the thirty-six members of the crew who reached the shore alive, out of the sixty-four on board. On October 29th the survivors were brought by the officials to be examined by the interpreter Wetterree. The latter was very rusty in his native language, but regained it in a month. Of course the first and last idea of the captives was how to escape. They made one effort to reach the sea shore, but were caught and severely punished, after which they were ordered to proceed to the capital. Wherever they went the Dutchmen were like wild beasts on exhibition. When they once reached the palace they were well treated, and were assigned to the body guard of the king as petty officers. Each time that the Manchoo envoy made his visit to the capital the captives endeavored to enlist his sympathy and begged to be taken to Peking, but all such efforts resulted in failure and punishment. The suspicions of the government were aroused by the studies which the Dutchmen pursued, of the climate, the topography, and the products of the country, and by their attempts to escape, and in 1663 they were separated and put into three different towns. By this time fourteen of the number were dead and twenty-two remained.

Finally, early in September 1667, as their fourteenth year of captivity was drawing to a close, the Dutchnene scaped to the seacoast, bribed a Corean to give them his fishing craft, and steered out into the open water. A few days later, they reached the northwestern islands in the vicinity of Kiushiu, Japan, and landed. The Japanese treated them kindly and sent them to Nagasaki, where they met their countrymen at Desima. The annual ship from Batavia was then just about to return, and in the nick of time the waifs got on board, reached Batavia, sailed for Holland, and in July, 1668, stepped ashore at home. Hendrik Hamel, the supercargo of the ship, wrote a book on his return recounting his adventures in a simple and straightforward style. It has been translated into English and is a model work of its sort.

The modern introduction of Christianity in Corea dates little more than a hundred years ago. Some Corean students studying with the famous' Confucian professor Kwem, during the winter of 1777, entered into discussion of some tracts on philosophy, mathematics, and religion just brought from Peking. These were translations of the writings of the Jesuits in the imperial capital. Surprised and delighted, they resolved to attain if possible to a full understanding of the new doctrines. They sought all the information that they could from Peking. The leader in this movement was a student named Stonewall. As his information accumulated, he gave himself up to fresh reading and meditation and them began to preach. Some of his friends in the capital, both nobles and commoners, embraced the new doctrines with cheering promptness and were baptized. Thus from small beginnings, but rapidly, were the Christian ideas spread.

But soon the power of the law and the pen were invoked to crush out the exotic faith. The first victim was tried on the charge of destroying his ancestral tablets, tortured, and sent into exile, in which he soon after died. The scholars now took up weapons, and in April, 1784, the king's preceptor issued the first public document officially directed against Christianity. In it all parents and relatives were entreated to break off all relations with Christians. The names of the leaders were published, and the example of Thomas Kim, the first victim, was cited. Forthwith began a violent pressure upon the believers to renounce their faith. Then began an exhibition alike of steadfast faith and shameful apostasy, but though even Stonewall lapsed, the work went on. The next few years of Christianity were important ones. The leaders formed an organization and as nearly as they could on the lines of the Roman Catholic church. Instructions mere sent from Peking by the priests there, and the worship in Corea became quite in harmony with that of the Western church. But the decision that the worship of ancestors must be abolished, was, in the eyes of the Corean public, a blow at the framework of society and state, and many feeble adherents began to fall away. December 8,1791, Paul and Jacques Kim were decapitated for refusing to recant their Christian faith. Thus was shed the first blood for Corean Christianity. Martyrdom was frequent in this early history of the Christian church in Corea, but in the ten years following the baptism of Peter in Peking in 1783, in spite of persecution and apostasy, it is estimated that there were four thousand Christians in the peninsula.

The first attempt of a foreign missionary to enter the Hermit kingdom from the west was made early in 1791. This was a Portuguese priest who endeavored to cross the Yalu River to join some native Christians, but was disappointed in meeting them and returned to Peking. Two years later a young Chinese priest entered the forbidden territory, and was hidden for three years in the house of a noble woman, where he preached and taught. Three native Christians who refused to reveal his whereabouts were tortured to death and were thrown into the Han River. From the beginning of this century the most bitter general persecutions against Christians was enforced. The young Chinese priest, learning that he was outlawed, surrendered himself to relieve his friends of the responsibility of protecting him, and was executed. The woman also who had so long sheltered him was beheaded. Four other women who were attendants in the palace, and an artist who was condemned for painting Christian subjects were beheaded near the "Little Western Gate" of Seoul. The policy of the government was shown in making away with the Christians of rank and education who might be able to direct affairs in the absence of the foreign priests, and in letting the poor and humble go free.

It is impossible to catalogue the martyrs and the edicts against Christianity. The condition of the Christians scattered in the mountains and forests, suffering poverty, hunger, and cold, was most deplorable. In 1817 the Corean converts addressed letters to the Pope begging aid in their distress. These however could not be answered in the way they desired, for the Pope himself was then a prisoner at Fontainebleau and the Roman propaganda was nearly at a standstill.

In 1817 the king and court were terrified by the appearance off the west coast of the British vessels Alceste and Lyra, but beyond some surveys, purchases of provisions, and interviews wit

COREAN MANDARINS

Rome local magistrates, the foreigners departed without opening communication with them. Fifteen years later the British ship Lord Amherst passed along the coasts of Chulla, seeking commercial connections. On board was a Protestant missionary, a Prussian. He landed on several of the islands and attempted to gain some acquaintance with the people, but made little progress. The year 1834 closed the first half century of Corean Christianity. It is not strange that persecutions resulted from the advance of Roman Catholic strength in Corea, for the Corean Christians assumed naturally the righteousness of the Pope's claim to temporal power as the vicar of heaven. The Corean Christians not only deceived their magistrates and violated their country's laws, but actually invited armed invasion. Hence, from the first, Christianity was associated in patriotic minds with treason and robbery.

After the restoration of the Bourbons in France and the strengthening of the Papal throne by foreign bayonets, the missionary zeal in the church was kindled fresh, and it was resolved to found a mission in Corea. The first priest to make entrance was Pierre Philibert Maubant who, reached Seoul in 1836, the first Frenchman who had penetrated the Hermit Nation. A few months later another joined him, and in December, 1838, Bishop Imbert ran the gauntlet of wilderness, ice, and guards at the frontier, and took up his residence under the shadow of the king's palace. Work now went on vigorously, and in 1838 the Christians numbered nine thousand. At the beginning of the next year the party in favor of extirpating Christianity having gained the upper hand, another persecution broke out with redoubled violence. To stay the further shedding of blood, Bishop Imbert and his two priests came out of their hiding places and delivered themselves up. They mere horribly tortured, and decapitated September 21,1839. Six bitter years passed before the Christians again had a foreign pastor.

Since 1839 the government had tripled its vigilance and doubled the guards on the frontier. The most strenuous efforts to pass the barriers repeatedly failed. Andrew Kim is a name to be remembered in the history of Christianity in Corea. Year after year he worked to enter Corea, or once in, to advance the cause, or when rejected to help others in the work. He was ordained to the priesthood in Shanghai, and finally in company with two French priests, in September, 1845, sailed across the Yellow Sea, and handed on the coast of Chulla, to make his final effort to spread Christianity among the Coreans. During July of the same year, the British ship Samarang was engaged in surveying off Quelpaert and the south coast of Corea. Beacon fires all over the land telegraphed the news of the presence of foreign ships, and the close watch that was kept by the coast magistrates made the return of Andrew Kim doubly dangerous.

These records of perseverance, of distress, of martyrdom, from the pages of missionary work in Corea, written in the blood of native converts, who bore their cross with equal bravery to that of the Roman fathers, may be surprising to some who have been unfamiliar with the history of the Corean peninsula. But they are convincing testimony to controvert the assertions of some incredulous ones who affirm that the "heathen" are never really Christianized, but are always ready to return to their idols in times of trial. There is no country that can show braver examples of fortitude, in enduring trial for the support of the faith, than the "Hermit Nation."

Three priests in disguise were now secretly at work in Corea, Andrew Kim, a native convert, and the Frenchmen, Bishop Ferreol, and his companion Daveluy. Kim was captured and in company with half a dozen others was executed September 16th. While he was in prison the Bishop heard of three French ships which were at that time vainly trying to find the mouth of the Han River and the channel to the capital. Ferreol wrote to Captain Cecile, who commanded the fleet, but the note arrived too late and Kim's fate was sealed. The object of the fleet's visit was to demand satisfaction for the murder of the two French priests in 1839, but after some coast surveys were made and a threatening letter was dispatched the ships withdrew.

During the summer of 1845, two French frigates set sail for the Corean coast, and August 10th went aground, and both vessels became total wrecks. The six hundred men made their camp at Kokun island, where they were kindly treated and furnished with provisions, although rigidly secluded and guarded against all commutation with the main land. An English ship from Shanghai rescued the crews. During the ensuing eight years repeated efforts were made by missionaries and native converts to enter Corea and advance the work there, and the labor of propagation progressed. A number of religious works in the Corean language were printed from. a native printing press and widely circulated. In 1850 the Christians numbered eleven thousand, and five young men were studying for the priesthood. Regular mails sewn into the thick cotton coats of the men in the annual embassy were sent to and brought from China. The western nations were beginning to take an interest in the twin hermits of the east, Corea and Japan. In 1852, the Russian frigate Pallas traced and mapped a portion of the shore line of the east coast, and the work was continued three years later by the French war vessel Virginie. At the end of this voyage the whole coast from Fusan to the Tumen was known with some accuracy and mapped out with European names.

It was in the intervening years, 1853 and 1854, that commodore. Perry and the American squadron were in the waters of the far east, driving the wedge of civilization into Japan. The American flag, however, was not yet seen in Corean waters, though the court of Seoul was kept informed of Perry's movements.

A fresh reinforcement of missionaries reached Corea in 1857. When three years later the French and English forces opened war with China, took the Peiho forts, entered Peking, and sacked the summer palace of the Son of Heaven, driving the Chinese emperor to flight, the loss of Chinese prestige struck terror into all Corean hearts. For six centuries China had been in Corean eyes the synonym and symbol of invincible power. Copies of the treaties made between China and the allies, granting freedom of trade and religion, were soon read in Corea, causing intense alarm. But the most alarming thing was the treaty between China and Russia, by which the Manchoo rulers surrendered the great tract watered by the Amoor river and bordered by the Pacific, to Russia. It was a rich and fertile region, with a coast full of harbors, and comprising an area as large as France. The boundaries of Siberia now touch Corea. With France on the right, Russia on the left, China humbled, and Japan opened to the western world, it is not strange that the rulers in Seoul trembled. The results to Christianity were that within a few years thousands of natives fled their country and settled in the Russian villages. At the capital, official business was suspended and many families of rank fled to the mountains. In many instances people of rank humbly sought the good favor and protection of the Christians, hoping for safety when the dreaded invasion should come. In the midst of these war preparations, the French missionary body was reinforced by the arrival of four of their countrymen who set foot on the soil of their martyrdom, October, 1861.

The Ni dynasty, founded in 1392, came to an end January 15, 1864, by the death of King Chul-chong, who had no child, before he had nominated an heir. Palace intrigues and excitement among the political parties followed. The widows of the three kings who had reigned since 1881 were still living. The eldest of these, Queen Cho, at once seized the royal seal and emblems of authority, which high-handed move made her the mistress of the situation. A twelve-year-old lad was nominated for the throne, and his father, Ni Kung, one of the royal princes, became the actual regent. He held the reins of government during the next nine years, ruling with power like that of all absolute despot, He was a rabid hater of Christianity, foreigners, and progress.

The year 1866 is phenomenal in Corean history. It seemed to the rulers as if the governments of many nations had conspired to pierce their walls of isolation. Russians, Frenchmen, Englishmen, Americans, Germans, authorized and unauthorized, landed to trade, rob, kill, or what was equally obnoxious to the regent and his court, to make treaties. This and the rapid progress of Christianity now excited the anti-Christian party, which was in full power at the court, to clamor for the enforcement of the old edict against the foreign religion.

Vainly the regent warned the court of the danger from Europe. Forced by the party in power, he signed the death warrants of bishops and priests and promulgated anew the old laws against the Christians. Within a few weeks fourteen French priests and bishops were tortured to death, and twice as many native missionaries and students for the priesthood suffered like fate. Scores of native Christians were put to death, and hundreds more were in prison. In a little over a month, all missionary operations came to a standstill. The three French priests who remained alive escaped from the peninsula in a Chinese junk, and finally reached Chefoo October 26. Not one foreign priest now remained in Corea, and no Christian dared openly confess his faith. Thus after twenty years of nearly uninterrupted labors, the church was again stripped of her pastors, and at the end of eighty-two years of Corean Christianity the curtain fell in blood.

With Bishop Ridel as interpreter and three of his converts as pilots, three French vessels were sent to explore the Han River and to make effort to secure satisfaction for the murder of the French bishops and priests in the previous March. They entered the river September 21, and two of the vessels advanced to Seoul, leaving one at the mouth of the river. One or two forts fired on the vessels as they steamed along, and in one place a fleet of junks gathered to dispute their passage. A well-aimed shot sunk two of the crazy craft, and a bombshell dropped among the artillerists in the redoubt, silenced it at once. On the evening of the 25th, the two ships cast anchor and the flag of France floated in front of the Corean capital. The hills were white with gazing thousands, who for the first time saw a vessel moving under steam. The ships remained' abreast of the city several days, the officers taking soundings and measurements, computing heights, and making plans. Bishop Ridel went on shore in hopes of finding a Christian and hearing some news but none dared to approach him. While the French remained in the river not a bag of rice nor a fagot of wood entered Seoul. Eight days of such terror, and a famine would have raged in the city. Seven thousand houses were deserted by their occupants. When the ships returned to the mouth of the river two converts came on board. They informed Ridel of the burning of a "European" vessel, the General Sherman, at Ping-Yang, of the renewal of the persecution, and of the order that Christians should be put to death without waiting for instructions from Seoul. Sailing away, the ships arrived at Chefoo, October 3.

The regent, now thoroughly alarmed, began to stir up the country to defense. The military forces in every province were called out, and the forges and blacksmith shops were busy day and night in making arms of every known kind. Loaded junks were sunk in the channel of the Han to obstruct it. Word was sent to the tycoon of Japan informing him of the trouble, and begging for assistance, but the Yeddo government had quite all it could do at that time to take care of itself. Instead of help two commissioners were appointed to go to Seoul and recommend that Corea open her ports to foreign commerce as Japan had done, and thus choose peace instead of war with foreigners. Before the envoys could leave Japan the tycoon had died, and the next year Japan was in the throes of civil war, the shogunate was abolished, and Corea was for the time utterly forgotten.

Another fleet of French vessels sailed from China to Corea, consisting of seven ships of various kinds, and with six hundred soldiers. The force landed before the city of Kang-wa on the island of the same name, and captured the city without difficulty on the morning of October 16. Several engagements in the same vicinity followed, all of them successful to the French until they came to attack a fortified monastery on the island some ten days later. Here they were repulsed with heavy loss to themselves and to the foe. The next morning to the surprise of all and the anger of many, orders were given to embark. The troops in Kang-wa set fire to the city which in a few hours burned to ashes. The departure of the invaders was so precipitate that Corean patriots to this day gloat over it as a disgraceful retreat.

In the palace at Seoul the resolve was made to exterminate Christianity, root and branch. Women and even children were ordered to the death. Several Christian nobles were executed. One Christian who was betrayed in the capital by his pagan brother, and another fellow believer, were taken to the river side in front of the city, near the place where the two French vessels had anchored. At this historic spot, by an innovation unknown in the customs of Cho-sen, they were decapitated and their headless trunks held neck downward to spout out the hot life blood, that it might wash away the stain of foreign pollution. Upon the mind of the regent and court the effect was to swell their pride to the folly of extravagant conceit. Feeling themselves able almost to defy the world, they began soon after to hurl their defiance at Japan. The results of this expedition were disastrous all over the east. Happening at a time when relations between foreigners and Chinese were strained, the unexpected return of the fleet filled the minds of Europeans in China with alarm. The smothered embers of hostility to foreign influence, steadily gathered vigor as the report spread through China that the hated Frenchmen had been driven away by the Coreans. The fires at length broke out in the Tien-tsin massacre of 1870.

It was this same year, 1866, that witnessed the marriage of the young king, now but fourteen years old, to Min, the daughter of one of the noble families. Popular report has always credited the young queen with abilities not inferior to those of her royal husband. The Min or Ming family is largely Chinese in blood and origin, and beside being preeminent among all the Corean nobility in social, political, and intellectual power, has been most strenuous in adherence to Chinese ideas and traditions with the purpose of keeping Corea unswerving in her vassalage and loyalty to China.

American associations with Corea have been peculiarly interesting. The commerce carried on by American vessels with Chinese and Japanese ports made the navigation of Corean waters a necessity. Sooner or later shipwrecks must occur, and the question of the humane treatment of American citizens cast on Corean shores came up before our government for settlement, as it had long before in the case of Japan. Within one year the Corean government had three American cases to deal with. June 24, 1866, the American schooner Surprise, was wrecked off the coast of Wang-hai. The approach of any foreign vessel was especially dangerous at this time, as the crews might be mistaken for Frenchmen and killed by the people from patriotic impulses. Nevertlieless, the captain and Iris crew, after being well catechised by the local magistrate and by a commissioner sent from Seoul, were kindly treated and well fed and provided with the comforts of life. By orders of Tai-wen Kun, the regent, they were escorted on horseback to Ai-chiu and after being feasted there were conducted safely to the border gate. Thence after a hard journey via Mukden they got to Ninchwang and to the United States consul.

The General Sherman was an American schooner that had the second experience with the Coreans. The vessel was owned by a Mr. Preston who was making a voyage for health. At Tien-tsin the schooner was loaded with goods likely to be salable in Corea, and she was dispatched there on an experimental voyage in the hope of thus opening the country to commerce. The complement of the vessel was five white foreigners and nineteen Malay and Chinese sailors. The white men were Mr. Hogarth, a young Englishman, Mr. Preston, the owner, and Messrs. Page and Wilson, the master and mate of the vessel, and the Rev. Mr. Thomas, a missionary, who were Americans. From the first the character of the expedition was suspected, because the men were rather too heavily armed for a peaceful trading voyage. It was believed in China that the royal coffins in the tombs of Ping-Yang were of solid gold, and it was broadly hinted that the expedition had something to do with these.

The schooner, whether merchant or invader, sailed from Chefoo and made for the mouth of the Tatong River. There they met the Chinese captain of a Chefoo junk who agreed to pilot them up the river. He stayed with the General Sherman for two days, then leaving her he returned to the river's mouth, and sailed back to Chefoo. No further direct intelligence was ever received from the unfortunate party. According to one report the hatches of the schooner were fastened down after the crew had been driven beneath, and set on fire. According to another, all were decapitated. The Coreans burned the woodwork for the iron and took the cannon for models.

The United States steamship Wachusett, dispatched by Admiral Rowan to inquire into the matter, reached Chefoo January 14, 1867, and took on board the Chinese pilot of the General Sherman. Leaving Chefoo they cast anchor two days later at the mouth of the large inlet next south of the Tatong River, thinking that they had reached their destination. A letter was dispatched to the capital of the province demanding that the murderers be produced on the deck of the vessel. Five days elapsed before the answer arrived, during which the surveying boats were busy. Many natives were met and spoken with, who all told one story, that the Sherman's crew were murdered by the people and not by official instigation. In a few days an officer from one of the villages appeared. He would give neither information nor

COLOSSAL COREAN IDOL—UN-JIN MIRIOK

satisfaction, and the gist of his reiteration was "go away as soon as possible." Commander Shufeldt, bound by his orders, could do nothing more, and being compelled also by stress of weather came away.

Later in the year Dr. Williams Secretary of the United States Legation at Peking, succeeded in obtaining an interview with a member of the Corean embassy, who told him that after the General Sherman got aground she careened over as the tide receded, and her crew landed to guard or float her. The natives gathered around them, and before long an altercation arose. A general attack began upon the foreigners, in which every man was killed by the mob. About twenty of the natives lost their lives. Dr. Williams' comment is, "The evidence goes to uphold the presumption that they invoked their sad fate by some rash or violent act towards the natives."

The United States steamship Shenandoah was sent to make further investigation, and this version of the story was given to the commander. The Coreans said that when the Sherman arrived in the river, the local officials went on board and addressed the two foreign officers of the ship in respectful language. The latter grossly insulted the native dignitaries. The Coreans treated their visitors kindly, but warned them of their danger and the unlawfulness of penetrating into the country. Nevertheless, the foreigners went up the river to Ping-Ysng where they seized the ship of one of the city officials, put him in chains, and proceeded to rob the junks and their crews. The people of the city aroused to wrath, attacked the foreign ship with firearms and cannon; they set adrift fire rafts and even made a hand to hand fight with knives and swords. The foreigners fought desperately, but the Coreans overpowered them. Finally the ship caught fire and blew up with a terrible report. This story was not, of course, believed by the American officers, but even the best wishers and friends of the Sherman adventurers cannot stifle suspicion of either cruelty or insult to the natives. Remembering the kindness shown to the crew of the Surprise it is difficult to believe that the General Sherman's crew was murdered without cause.

In 1884 Lieutenant J.B. Bernadon, of the United States navy, made journey from Seoul to Ping-Yang, and being able to speak

Corean, secured the following information from native Christians: The governor of Ping-Yang sent officers to inquire the mission of the Sherman. To gratify their curiosity large numbers of the common people set out also in boats which the Sherman's crew mistook for a hostile demonstration and fired guns in the air to warn them off. When the river fell the Sherman grounded and careened over, which being seen from the city walls, a fleet of boats set out with hostile intent and were fired upon. Officers and people now enraged, started fire rafts, and soon the vessel, though with white flag hoisted, was in flames. Of those who leaped into the river most were drowned. Of those picked up one was the Rev. Mr. Thomas, who was able to talk Corean. He explained the meaning of the white flag, and begged to be surrendered to China. His prayer was in vain. In a few days all the prisoners were led out and publicly executed.

In the spring of 1867 an expedition was organized by a French Jesuit priest who spoke Corean, having been a missionary in the country a German Jew named Ernest Oppert; and the interpreter at the United States consulate in Shanghai, a man named Jenkins. These worthies, it is said, conceived a plan to steal the body of one of the dead Corean monarchs, and hold it for ransom. With two steam vessels and a crew of sailors, laborers, and coolies, the riffraff of humanity, such us swarm in every Chinese port, they left Shanghai the last day of April, steamed to Nagasaki, and then to the west coast of Corea, landing in the river which flows into Prime Jerome Gulf. The steam tender which accompanied the larger vessel took an armed crowd up the river as far as possible, and from this point the march across the open country to the tomb was begun. Their tools were so ineffective that they could not move the rocky slab which covered the sarcophagus, and they were compelled to give up their task. During their return march they were attacked by the exasperated Coreans, but were able to protect themselves without great difficulty. During the remainder of their buccaneering trip, which lasted ten days, they had various skirmishes d two or three of their party were killed. On their return to Shanghai the American of the party was arrested and tried before the United States consul, but it was impossible to prove the things with which Jenkins was charged, and he was dismissed. A few years later Oppert published a work in which he told the story of his different voyages to Corea, including this last one. In writing of the last he takes pains to gloss over the intentions of his journey and to explain the good motives behind it.

The representations made to the department of state at Washington by the United States diplomatic corps in China concerning these different attempts to enter Corea, directed the attention of the United States government to the opening of Corea to American commerce The state department in 1870 resolved to undertake the enterprise. Frederick F. Low, minister of the United States to Peking and Rear Admiral John Rodgers, commander in chief of the Asiatic squadron, were entrusted with the delicate mission. The American squadron consisted of the flagship Colorado, the corvettes Alaska and Dimitia, and the gunboats Monocacy and Palos. In spite of the formidable appearance of the navy, the vessels mere either of an antiquated type, or of too heavy a draft, with their armament defective. All the naval world in Chinese waters wondered why the Americans should be content with such old fashioned ships unworthy of the gallant crews who manned them.

The squadron anchored near the mouth of the Han River May 30, 1871. Approaching the squadron in a junk, some natives made signs of friendship and came on board without hesitation. They bore a missive acknowledging the receipt of the letter which the Americans had sent to Corea some months before, by a special courier from the Chinese court. This reply announced that three nobles had been appointed by the regent for a conference. The next day a delegation of eight officers of the third and fifth rank came on board, evidently with intent to see the minister and admiral to learn all they could and gain time. They had little authority and no credentials, but they were sociable, friendly and in good humor. Neither of the envoys would see them, because they lacked rank and credentials and authority. The Corean envoys were informed that soundings would be taken in the river and the shores would be surveyed.

The best judges of eastern diplomacy think that this mission was very poorly managed. These envoys were sent ashore, and at noon on the 2nd of June the survey fleet moved up the river. The fleet consisted of four steam launches abreast, followed by the Palos and Monocacy. But a few minutes passed until from a fort on the shore a severe fire was opened on the moving boats. The Americans promptly returned the fire, with the result that the old Palos injured herself by the cannon kicking her sides out. The Molocacya also struck a rock and began to leak badly, but after hammering at the forts until they were all silenced, the squadron was able to return down the river and not greatly injured. Strange to say only one American was wounded and none were killed. It was a strong evidence of the poor marksmanship of Corean gunners.

Ten days were now allowed to pass before further action was taken, then the same force started up the river again, enlarged by twenty boats conveying a landing force of six hundred and fifty men. These were arranged in ten companies of infantry and seven pieces of artillery. The squadron proceeded up the river on the morning of the 10th of June, and soon after noon, having demolished and emptied the first fort, the troops were landed. The next day they began the march and soon reached another fortification which was deserted. Here all of the artillery was tumbled into the river and the fort was named Monocacy. In another hour, another citadel was reached, attacked, and conquered by the united efforts of the troops on shore and the vessels in the stream. The final charge of the American troops up a steep incline met a terrible reception. The Coreans fought with furious courage in hand to hand conflict. Finally the enemy was completely routed, some three hundred and fifty of them being killed. On the American side three were killed, and ten wounded. Before the day was over two more forts were captured. The result of the forty-eight hours on shore, of which only eighteen were spent in the field, was the capture of five forts probably the strongest in the kingdom, fifty flags, and four hundred and eighty-one pieces of artillery. The work of destruction was carried on and made as thorough as fire, are and shovel could make it, and this was all on Sunday, June 11.

Early on Monday morning the whole force was re-embarked ill perfect order, in spite of the furious tide. The fleet moved down the stream with the captured colors at the mast heads, and towing the boats laden with the trophies of victory. Later in the day the men slain in the fight were buried on Boisee Island, and the first American graves rose on Corean soil.

Admiral Rodgers, having obeyed to the farthest limit the orders given him, and all hope of making a treaty being over, the fleet sailed for Chefoo on the 3rd of July, after thirty-five days' stay in Corean waters.

"Our little war with the heathen," as the New York Herald styled it, attracted slight notice in the United States. In China the expedition was looked upon as a failure and a defeat. The popular Corean idea was that the Americans had come to avenge the death of pirates and robbers, and after several battles had been so surely defeated that they dare not attempt the task of chastisement again.

When the mikado was restored to supreme power in Japan, and the department of foreign affairs was created, one of the first things attended to was to invite the Corean government to resume ancient friendship and vassalage. This summons, coming from a source unrecognized for eight centuries, and to a regent swollen with pride at his victory over the French and his success in extirpating the Christian religion, was spurned with defiance. An insolent and even scurrilous letter was returned to the mikado's government. The military classes, stung with rage, formed a war party, but the cabinet of Japan vetoed the scheme and in October, 1873, Saigo, the leader of the war party, resigned and was returned to Satsuma to brood over his defeat.

In 1873 the young king of Corea attained his majority. His father Tai-wen Kun, the Regent, by the act of the king was relieved of office and his bloody and cruel lease of power came to an end. The young sovereign proved himself a man of some mental vigor and independent judgment, not merely trusting to his ministers, but opening important documents in person. He was ably seconded by his wife, to whom was born in the same year an heir to the throne.

The neutral belt of land, long inhabited by deer and tigers, had within the last few decades been overspread with squatters, brigands, and outlaws. The depredations of these border ruffians had become intolerable both to China and Corea. In 1875 Li Hung Chang sending a force of picked Chinese troops with a gunboat to the Yalu broke up the nest of robbers and allowed settlers to enter the land. Two years later the Peking government shifted its frontier to the Yalu River, and Corean and Chinese territory was separated only by flowing water. The neutral strip was no more.

In 1875 some sailors of one of the Japanese ironclads, landing near Kang-wa for water, were fired on by Corean soldiers under the idea that they were Americans or Frenchmen. The Japanese before this time had adopted uniforms of foreign style for their navy. Retaliating, the Japanese two days later stormed and dismantled the fort, shot most of the garrison, and carried the spoils to the ships. The news of this affair brought the wavering minds of both the peace and the war party of Japan to a decision. An envoy was dispatched to Peking to find out the exact relation of China to Corea, and secure her neutrality. At the same time another was sent with the fleet to the Han River, to make if possible a treaty of friendship and open ports. General Kuroda having charge of the latter embassy, with men of war, transports, and marines, reached Seoul February the 6th, 1876. About the same time a courier from Peking arrived in the capital, bearing the Chinese imperial recommendation that a treaty be made with the Japanese. The temper of the young king had been manifested long before this by his rebuking the district magistrate of Kang-wa for allowing soldiers to fire on peaceably disposed people, and ordering the offender to degradation and exile. Arinori Mori in Peking had received a written disclaimer of China's responsibility over Corea, by which stroke of policy the Middle Kingdom freed herself from all possible claims of indemnity from France, the United States, and Japan.

After several days of negotiation the details of the treaty were settled, and on February 27 the treaty in which Chosen was recognized as in independent nation was signed and attested. The first Corean embassy which had been accredited to the mikado's court since the Twelfth century, sailed from Fusan in a Japanese steamer, landing at Yokohama, May 29. By railroad and steam cars they reached Tokio, and on the first of June the envoy had audience of the mikado. For three weeks the Japanese amused, enlightened and startled their guests by showing them their war ships, arsenals, artillery, torpedoes, schools, buildings, factories, and offices, equipped with steam and electricity, the ripened fruit of the seed planted by Perry in 1854. All attempts of foreigners to hold any communication with them were firmly rejected by the Coreans. Among the callers with diplomatic powers from the outside world in 1881, each eager and ambitious to be the first in wresting the coveted prize of a treaty, were two British captains of men-of-war and a French naval officer, all of whom sailed away with rebuffs.

Under the new treaty Fusan soon became a bustling place of trade with a Japanese population of some two thousand. Public buildings were erected for the Japanese consulate, chamber of commerce, bank, steamship company, and hospitals. A newspaper was established, and after a few years of mutual contact at Fusan the Coreans, though finding the Japanese as troublesome as the latter discovered foreigners to be after their own ports were opened, with much experience settled down to endure them for the sake of a trade which was undoubtedly enriching the country. Gensan was opened May 1, 1880. An exposition of Japanese, European, and American goods was established for the benefit of trade with the Coreans.

Russia, England, France, Italy, and the United States all made efforts in the next few months to make treaties with Corea, and all were politely rejected. Early in 1881 Chinese and Japanese influence began to be enlisted in favor of the United States in the effort to make a treaty. Li Hung Chang, China's liberal statesman, wrote a letter to a Corean gentleman in which he advised the country to seek the friendship of the United States. The Chinese secretary of legation at Tokio also declared to the Coreans that Americans were the natural friends of Asiatic nations, and should be welcomed. It began to look more hopeful for the United States to secure her treaty through the influence of the Chinese than that of the Japanese, on whom we had previously depended. One of the most important moves in the advancement of Corea's civilization mas the sending of a party of thirty-four prominent men to visit Japan, and further study the problem of how far western ideas were adapted to an oriental state. The leader of this party, after his return from Japan, was dispatched on mission China, where his conference was chiefly with Li Hung Chang. He had now a good opportunity of judging the relative merits of Japan and China. The result of this mission were soon apparent, for shortly after, eighty young men were sent to Tien-tsin where hey began to diligently pursue their studies of western civilization as it had impressed itself on China in the arsenals and schools.

The spirit of progress made advance from the beginning of 1882, but discussion reached fever heat in deciding whether the favor of Japan or China should be most sought, and which foreign nation should be first admitted to treaty rights. An event riot unlooked-for, increased the power of the progressionists. Kozaikai urged the plea of expulsion of foreigners in such intemperate language that he was accused of reproaching the sovereign. At the same time a conspiracy against the life of the king was discovered. Kozaikai was put to death, many of the conspirators were exiled, and the ringleaders were sentenced to be broken alive on the wheel. The progressivists had now the upper hand, and early in the spring two envoys went to Tien-tsin to inform Americans and Chinese that the Corean government was ready to make a treaty. Meanwhile Japanese officers were drilling the Corean soldiers in Seoul.

The American diplomatic agent, Commodore R.W. Shufeldt, arrived in the Swatara off Chemulpo May 7. Accompanied by three officers he went six miles into the interior, to the office of the Corean magistrate, to formulate the treaty. Two days afterward the treaty document was signed, in a temporary pavilion on a point of land opposite the ship. Both on the American and Corean side thin result had been brought about only after severe toil and prolonged effort.

Four days after the signing the American treaty, the crown-prince, a lad of nine years old, was married in Seoul. This year will be forever known as the year of the treaties. Within a few months treaties were signed by Corea with Great Britain, France, Germany, Italy and China. Within a week there appeared in the harbor of Chemulpo two American, three British, one French, one

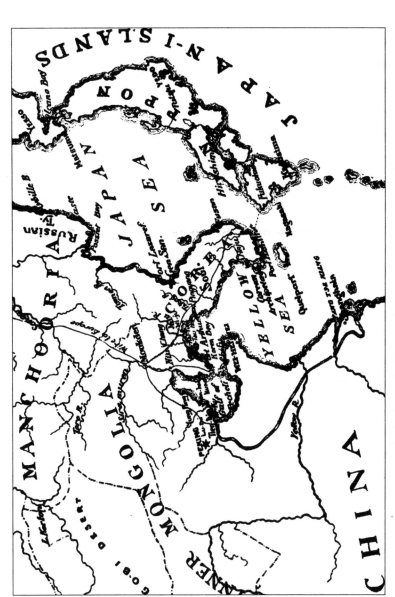

MAP SHOWING JAPAN, COREA AND PART OF CHINA

Japanese, one German and five Chinese armed vessels; all of them except the French had left by June 8, to the great relief of the country people, many of whom had fled to the hills when the big guns began to waste their powder in salutes.

The Japanese legation in Seoul now numbered about forty persons. They seemed to suspect no imminent danger, although the old fanatic and tyrant Tai-wen Kun was still alive and plotting. He was the centre of all the elements hostile to innovation, and being a man of unusual ability, was possessed of immense influence. During the nine years of his nominal retirement from office, this bigoted Confucianist who refused to know anything of the outer world waited his opportunity to make trouble. Just then the populace was most excited over the near presence of the foreigners at Chemulpo, the usual rainfall was withheld, and in the consequent drought the rice crop was threatened with total failure. The sorcerers and the anti-foreign party took advantage of the situation to play on the fears of the superstitious people. The spirits displeased at the intrusion of the western devils were angry and were cursing the land.

While the king was out in the open air praying for rain July 23, a mob of sympathizers with the old regent attempted to seize him. The king escaped to the castle. Some mischief-maker then started the report that the Japanese had attacked the royal castle and had seized the king and queen. Forthwith the mob rushed with frantic violence upon the legation, murdering the Japanese policemen and students whom they met on the streets, and the Japanese military instructors in the barracks. Not satisfied with this, the rioters, numbering four thousand men, attacked and destroyed the houses of the ministers favoring intercourse. Many of the Mins and seven Japanese were killed. The Japanese legation attaches made a brave defence to the night attack which was made on them. Armed only with swords and pistols, the Japanese formed themselves into a circle, charged the mob, and cut their way through it. After an all night march through a severe storm, the tittle band fighting its way for much of the time, reached In-chiun at three o'clock the next day. The governor received them kindly and supplied food and dry clothing, then posting sentinels to watch so that the Japanese could get some rest.

In an hour the mob attacked them there, and they were again compelled to cut their way out. They now made for Chemulpo, the seaport of the city, and about midnight, having procured a junk, they put to sea. The next morning they were taken on board a British vessel which was surveying the coast, and a few days later were landed at Nagasaki.

Without hesitation the Japanese government began preparations for a military and naval attack. Hanabusa, the minister to Corea and his suite were sent back to Seoul, escorted by a military force. He was received with courtesy in the capital whence he had been driven three weeks ago. The fleet of Chinese war ships was also at hand, and everything was apparently under the control of Tai-wen Kun, who now professed to be friendly to foreigners. At his audience with the king, Hanabusa presented the demands of his government. These were nominally agreed to, but several days passing without satisfactory action, Hanabusa having exhausted remonstrance and argument left Seoul and returned to his ship. This unexpected move, a menace of war, brought the usurper to terms. On receipt of Tai-wen Kun's apologies, the Japanese envoy returned to the capital and full agreement was given to all the demands of Japan by the Corean government. The insurgents were arrested and punished, the heavy indemnity was paid, and apology was sent by a special embassy to Japan. Within the next few days Tai-wen Kun was taken on board a Chinese ship at the orders of Li Hung Chang and taken to Tien-tsin. It is generally believed that this action was practically a kidnapping, but whether to rescue Tai-wen Kun from the dangers which threatened him or to maintain China's old theory of sovereign control over Corean rulers it is hard to know.

The treaty negotiated with the United States was duly ratified by our senate, and Lucius H. Foote was appointed minister to Corea. General Foote reached Chenulpo in the United States steamship Monocacy May 13, and the formal ratifications of the treaty were exchanged in Seoul six days later. The guns of the Monocacy, the same which shelled the Han forts in 1870, fired the first salute ever given to the Corean flag. The king responded by sending to the United States an embassy of eleven persons led by

Min Yong Ik and Horig Yong Sik, members respectively of the conservative and liberal parties.

Their interview with President Arthur was in the parlors of the Fifth Avenue Hotel, New York, on September 17. All the Coreans were dressed in their national custom, which they wore habitually while in America. After spending some weeks in the study of American Institutions in several cities, part of the embassy returned home by way of San Francisco, leaving one of their number at Salem, Mass., to remain as a student; while Min Yong Ik and two secretaries embarked on the United States steamship Trenton, and after visiting Europe, reached Seoul in June, 1884.

We have now reached a point in Corean history from which a continuance can be better made in a later chapter. Almost from the time of the return of the Corean embassy from the United States, the political ferment increased, until a few months after began the disorders which culminated ten years later in the present Japanese-Chinese war. These events will therefore be related in the chapter which is to follow, descriptive of the causes of the war, and the relations of the three oriental nations at the outbreak of hostilities.

GEOGRAPHY, GOVERNMENT, CLIMATE AND
PRODUCTS OF COREA

Geographical Limits of Corea—Characteristies of the Coast Line—The Surface Configuration of the Country—Isolation Made Easy by the Character of its Boundaries—Rivers of the Peninsula—The Climate—Forests, Plants, and Animals—Products of the Soil and of the Mine—Extent of foreign Trade—The Eight provinces of Corea, Their Extent, Cities, and History—Government of the Corean Kingdom—The Dignitaries and their Duties—Corruption in the Administration of Official Duties—Buying and Selling Office—The Executive and the Judiciary.

For many a year the country of Corea has been known in little more than name. Its territory is a peninsula on the east coast of Asia, between China on the continent, and the Japanese islands to the eastward. It extends from thirty-four degrees and thirty minutes to forty-three degrees north latitude, and from one hundred and twenty-four degrees and thirty minutes to one hundred and thirty degrees and thirty minutes east longitude, between the Sea of Japan and the Yellow Sea. The Yellow Sea separates it from the southern provinces of China, while the Sea of Japan and the Strait of Corea separate it from the Japanese island. It has a coast line of about one thousand seven hundred and forty miles, and a total area of about ninety thousand square miles. The peninsula, with its outlying islands, is nearly equal in size to Minnesota or to Great Britian. In general shape and relative position to the Asiatic continent it resembles Florida. Tradition and geological indications lead to the belief that anciently the Chinese promontory and province of Shan-tung, and the Corean peninsula were connected, and that dry land once covered the space filled by the waters joining the Gulf of Pechili and the Yellow Sea. These waters are so shallow that the elevation of their bottoms but a few feet would restore their area to the land surface of the globe. On the other side also, the Sea of Japan is very shallow and the Straits of Corea at their greatest depth have but eighty-three feet of water.

The east coast is high, mountainous, and but slightly indented, with very few islands or harbors. The south and west shores are deeply and manifoldly scooped and fringed with numerous islands. From these island-skirted shores, especially on the west coast, mud banks extend out to sea beyond sight. While the tide on the east coast is very slight, only two feet at Gensan, it increases on the south and west coasts in a north direction, rising to thirty-three feet at Chemulpo. The rapid rise and fall of tides, and the vast area of mud left bare at low water, cause frequent fogs, and render the numerous inlets little available except for native craft. On the west coast the rivers are frozen in winter, but the east coast is open the whole winter through.

Quelpaert, the largest island, forty by seventeen miles, lies sixty miles south of the main land. Port Hamilton, between Quelpaert and Corea, was for a time an English possession, but in 1886 was given to China. The Russians are generally believed to have an overweening desire for the magnificent harbor of Port Lazaref on the east coast of the Corean mainland. In its policy of exclusion of all foreigners, the government has had its tasks facilitated by the inaccessible and dangerous nature of the approaches to the coast. The high mountain ranges and steep rocks of the east coast, and the thousands of islands, banks, shoals and reefs extending for miles into the sea on the western and southern shores, unite to make approach exceedingly difficult, even with the best charts and surveys at hand.

In the middle of the northern boundary of Corea, is the most notable natural feature of the peninsula. It is a great mountain, the colossal Paik-tu or "ever white" mountain, as it is known from the snow that rests upon its summit. When the Manchoorians pushed the Coreans farther and farther back, they reached this mountain, which marked the natural barrier which they were able to make their permanent boundary line. According to native account, which in Corea is seriously believed, the highest peak of this mountain reaches the moderate elevation of forty-four miles. It is famous as the birthplace of Corean folk lore, and a great deal that is mythical hangs about it still. On the top of the peak is a lake thirty miles in circumference. From this lake flow two streams, one to the north-east, the Tumen, which enters the Sea of Japan; and the other to the south-west, the Yalu river, which flows into the Corean bay at the head of the Yellow Sea. Corea is therefore in reality an island. These two rivers and the lake forming the northern boundary are about four hundred and sixty miles from the ocean at the southern end of the peninsula. The greatest width of the country is three hundred and sixty miles and its narrowest about sixty miles.

The Tumen river separates Corea from Manchooria, except in the last few miles of its course, when it flows by Russian territory, the south-eastern corner of Siberia. The Yalu river also divides Corea from Munchooria. The rivers of Corea are not of great importance except for drainage and water supply, being navigable but for short distances. On the west coast the chief rivers are the Yalu, the Ching-chong, the Tatong, the Han, the Kum; the Yalu is navigable for about one hundred and seventy miles and is by far the greatest of all in the peninsula. The Han is navigable to a little above Seoul, eighty miles; the Tatong to Ping-Yang, seventy-five miles; and the Kum is navigable for small boats for about thirty miles. In the south-eastern part of the peninsula the Nak-tong is navigable for small boats to a distance of one hundred and forty miles. The Tumen river, which forms the northeastern boundary between Corea and Siberia, is not navigable except near the mouth. It drains a mountainous and rainy country. Ordinarily it is shallow and quiet, but in spring its current becomes very turbulent and swollen.

Occupying about the same latitude as Italy, Corea is also, like Italy, hemmed in on the north by mountain ranges, and traversed from north to south by another chain. The whole peninsula is very mountainous, some of the peaks rising to a height of eight thousand feet.

The climate of the country is excellent, bracing in the north, with the south tempered by the ocean breezes in summer. The winters in the north are colder than those of American states in the same latitude, and the summers are hotter. The heat is tempered by sea breezes, but in the narrow enclosed valleys it becomes very intense. The Han is frozen at Seoul for three months in the year, sufficiently to be used as a cart road, while the Tumen is usually frozen for five months.

Various kinds of timber abound, except in the west, where,

wood is scarce' and is sparingly used; and in other parts the want of coal has caused the wasteful destruction of many a forest. The fauna is very considerable and besides tigers, leopards, and deer, includes pigs, wild cats, badgers, foxes, beavers, otters, martens, bears, and a great variety of birds. The salamander is found in the streams as in western Japan. The domestic animals are few. The cattle are excellent, the bull being the usual beak of burden, the pony very small but hardy, fowls good, the pigs inferior.

Immense numbers of oxen are found in the south, furnishing the meat diet craved by the people, who eat much more of fatty food than the Japanese. Goats are rare. Sheep are imported from China only for sacrificial purposes. The dog serves for food as well as for companionship and defense. Of birds the pheasants, falcons, eagle, crane, and stork are common. Among the products are rice, wheat, beans, cotton, hemp, corn, sesame, and perilla. Ginseng grows wild in the Kange mountains and is also

COREAN BULL HARROWING

much cultivated about Kai-seng, the duties upon it, notwithstanding much smuggling, yielded about half a million dollars annually.

Iron ore of excellent quality is mined; and there are copper mines in several places. The output of the silver mines is very small, but the customs returns for 1886 show the value of gold exported that year to be $503,296. The principal industries are the manufacture of paper, mats woven of grass, split-bamboo blinds, oil paper, and silk. The total value of the foreign imports in 1887 was $2,300,000, two-thirds representing cotton goods; the native exports reached about $700,000, chiefly beans and cow hides. The foreign vessels entering the treaty ports yearly number about seven hundred and fifty, of some two hundred thousand tons burden. Three-fourths of the trade is with Japan and more than one-fifth with China; British goods go by way of these countries. Until 1888 business was done chiefly by barter, imports being exchanged largely for gold dust, and Japanese silk piece goods being a current exchange for trade inland. In that year the mint at Seoul was completed, and a beneficial effect on commerce resulted from the introduction of a convenient and sufficient coinage. Seoul is connected by telegraph with Taku Port Arthur, Chemulpo, Gensan, and Fusan.

Corea is divided into eight provinces, three on the east coast and five on the west coast. These provinces are divided into sixty districts with about three hundred and sixty cities, only sixty of which however are entitled to the name, the remainder distinguishing themselves from the larger hamlets and villages merely by the walled-in residence of the chief government official. Only a portion of each real city is walled in; but it

COREAN CITY WALL

must not be thought that these walls are in any way similar to those to be found in China, where even second and third rate cities are protected by high and strong fortifications with moats. Corean walls are usually about six feet high, miserably constructed, of irregular and uneven stone blocks, and nearly every one of them would tumble down at the first shock of a ball fired from a modern gun.

CHINESE PROTECTED CRUISER CHEN-YUEN
SUNK AT THE BATTLE OF THE YALU

Corea has for centuries successfully carried out the policy of isolation. Instead of a peninsula, her ruled strove to make her an accessible island, and insulate her from the shock of change. She has built, not a great wall of masonry, but a barrier of sea and river-flood, of mountain and devastated land, of palisade and cordon of armed sentinels. Frost and snow, storm and winter, she hailed as her allies. Not content with the sea border, she desolated her shores lest they should tempt the foreigner to land. In addition to this, between her Chinese neighbor and herself she placed a neutral space of unplanted, unoccupied land. This strip of forest and desolated plain twenty leagues wide, has stretched for three centuries between Corea and Manchooria. To form it, four cities and many villages were suppressed and left in ruins. The soil of these former solitudes is very good, the roads easy, and the hills not high. The southern boundary of this neutral ground has been the boundary of Corea, while the northern boundary has been a wall of stakes, palisades and stone. Two centuries ago, this line of walls was strong, high, guarded and kept in repair, but year by year at last, during a long era of peace, they were suffered to fall into decay, and except for their ruins exist no longer. For centuries only the wild beasts, fugitives from justice, and outlaws from both countries have inhabited this fertile but forbidden territory. Occasionally borders would cultivate portions of it, but gathered the produce by night or stealthily by day, venturing on it as prisoners would step over the dead line. Of late years the Chinese government has respected the neutrality of this barrier less and less. Within a generation large portions of this neutral strip have been occupied; parts of it have been surveyed and staked by Chinese surveyors, and the Corean government has been too feeble to prevent the occupation. Though no towns or villages are marked on the map of this neutral territory yet already a considerable number of small settlements exist upon it, and it was through them that the over land marches of the Japanese army from Corea into Manchooria had to be made.

The province which borders this neutral territory, is that of Ping-Yang or "Peaceful Quiet." It is the border land of the kingdom, containing what was for centuries the only acknowledged gate of entrance and outlet to the one neighbor which Corea willingly acknowledged as her superior. The battle of Ping-Yang recently fought, is only one of many which have interrupted the harmony of the province of "Peaceful Quiet." The town nearest the frontier and the gateway of the kingdom is Wi-ju. It is situated on a hill overlooking the Yalu river, and surrounded by a wall of light colored stone. The annual embassy always departed for its overland journey to China through its gates. Here also are the custom house and vigilant guards, whose chief business it was to scrutinize all persons entering or leaving Corea. Nevertheless most of the French missionaries have entered the mysterious peninsula through this loophole, disguising themselves as wood cutters, crossing the Yalu river on the ice, creeping through the water drains in the grind wall, and passing through this town, or they have been met by friends at appointed places along the border, and thence have traveled to the capital. Further details as to the political condition of this neutral strip will be included in a succeeding chapter, preliminary to the outbreak of the war. The Tatong river, which forms the southern boundary of the province, is the Rubicon of Corean history. At various epochs in ancient times it was the boundary river of China or of the rival states within the peninsula. About fifty miles from its mouth is the city of Ping-Yang, the metropolis and capital of the province and the royal seat of authority from before the Christian era to the tenth century. Its situation renders it a natural stronghold. It has been many times besieged by Chinese and Japanese armies, and near it many battles have been fought.

The next province to the south is that of Hwanghai or the "Yellow Sea" province. This is the land of Corea that projects into the Yellow Sea directly opposite the Shan-tung promontory of China, on which are the ports of Chefoo and Wei-hai-wei. Tien-tsia, the seaport of Peking, is a little farther east. From these ports since the most ancient times, the Chinese armadas have sailed and invading armies have embarked for Corea. Over and over again has the river Tatong been crowded with fleets of junks, fluttering the dragon banners at their peaks. To guard against these invasions signal fires were lighted on the hill-tops which formed a cordon of flame and sped the alarm from coast to capital in a few hours. This province has been the camping ground of the armies of many nations. Here, beside the border forays which engaged the troops of the rival kingdom, the Japanese, Chinese, Mongols, and Manchoos have contended for victory again and again. The principal cities of this province are Hai-chiu the capital, Hwang-ju an old baronial walled city, and the commercial city of Sunto or Kai-seng. Rock salt, flints, ginseng, varnish, and brushes made of the hair of wolf tails, are the principal products of the province.

Kiung-kei is the province which contains the national capital, although it is the, smallest of all. The city of Han Yang, or Seoul, is on the north side

GATE OF SEOUL

of the river, forty or fifty miles from its mouth. The name "Han Yang means the fortress on the Han river," while the common term applied to the royal city is Seoul, which means "the capital." The population of the city is between two hundred thousand and two hundred and fifty thousand. The natural advantages of Seoul are excellent, as it is well protected by surrounding mountains, and its suburbs reach the navigable river. The scenery from the city is magnificent. The walls are of masonry, averaging about twenty feet in height, with arched stone bridges over the water courses. The streets are narrow and tortuous. The king's castle is in the northern part. The islands in the river near the capital are inhabited by fishermen.

Four great fortresses guard the approaches to the royal city, all of which have been the scene of siege and battle in time past. The fortresses in succession are Suwen to the south, Kwang-chiu to the southeast, Sunto to the north and Kang-wa to the west. On the walls of the first three have been set the banners of the hosts of Ming from China and of Taiko from Japan, in the wars at the close of the sixteenth century. The Manchoo standard in 1637 and the French eagles in 1866 were planted on the ramparts of Kang-wa. Beside these castled cities there are forts and redoubts along the river banks crowning most of the commanding headlands. Over these the stars and stripes floated for three days in 1871 when the American forces captured the strongholds.

Sunto is one of the most important, if not the chief commercial city in the kingdom, and from 960 to 1392 it was the national capital. The chief staple of manufacture and sale is the coarse cotton cloth which forms the national dress. Kang-wa on the island of the same name, at the mouth of the Han river, is the favorite fortress to which the royal family are sent for safety in time of war, or are banished in case of deposition.

The province Chung Chong or "Serene Loyalty" is the next one to the southward facing the Yellow Sea. In the history of Corean Christianity this province will be remembered as the nursery of the faith. Here were made the most converts to the teachings of the French missionaries, and here persecutions were most violent. When the Japanese armies of invasion reached the capital in 1592, it was over the great highways from Fusan which cross this province. Chion-Chiu, the fortress on whose fate the capital depended, lies in the northeast of the province. The province contains tin walled cities, and like all its fellows it is divided into departments, right and left.

The most southern of the eight provinces, "Chulla or Complete Network" is also the warmest and most fertile. It is nearest to Shanghai and to the track of foreign commerce. Considerable quantities of hides, bones, horns, leather, and tallow are exported to Japan. The beef supplied from the herds of cattle in the pastures of Chulla is famous, and troops of horses graze on the pasture land. The province is well furnished with ports and harbors. Christianity had quite a hold this province, and when Corea

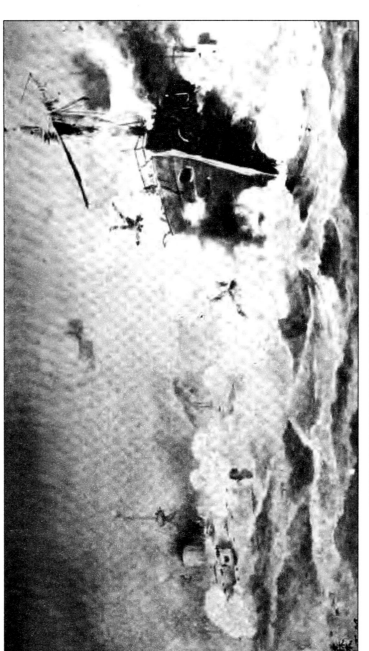

NAVAL ATTACK ON THE CHEN-YUEN BEFORE CHEMULPO
JAPANESE DRAWING

was partly opened to the world there were many believers found in the north who were descendants of Christian martyrs. The capital is Chon. chiu. The soil of the province was the scene of many battles during the Chinese invasions of 1592-97.

The island of Quelpaert is about sixty miles south of the mainland. It is mountainous, with one peak called Han-ra more than six thousand five hundred feet high. On its top are three extinct craters within each of which is a lake of pure water. Corean children are taught to believe that the three first created men of the world still dwell on these lofty heights.

The most south-easterly province of Corea, and therefore the nearest to Japan, is Kiung-sang or the "Province of Respectful Congratulation." It is one of the richest of the eight provinces as well as the most populous, and the seat of many historical associations with Japan. The city of Kion-chiu was the capital of the ancient kingdom of Shinra, and from here to Kioto, from the third to the tenth century, the relations of war and peace, letters and religion were continuous and fruitful. The province has always been the gateway of entrance and exit to the Japanese. Fusan, the port which was held by the Japanese from very ancient times, is well at the south eastern extremity of the peninsula. Its fortifications are excellent, and its harbor well protected. Populous cities encircle the bay on which Fusan stands, and from this point extend two great roads to Seoul. The influence of centuries of close intercourse with their neighbors, the Japanese, is strongly marked in this province.

The "River Meadow," or Knng-wen provinces fronts Japan from the middle of the eastern coast directly north of Kiung-sang. It is a province of beautiful scenery and precipitous mountains. The capital is Wen-chiu. The women of the province are said to be the most beautiful in Corea.

Ham-kiung, or complete view, is that part of Corean territory adjoining the boundary of Russia. The south-eastern boundary of Siberia, which has been pushed farther south after every European war with China, touched the Tumen river, the northern boundary of Corea, in 1858. It is but a little ways from the mouth of the Tumen river to the forts of Vladivostok and Possiet in Russian territory. From these cities extends a telegraph across Siberia to the cities of European Russia, and here will be the terminus of the great Trans-Siberian railway now under construction. Possiet is connected with Nagasaki by an electric cable. In the event of a war between China and Russia, the Czar would most probably make Corea the basis of operations. Thousands of Coreans have left their own country to dwell in the neighboring portions of Siberia, and most of them are from the province of Ham-kiung. Persecuted Christians from all over the Corean peninsula have however escaped to Russia for protection for many years. The port of Gensan near Port Lazaref, fronting Brouglton's Bay has been opened for trade since May 1,1880, and has been in important strategic and commercial point ever since. The capital city of this province is Ham-hung and there are fourteen other walled cities within its limits. Until the Russians occupied the adjoining territory, an annual fair was held at the Corea city of Kion-wen which lies close to the border. Here the Manchoo and Chinese merchans bartered their wares for those of Corean, the traffic lasting but two or three days and sometimes only one day. At the end of the fair any lingering Chinese not soon across the border was urged over at the point of a spear. Foreigners found within the Corean limits at any other time were apt to he ruthlessly murdered.

The government of Corea, since the amalgamation of the different tribes and union of the various states five hundred years ago, has devolved upon an independent king, an hereditary monarch whose rule was absolute and supreme. Next in authority to the king are the three Chong, or high ministers. The chief of these is the greatest dignitary of the kingdom, and in time of minority or inability of the king wields royal authority. The father of the present king ruled as regent up to the time when his son reached his majority in 1874. After the king and the three prime ministers, come the six heads of departments of government which rank next. These six-department ministers are assisted by two other associates, the Cham-pan and the Cham-e. These four grades and twenty-one dignitaries constitute the royal council of Dai-jin, though the actual authority is in the three ministers. All of the department ministers make daily reports of their affairs, and refer matters of importance to the supreme council. There are also three chamberlains who record every day the acts and words of the king. A daily government gazette called the Cho-po is issued for information on official matters. The general cast and method of procedure in the court and government were copied in the beginning after the great model in Peking. The rule of the king in Corea is absolute, and his will alone is law. There has always existed, indeed, the office of a high functionary whose special duty

consists in watching and controlling the royal actions. Formerly this office really had some significance, but of late years it has possessed none whatever. Another very curious institution has been that of the declared or official favorite, a position generally filled by some member of a noble family, or by one of the ministers whose influence for good or for evil was paramount with his royal master.

The titles of the prime ministers are Chief of The Just Government, The Just Governor of the Left, and The Just Governor of the Right. The six department ministers are those of the interior, or office and public

COREAN MAGISTRATE AND SERVANT

employ, finance, war, education, punishments or justice, and public works. The duties of the minister of foreign affairs devolved on the minister of education.

Each of the eight provinces is under the direction of a Kam-sa or governor. The cities ate divided into six classes, and are governed by officers of corresponding rank. Towns are given in charge of the petty magistrates, there being twelve ranks or dignities in the official class. In theory, any male Corean able to pass the government examination is eligible to office, but the greater number of the best positions are secured by the nobles and their friends. The terms of office in these posts, from that of provincial governorship down to the lowest are only for two or three years. At the end of that time the incumbent pays purchase money and is removed to another place. The natural result of this system is that the officials take little interest in their offices except to extort as much profit as possible from the people whom they are governing. With offices and honors old to the highest bidder, the high officers sell justice and plunder their subordinates, while these again try to indemnify themselves by further extortion.

The magistrates lay great stress on the trifles of etiquette, and sumptuary laws exist referring to all sorts of the small things of life. The rule of the local authorities is very minute in all its ramifications. The system of making ever five houses a social unit is universal. Every subject of the sovereign except nobles of rank must possess a passport testifying to his personality and must show his ticket on demand.

Civil matters are decided by the ordinary civil magistrate, while criminal cases are tried by the military commandant. Very important cases are referred to the governor of the province, and thence appealed to the high court in the capital.

JAPANESE NAVAL ATTACK ON THE FORTS AT WEI-HAI-WEI, FEBRUARY 3rd

COREAN CHARACTERISTICS AND MANNERS OF LIFE

Physique of the People—Rigid Caste System—Silvery—Guilds and Trade Unions—Position of Women—Nameless and Oppressed—Marriage and Family Life—Burial and Mourning Customs—Dress and Diet—Homes—Home Life—Children—Education—Outdoor Life—Music—Literature—Language—Religion.

The Corean people are mainly of a Mongolian type, though there is some evidence that there is a Caucasian element in the stock. They are a little larger and steadier of physique than the Japanese, or the Chinese of the south, more nearly approaching to the northern Chinese and even to the tribes in the northeast of Asia. Frequently individuals are met, with hair not quite black, and even blue eyes and an almost English style of face. The characteristics of the people are distinguished to advantage from that of their Chinese neighbors by the openness and frankness of their demeanor. The Coreans, even of the lower classes, are grave and sedate by nature, which, however, does not exclude a spirit of frank gayety shown on nearer acquaintance. They are thoroughly honest, faithful and good natured, and attach themselves with an almost childlike confidence even to strangers and foreigners, when once they begin to trust in their sincerity.

Firm, sure, and quick in his walk, the Corean possesses greater ease and a freer motion than the Chinese, whom they are superior in height and bodily strength. On the other hand it cannot be denied that the Coreans rank considerably below the Chinese in cultivation of good manners, and they are wanting in that little polish which is not absent even among the lower classes of China and Japan.

The peculiarity of the Corean race and the difference between the same and the neighboring nations, shows itself mainly in the strict and rigid division of the castes which part the various ranks of the population of the peninsula from each other, showing some analogy to the caste institutions prevailing among the Hindus in India. There exists, however, this notable difference between the two, that while with the latter this separation is based upon religious principles and customs, no religious movement appears as its cause in Corea, where its origin seems solely attributable to political reasons, which have been maintained and kept up to our times by the government for reasons of its own. The forms of Corean society to this day are derived from feudal ranks and division. The fruit and legacy of feudalism are seen in the serfdom or slavery which is Corea's peculiar domestic situation.

Speaking in general terms, society has four grades, following the king. These are the nobles and the three classes which come after them, in the last of which are "the seven low callings." In detail the grades may be counted by the scores. In the lowest grade of the fourth class are "the seven vile callings," that is, the merchant, boatman, jailer, postal or mail slave, monk, butcher, and sorcerer. The first and foremost rank, immediately after the king and the members of the royal family, who stand absolutely above and beyond these castes, is taken up by the so-called nobles, descendants of the old families of chieftains, who are again subdivided into two degrees, the civil and the military nobility. These two classes of nobles, in the course of time, had possessed themselves of the exclusive right of occupying public office. Following upon these we find the caste of the half nobles, numerically a very weak class, which forms the transition from the nobility to the civic classes. These also enjoy the right to fill certain offices from their ranks, principally those of government secretaries and translators of Chinese. After these come the civic caste, which consists of the better and wealthier portion of the city inhabitants. This class counts amongst its numbers the merchants, manufacturers, and most kinds of artisans. Next follows the people's caste, which comprising the bulk of the people is naturally the most numerous of all and includes all villagers, farmers, shepherds, huntsmen, fishermen, and the like.

The nobles are usually the slave holders, many of them having in their households large number whom they have inherited along with their ancestral chattels. The master has a right to sell or otherwise dispose of the children of his slaves if he so choose. Slavery or serfdom in Corea is in a continuous state of decline, and the number of slaves constantly diminishing. The slaves are those who are born in a state of servitude, those who sell themselves as slaves, and those who are sold to be such by their parents in times of famine or for debt. Infants exposed or abandoned that are picked up and educated become slaves, but their offspring are born free. The serfdom is really very mild. Only the active young men are held to field labor, the young women being kept as domestics. When old enough to marry, the males are let free by an annual payment of a sum of money for a term of years. Outside of private ownership of slaves,

STATESMAN ON MONOCYCLE—NATIVE DRAWING

there is a species of government slavery which illustrates the persistency of one feature of the ancient kingdom of Korai perpetuated through twenty centuries. It is the law that in case of the condemnation of a great criminal, the ban shall fall upon his wife and children, who at once become the slaves of the judge. These unfortunates do not have the privilege of honorably serving the magistrate, but usually pass their existence in waiting on the menials in the various government offices. Only a few of the government slaves are such by birth, most of them having become so through judicial condemnation in criminal cases; but this latter class fare far worse than the ordinary slaves. They are chiefly females, and are treated little better than beasts. Nothing can equal the contempt in which they are held.

By union and organization it has come to pass that the common people and the serfs themselves in Corea have won a certain degree of social freedom that is increasing. The spirit of association is spread among the Coreans of all classes, from the highest families to the meanest slaves. All those who have any kind of work or interest in common, form guilds, corporations or societies which have a common fund contributed to by all for aid in time of need. Very powerful trade union exist among the mechanics and laborers, such as hat-weavers, coffin-makers, carpenters, and masons. These societies enable each class to possess a monopoly of trade which even a noble vainly tries to break. Sometimes they hold this right by writ purchased or obtained from government, though usually

COREAN BRUSH CUTTER-*Native Drawing*

it is by prescription. Most of the guilds are taxed by the government for their monopoly enjoyed. They have their chief or head man who possesses almost despotic power, even in some guilds of life and death.

One of the most powerful and best organized guilds is that of the porters. The interior commerce of the country being almost entirely on the backs of men and pack horses, these people have the monopoly of it. They number about ten thousand, and are divided by provinces and districts under the orders of chiefs and inspectors. They have very severe rules for the government of their guild, and crimes among them are punished with death at the order of their chief. They are so powerful that they pretend that even the government dare not interfere with them. They are honest and faithful in their business, delivering packages with

PORTERS WITH CHAIR—*Native Drawing*

certainty to the most remote places in the kingdom. When they have received an insult, or injustice, or too low wages, they "strike" in a body and retire from the district. This puts a stop to all travel and business until the grievances are settled, or submission to their own terms is made. Owing to the fact that the country at large is so lacking in the shops and stores common in other countries, and that instead fairs on set days are so numerous in the towns and villages, the guild of peddlers and hucksters is very large and influential. This class includes probably two hundred thousand able bodied persons who in the various provinces move freely among the people, and are thus useful to government as spies, detectives, messengers, and in time of need, soldiers.

The Corean woman has little moral existence. She is an instrument of pleasure or of labor, but never man's companion or equal. She has no name. In childhood she receives indeed a surname by which she is known in the family and by near friends, but as she grows up none but her father and mother employ this appellation; to all others she is "the sister" of such a one or "the daughter" of so and so. After her marriage her name is buried, and she is absolutely nameless. Her own parents allude to her by employing the name of the district or ward in which she is married. When she bears children she is "the mother" of so and so. When a woman appears for trial before a magistrate, in order to save time and trouble she receives a special name for the time being.

In the higher classes of society etiquette requires that the children be separated after the age of eight or ten years. After that time the boys dwell entirely in the men's apartments to study and even to eat and drink; the girls remain secluded in the women's quarters. The boys are taught that it is a shameful thing even to set foot in the female part of the house. The girls are told that it is disgraceful even to be seen by males, so that gradually they seek to hide themselves when any of the male sex appear. These customs continued from childhood to old age, result in destroying the family life. A Corean of good taste only occasionally holds conversation with his wife, whom he regards as being far beneath him. The men chat, smoke, and enjoy themselves in the outer rooms, and the women receive their parents and friends in the inner apartments. The men seek the society of their male neighbors, and the women on their part unite together for local gossip. In the higher classes, when a young woman has arrived to marriageable age none even of her own relatives except those nearest of kin, is allowed to see or speak to her. After their marriage women are inaccessible. They are nearly always confined to their apartments, nor can they even look out into the streets without permission from their lords.

There is, however, another side. Though counting for nothing in society, and nearly so in their family, they are surrounded by a certain sort of exterior respect. They are always addressed in the formulas of the most polite language. The men always step aside in the street to allow a woman to pass, even though she be of the poorer classes. There is also a peculiar custom which exists in Seoul which exhibits deference to the comfort of the women. A bell in the castle is struck at sunset, after which male citizens are not allowed to go out of their houses even to visit their neighbors. Women, on the contrary are permitted the freedom of the streets after this time, consequently, as they are assured of safety, from seeing men or being seen by them, they take their exercise and enjoy the outdoors most heartily and freely at night.

Marriage in Corea is a thing with which a woman has little or nothing to do. The father of the young man communicates with the father of the girl he wishes his son to marry. This often done without consulting the tastes or character of either, and usually through a middleman or go-between. The fathers settle the time of the wedding, and a favorable day is appointed by the astrologers. Under this aspect marriage seems an affair of small importance, but it reality it is marriage only that gives one any civil rank or influence in society. Every unmarried person is treated as a child. He may commit all sorts of foolishness without being held to account. His capers are not noticed, for he is not supposed to think or act seriously. Even the unmarried young men of twenty-five or thirty years of age can take no part in social reunions or speak on affairs of importance. But marriage is emancipation. Even if mated at twelve or thirteen years of age, the married are adults. The bride takes her place among the matrons and the young man has a right to speak among the men and to wear a hat.

The badge of single or married life is the hair. Before marriage the young man who goes bareheaded, wears a simple tress hanging down his back. In wedlock the hair is bound up on the top of the head and is cultivated on all parts of the scalp. Young persons who insist on remaining single, or bachelors who have not yet found a wife, sometimes, however, secretly cut of their hair or get it done by fraud in order to pass for married folks and avoid being treated as children. Such a custom however is a gross violation of morals and etiquette.

On the evening before the wedding the young lady who is to be married invites one of her friends to change her virginal coiffure to that of a married woman. The bridegroom-to-be, also invites one of his acquaintances to do up his hair in manly style. On the marriage day in the house of the groom a platform is set up and richly adorned with decorative cloths. Parents, friends, and acquaintances assemble in a crowd. The couple to be married, who may never have seen or spoken to each other, are brought in and take their places on the platform face to face. There they remain for a few minutes. They salute each other with profound obeisance but utter not a word. This constitutes the ceremony of marriage. Each then retires upon either side; the bride to the female, and the groom to the male apartments, where feasting and amusement after fashions in vogue in Chosen take place. The expense of a wedding is considerable and the bridegroom must be unstinting in his hospitality. Any failure in this particular may subject him to unpleasant practical jokes. On her wedding day the young bride must preserve absolute silence both on the marriage platform and in the nuptial chamber. Etiquette requires this at least among the nobility. Though overwhelmed with questions and compliments, silence is her duty. She must rest mute and impassive as a statue.

It is the reciprocal salutation before witnesses on the wedding dais that constitutes legitimate marriage. From that moment a husband may claim a woman as his wife. Conjugal fidelity, obligatory on the woman, is not required of the husband, and a wife is little more than a slave of superior rank. Among the nobles the young bridegroom spends three or four days with his bride, and then absents himself from her for a considerable time to prove that he does not esteem her too highly. To act otherwise would be considered in very bad taste and highly unfashionable.

Habituated from infancy to such a yoke and regarding themselves as of an inferior race, most women submit to their lot with exemplary resignation. Having no idea of progress or of an infraction of established usage they bear all things. They become

JAPANESE WAR SHIP "YOSHINO"
(During the Attack on Wei-hai-wei, February 3rd, 1895)

devoted and obedient wives, jealous of the reputation and wellbeing of their husbands. The woman who is legally espoused, whether widow or slave, enters into and shares the entire social estate of her husband. Even if she be not noble by birth she becomes so by marrying a noble. It is not proper for a widow to remarry.

The fashion of mourning, the proper time and place to shed tears, and express grief, according to regulations, are rigidly prescribed in an official treatise, or "Guide to Mourners," published by the government. The corpse must be placed in a coffin of very thick wood, and preserved during many months in a special room prepared and ornamented for this purpose. It is proper to weep only in this death chamber but this must be done three or four times daily. Before entering it the mourner must don a special suit of mourning clothes. At the new and full moon all the relatives are invited and expected to assist in the ceremonies. These practices continue more or less even after burial, and at intervals during several years. Often a noble will go out to weep at the tomb, passing days and nights in this position. Among the poor, who have not the means to provide a death chamber and expensive mourning, the coffin is kept outside their houses covered with mats until the time for its burial.

Though cremation is known in Corea, the most usual form of disposing of the dead is by burial. Children are wrapped up in the clothes and bedding in which they die and are thus buried. As all unmarried persons are reckoned as children their shroud and burial are the same. With the married the process is more costly, and more detailed and prolonged. The selection of a proper site for their tomb is a matter of profound solicitude, time, and money; for the geomancers must be consulted with a fee. The tombs of the poor consist only of a grave and a low mound of earth. With the richer class monuments are of stone, sometimes neat or even imposing, sometimes grotesque.

Mourning is of many degress and lengths, and in betokened by dress, abstinence from food and business, visits to the tomb, offerings, tablets, and many visible indications detailed even to absurdity. Pure or nearly pure white is the mourning color, as a contrast to red, the color of rejoicing. When noblemen don the peaked hat which covers the face as well as the head, they are as dead to the world, not to be spoken to, molested, or even arrested, if charged with crime. This Corean mourning hat proved the helmet of salvation to Christians and explains the safety of the French missionaries who lived so long in disguise under its shelter, unharmed in the country where the police were ever on their track. The Jesuits were not slow to see the wonderful protection promised for them, and availed themselves of it at once and always, both while entering the well-guarded frontier and while residing in the country.

Corean architecture is in a very primitive condition. The castles, fortifications, temples, monasteries, and public buildings cannot approach the magnificence of those of Japan or China. The dwellings are tiled or thatched houses, almost invariably one story high. In the smaller towns these are not arranged in regular streets but are scattered here and there. Even in the cities the streets are narrow and tortuous. In the rural parts the houses of the wealthy are surrounded by beautiful groves, with gardens circled by hedges or fences of rushes or split bamboo. The cities show a greater display of red-tiled roofs, as only the officials and nobles are allowed this honor. Shingles are not much used. The thatchings are rice or barley straw. A low wall of uncemented stone five or six feet high, surrounds the dwellings. The foundations are laid on stone set in the earth, and the floor of the humble is the ground itself. The people one grade above the poorest, cover the hard ground with sheets of oiled paper which serve as a carpet. For the better class a floor of wood is raised a foot or so above the earth.

Bed clothes are of silk, wadded cotton, thick paper, and furs. Cushions or bags of rice-chaff form the pillows of the rich. The poor man uses a smooth log of wood or slightly raised portion of the floor to rest his head upon. In most families of the middle class, "the kang" forms the vaulted floor, bed, and stove. It is as if we should make a bedstead of bricks and put foot-stoves under it. The floor is bricked over or built of stone, over flues which run from the fireplace at one end of the house to the chimney at the other. The fire which does the cooking is thus used to warm those sitting or sleeping in the room beyond.

Three rooms are the rule in an average house, and these are for cooking, eating, and sleeping. In the kitchen the most notable articles are the large earthen jars for holding rice, barley or water. Each of them is big enough to hold a man easily. The second room, containing the "kang," is the sleeping

COREAN BOAT—*Native Drawing*

apartment, and the next is the best room or parlor. Little furniture is the rule. Coreans, like the Japanese, sit not cross-legged but on their heels. Aong the well-to-do dog skins cover the floor for a carpet, or tiger skins serve as rugs. Matting is common.

The meals are served on the floor on small low tables, usually one for each guest, but sometimes one for a couple. The best table service is of porcelain and the ordinary sort of earthenware with white metal or copper utensils. The tablecloths are of fine glazed paper and resemble oiled silk. No knives or forks are used; but instead chopsticks and what is more common than in

China or Japan, spoons are used at every meal. The walls range in quality of decoration from plain mud to colored plaster and paper. Pictures are not known. The windows are square and latticed without or within, covered with tough oiled paper, and moving in grooves. The doors are of wood, paper, or plaited bamboo. Glass was till recently a nearly unknown luxary in Corea.

The Corean liquor by preference is brewed or distilled from rice, millet, or barley. These alcoholic drinks are of various strength, color, and smell, ranging from beer to brandy. No trait of the Coreans has more impressed their numerous visitors than their love of all kinds of strong drink. No sooner were the ports of Corea opened to commerce than the Chinese established liquor stores, while European wines, brandies and whiskeys have entered to increase the national drunkenness. Although the Corean lives between the two great tea-producing countries the world, he scarcely knows the taste of tea and the fragrant herb is little used on the peninsula.

The staple diet has in it much more of meat and fat than that of the Japanese, and the average Corean can eat twice as much as the Japanese. Beef, pork, fowls, venison, fish, and game are consumed without much waste and rejected material. Dog flesh is on sale among the common butcher's meat. The women cook rice beautifully, and other well-known dishes are barley, millet, beans, potato, lily-bulbs, seaweeds, acorns, radishes, turnips, macaroni, vermicolli, apples, pears, plums, grapes, persimmons, and various kinds of berries. All kinds of condiments are much relished.

One striking fault of the Coreans at the table is their voracity. In this respect there is not the least difference between the rich and poor, noble or plebeian. To eat much is an honor, and the merit of a feast consists not in the quality but in the quantity of the food served. Little talking is done while eating, for each sentence might lose a mouthful. Hence, since a capacious stomach is a high accomplishment, mothers use every means to develop as elastic a capacity as possible in their children from very infancy. The Coreans equal the Japanese in devouring raw fish, and uncooked food of all kinds is swallowed without a wry face. Fish

THE BATTLE AT ASAN
Japanese Drawing

bones do not scare them. These they eat as they do the small bones of fowls.

Nationally and individually the Coreans are very deficient in conveniences for the toilet. Bath tubs are rare, and except in the warmer days of summer, when the river and sea serve for immersion, the natives are not usually found under water. The need of soap and hot water has been noticed by travelers and writers of every nation. The men are very proud of their beards, and honor them as a distinctive glory and mark of their sex. Women coil their glossy black tresses into massive knots and fasten them with pins, or gold and silver rings.

COREAN EGG-SELLER—*Native Drawing*

Corea is famous as the land of big hats. Some of these head-coverings are so immense that the human head encased in one of them seems as but a hub in a cart wheel. In shape the gentleman's hat resembles a flowerpot inverted in the center of a round table. Two feet is a common diameter, and the top, which rises in a cone nine inches higher, is only three inches wide at the apex. The usual material is bamboo, split to the fineness of a thread and woven. The fabric is then varnished or lacquered, and becomes perfectly weatherproof. The prevalence of cotton clothing, easily soaked and rendered uncomfortable, requires the ample protection for the back and shoulders which these umbrella-like hats furnish.

The wardrobe of the upper classes consists of the ceremonial and the house dress. The former as a rule is of fine silk, and the latter of coarser silk or cotton. They are of pink, blue, and other rich colors. The official robe is a long garment like a wrapper, with loose baggy sleeves. There are few tailors' shops, the women of each household making he family outfit. The underdress of both sexes is a short jacket with tight sleeves, which for men reaches to the thighs, and for women only to the waist, and a pair of drawers reaching from waist to ankle. The females wear a petticoat over this garment, so that the Coreans say they dress like western women, and foreign-made hosiery and undergarments are in demand. Their general style of costume is that of the wrapper, stiff, wide, and inflated, with abundant starch in summer, but clinging and baggy in winter. The white dress of the Corean makes his complexion look darker than it really is. Footgear is either of native or of Chinese make. The laborer contents himself with sandals woven from rice-straw, which usually last but a few days. Small feet do not seem to be considered a beauty, and the foot binding of the Chinese is unknown in Cho-sen.

Judging from a collection of the toys of Corean children, and from their many terms of affection, and words relating to games and sports, festivals and recreation, and nursery stories, the life of the little ones must be pleasant. In the capital and among the higher classes, childern's toys are very handsome, ranking as real works of art. They have many games played by the little ones quite similar to those of our own babies, and they delight in pets, such as monkeys and puppies.

At school the pupils study out loud and noisily, according to the method all over Asia. Besides learning the Chinese characters and the vernacular alphabet, the children master arithmetic and writing. The normal Corean is fond of his children, especially of sons, who in his eyes are worth ten times as much as daughters. Such thing as exposure of children is little known. The first thing inculcated a child's mind is respect for his father. All insubordination is immediately and sternly is pressed. Far different is it with the mother. She yields to her boy's caprices, and laughs at his faults and vices without rebuke, while the child soon learns that a mother's authority is next to nothing.

Primogeniture is the rigid rule. Younger sons at the time of their marriage, or at other important periods of life receive paternal gifts, but the bulk of the property belongs to the oldest son on whom the younger sons look as their father. He is the head of the family, and regards his father's children as his own. In all eastern Asia the bonds of family are much closer than among Caucasian people of the present time. All the kindred, even to the fifteenth or twentieth degree, whatever their social position, rich or poor, educated or illiterate, officials or beggars, form a clan or more properly one single family, all of whose members have mutual interests to sustain. The house of one is the house of the other, and each will assist to his utmost, another of the clan to get money, office, or advantage. The law recognizes this system by levying on the clan the taxes and debts which individuals of it cannot pay, holding the clan responsible for the individual. To this they submit without complaint protest. Instead of the family being a unit, as with us, it is only the fragment of a clan, a segment in the great circle of kindred. The Coreans fully as clannish as the Chinese, and in this lies one great obstacle to Christianity or to any kind of individual reform.

China gave her culture to Corea and Corea passed it on to Japan. If we may believe Corean tales, then the Coreans have possessed letters and writing during three thousand years. It is certain that since the opening of the Christian era the light of China's philosophy has shone steadily among Corean scholars. In spite of their national system of writing, the influence of the finished philosophy and culture of China has been so great that the hopelessness of producing a copy equal to the original became at once apparent to the Corean mind. The culture of their native tongue has been neglected by Corean scholars. The consequence is that after so many centuries of national life Corea possesses no literature worthy of the name.

At present Corean literary men possess a highly critical

knowledge of Chinese. Most intelligent scholars read the classics with ease and fluency. Penmanship is an art as much prized and as widely practiced as in Japan, and reading and writing constitute education. Corea has most closely imitated her teacher, China, in the use of education. She fosters education by making scholastic ability as tested in the literary examination, the basis of appointment to office. This civil service reform was established by the now ruling dynasty early in the fifteenth century. The Corean child, neglecting his own language, literature, and history, studies those of China and the philosophy of Confucius, so that his education is practically that of the young man in China. The same classics are studied and the same attention is paid to memory cultivation. The competitive examinations too are very similar to those of China, and corresponding degrees are granted. The system of literary examinations, which for two or three centuries after its establishment was vigorously maintained with impartiality, is at present in a state of decay, bribery and official favor being the causes of its decline.

The special schools of languages, mathematics, medicine art, etc., are under the patronage of the government, but amount to very little. The school of astronomy and the choice of fortunate days for state occasions is for the special service of the king. There is also a school of interpreters, charts, law, and horology.

Although the Chinese language, writing and literature form the basis of education and culture in Chosen, yet the native language is distinct in structure from the Chinese, having little in common with it. The latter is monosyllabic, while the Corean is polysyllabic, as is the Japanese which the Corean closely resembles. No other language is so nearly affiliated to the Japanese as is the Corean. The Corean alphabet, one of the most simple and perfect in the world, consists of twenty-five letters, eleven vowels and fourteen consonants. They are made with easy strokes in which straight lines, circles, and dots only are used.

As in Japan, so in Corea three styles of languages prevail, and are used as follows: Pure Chinese without any admixture of Corean, in books and writings on science, history and government and in the theses of the students and literary men; in the books composed in the Corean language the vernacular syntax

JAPANESE SOLDIERS DESCENDING FROM THE CASTLE AT FENG-HWANG
Japanese Drawing

serves as the framework, but the vocabulary is largely Chinese; the Corean book style of composition which is written in the pure Corean language. Every one in Corea speaks the vernacular and not Chinese.

The books which have been written in Corean, are chiefly primers or manuals of history, books on etiquette and ritual, and geography. There are also a few works of poetry written in the vulgar dialect.

COREAN BAND OF MUSICIANS—*Native Drawing*

In passionate fondness for music the Coreans decidedly surpass all other Asiatic nations. Their knowledge is indeed primitive, however, not superior to that of their neighbors, and their instruments are of rude workmanship and construction. The principal of these instruments are the gong, the flute, and the two-stringed guitar, combining to make a music anything but harmonious. They always sing in falsetto, like the Chinese, in a monotonous and melancholy manner. The Coreans however possess a musical ear, and they know how to appreciate and like to listen to foreign music very much, while the Chinese have not the slightest idea of harmony, and placing our music far below their own, look down upon our art with something like a feeling of pity.

The fibres of Corean superstition, and the actual religion of the people of to-day, have not radically changed during twenty centuries in spite of Buddhism. The worship of the spirits of nature and the other popular gods is still reflected in superstition and practice. The Chinese Fung Shuy, which in Corean becomes Pung-siu, is a system of superstition concerning the direction of the everyday things of life, which is nearly as powerful in Corea as in the parent country. Upon this system, and perhaps nearly equal in age with it, is the cult of ancestral worship which has existed in Chinese Asia from unrecorded time. Confucius found it in his day and made it the basis of his teachings, as it had already been of the religious and ancient documents of which he mas the editor. The Corean system of ancestral worship presents no feature radically different from the Chinese. Confucianism, or the Chinese system of ethics, holds about the same position that it does in China. Taoism seems to be little studied.

In Corean mouths Buddha becomes Pul and his "way" or doctrine Pul-to or Pul-chie. The faith from India has made thorough conquest of the southern half of the peninsula, but has only partially leavened the northern portion where the grosser heathenisn prevails. The palmy days of Corean Buddhism were during the era of Korai, 905 to 1392 A. D. In its development, Corean Buddhism has frequently been a potent influence in national affairs, and the power of the bonzes has at times been so great as to practically control the court and nullify decrees of the king. As in Japan the frequent wars have developed the formation of a clerical militia, able to garrison and defend their fortified monasteries, and even to change the fortune of war by the valor of their exploits. There are three distinct classes or grades of the bonzes or priests. The student monks devote themselves to learning and to the composition of books and to Buddhist rituals. Then there are the mendicant and traveling bonzes who solicit alms and contributions for the erection and maintenance of the temples and monastic establishments. Finally the military bonzes act as garrisons, and make, keep in order, and are trained to use weapons. Even at the present day Buddhist priests are made high officers of the government, governors of provinces, and military advisers. In the nunneries are two kinds of female devotees, those who shave the head and those who keep their locks. The vows of the latter are less rigid. Excepting in its military phases, the type of Corean Buddhism approaches that of China rather than of Japan.

The great virtue of the Coreans is their innate respect for and daily practice of the laws of human brotherhood. Mutual assistance and generous hospitality among themselves are distinctive national traits. In all the important events of life, such as marriages and funerals, each person makes it his duty to aid the family most directly interested. One will charge himself with the duty of making purchases; others with arranging the ceremonies. The poor, who can give nothing, carry messages to friends and relatives in the near or remote villages, passing day and night on foot and giving their labors gratuitously. When fire, flood or other accident destroys the house of one of their number, neighbors make it a duty to lend a hand to rebuild. One brings stone, another wood, another straw. Each in addition to his gifts in material devotes two or three days' work gratuitously. A stranger coming into a village is always assisted to build a dwelling. Hospitality is considered as one of the most sacred duties. It would be a grave and shameful thing to refuse a portion of one's meal to any person, known or unknown, who presents himself at eating time. Even the poor laborers at the side of the roads are often seen sharing their frugal nourishment with the passer-by. The poor man making a journey does not need elaborate preparations. At night, instead of going to a hotel, he enters some house whose exterior room is open to any comer. There he is sure to find food and lodging for the night. Rice will be shared with the stranger, and at bedtime a corner of the floor mat will serve for a bed, while he may rest his head on the long log of wood against the wall, which serves as a pillow. Even should he delay his journey for a day or two, little or nothing to his discredit will be harbored by his hosts.

It is evident after this glance at the history, the conditions, and the customs of the Coreans, that they have many excellent qualities, which require but the leavening influence Christianity and western civilization to make them worthy members of the family of nations. It is quite possible that the influence of the Japanese-Chinese war, in its ultimate results, may reach this desirable consummation.

THE WAR

JAPANESE COOLIES FOLLOWING THE ARMY

CAUSES OF THE WAR BETWEEN JAPAN AND CHINA

Inception Must be Sought Far Back In History—Old Time Animosity Between the two Nation Chiefly Responsible—Formal Recognition of Corean Independence by Japan—The Riots of 1882 and Their Result — Return of the Corean Embassy from a Trip Around the World—Advance of American Ideas and Influence—Plots of the Progressionists—The Coup d'Etat and Its Fatal Results—Flight of the conspirators to Japan and America—Decoying of Kim-ok-Kiun to Shanghai—Assassinations of Kim—Rebellion in Northern Corea—Aid Asked From China—China Sends Troops—Violation of Treaty with Japan—Army from Japan Arrives—Japanese in the Capital—Scheme of Reform Proposed by Japan and Rejected by China—A Diplomate Campaign.

In its broadest sense no war between nations can be ascribed to a single cause, defined by exact limits of time and place. A cause of war always suggests the question as to what has made it such; and so we find that for an intelligent understanding of the present war we have to go back, beyond the Corean rebellions of the early spring of 1894, and take in the whole range of the relations of China and Japan to Corea and to each other. An understanding of the history of the three nations is necessary to a proper understanding of the war.

The first formal recognition of Corean independence is found in the earliest treaty between Japan and Corea, that of 1876, by which the Coreans agreed to pay indemnity for an unwarranted attack which had been made upon a Japanese vessel, and to open several ports to Japanese traders. It was through this treaty that Corea was first introduced to the comity of nations. One of the professed objects of Japan during the war, has, therefore, been to establish the independence of Corea, which she has recognized in her treaties, against the Chinese claim of suzerainty. Sooner or later a war between Japan and China was inevitable. The hereditary animosities between the two nations have been aggravated by the marked differences which have arisen of late years between their civilizations; by the impatience under which Japan has struggled against an anomalous position among the powers, forced upon her by foreign treaties, while she has beheld her mediaeval rival holding precedence and predominances; and by the jealousy and fanatic contempt with which the subjects of the "Son of Heaven" have watched the growing political aspirations of Japan, her conciliatory attitude towards foreigners, and her apostate abandonment of the manners and customs of oriental life.

For years, moreover, an excuse for a collision has been developing 'in the relations of the two states to Corea. In spite of the liberal sympathies of the Corean king himself, the ascendant force in the government has long been the Ming faction, to which family the queen belongs, which is pro-Chinese in its sympathies, foe to everything savoring western liberal progress. Under the sway of this faction, which has monopolized the highest magistracies, government in Corea has been nothing more nor less than systematic plunder of the masses, for the benefit of a few privileged nobles. The admitted misgovernment of the country, which has always jeopardized the lives and property of aliens; the suzerain claims of China; the vast commercial interests of Japan in the peninsula and her large colonies; and finally the complicated treaty arrangements which have grown up between Tokio and Peking with regard to the "Hermit Kingdom"—these have long' constituted a source of friction, in the knowledge of which the present conflict between the mandarins and the daimios is more readily understood. It is significant that while China has never formally given up her claim to lordship over Corea, she has refused to stand by her vassal on certain occasions, and has encouraged the latter to conduct negotiations on her own account. This was indeed the action of China in 1876, when the treaty with Japan was made, and the latter seized the opportunity to recognize the king of Corea as an independent sovereign prince. The immediate cause of the war is centered around the disputed question of the right of both parties to keep troops on Corean soil, a right which both have exercised more than once. It is the origin of this right and the complications that have arisen from it, that we must now trace with reference to the outbreak of the war.

Corea for ages has been the pupil of China, whence nearly everything that makes up civilization has been borrowed. Of patriotism in its highest sense, of pure love of country, of willingness to make sacrifices for native land, there have been little in the

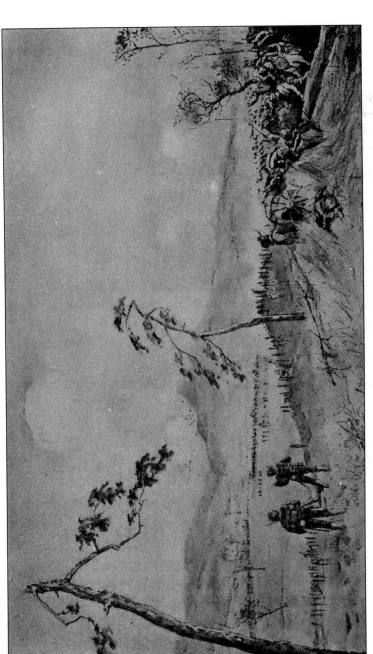

JAPANESE ARMY AT CHIU-LIEN-CHENG
Japanese Drawing

kingdom. Such things are new thoughts nourished by a few farseeing patriots. But leavening the multitude of Confucian fanatics and time-servers of the men in power at Peking, there are also men who have drunk at other fountains of thought, entered new worlds of knowledge, and seen the light of modern science, of Christianity, and of western civilization in other lands. The numbers of enlightened men are increasing who believe in national progress, though to their demands there has ever been the defiance of vigilant conservation. Even within the two broadly defined parties, there are factional and family differences. Against the craft of the Ming clan the other noble families, Ni, So, Kim, Hong, and others, have been able to make headway only by adroit combination.

In 1875 the two noblemen Kim-ok-Kiun and So Kwang Pom secretly left Corea and went to Japan, being the first men of rank in recent times to travel in lands beyond China. On their return they sought the king and boldly told him what they had seen. Other noblemen followed their example, but the brother-in-law of the king, Pak Hong Hio, was the first who at risk of reputation and life openly advocated the adoption of western civilization. In 1882 Kim and So in earnest consideration of the opening of their country to modern ideas, endeavored to persuade Min Yong Ik to join them and also win over his powerful Ming relatives to a liberal policy. When this came to the ears of the Tai-wen Kun the young men were forthwith charged with intent to introduce Christianity, and the two liberals narrowly escaped being put to death by the old regent who had already shed the blood of thousands.

The men of the Ming faction held aloof from treaty negotiations with the United States until China gave the nod. When at last Li Hung Chang advised Corea to treat with Admiral Shufeldt, the Ming nobles obeyed and exhibited so much energy in the matter as to seem to foreigners to be the leaders of the party of progress. The old regent at once felt it his duty to overthrow both the Mings and the treaty. His opportunity came in July, 1882, the year of the treaties. When on account of the short rice crop the soldiers' rations were cut down by the father of Min Yong Ik, the artful politician directed their revolt against this pro-

Chinese family, and after destroying, as he imagined, the queen and the leading men of the Ming clan, he seized the government itself and for a few days enjoyed full power. When the news of the usurpation reached China and Japan there were in Tien-tsin three Corean nobles, Cho Yong Ha, Kim Yun Sik, and O-Yun Chung; and in Tokio Kim-ok-Kiun and So Kwang Pom. The former, notified by telegram from the Chinese consul at

THE COREAN REGENT

Nagasaki of the movements of the Japanese, obtained a Chinese military and naval force, and the ships of these two foreign nations met at Chemulpo. Before either the Chinese or Japanese troops were disembarked, the two groups of Corean noblemen had a conference, and after a long and warm discussion it was agreed to submit the question whether the Chinese should land and proceed to Seoul, to the king himself. Accordingly Kim-ok-Kiun in disguise penetrated to the capital, but only to find the royal person in possession of his old and chief enemy Tai-wen Kun, his friends driven away, and approach to the palace impossible. On learning the failure of Kim's mission the Chinese force at once landed, marched to Seoul, abducted the regent, built forts to command the river against the Japanese, and established their camp inside the walls. This act of China gave her a new lien on Corea. The father of Min Yong Ik, Min Thai Ho, who had been supposed to have been mortally wounded, recovered and resumed office. Min Yonk Ik, who after fleeing to the mountains, shaved his head and in the disguise of a priest had fled to Japan, returned smiling after temporary defeat. The queen, for whom a palace maid had suffered vicarious death, re-entered the capital and palace, and the star of the Mings was again in the ascendant.

Two years later, in June, 1884, Min Yong Ik and So Kwang Pom, the first Coreans to go around the world, reached home followed by Kim-ok-Kiun and the Tokio students from Japan. After an enthusiastic reception of the returned envoys and the Anlerican officers of the Trenton in Seoul, the public opinion in favor of progress was greatly stimulated. Min Yong Ik was made vice-president of the Foreign office and the others of the embassy were elevated in rank. The Chinese military instructors were dismissed by the king. A model farm sown with American seeds, and for which California live stock was ordered, Edison electric lights, American rifles and Gatling guns, Japanese artisans to establish potteries and other industries, gave indications of the new path of national progress upon which Corea had entered.

Min Yong Jk while abroad has passed for an enlightened man, susceptible to modern ideas and in favor of opening Corea to commerce. Yet falling under the influence of his clan he had been home but a few weeks when he came to open rupture with Hong Yong Sik. Resigning from the foreign office he assumed command of the palace guard battalion and restored Chinese drill masters, the military students from Japan being left to gain their support as subordinates in the proposed postal department. By autumn the late envoy to the United States had surrounded himself with Chinese and pro-Chinese conservatives, the progressive men had been hampered in their action, and the revenues for the promised enterprises and industries had been diverted to warlike preparations, that looked as if Corea, as a vassal, was to help China against France in the Tonquin complication.

The situation in Seoul became alarming. A state of hostility existed between the leaders of the two political parties, one of which had at their call a rabble of rapacious militia, eager to try their new tools upon their hereditary enemies, the Japanese, while the other knew full well the sterling quality of the little body of Japanese infantry. Fifteen hundred Chinese soldiers were still in the camp under General Yuen. In such a situation, the government being in the hands of their rivals and committed to the pro-Chinese policy, the liberals felt that their heads were likely to remain on their shoulders only so long as it pleased their enemies to bring no charge against them. In nations without representative institutions, revolutions and outbreaks must be expected when a change of policy is decided upon.

Let us see how the Corean liberals attempted, when beset and thwarted, to save their own lives and reverse the policy of the government. On October 25, one of the liberal leaders intimated to an American that "for the sake of Corea" about ten of the prominent conservatives "would have to be killed." The idea was to remove their rivals by removing the heads of the same, seize the government, inaugurate new schemes of progress, open new ports, and otherwise commit Corea to the same course as that upon which Japan had entered. They supposed that the treaty powers would condone and approve their action, make further favorable treaties, and loan money for national improvement. Further, they claimed to have had the royal sanction. The autumn passed by and the moment seemed ripe for the plot. China, pressed by France, had withdrawn half her troops from Seoul, and Japan, with a view to strengthening her influence in the peninsula, had a few days before remitted $400,000 of the indemnity exacted for the riot of 1882. The time to strike a blow for Corean independence and to break the shackles of China forever seemed to have come.

On the evening of December 4, the foreign envoys and several high officers of the government were invited to a banquet to celebrate the inauguration of the postal service. When it was nearly over, an alarm of fire was given from the outside, according to arrangement of the conspirators, and Min Yong Ik, going out to look, was set upon by assassins, but instead of being killed as was intended, was only wounded. Thereupon the liberal leaders hastened to the palace, and assuring the king that be was in great danger, in his name sent to the Japanese minister for the Japanese legation guard. At the same time the conservative leaders were summoned, as they supposed by the king; as fast as they stepped out of their sedan chairs at the palace gates, they were relieved of their heads. Meanwhile the Japanese infantry commanded the inner gates of the palace, and during the next day the new ministers of government, the liberals whose names have already become familiar to us, prepared edicts to be issued by the king reforming ancient abuses and customs, and instituting new and radical measures of national policy. The city was in a state of commotion, but despite the surging crowd no actual outbreak occurred.

On the morning of the 6th the cry was raised "death to the Japanese," and then began a wild revelry of outrage, butchery, and incendiarism, in

COREAN NATIVES VIEWING JAPANESE SOLDIERS

which the newly-trained militia were conspicuous. The white foreigners in Seoul, nine in number, of whom three were ladies, had gathered at the American legation, which under Lieutenant Bernadon's directions was put in a state of defense. In it twenty-two Japanese also found refuge.

That afternoon the Chinese troops, six hundred strong, commanded by General Yuen and backed by three thousand Coreans, moved upon the palace to drive out the Japanese. With superb discipline and skill Captain Murakami and his little band drove off their assailants, and through the narrow streets reached the legation at 8:00 P.M. after forty-eight hours' absence. The score of soldiers left behind, aided by the hundred or so of civilians who had gathered within, had successfully defended the enclosure from the mob. Provisions being exhausted, the Japanese with admirable coolness, discipline, and success began the march to the sea on the afternoon of the next day. Despite hostile soldiery with rifles and cannon, armed men firing from roof and wall, barred city gates, and a mob following them to the Han river, they crossed with their wounded and reached Chemulpo on the morning of the 8th. There they were fed by the sailors of the men-of-war, while a Japanese steamer carried the news to Nagasaki.

The short-lived liberal government came to an end after an existence of less than forty-eight hours. Hong Yong Sik, refusing to leave the king, was taken with him to the Chinese camp and there beheaded. The other conspirators fled to Japan, whence they were demanded by the Corean ministerial council, which demand was by the Japanese promptly refused. The torture and trial of twelve persons implicated in the affair was concluded January 27, 1885, and eleven were executed in the usual barbarous manner. Their bodies were chopped in pieces and the flesh and bones distributed in fragments through the streets of the city and the different provinces. The refugees ultimately reached America, except Kim-ok-Kiun who settled in Japan.

Count Inouye of Japan and Kim Hong Chip of Corea on January 9; and Inouye and Li Hung Chang, of China, on May 7 concluded conventions by which the troubles were settled. The chief points in the diplomacy were the payment of indemnity by Corea to Japan, and a joint agreement between China and Japan to withdraw their troops. Both camps were emptied on the 20th, and on the 21st of May the troops left Chemulpo for their respective countries. October 5 the Tai-wen Kun, now sixty-eight years old, but fresh as a man of forty and able as ever to be a disturbing element, returned from China and re-entered Seoul under a guard of Chinese warriors and many thousands of Coreans.

The affair was in its origin an anti-Chinese uprising of radical progressives, but in its ending an anti-Japanese demonstration. About three hundred lives were lost by battle and murder. The conduct of the American minister, General Foote, during this trying occasion, was most admirable, and the legation, which sheltered all the foreigners and many Japanese, was kept open and the American flag was never lowered.

Even in these troublous times a way was opened for the entrance of western science and reformed Christianity. Dr. Henry N. Allen, a missionary physician from Ohio, was called upon to attend Min Yong Ik and the wounded Chinese soldiers. The superiority of modern methods being at once manifest, the government became interested, and the dwelling occupied by Hong Yong Sik, who had been beheaded, was set aside as a hospital under Dr. Allen's charge. From that time forward several missionaries from American churches have entered active work in Corea, and three American young men engaged by the Corean government as teachers have begun to devise an educational system for the kingdom. There are now native Christian churches in Seoul, a hospital, schools, orphanages, and a college. Americans were chosen as advisers and assistants of the nation. Three military officers to organize her army, naval officers to inaugurate a navy, commissioners of customs, and a counsellor in the foreign office were among these.

Renouncing the idea of the suzerainty of China over Corea, the king and government sent embassies to Japan, Europe, and the United States, to establish permanent legations. This movement was opposed by the Chinese, and especially by the Minister Yuen in an active, impudent, and even villainous manner. Yuen, who led the Chinese troops during the riot of December, 1884, and who escorted the Tai-wen Kun to Corea, is believed to have plotted to dethrone the king and set up another son of the old regent as a pro-Chinese partisan on the throne. Expecting to make use of the Corean military, whom he had drilled in person, his plot was exposed by Min Yong Ik. To checkmate any design of China, to prevent the departure of the envoys, or to convert her nominal authority into assertions of sovereignty or suzerainty, the Honorable Hugh N. Densmore, our minister, by the orders of the United States government, invited the embassy to take passage from Chemulpo in the United States Steamship Omaha, which was done. In charge of Dr. H.N. Allen, Pak Chung Yang, a noble of the second rank, envoy extraordinary and minister plenipotentiary of the king of Corea, arrived in Washington and had audience of President Cleveland in January, 1888.

When Kim-ok-Kiun, the leader of the insurrection of 1884, fled to Japan, he was welcomed by the Japanese and received as a protege of the emperor. Repeated demands were made by Corea upon the mikado to surrender him, and the demands were as repeatedly refused. In the spring of 1894 he was lured by means of a dummy draft on a non-existing bank in China, to Shanghai, where on March 28, at the Japanese hotel, and in the absence of his Japanese attendant, he was foully murdered by his pretended friend, Hong Tjyong On, a tool of the Ming faction. This man had been in the employ of the Ming faction of the Corean government with the mission of the assassination entrusted to him, and if the crime was not committed by order of the king of Corea, as was popularly believed, it was surely by order of the queen, who has been strong in her influence. The murderer was arrested; but instead of being tried by the Chinese was handed over to a Corean official, who, with the assassin and the corpse, was sent to Corea. There in spite of the protestations of foreign representatives, the body of Kim was horribly mutilated, parts of it being sent to the different provinces, while the murderer was rewarded with high official honor.

This murder of a Corean by another Corean in a port under Chinese jurisdiction, though coupled with the subsequent brutalities at Seoul, could not be made a subject of diplomatic remonstrance; but it served in Japan to rouse the deepest public indignation and intense disgust. The Japanese government was not only outraged by the assassination of Kim, but by the conduct of Yu, the Corean minister at Tokio. Two brothers named Ken, at the time of Kim's murder, attempted to bring the same fate upon Boku Eiko, Kim's fellow conspirator. Their plot having been discovered, they fled to Yu for protection. For

SINKING OF THE KOW-SHING

three days he refused to give them up, but finally surrendered them and took a hasty and undignified departure from the country. The Japanese foreign office, having in vain sought an explanation of the motives of the king of Corea in connection with Kim's assassination, and of the precipitate and undiplomatic flight of the Corean representative, was glad to seize the first opportunity which arose before long, when other events occurred which gave Japan occasion to act.

For some time past the peninsular kingdom has been in a disturbed condition, owing to the spread of rebellious confederacies among the people. There was now quite a general uprising of Coreans, caused by their want of sympathy with the government, and focussed by their indignation at the horrible fate of Kim. In May, a formidable peasant uprising occurred in northern Corea, caused mainly by the official extortion practiced by tax-gatherers, but having in it elements of remonstrance against the assassination of Kim. The government troops were defeated May 16 at Reisan; and on May 31 Zenshu fell into the hands of the insurgents. Later Chung Jui was captured, and Seoul, the capital, was in a state of great commotion. The discovery of a plot to blow up the government building during the annual official meeting of the king and his ministers caused immense excitement. The plot was confessed by one of the conspirators, and warrants were issued for the arrest of one thousand persons implicated or suspected.

In alarm the government appealed to China for assistance, and early in June an armed Chinese force numbering about two thousand was dispatched, from Chefoo to Asan, a port lying a little southwest of Seoul, where it encamped.

In the treaty of Tien-tsin, both Japan and China agreed to withdraw their troops from the peninsula, neither power to send soldiers thither again, without giving to the other power preliminary notice of the intended action. In the present struggle, Japan has declared from the beginning that she intended to carry her action into Corea no further than the treaty of 1885 allowed, and the necessity for restoring order and stability required her to do. When these troops were sent, the stipulated notification to Japan it is declared, was delayed until after their departure.

Actuated by distrust of Chinese motives, and looking to the protection of her commercial interests and the safety of the Japanese residents and traders in Cores, the authorities at Tokio quickly followed by landing a force of six thousand troops on the western coast. A strong force was soon stationed in Seoul, for the protection of the Japanese legation, and the approaches to the capital were securely occupied.

Then began the diplomatic campaign, Japan seizing the opportunity

MR. OTORI BEFORE THE COMMISSIONERS

offered to insist on a final understanding with both China and the Corean government, regarding the matters whir had long been the source of friction, and a constant menace to tranquility in the peninsula. On June 28 a communication passed between Mr. Otori, the Japanese minister, and the Corean foreign office, regarding the tributary relations between Corea and China. To this the Corean government returned an evasive reply. July 8, Mr. Otori laid before the Corean government in a courteously worded note, the draft of a scheme of reforms which Japan proposed, as a remedy for the disorders of the country, under the following five general heads:

1. The civil government in the capital and in the provinces to be thoroughly reformed, and the departments arranged on a new basis under proper responsible heads.

2. The resources of the country to be developed, mines opened, railways constructed, etc.

3. The laws of the country to be radically reformed.

4. The military establishments to be reorganized under competent instructors, so as to render the country secure alike from internal disorder and external attack.

5. Education to be thoroughly reformed on modern lines.

Mr. Otori asked for the appointment of a commission to discuss details, and on July 10, unfolded before the three commissioners, in twenty-five proposals, the details of the contemplated reforms. They were of such a character as to weaken greatly the influence of the queen and the dominant Ming party. Personages of too great influence were to be removed; the foreign customs establishment to be abolished; all foreign advisers to be dispensed with; the resources of the country to be developed; railways, telegraphs and a mint to be established; the legal and judicial systems to be radically reformed, and a school system to be adopted, beginning with primary schools and culminating in universities, with provisions for sending pupils abroad.

These reforms were declared to be as essential to the true welfare of Corea and China, as to the interests of Japan. It being impossible, however, for the Coreans to effect them themselves, Japan proposed joint action on the part of herself and China with a view to the desired object. This proposal however. China curtly refused even to discuss, so long as any Japanese troops remained in Corea. She assured Japan that the peasant rebellion had been quieted, which was true in a sense, for the insurgents, after the landing of the Chinese regulars, had temporarily stayed their onward progress; but the cause of the trouble still remained. From the moment of this deadlock we may date the unofficial beginning of the war. The formal declaration was not made until about two weeks later.

JAPANESE ARMY ON THE MARCH

THE BEGINNINGS OF HOSTILITIES

Japan Decides to Reform Corea without China's Aid—Corean Palace Guards Fire on the Japanese Escort of Minister Otori—Momentous Result of the Skirmish—Announcement of Corean Independence—Tai-wen Kun as Prime Minister—The First Collision at Sea—Sinking of the Kow-shing—Fighting Around Asan—Defeat of the Chinese—Li Hung Chang Declares that the War will be Fought to the Bitter end—Japan's Formal Declaration of War—China's Response—The Conflict Begun.

Failing to secure China's co-operation, Mr. Otori told the officials at Seoul that the government was now determined of her own accord to see the needed reforms carried out. The Corean government still showing no disposition to acquiesce in his proposals, the Japanese minister determined to have a personal interview with the king, of whose sympathy with the policy of the Ming party, there was some doubt. The minister had regarded the reply of the Corean government to his demands as insolent, and knowing that its substance had been made known to the Corean officers, he felt an apprehension 'of violence toward himself and the members of the legation. He therefore insisted on being accompanied by a strong escort of Japanese on the occasion of any further visits to the palace.

On the morning of July 23, attended by this escort of Japanese guards, and accompanied by the father of the king, Mr. Otori set out from the legation for the purpose of having another interview with the Corean monarch. As the minister with his fully armed escort approached the palace, they were fired upon by troops in the service of the Ming ministry, some of whom were stationed within the palace walls. The fire was promptly returned by the Japanese, and a sharp skirmish ensued which lasted twenty minutes. One Japanese cavalryman and two footsoldiers were wounded; while the Corean loss was seventeen killed and seventy wounded. When quiet was restored, the Japanese were in possession of the palace. The result of the fight was momentous-the complete overthrow of the Ming, or pro-Chinese faction in the Corean government.

On the same day the Corean king formally announced his independence of China. One of his first acts was to request an interview with Mr. Otori, and before the interview had ended that day the Japanese ministers saw the Tai-wen Kun, father of the king, and formerly regent during the latter's minority, formally installed as prime minister and instructed to introduce administrative reforms such as Japan had proposed. A written pledge was signed by the king, guaranteeing that the remedying of social and political abuses should begin as soon as the proper machinery could be put in operation; the old counsellors of the king were replaced by men believed to be in sympathy with progressive principles. Japan on her part made herself responsible for the execution of these pledges. The part taken by the king in the reforms is somewhat uncertain. One of the most eminent authorities on Corean affairs has declared that the king himself cannot be looked upon as a potent factor in the struggle; that he is a weak, amiable, nervous man, whose only importance consists in the fact that he is a king and in the sanction that his presence, and authority, and seal may be considered to lend to the party with which he sides. He has not been on good terms with his father, and when the Japanese placed the latter in charge there was considerable uncertainty as to the results that would follow.

The same day that this skirmish at the palace occurred between Corean and Japanese troops, a report mas sent out which might have involved Great Britain in the eastern war. It mas alleged that ill-treatment had been offered by the Japanese troops to the British consul-general at Seoul, Mr. Gardner and his wife. The assertion was that the Japanese troops forbade their passing the line of sentries which had been drawn around an encampment, and that unnecessary force had been used to accomplish this. The falsity of the charges, or the fact that they were very much overdrawn, was proved upon the first investigation, no regulations being in force except those natural and proper in such times.

The situation in Corea developed very slowly. The ways of the east are not as the ways of the west, and one of the most deeply-rooted and highly-prized instincts which oriental diplomatists have inherited from a long line of their ancestors is a profound belief in the merits of procrastination.

The first important collision at sea occurred in Prince Jerome gulf, about forty miles off Chemulpo, on July 25, one week before the formal declaration of war. Up to the night of July 19, the highest authorities at Tien-tsin did not anticipate war, but as a matter of watchful policy the war-office chartered the British steamers Irene, Fei Ching, and Kow-shiug, belonging to the Indo-Chinese Steam Navigation company, and a number of Chinese merchant steamers, for the transportation of troops. The object was to transport the second division from Taku to Asan, to reinforce the Chinese army in that Corean city. The Irene was the first to leave Taku,

PROCESSION IN SEOUL

July 21, with one thousand one hundred and fifty troops, with one of the owners and his wife on board; the other two vessels were to leave on the 22nd and 23rd.

The Kow-shing was an iron vessel, schooner-rigged, of one thousand three hundred and fifty tons, built at Barrow and belonging to the port of London. She sailed from Taku July 23, with no cargo, but with one thousand two hundred Chinese troops on board. All went well with the transport until the second morning, July 25, when about nine o'clock the vessel was sighted by a Japanese man-of-war, the Naniwa Kan. The Naniwa was accompanied by two other men-of-war, one of which was the Matsusima, on board of which was the Japanese admiral. The Kow-shing was ordered by signal, "Stop where you are or take the consequences." She promptly anchored. Then the Naniwa steamed up and sent a boarding party to the Kow-shing.

The officers in command made a strict scrutiny of the ship's papers, and after some hesitation as to his course of action, peremptorily ordered the Kow-shing to follow. This caused great excitement amongst the troops, who said to the English officers of the ship, "We refuse to become prisoners and would rather die here. If you move the ship, except to return to China, we will kill you." The Japanese having returned to their own vessel, the European officers on the Kow-shing argued with the Chinese to convince them that it would be wiser to surrender, thus saving the life of all and the ship itself. These arguments had no effect on the Chinese, and the Kow-shing then signalled to the Naniwa to send another boat.

Captain Von Hannecken explained the situation to the Japanese boarding officer, pointing out that there had been no declaration of war, that the Kow-shing was a British ship under the British flag, and that owing to the position taken by the Chinese it was physically impossible for the officers of the vessels to obey the Naniwa's order. He claimed that the flag should be respected, and that the ship should be escorted back to the Chinese coast. The boarding party then returned to the Naniwa, which thereupon signalled "Quit the ship as soon as possible." The Kow-shing officers replied that it was impossible to quit the ship, owing to the threats of the Chinese. The Naniwa threw an answering pennant, and steamed quickly into position, broadside on, at a distance of about two hundred yards. Mr. Tamplin, the chief officer of the Kow-shing, tells a graphic story of the scene that followed."

"The Chinese were greatly excited, and kept drawing their fingers across their throats in order to show us what we might expect. The British officers, and Captain Von Hannecken, were anxiously gathered on the bridge, and the bodyguards were at the bottom of the ladder watching us like cats. Two executioners fully armed were told off to follow the captain and myself, and

AFTER THE BATTLE
From a Sketch by Japanese Artist

they clogged us everywhere with drawn scepters. About one o'clock the Naniwa opened fire, first discharging a torpedo at the Kow-shing, which did not strike her. The man-of-war then fired a broadside of five heavy guns, and continued firing both heavy and machine guns from deck and tops until the Kow-shing sank about an hour later. The Kow-shing was first struck right amidships, and the sound of the crashing and splintering was almost deafening. To add to the danger, the Chinese rushed to the other side, causing the ship to heel over more than ever. As soon as the Kow-shing was struck the soldiers made a rush. I rushed from the bridge, got a life-belt, and jumped overboard forward. While in the wheel house selecting a life-belt I passed another European, but I had no time to see who it was. It was a regular *sauve qui peut*. Mr. Wake, our third officer, said it was no use for him to take to the water, as he could not swim, and he went down with the ship.

"After jumping into the water I came foul of the chain, down which the Chinese were swarming. As I came to the surface the boiler exploded with terrific noise. I looked up and saw Captain Von Hannecken striking out vigorously. Captain Galsworthy, the master of the vessel, was also close by, his face perfectly black from the explosion. All of us went in the direction of the island of Shotai-ul, which was about a mile and a half to the northeast, swimming through the swarm of dead and dying Chinamen. Bullets began to strike the water on every side, and turning to see whence they came, I saw that the Chinese herding around the only part of the Kow-shing that was then out of water, were firing at us. I was slightly hit on the shoulder, and in order to protect my head covered it with the life-belt until I got clear of the sinking vessel. When I succeeded in doing this, and got away from the swarms of Chinamen, I swam straight for the Naniwa. I had been in the water nearly an hour when I was picked up by one of the Naniwa's boats. While in the water I passed two Chinese warriors clinging to a sheep which was swimming vigorously. As soon as I was on board the Naniwa's boat, I told the officer in which direction the captain had gone, and he said that he had already sent another boat to pick him up. By this time only the Kow-shing's masts were visible. The water was however covered with Chinese, and there were two lifeboats from the Kow-shing crowded with soldiers. The Japanese officer informed me that he had been ordered by signal from the Naniwa to sink these boats. I remonstrated, but he fired two volleys from the cutter, turned back, and steamed for the Naniwa. No attempt was made to rescue the Chinese. The Naniwa steamed about until eight o'clock in the evening, but did not pick up any other Europeans."

The Irene, which had been the first vessel to leave Taku, herself had a narrow escape from an attack. She sighted a war vessel at eleven o'clock on the night of July 23, but by at once putting out all her lights was enabled to escape, and reached Asan early the next morning. The Chinese cruisers Chih Yuen and Kwang Kai, and the training ship Wei Yuen were at anchor. The troops were at once disembarked, and about nine o'clock the same morning the Irene left for Chefoo, arriving at four o'clock the afternoon of the 25th. Being under orders to proceed to Chemulpo to bring back refugees, she sailed at noon the next day in company with the British ship Archer. When some distance from Chefoo, the Irene was hailed by the Fei Ching, and informed that the troop ship Kow-shing had been sunk by Japanese war vessels. It was decided to take the Irene into Wei-hai-wei and confer with Admiral Ting as to the advisability of her going to Chemulpo; he advised her return to Chefoo.

The same morning, July 26, the cruiser Chih Yuen arrived at Wei-hai-wei from Asan, and reported that shortly after leaving that port, the new Japanese cruiser Yoshino fired on her and her consort, the Kwang Kai, unexpectedly, and a shell, piercing the bow turret, exploded, killing the entire crew serving one gun, and disabling the turret. As soon as the Chih Yuen got a little sea-room, her steering-gear having been disabled, she maneuvered and fought with her stern gun, one shell from which swept away the entire bridge of her opponent. A second shell striking the same place, the Japanese ceased firing and hoisted a white flag over a Chinese ensign, but Captain Hong, of the Chih Yuen, having his bow guns and his steering gear disabled, and other Japanese coming up, decided to make for Wei-hai-wei and report to the admiral. The first lieutenant of the Chih Yuen was speaking through the tube, directing the men, when a shot struck him and he fell dead. Twelve of the crew were killed and thirty wounded. The Japanese vessel suffering somewhat less.

The Kow-shing affair caused a complete change in the attitude of the Chinese government and in the foreign mind. The viceroy, Li Hung Chang, declared in an interview that if war was once provoked, China would fight to the bitter end. Japan was attacked in the European press for having sent a British ship to the bottom, even though it were loaded with Chinese soldiers, inasmuch as war had not been declared. The Japanese government at once instructed the minister in London to apologize to Great Britain for firing on the British flag, which was floating over the Kow-shing, and it was talked in every quarter that a heavy indemnity would be required from Japan. As further details became known, however, European and American sentiment began to shift. A British consular court of inquiry called to investigate the matter, decided that inasmuch as the two nations were virtually in a state of war at the time, though no formal declaration had been made, the Japanese commander was justified in his action on the ground that the Kow-shing was violating neutrality. The demand for an indemnity was practically abandoned on account of a clause contained in the ship's charter to the effect that in the event of an outbreak of hostilities between China and Japan, the Kow-shing should be considered Chinese property. The case was therefore ended, so far as the action of nations outside of China and Japan was concerned. Less than two hundred were saved, out of nearly twelve hundred souls who were on board the vessel. French, German, and Italian gunboats which were cruising near, brought to Chefoo the few Chinese survivors, and several of the European officers were saved by the Japanese. Captain Von Hannecken was rescued by a fisherman's boat, and made his way back to China.

Immediately following the date of these sea battles, hard fighting began at and around Asan, where the body of Chinese troops was intrenched. Early on the morning of July 29 the Chinese troops, who had left their fortifications at Asan, were attacked by General Oshima, the commander of Japanese armies in Corea, at Seikwan. The Japanese gained a decisive victory. After a hard fought battle in which one hundred Chinese were killed and five hundred wounded, out of twenty-eight hundred troops engaged, while the Japanese lost less than one hundred, the Chinese were forced back towards Asan, their entrenchment at Chan Hon having been captured. During the night the Chinese evacuated Asan, abandoning large quantities of ammunition and some guns, and fled in the direction of Koshu. When the Japanese reached Asan early in the morning of the 30th they found the trenches deserted. Many flags, four cannon, and a quantity of other munitions of war were captured, and the victorious troops took possession of the enemy's headquarters.

Elated by the results of the actions which had occurred, Japan was now hurrying troops into the field. Thousands of soldiers were shipped in transports and stationed in Chemulpo, in Seoul, along the Great Northern road in Fusan, and finally around Asan, sixty miles south of Chemulpo, out of which the Chinese had just been driven. Three attempts at mediation had been made with a desire to avert war by diplomatic interference, first by Russia, then by England, and lastly by England supported by all the powers, but Japan was ready and anxious to prove her prowess over her ancient enemy, and to show to western nations the strength that she had acquired; while there were ample and strong reasons which appeared to the Japanese worthy ones why they should wage war upon China. They asserted that the best interests of civilization and humanity demanded this action and the time had come to begin. Belligerent acts had multiplied and formal action became necessary, without further delay. August 3 was the important date which marked the formal beginning of warlike operations.

The announcements to the world that an oriental war was actually to be waged, were in every way characteristic of the people and the habits of the two belligerent nations. Each one took pains to declare its power and the age of the reigning dynasty. Japan however took its greatest pride, very evidently, in the advance of its civilization, and the introduction of western methods in diplomacy as well as elsewhere. China, on the other hand, was more verbose, and at the same time very scornful of the fighting strength of the ancient rival. Each of course took pains to justify her own actions and cast all the odium of the war on the other.

THE ATTACK ON PING-YANG

(Japanese Entering at the Gate of the Taiong River Bridge)

Japan's formal declaration of war appeared in the "Official Gazette," and in substance was as follows:

"We, by the grace of heaven, Emperor of Japan, seated on a throne occupied by the same dynasty from time immemorial, do hereby make proclamation to all our loyal and brave subjects as follows: We hereby declare war against China, and we command each and all of our competent authorities, in obedience to our wish, and with a view to the attainment of the national aim, to carry on hostilities by sea and land against China, with all the means at their disposal, consistently with the law of nations.

Over twenty years have now elapsed since our accession to the throne. During this time we have consistently pursued a policy of peace, being deeply impressed with a sense of the undesirability of being in strained relations with other nations, and have always directed our officials diligently to endeavor to promote friendship with all the treaty powers. Fortunately our intercourse with the nations has continued to increase in intimacy.

"We were therefore unprepared for such a conspicuous want of amity and of good faith, as has been manifested by China in her conduct towards this country in connection with the Corean affairs. Corea is an independent state. She mas first introduced into the family of nations by the advice and under the guidance of Japan. It has however, been China's habit to designate Corea as her dependency, and both openly and secretly to interfere with her domestic affairs. At the time of the recent civil insurrection in Corea, China dispatched troops thither, alleging that her purpose was to afford succor to her dependant state. We, in virtue of the treaty concluded with Corea in 1882, and looking to possible emergencies, caused a military force to be sent to that country, wishing to procure for Corea freedom from the calamity of perpetual disturbance, and thereby to maintain the peace of the east in general. Japan invited China's co-operation for the accomplishment of that object; but China, advancing various pretexts, declined Japan's proposal.

"Thereupon Japan advised Corea to reform her administration, so that order might be preserved at home, and so that the country might be able to discharge the responsibilities and duties of an independent state abroad. Corea has already consented undertake the task, but China has insidiously endeavored to circumvent and thwart Japan's purpose. She has further procrastinated and endeavored to make warlike preparations, both on land and at sea. When these preparations were completed, she not only sent large re-enforcements to Corea with a view to the attainment of her ambitions designs, but even carried her arbitrariness and insolence to the extent of opening fire upon our ships in Corean waters.

"China's plain object is to make it uncertain where the responsibility resides for preserving peace and order in Corea, and not only to weaken the position of that state in the family of nations a position obtained for Corea through Japanese efforts-but also to obscure the significance of the treaties recognizing and confirming that position. Such conduct on the part of China is not only a direct injury to the rights and interests of this empire, but also a menace to the permanent peace and tranquility of the Orient. Judging from her action, it must be concluded that China from the beginning has been bent upon sacrificing peace to the attainment of her sinister objects. In this situation, ardent as our wish is to promote the prestige of the country abroad by strictly peaceful methods, we find it impossible to avoid a formal declaration of war against China. It is our earnest wish that by the loyalty and valor of our faithful subjects, peace may soon, be permanently restored, slid the glory of the empire be augmented and completed."

China promptly accepted the issue thus formally raised, and published a declaration in substance as follows:

"Corea has been our tributary for the last two hundred odd years. She has given us tribute all of this time, which is a matter known to the world. For the last dozen years or so Corea has been troubled by repeated insurrections; and we in sympathy with our small tributary have as repeatedly sent succor to her aid, eventually lacing a resident in her capital to protect Corea's interests. In the fourth moon (May) of this year, another rebellion was begun in Corea, and the king repeatedly asked again for aid from us to put down the rebellion. We then ordered Li Hung Chang to send troops to Corean, and they having barely reached Asan, the rebels immediately scattered, but the Wojen (the ancient epithet for the Japanese expressive of contemp translated 'pigmies' or more strictly according to usage 'vermin'), without any cause whatever sent their troops to Corea and entered Seoul, the capital of Corea, re-enforcing them constantly until they have exceeded ten thousand men.

"In the meantime the Japanese forced the Corean king to change his system of government, showing a disposition in every way of bullying Coreans. It was found a difficult matter to reason with the 'Wojen'. Although we have been in the habit of assisting our tributaries, we have never interfered with their internal government. Japan's treaty with Corea was as one country with another. There is no law for sending large armies to bully a country in this way and to tell it to change its system of government. Various powers are united in condemning the conduct of the Japanese, and can give no reasonable name to the army she now has in Corea. Nor has Japan been amenable to reason, nor will she listen to an exhortation to withdraw her troops and confer amicably upon what should be done in Corea. On the contrary, Japan has shown herself belligerent without regard to appearances, and has been increasing her forces there. Her conduct alarmed the people of Corea as well as our merchants there, and so we sent more troops over to protect them. Judge of our surprise then, when half way to Corea a number of the ' Wojen ' ships suddenly appeared, and taking advantage of our unpreparedness opened fire on our transports at a spot on the sea coast near Asan, and damaged them, thus causing us to suffer from their treacherous conduct which could not be foretold by us.

"As Japan has violated the treaties and not observed the international laws, and is now running rampant with her false and treacherous actions, beginning hostilities herself, and laying herself open to condemnation by the various powers at large, we, therefore, desire to make it known to the world that we have always followed the paths of philanthropy and perfect justice throughout the whole complications, while the 'Wojen' and others have broken all the laws of nations and treaties which it passed our patience to bear with. Hence we command Li Hung Chang to give strict orders to our various armies to hasten with all speed to root the Wojen 'out of their lairs. He is to send successive armies of valiant men to Corea, in order to have the Coreans freed from bondage. We also command Manchoo generals, viceroys, and governors of the maritime provinces, as well as the commanders in chief of the various armies to prepare for war and to make every effort to fire on the 'Wojen' ships if they come into our ports, and utterly destroy them. We exhort our generals to refrain from the least laxity in obeying our commands, in other to avoid severe punishment at our hands. Let all know this edict as if addressed to themselves individually.

Immediately following China's declaration of war, the Chinese Imperial Foreign Office addressed an important circular letter to the ministers of the various Europeat countries, and of the United States, to be forwarded to their respective governments. The message began abruptly with the announcement that some time ago a rebellion broke out in the district of Cliurig in Corea, and the king of that country sent a written application for Chinese assistance through Li Hung Chang, Viceroy of the North.

"Our Imperial Majesty," the message continued, considering that on previous occasions rebellion in Corea had been suppressed by our assistance, dispatched troops, which did not however enter Seoul, but went direct to the scene, with n view to exterminating the rebellion. At the first rumor of their approach the rebels dispersed, and our army, having brought merciful relief to the distressed people, meditated a victorious 'retirement. To our astonishment Japan also dispatched troops to Corea, pretending that it was for the purpose of assisting to quell the rebellion, but their real object being to occupy Seoul, which they did, posting themselves at all the important passes. They continued to re-enforce themselves, until the number of their troops rose to upwards of ten thousand, when they demanded that Corea should repudiate her allegiance to China, and declare herself dependent. Japan further drew up many rilles and regulations for or the alteration of the Corean government, which they required the king to conform to in every detail. That Corea has been a dependency of China from time immemorial is known to dl the world, and therefore when your different

OPENING THE GATES AT PING-YANG
Japanese Drawing

respective governments established treaties with that nation, such treaties were approved and recorded by ourselves. For Japan to ignore this in so high handed a manner, is an offense against the dignity and authority of China, and a grave breach of the pre-existing harmonious relations."

The message comments upon the doubtful right of any country to interfere with the internal administration of the affairs of the neighboring states, and adds that while friendly counsel and exhortation may sometimes be permissible, the enforcement of suggestions of reform by direct and strenuous coercion and armed invasion cannot be tolerated. It is impossible, the message declares, for China to submit to such ignominious treatment, which would be equally intolerable to any of the respective governments to which the message is addressed. Reference is next made to the efforts of the British and Russian governments through their representatives to induce Japan to withdraw her forces from Seoul, thus making possible the peaceful negotiation of Corean affairs.

"This," says the circular, "was an extremely fair and just proposal, but Japan stubbornly refused to take it into consideration, and on the contrary strengthened her forces to such an extent that the people of Corea and resident Chinese merchants there became daily more alarmed and disturbed. China, out of consideration for the commendable efforts of the different governments to effect a peaceful solution of the Corean question, rigidly abstained from any act of bloodshed, which would have led to great suffering and serious injury to commerce, and through it became necessary to send further forces for the protection of the country, we placed them at a careful distance from Seoul, studiously avoiding a collision with the Japanese troops, which mould have occasioned the commencement hostilities. Notwithstanding all this, and by a most unexpected and treacherous scheme, the Japanese on July 25, collected a number of their war vessels outside the port of Asan, and began hostilities by firing on our transports and attacking and sinking the British steamer Kow-Shing, flying the English flag. Thus, therefore, the commencement of the war on their part was beyond all justification, and China, having done her utmost hitherto to preserve the good fellowship of nations, can carry forbearance no further, but feels constrained to adopt different counsels and to take effectual measures for the management of affairs.

"We anticipate," says the message in conclusion, "that the various governments of the world will hear of these extraordinary proceedings with wonder and surprise, but they will know where to lay the entire blame attaching to them. This full statement of the circumstances tinder which Japan has iniquitously and unlawfully commenced war, is presented to your excellency for communication to your respected government for its inspection.

"The two great nations of the orient were now at war, one with forty millions of inhabitants, the other with four hundred millions, fighting on the soil of their helpless neighbor, a nation which was to act as little more than a buffer for the shock of war from either ride to strike.

Preparations for War in the two Nations—Activity to Provide Defense for Southern China—Chinese Arsenals—War Spirit Among the Japanese—Armies of China, Their Organization and Administration—Burdens upon Li Hung Chang—Manner of Campaign followed by Chinese Armies—Seeking a Commander for the Chinese Troops in Corea—Complications with European and American Interest—Trade Relation—The Chung king Affair—Arrest of Japanese Students in Shanghai—Efforts of American Representatives to Save their Lives—Delivered to the Chinese by Order from Washington—Tortured to Death—Operations in Corea—The Masterly Retreat from Asan—Engagements in the North—The Lines of the Japanese Drawing Around Ping-Yang.

As soon as the formal declaration of war was made public in the rival nations, the preparations for aggression and defense which had been in progress in China for a few weeks, and in Japan for several months, began to be multiplied with unceasing activity. The conditions which existed in the two nations were very different, and required different treatment.

Immediately following the outbreak of hostilities, the viceroy at Canton, Li Han Chang, brother of Li Hung Chang, began to make great efforts to put the southern part of the empire in something like an efficient state of defense. The first definite word of warning that reached him, through an official channel, was a cipher telegram from Peking informing him of the sinking of the Kowshing and the other engagements on sea and land, immediately prior to July 30. Li Han Chang was mainly responsible for the series of indignities which led to the resignation of the last British officers remaining in the Chinese naval service in 1891, so that China's defeat at sea was to a certain extent his fault. For this reason he was placed in a position to be peculiarly anxious to make a good showing now. It was incumbent upon him to send forces to Formosa, the favorite point of attack in every important war that has been waged against China, and also to guard practically the whole southern coast, of which Canton with the naval station and arsenal at Whainpoa, forms the principal point.

In times of peace the defenses of Canton consist of the southern

squadron, the river forts, and the Manchoo or Tartar garrison, supposed
to number four thousand, but really of very indefinite strength. The
sqadron at this time, however, was in the north, except about a dozen river
gunboats, belonging to the navy and various revenue offices. The forts were
in fairly satisfactory state, although insufficiently supplied for war, and the
army sought recruits' to increase its numbers as rapidly as possible. The
investigation of the Whampoa arsenal, however, was highly unsatisfactory
as to its results. When orders were given to the various arsenals to get to
work building ships and making guns, the Shanghai and Nanking stations
were found in readiness, and the Foochow arsenal, the largest and only
one that had ever done any shipbuilding on a serious scale, was also in
reasonably good condition. But Whampoa arsenal was in a lamentable
state of unfitness, and all that remained of it was its naval training college,
torpedo depot, and warehouse for guns and ammunition. The responsible
officials whose negligence and dishonesty had resulted in this unfortunate
condition, had good cause to anticipate severe punishment.

In the north of China, where the administration had been more closely
under the eye of Li Hung Chang, things were in somewhat better condition,
although still not what they ought to be to meet a great war.

The Japanese nation at the same moment presented a rare spectacle. To
a man, ay, to a woman, the whole people were for war to the knife. They
scarcely knew, nor did they greatly care, for what, but having been without
the luxury of a serious foreign war for two hundred or three hundred years,
their military and patriotic spirits were raised over the invasion of Corea
and the prospective conflict with China. Never was a stronger antithesis
than that between Japanese and Chinese at the beginning of this conflict.
It was the perfection of order and of precision against slovenliness and
carelessness; the pitting of a trained athlete against a corpulent brewer who
hated fighting. China has in her history had good soldiers, but her system
does not produce nor encourage them. Despised by the literary class,
which has been in absolute control of everything, the soldier, having little
chance of fame, and feeling himself as belonging to a degraded class, has

taken naturally to pillage. If he has hoped to succeed to honors, it has been as likely to be by corrupt interest as by meritorious service, for the Chinese have had no appreciation of military excellence. Of course an army, however numerous, composed of such unkindly material, is but a mob, and if the Chinese had the spirit of soldiers they lacked the arms, for in a service built up on corruption it was natural to expect that the funds allotted for equipment would find other destinations.

After the war broke out, immense efforts were made by Japan ill mobilizing troops and transporting them across the straits to Corea. The reserve was called out, and from every house and every shop some one was drafted to serve with the colors. So perfect, however, was the machine, that all this was accomplished without the least visible disturbance to the internal business of the country, and with such secrecy that it was only through reports of trains full of troops passing at night, and occasional train loads of war material, that any inkling was obtained of what was going on. The embarkation was kept equally secret, even when whole fleets of transports were engaged.

One was constrained more and more to admire the organization of the Japanese, and the perfect order which everywhere prevailed. In a country so strictly policed, the police need never be called on to quell a disturbance, and the force itself constituted another military reserve, drilled and disciplined for any service. So complete was their network of armed watchmen, that a sparrow could hardly cross the road without its name and destination being recorded in the archives of the prefecture. Everything about every individual, whether foreign or native, was known to this intelligent government. Every foreigner's house was frequented by spies, in the guise of peddlers or servants, who reported minutely to their official employers. It was the same abroad. Japanese spies had examined every Chinese ship and fort, had measured the fighting power of every Chinese regiment. Japan knew the rottenness of Chinese naval and military administration better perhaps than the Chinese themselves. Japan was, in short, one great intelligence department, and it began to prove in a most unexpected way that "knowledge is power."

Coming fresh from Japan to Tientsin, the port of Peking,

whence the direction of the war was to be carried on, one would be astounded at the aspect of China. The Celestial Empire in war times contrasted so completely with its hostile neighbor that one might imagine oneself in another planet. The silent, stolid action of the one country and the confused bustle of the other were the strongly evident contrasts. Coming from war ministries, marine ministries, finance ministries, an executive as elaborate and perfect as the machinery of a gun factory, every individual knowing and doing his duty without hurry and without friction, into China where there were none of these things at all, one would be puzzled to conceive how any war could be carried on between these countries except one of ultimate subjugation. China was in a sense full of troops, mostly disbanded without pay, but in such loose fashion as to enable them even to carry off the honors of war, in the shape of their rifles and accoutrements. Some of these had sought and found an honest living, but many had gone to swell the ranks of brigandage. The troops in active service belonged to the great system of sham in which China revelled. The levies on paper and on pay rolls bore no direct correspondence with either the men or the arms. Neither the army nor the navy was a fighting service, but a means of living; and while generals, colonels and captains practically absorbed the naval and military expenditure, the custom of the country permitted the ranks to be robbed and starved, while those officials grew rich.

Vast as mere the numbers of the fighting men of China on paper, they were but a very small proportion to the huge population of that empire. The old Chinese army in its three divisions of Manchoo, Mongol, and native Chinese did not exceed the nominal strength of one million, and all the efforts of military reformers have been devoted to increasing the efficiency and not the size of that force. The Green flag or Luh-ying corps, still represented the bulk of the army, furnishing on paper a total of six hundred and fifty thousand men scattered through the nineteen provinces, excluding the new province of Manchooria. It has been controlled by the local viceroys and governors who may in some instances have attempted to improve its efficiency, but as a general rule the force has had little or no military value.

When the Tai-Ping rebellion was finally crushed, the Ever Victorious army was disbanded", and the Viceroy Li Hung Chang, took into his pay a considerable number of these disciplined and experienced soldiers who had taken their part in a succession of remarkable achievements. When he was transferred to Pechili he took with him these men as a sort of personal bodyguard, and with the avowed intention of organizing an army that would bear comparison with European troops. He was engaged on this task for nearly twenty-five years. At the commencement this force numbered about eighteen thousand men. In 1872 the viceroy took into his service several German officers, who devoted themselves with untiring energy to the conversion of what was not unpromising material into a regular army of the highest standard. The training of this force was carried on with the greatest possible secrecy, and no European officers except those serving with it had any opportunity of forming an opinion. But it was known at the beginning of the war that the Black Flag army, as it was called, numbered about fifty thousand men.

After Li Hung Chang's army, and scarcely inferior to it in strength and importance, came the two branches of the old Tartar army, both of which were recently subjected to some military training, and more or less equipped with modern weapons. These were the old Banner army, and the army of Manchooria, the total strength of the former being some three hundred thousand. Up to a comparatively recent time nothing had been done to make this force efficient. Many of the troops were armed with nothing but bows and arrows, and a kind of iron flail. In the last fifteen years, however, part of the Banner army, called the Peking Field force, was organized by the late Prince Chun, father of the reigning emperor and raised to a fair degree of efficiency. The second Tartar force, the army of Manchooria, contained some eighty thousand men who had received training and approximately modern weapons. Out of these, thirty thousand men, all armed with rifles, have made their headquarters at Mukden, the old capital of the Manchoos.

The Japanese reproached the Chinese with having no commissariat. Neither had they telegraphs, ambulance, or hospital services. Their habit was to live on the country in which they happened to be, and make it a desert. The Corean campaign was expected to form no exception to this rule, and the plains in the northwest, in the region first occupied by the Chinese after the abandonment of Asan, were early deserted by their inhabitants, Yet there were exceptions to this method of procedure. The force that was sent under General Yeh to Asan to quell the insurrection there, treated the natives with kindness and were consequently much liked. The general had funds entrusted to him, to distribute among the poor people who were suffering from want, and miraculous to say he did not steal the money, but spent all, and even, it is said, some of his own, in benevolence to the Coreans.

At the opening of the war the functions of a war ministry, marine ministry, finance ministry, with their staff of experts, were in China discharged by one old man, without any staff, who had stood for thirty years between the living and the dead. The emperor issued edicts without providing the means of carrying them out; all the rest, whether in gross or in detail, devolved on Li Hung Chang, who like another Atlas was bearing the whole rotten fabric of Chinese administration on his shoulders.

The supreme command of the Corean expeditions was first offered to Liu Ming-Chuan, who defended Formosa in 1884, but that astute old soldier declined on the ostensible ground of age and defective sight, but really because, as he said, peace would be made before he could reach Tein-tsin. The command was next offered to Liu Kin-tang, the real conqueror of Kashgar, for which the Governor-General Tso obtained the credit. He also declined, but was overruled by the emperor, and started from his home in the interior. His journey in the height of the summer heat was too much to endure, and he died in his boat before reaching the coast. The command was then entrusted to a civilian, Wu Ta-cheng, who distinguished himself in closing a great breach on the Yellow River some years ago, and who has lately been governor of Hu-nan. This promising official was therefore chosen to go to Corea as imperial commissioner to command the generals, no one of whom had been in authority over another.

It was natural to expect that complications would arise between the belligerent nations and the European and American nations having commercial interests in the orient. Japan and

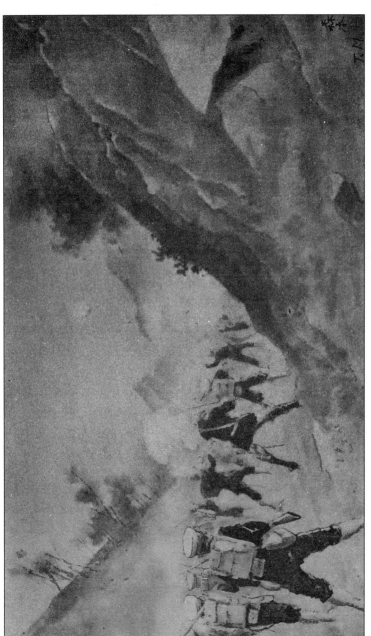

FIGHTING AT FOO CHOW
Japanese Drawing

China had not been long enough acquainted with the rules of international comity and international war to be familiar with the exactions that would be made by the other nations which might be affected. The diplomatic representatives from the west lost no time in stipulating the neutrality of the more important treaty ports where foreigners were settled, and in arranging that certain branches of commerce should not be interfered with. Trade, however, was seriously affected and the price of coal doubled at one leap. China prohibited the export of rice from its own ports whence large quantities are usually shipped to Japan. Chinese lighthouses were darkened, and pilots were specifically warned not to assist Japanese vessels.

The term contrabrand was found to apply to many articles the transport of which in time of peace gave employment to many steamers, mainly coal, rice, and materials for building and repairing ships. The British government published a declaration that rice would not be recognized as contrabrand, and the prices of grain and rates for freight and insurance ruled high. The whole trade was, therefore, dislocated, for the Yang-tsze is the chief granary for the far east.

The British steamer Chungking suffered an aggression from the Chinese that drew upon them a severe rebuke and punishment. The vessel was at anchor in the harbor of Tongku, and among its passengers were sixty Japanese, many of them women and children, who were leaving China to return to Japan for safety during the impending troubles. While the vessel lay in the harbor a large number of Chinese soldiers forced their way on board with hostile intent. They began chasing the Japanese with threats of punishment, and the women and children fled to hide themselves. Many were found and were dragged from their places of concealment with violence. When they were found, their feet were tightly fastened together and their hands were tied behind their backs. They were then thrown upon the wharf, where they lay helpless, and several of them fainted under the severe treatment. As soon as the report of the outrage reached the superior officer commanding the district, he commanded the release of the victims, and the ship moved on to Shanghai where it arrived August 7. Viceroy Li Hung Chang tendered a most humble apology to the British consul for the aggression, the soldiers who committed the outrage were severely punished, and the officers who were responsible for it were degraded and sent into the interior.

The Japanese who were living in various Chinese treaty ports, engaged in business or connected with the various foreign concessions, took pains during the early period of the war to keep themselves as much as possible sequestered from Chinese view, to avoid giving offense to the people. Many of them had for years worn Chinese dress, and others now adopted the same costume, thinking thus to lessen the danger to which they were undoubtedly exposed. The Chinese authorities of Shanghai became convinced that the Japanese remaining there, under the protection of various foreign flags, constituted so many menaces to the national security. The precaution which the Japanese took in adopting Chinese costume, was made the pretext for a demand upon the consuls for the arrest of all who had resorted to it, but in each instance the demand was refused.

The first complication of American diplomatic interests with those of China came in this connection. On the morning of August 18, two Japanese who were walking within the limits of the French concession were pounced upon by Chinese guards and carried off to prison, charged with being spies in the service of the Japanese government. The accused were young men of good position and repute, and it seemed without the opportunity of spying, even if they were prepared to take the risk. They were placed in prison, however, pending, it was explained, the appointment of a proper tribunal to try them, and it was alleged by the Chinese authorities that there were found concealed about their clothes, plans of Chinese fortifications and cipher notes on Chinese movements. The following day the Japanese residing in Shanghai moved from the Chinese quarters into the American concession, where they placed themselves formally under the protection of the United States. The two who were arrested were immediately handed over to the American consul-general at his demand, he agreeing to keep them until charges should be formulated and presented. After a careful examination of the merits of the case, the consul, Mr. Jernigan, and the United States minister to China, Mr. Denby, became convinced that the charges were groundless, and that the young men were innocent of any guilt or evil intent. They were mere boys, students at the schools maintained in the American and French concessions, where they had resided for many years. The fact that they were dressed in Chinese costume proved nothing, inasmuch as they had worn that costume for many years The charges that plans and notes had been found upon them, were also discredited by the American representatives. Americans in private life in Shanghai, as well as Europeans, both in official and private position, united to sustain the position taken by the American representatives. These representations were submitted to the state department at Washington, where Secretary Gresham gave them careful and painstaking review. He lost no time in deciding that the opinions of the diplomatic representatives of the United States, who were on the ground and able to make a personal investigation of the merits of the case, were worthless, and that the allegations of the Chinese officials were those which were to be accepted in their entirety. The result was that the United States consul general at Shanghai was commanded by the state department at Washington to surrender to the Chinese officials these students, without delay. He did, however, delay sufficiently to make a strenuous protest against this action, offering further explanations why it should not be done, and in all he was sustained by the other diplomats in Shanghai. He declared that the surrender of these young men to China would be the signal for the torture, and that the only true wisdom and kindness would be to send them back to Japan. His protests were unavailing, and he was again instructed to deliver them at once, only exacted from the Chinese a promise that they should have fair trial and kind treatment.

To the distress of every friend of civilization in China, these two students were therefore surrendered to the Chinese, and two days later, after a trial which would be considered a mockery among ourselves, without the semblance of judicial fairness, they were condemned to death. The sentence was executed by means of the most shocking tortures which Chinese fiendish barbarity has been able to devise, to the horror of all foreigners living in that dark empire. The blot thus placed on American state-craft as exemplified in its first test daring this war, can never be eradicated from the minds of those familiar with the circumstances of the sad case.

The surrender of the two Japanese to the Chinese officials, by the United States consul-general, threw the Japanese of Shanghai into a state of the greatest consternation, as they had hitherto believed themselves to be perfectly secure under the protection of the American government. Their dismay was doubled a month later, when on October 8, the two students were tortured to death, in spite of the promise which had been made to Secretary Gresham by the Chinese minister at Washington, that they should be properly treated. The pledge given by the Chinese government was that these students should be treated as prisoners of war, and tried by a competent court, after the manner of civilized countries; and that their trial would be postponed until Colonel Denby, the United States minister, could be present. Information furnished to the American state department at Washington, its representative in China, the American minister and the American consul-general at Shanghai, was to the effect that the young men were not spies, but were students in a commercial school established in Tokio with a branch at Shanghai, the chief object of which was to impart a knowledge of the commerce of China and Japan, and promote the trade relations between the two countries. Under date of September 1, Colonel Denby wrote to the secretary of state as follows:

"To give up these boys unconditionally is generally believed to be to give them up to death. The viceroy of Nanking has, I am informed, already demanded of the taotai of Shanghai why the heads of the two spies have not been sent to him. They are judged and condemned in advance. The governor of Formosa has posted a proclamation offering prizes for Japanese heads. In a country where such a thing is possible, it is needless to inquire what chance a Japanese accused as a spy would have for his life. This case has attracted much attention in Japan. The American minister at Tokio telegraphed this legation that these men were innocent. Should any harm befall them, retaliation is inevitable. These young men have the fullest sympathy of all foreigners in

CAPTURE OF PING-YANG, SEPTEMBER 16TH

China, and the advice of the high officials of all nationalities has been not to give them up without conditions.

Mr. Jernigan, the United States consul-general at Shanghai, wrote as follows:

"Had it been known to the Chinese authorities that the limits of my power as a protector of Japanese interests extended only to an inquiry after arrest, all the students, fifty, would have been summarily arrested, and it is believed here, as summarily dealt with as were their two fellow students. I do not hesitate to conclude that the delay caused by the course of this consulate-general in the case of the two Japanese students, prevented the arrest of as many as two hundred Japanese upon mere suspicion, and has probably saved many from being executed and others from being held for ransom."

With this sort of a warning before them, the remaining Japanese residents in Shanghai, who numbered about seven hundred persons, consequently determined to quit the place at the earliest possible moment. The Yokohama Specie bank transferred its business for the time to a French bank and closed its doors. The Japanese storekeepers sold off their stocks with all speed, and prepared to leave in the first steamer for their native country.

Let us turn now to the hostile operations in Corea involving the rival forces. In the last chapter the operations were related up to July 30, on which date the Japanese drove the Chinese troops out of their intrenched position at Asan. Five days later, on the 4th of August, the conquerors re-entered Seoul in triumph, leaving the retreating Chinese to make their way to their friends far to the northward. Barbarous as it might have been in the Chinese to have no commissariat, they had in such an encounter the advantage in marching, and were able to make a retreat so successfully as to win the admiration of those who can recognize even that sort of merit.

To understand the movements of forces from this period of the war, it must be remembered that we have to do with a single Japanese force, landing at Chemulpo and commanding and occupying Seoul, from which center the movements were carried on. There were, however, two Chinese forces, the original garrison of Asan, a port forty miles south of Seoul, and a large force advancing by the road which enters Corea at its northwest corner at Wi-ju. China anxious to meet and annihilate at one blow if possible her despised foe, threw the latter body of troops, drawn largely from the Manchoo garrisons, into the Corean peninsula, where they advanced about one hundred and seventy miles inside the border to the banks of the Tatong River at Ping-Yang. The Japanese were awaiting the shock a little to the north of Seoul, and such was the strength of their position that the Chinese, instead of advancing upon them, halted at the capital city of the province, Ping-Yang, assuming the defensive there and strongly fortifying it. One week after the capture of Asan and the beginning of the retreat of the Chinese, the van of the victorious army started from Seoul, marching towards Ping-Yang, one hundred and forty miles distant, whence they were destined five weeks later to be once more victorious in expelling the Chinese.

General Yeh, with his four thousand Chinese, made, as has been said, a masterly retreat. Accompanied by many Coreans who joined his standard when he was compelled to abandon his untenable position, he struck northeastward and after twenty-five days effected a junction with the Chinese main body at Ping-Yang, August 23. His column kept to the mountains, where travel was difficult, and it was harassed by the enemy all along the route. Nevertheless, the troops marched three hundred and fifty miles through this almost impassable country, breaking through the Japanese lines at Chong-ju, and reaching their friends at last.

The Japanese army, advancing on Ping-Yang at the same time, was approaching that position by a course parallel with that of the Chinese, but to the westward of it. The opposing forces were near enough to one another that detached bodies frequently met in conflict, and the skirmishes resulting were reported by whichever band happened to be victorious, as a brilliant victory for the army. Because of this condition of affairs, many battles were reported from one side or the other that were scarcely mentioned by the opponents, whichever force it might be, and the war spirit was thus constantly fed in China and Japan without anything of considerable importance really happening.

About the middle of August the Japanese scouts pressing forward from Pongsan came across an advance guard of the Chinese, who had seized the telegraph line. A brisk skirmish ensued and the scouts fell back. A few days later the Chinese advance guard, numbering five thousand men, encountered the Japanese troops guarding the Ping-Yang passes, and drove them out. Two days later an advance was made on the Japanese

FIRST SIGHT OF PING-YANG

skirmish lines, and the Japanese were again defeated, this time being turned back as far as Chung-Law some twenty miles south of Ping-Yaag.

When the Japanese troops started from Chemulpo and Seoul to advance on Ping-Yang, a force of thirteen transports, protected by a strong convoy of war vessels, also started for Ping-Yang, carrying some six thousand troops who were intended to co-operate with the forces advancing by land. On the 18th of August these troops were landed in Ping-Yang inlet, and they immediately began their march up the cultivated valley of the Tatong River in the direction of the city. When the force had proceeded some distance, it was suddenly attacked by one thousand Chinese cavalry, who succeeded in dividing the column into two parts. The Chinese artillery at the same time caused great havoc among the Japanese. The latter were thrown into complete disorder, and considerably reduced in numbers they fled to the seashore, pursued by the cavalry who cut down many of the fugitives. As they reached the coast the Japanese came within the shelter of the guns of their war vessels, and the Chinese were consequently compelled to desist from further pursuit.

The land skirmishes of which mention has been made, involved none except the extreme van of the Japanese forces and the outposts of the Chinese. The main body of the Japanese troops, some fifteen thousand strong, found that the daily rate of progress northward did not exceed six miles, so broken was the road by mountains and streams, the passage of which presented great obstacles. This being the rate of advance, the army had pushed some ninety miles from Seoul, when it was decided that a change of military plan must be made. The Chinese assembling in such great force at Ping-Yang, by the union of the two armies, threatened Gensan, on the east coast of Corea. At Gensan there was an important Japanese colony, and from there a trunk road led southward to Seoul. The destruction of the colony, a flanking movement against the Japanese army, and an irruption of Chinese troops into the Corean capital, might have been the result of not including Gensan in the Japanese program of operations. A force of ten thousand men was accordingly transported to Gensan by sea, with instructions to move westward against Ping-Yang, timing its advance and attack with those of the army from Seoul, whose progress northward was suspended to allow time for the passage and disembarkation of this column, and of the column which had been sent from Chemulpo into the Ping-Yang inlet.

While these land operations were going on, there were also some naval movements under way, but the latter brought no very

BATTLE OF THE YALU—SINKING OF THE CHIN-YUEN

definite results. A fleet of Japanese vessels, including a few iron clads and some merchant steamships transformed into cruisers, made a reconnaissance of Wei-hai-wei and Port Arthur about the 10th of August. A few shots were exchanged at long range between the vessels and the forts at each of these places, and the fleet then withdrew. The operations were of little more importance than a mere ruse to draw fire and ascertain the position and strength of the enemy's guns. No submarine mines were exploded, or torpedoes launched. At the request of the British admiral, Sir Edmund Fremantle, the Japanese promised not to renew the attack upon Wei-hai-wei or to bombard Chefoo without giving forty-eight hours' notice to him, so that measures might be taken to protect the lives of foreign residents.

The emperor of China, taking personal interest in affairs to greater extent than had been his custom, insisted on a full daily report of the warlike operations and plans. He studied special official reports of the naval attack, and then wanted to know why his commanders allowed the enemy's vessels to escape. All this time the Japanese fleet was patrolling the China sea, the Gulf of Pechili and the Corean Bay, trying to reach a conflict with the enemy, and to prevent the tribute of rice from going north. Torpedoes were placed in the entrance to Tokio Bay and Nagasaki harbor, to guard against an attack by Chinese war vessels. The war spirit in Japan lost none of its warmth. The detachments sent across the straits into Corea in August numbered nearly fifty thousand men, and early in September the total number of Japanese troops available for activity in the peninsula was nearly one hundred thousand. A war loan of $50,000,000 was desired by the government, and so anxious were Japanese capitalists to subscribe for it that foreign subscriptions were refused and more than $80,000,000 were offered.

Chinese efforts continued also in great degree, but the results were scarcely as happy. Troops to the same number could not be sent into Corea. A very long land march was required before the forces could reach the seat of war by way of Manchooria and it was useless to attempt transporting them by water, so carefully did the Japanese cruisers patrol the sea routes.

Just at this time, when the lines were drawing closer and

closer for a decisive battle, the relations between Japan and Corea were more closely defined by a formal treaty of alliance signed at Seoul on August 26. The preamble of the treaty declared it to be the desire of the emperor of Japan and the king of Corea to determine definitely the mutual relations

BRINGING IN THE WOUNDED

of Japan and Corea, and to elucidate the relations between Japan and China with respect to the peninsula. The body of the treaty consisted of three articles:

"The object of the alliance is the strengthening and perpetuation of the independence of Corea as an autonomous state, and the promotion of the mutual interests of Corea and Japan, by compelling the Chinese forces to withdraw from Corea, and by obliging China to abandon her claims to the right to dominate the affairs of Corea.

"Japan is to carry on warlike operations against China both offensive and defensive; and the Corean government is bound to afford every possible facility to the Japanese forces in their movements, and to furnish supplies of provisions to them at a fair remuneration, so far as such supplies may be needed.

"The treaty shall terminate when a treaty of peace is concluded by Japan with China."

At this very time, however, the feeling of the Corean people against the Japanese was very intense and they were everywhere welcoming the Chinese as their friends. Except the strongly guarded positions in the provinces of Seoul and Hwanghai and the country around the treaty ports which were under Japanese influence, the peninsula was in the possession of armed Coreans and Chinese. The Japanese Marquis Saionji landed at Chemulpo, August 28, to congratulate the Corean monarch on his declaration of independence, and the king showed every disposition to co-operate with the Japanese in their efforts to introduce reforms into his country. His Majesty appointed a commissioner to visit Japan and thank the mikado for his promises to restore peace, and to establish a stable government in Corea. He further issued a decree introducing several reforms, including religious freedom, the establishment of a diplomatic service, the abolition of slavery, economies in the public service, the abrogation of the law whereby the whole family of a criminal is punished, and the granting of permission to widows to marry again.

Early in September the mikado established headquarters in Hiroshima with the ministers of war and marines and the general staff, deciding to direct the war operations from that city in the future. This had already been the place of assembly and embarkation for the troops ordered to the seat of war. At the same time Field Marshal Count Yamagata left for Corea to assume sole command of the Japanese army, which had now been augmented till its numbers were approximately one hundred thousand. Lines were drawing about the Chinese forces nearer and nearer. The indecisive battle which they had fought with the Japanese on August 16 had availed them nothing, and all their available troops were now massed together in Hwang-ju and Sing-chuen.

As the three advancing columns of Japanese drew nearer to the lines of the enemy, engagements multiplied and scarcely a day passed without some sort of a skirmish. The three divisions struck the Chinese simultaneously on September 5 and 6. The troops from Chemulpo struck the Chinese center at Chung-Hwa; those from Gensan came up with their enemies at Sing-chuen, where the left flank of the Chinese was strongly intrenched;

THE MIKADO REVIEWING THE ARMY

and the detachment from the mouth of the Tatong struck the right flank of the Chinese at Hwang-ju. The results from all of these engagements were favorable to the Japanese, and the Chinese were forced back in confusion upon Ping-Yang where they united to give final battle. In the retreat, the column advancing from the Tatong again caught up with the Chinese on the 7th and another stubborn engagement was fought. The Chinese did not give way until they were in danger of being surrounded, when they fled in redoubled haste towards Ping-Yang.

With the Chinese forces in Corea thus surrounded by the Japanese, after the sharp campaign; and the Chinese fleet of warships in perfect fighting trim collected at Wei-hai-wei, the time was now at hand for the two important conflicts, one on land and one at sea, which resulted in mid-September in the entire victory of the Japanese.

THE FIRST GREAT BATTLES OF THE WAR

Concentration of Japanese Troops to threaten Ping-Yang—Plan of attack—Poor defenses in the rear of the Chinese position—Night advance on the enemy—Swift and effective victory—Chinese Commander killed—Thousands of prisoners taken—Rejoicings in Japan—Honors for the dead Chinese Commander—Second great conflict in a Week—The Naval battle of the Yalu River—Another Victory for the Japanese Fleet—Many War Ships destroyed—Hundreds of Sailors drowned in sinking Vessels—Carnage and destruction—Elation of the Japanese over two successive victories—Depression in the Chinese Capital and Criticism of the Chinese Viceroy, Li Hung Chang.

The first serious engagement between the Chinese and the Japanese forces in Corea resulted, as competent judges foresaw all along, in the complete victory of the latter. The great battle was fought and won. The Chinese were utterly routed. The strong position of Ping-Yang lying just north of the Tatong river, on the road from Seoul to the frontier at the mouth of the Yalu river, was carried by assault in the small hours of Sunday morning September 16. The Chinese troops who held it were utterly defeated, with a loss in killed, wounded, and prisoners, estimated at nearly fourfifths of their entire force.

COREAN POLICE AGENT

On Thursday morning, September 13, began the attacks which resulted two days later in the brilliant victory. Three columns of Japanese troops had been centering for this attack for some weeks. The first of these came from Gensan, threatening a flank attack. The column marched from this port on the Sea of Japan almost directly west, approaching Ping-Yang by way of the mountain passes. The center column landed at Hwang-ju near the mouth of the Tatong river, and occupied a position to the westward of Ping-Yang on the right flank of the Chinese troops.

The infantry and artillery of the Japanese were in a high state of efficiency. The men themselves were hardy, active, brave and intelligent. Their drill and discipline had been carefully adapted from the best European models. Their arms were of the latest and most destructive patterns that science has been able to devlse, and every detail in

JAPANESE KITCHEN IN CAMP

their equipment and accoutrements had been thoroughly thought out and carefully provided. The officers who had the skill and the energy to create such a force were of course worthy to lead it. All of them had made scientific study of their profession, and some of them had spent years in close investigation of the more famous European military systems, under the guidance of distinguished strategists. But while it was generally anticipated that such an army, so led, would have an easy task in defeating and dispersing any force which the Chinese were likely to assemble against it at short notice in Corea, it was by no means certain that the Japanese could force an engagement before the Corean winter made serious operations impracticable. The Japanese commander showed that he had mastered the great secret of modern warfare. He knew how to move his troops with rapidity and with decision, and doing so he succeeded in dealing a heavy blow to China with trifling loss to himself.

The position held by the Chinese was one of great natural strength. Doubtless on this account it was protected by old works, which the Chinese had supplemented by new defenses. True, however, to the extraordinary practice so often adopted by the Chinese armies, they neglected to secure their rear to any adequate degree. The Japanese, who had fought the Chinese before, foresaw that this would be the case, and planned their measures accordingly.

Thursday the Japanese column from Pongsan, the centre, made a reconnaissance in force, drawing the fire from the Chinese fort, and ascertaining accurately the location of the defenses and the disposition of the troops. This having been accomplished, the Japanese forces fell back in good order and with very little loss, none of the other troops having entered the engagement. Friday was spent by the Japanese in taking up their final position, and by that evening all the Japanese forces were in position for the combined attack, the Pongsan column facing the Chinese centre to bear the brunt, as in the preliminary fighting, and the others arranged as heretofore described. The Hwang-ju column had been re-enforced the day before by marines and blue jackets from the fleet at the mouth of the Tatong river.

The battle opened Saturday morning at daybreak by a direct cannonade upon the Chinese works. This continued without cessation until the afternoon, the Chinese fighting their guns well and making good execution. At two o'clock in the afternoon a body of infantry was thrown forward, and these troops kept up a rifle fire upon the Chinese until dusk. The Japanese gained some advanced positions, but they mainly occupied the same ground as when the attack opened. Firing continued at intervals throughout the night.

Neither of the flanking columns took any part in the heavy fighting during Saturday, and thus no opportunity was given to the Chinese of measuring the real number of the forces opposed to them or of ascertaining the real plans of the enemy. Throughout the day the Chinese held their own without much loss except to their defenses, and they retired to rest with the satisfied feeling of men who have not unsuccessfully opposed a formidable adversary.

JAPANESE SOLDIER SALUTING AT FIELD CEMETERY

They had a rude awakening. During the night the two flanking columns drew a cordon around the Chinese forces, and at three o'clock on Sunday morning the attack was delivered simultaneously and with admirable precision. The Gensan and Hwangju columns were the ones who devoted themselves to the rear of the Chinese position, and the entrenched troops suddenly found themselves exposed to attacks from the force they had fought during the day and from new forces of fresh troops of unknown numbers.

The Chinese lines which were so strong in front, were found comparatively weak in the rear. The unsuspicious soldiers, taken completely by surprise, fell into panic and were cut down by hundreds. They were surrounded and at every point where they sought safety in flight they met the foe. It was of course a disgrace

CROWD IN TOKIO LOOKING AT PICTURES OF THE WAR

to the Chinese leaders to be completely out manoeuvred and surprised, but it was no disgrace to the Chinese soldiers to flee with but slight resistance when the surprise had been accomplished by an enemy outnumbering them nearly three to one.

The greatest Manchoo general, and some of the troops disciplined under Li Hung Chang's directions on the European system, fought stoutly, stood their ground to the last, and were cut down to a man. But their stand was useless. The Pongsan column, swarming over the damaged defenses in the front, completed the discomfiture of the Chinese. Half an hour after the night attack opened, the splendid position of Ping-Yang was in the possession of the Japanese.

JAPANESE AMBULANCE OFFICER

The Japanese victory was brilliant and complete. They captured the whole of the immense quantities of stores, provisions, arms and ammunition in the camp, besides hundreds of battle flags. The Chinese loss was about two thousand seven hundred killed and more than fourteen thousand wounded and prisoners. Less than a fourth of the Chinese army succeeded in escaping. The Japanese loss was thirty killed and two hundred and sixty-nine wounded, ambulance officer including eleven officers.

Among the officers of the Chinese killed was General Tso-paokwei, Manchoorian commander-in-chief of the army, who fought desperately to the last and was wounded twice. In this battle also, General Wei Jinkwoi, and General Sei Kinlin were captured and these practically comprise the effective Chinese staff.

Within ten hours of the great battles of Ping-Yang, the engineers had completed the military field telegraph between that place and Pongsan, and had messages on the wires to Seoul. The number of troops engaged in the battle on the side of the Japanese was about sixty thousand, and of the Chinese about twenty thousand, which in a measure explains and justifies the result of the conquest.

The news of this battle was welcomed most enthusiastically in Japan, and rejoicings were held in Tokio and the other large cities. Bells were rung and salutes fired. Field Marshal Count Yamagata, in command of the Japanese troops, received congratulations by telegraph from the emperor of Japan.

CHINAMAN MUTILATING REMAINS OF JAPANESE SOLDIERS

The emperor of China had occasion to take different measures. An imperial edict was promulgated in which he expressed his profound regret at the death of General Tso, who was killed while gallantly leading the Chinese troops. The emperor ordered that posthumous orders should be paid to the deceased, befitting his rank as a provincial commander of the Chinese Empire. The edict bestowed imperial favors upon the sons and family of the late general. After he had been severely wounded in the shoulder by a bullet, General Tso persisted in remaining at the head of his troops, and it was while leading his men in an unsuccessful charge that he was struck by another bullet and killed.

Just one day after the rout of the Chinese from their defenses at Ping-Yang, another meeting between Japanese and Chinese took place not may miles from the same point, but the second battle was on sea instead of land, and its results were not as definitive as those of the battle of Ping-Yang. There remained room for each contestant to lay claim to certain phases of the victory. But the opinion of independent and impartial authorities, naval

THE PING-YUEN

and military, has been that in the indirect results as well as the immediate lesson, Japan was well justified in claiming the contest to be hers.

Admiral Ting and his fleet were at Tien-tsin awaiting the orders of the Chinese war council which was sitting at that place. He was instructed to convoy a fleet of six transports to the Yalu river and protect them while landing troops, guns and stores at Wi-ju, from which base China intended to renew operations in Corea. The transports were ready Friday, September 14, and the following vessels escorted them to sea: Chen-Yuen and Ting-Yuen, speed fourteen knots, tonnage seven thousand four hundred and thirty; King-Yuen and Lai-Yuen, sixteen and one-half knots, two thousand eight hundred and fifty tons; Ping-Yuen, ten and one-half knots, two thousand eight hundred and fifty tons; Chih-Yuen and Ching-Yuen, eighteen knots, two thousand three hundred tons: Tsi-Yuen, fifteen knots, two thousand three hundred and fifty-five tons; Chao Yung and Yang Wei, sixteen and one-half knots, one thousand three hundred and fifty tons; Kwang Kai and Kwang Ting, sixteen and one-half knots, one thousand and thirty tons. The first five vessels named were armored battle ships, the first two built in 1881.2, the third and fourth in 1887, and the fifth in 1890. The seven following were cruisers with outside armor, all of them built since 1881 and some as late as 1890. There were also in the fleet six torpedo boats and two gun boats. It is evident that the fleet was of modern construction, and without going into details as to the armament it may be said that the guns were equally modern in pattern.

This splendid fleet arrived off the eastern entrance to the Yalu river on the afternoon of Sunday, September 16, and remained ten miles outside while the transports were to be unloaded. There were about seven thousand troops to be disembarked, composing the second Chinese army corps, which consisted almost entirely of Hunanese. The war council had realized that it was impossible to get the necessary re-enforcements to Corea with sufficient promptitude if they were marched overland, so the risk of sending them by transports was assumed.

The work of disembarking troops and discharging stores proceeded rapidly until about ten o'clock Monday morning, September 17. Very soon after that hour, the sight of a cloud of smoke upon the horizon indicated the approach of a large fleet. The enemy was at hand, and the battle was impending. Admiral Ting immediately weighed anchor and placed his ships in battle array. His position was a difficult one. If he remained near the shore, his movements were cramped. If he steamed out for sea room he ran the risk of a Japanese cruiser or torpedo boat running in amongst his transports. He chose the least of two evils and decided to remain near the shore.

By noon it was possible to distinguish twelve ships in the approaching Japanese squadron. The Chinese fleet steamed in the direction of the enemy and at a distance of five miles was able to distinguish the ships according to their types. Admiral Ting signalled his ships to clear for action and then brought them into a V-shaped formation, with the flagship at the apex of the angle. The Japanese had at first approached in double line, but when Admiral Ito saw the formation adopted by his opponent he changed his fleet into single line and so went into action.

The Ting-Yuen opened firing about twelve thirty P.M. at a range of five thousand seven hundred yards. The concussion of the first discharge threw every one off the bridge. As they came nearer, the Japanese appeared to form in quarter lines, to which the Chinese replied by turning two points to starboard, thus keeping their bows directed towards the enemy. Approaching within four thousand four hundred yards, the whole Japanese fleet seemed to turn eight points to port, thereby forming a single line ahead, and steaming across the Chinese line they turned its starboard wing.

The Japanese manoeuvred swiftly throughout the battle, and the Chinese scarcely had a chance for effective firing from beginning to end. When the Japanese were firing at the starboard section of the Chinese squadron, the ships of the port section were practically useless, and could not fire without risk of hitting their own ships. The Japanese cruisers attacked first one section and then the other. As soon as the Chinese on the port side had brought their guns to bear and had attained the range accurately, the Japanese would work around and attack the starboard side. At times as many as five Japanese vessels would bring the whole weight of their armament to bear upon one Chinese ship, their consorts keeping the attention of the other vessels of that line fully engaged, while the ships of the diverging line lay looking on almost as useless as hulks in the water.

As compared with that of the Japanese, the fire of the Chinese was very feeble and ineffective. The men fought bravely, however, and there appeared to be no thought of surrendering on either side, but a constant intention to fight to the end.

While the fleet was getting into its formation the Chao Yung and Yang Wei, which were slow in taking up stations, were disastrously exposed to the Japanese fire, and one of them in consequence began to burn. On the port wing the Tsi-Yuen and Kwang Kai, occupied a similar position behind the Chinese line. The Japanese steamed around by the stern at a distance of five thousand yards and cut off the Tsi-Yuen. The Kwang Kai, which was as yet keeping touch with the fleet, soon fell back.

Nothing more was seen of these two during the action, and they escaped unhurt.

The Chinese, unable to keep pace with the enemy, endeavored to follow their movements by keeping bow on to them, as they circled around, maintaining a heavy bombardment. The Chinese fleet that kept in the thick of the fight consisted of six ships of the Yuen class, including the ironclads. The Japanese, having completed one circle, hauled off to a distance of eight thousand yards, and went through an evolution with the object of separating in two divisions, the first consisting of the seven best known cruisers, and the second of five inferior ships which stood off to some distance.

The Japanese gunners were making much better practice than their enemy. Very few of the Chinese shots reached their mark, while the Japanese were constantly hitting the opposing vessels most effectively. After a time the Chinese admiral apparently became desperate. His formation was broken, and two or three of his ships advanced at full speed. The fighting became furious, but the weight of metal told and one of his ships, the Lai-Yuen, was crippled in this venture. Then for some unknown reason the Japanese ceased firing and cleared off, while the Chinese retired nearer the shore. The respite was a brief one, for the Japanese returned in about fifteen minutes, renewing the battle with great vigor and upon the same effective plan.

Late in the afternoon the Chinese cruiser Chih-Yuen, the captain of which had several times shown a disposition to disregard the admiral's signals, deliberately steamed out of line and, although again ordered to remain in the place assigned to her, went full speed at a Japanese cruiser. The latter received a slanting blow which ripped her up below the water line and it was believed she would founder. She succeeded however, in pouring several broadsides into her enemy at close quarters, and the Chih-Yuen was so injured by her fire and by the effects of the collision that she herself sank.

When the Chinese resumed their line formation, the Japanese guns were directed upon the disabled ships, particularly the Lai-Yuen. She had been riddled by shot and shell, and it was evident that she was sinking. The Chinese gunners worked their weapons to the last. Finally she went down slowly, stern first. Her bows rose clear out of the water and she remained in this position for a minute and a half before she disappeared in one last plunge. The Japanese had used no torpedoes upon her, but sunk her by fair shot and shell fire. It spurred all the men to additional effort, and the officers were naturally exultant. They regarded the sinking of a double bottomed ship like the Lai-Yuen by gun fire alone as no mean achievement.

The battle then arranged itself into two great groups, the four Chinese cruisers becoming engaged with the second division, while the ironclads attacked the first division. The fighting of the second division was irregular and difficult to follow, and ended in the Japanese disappearing in the direction of the island of Hai-yung-tao.

The first Japanese division carried on the fighting with the Chinese ironclads by circling round at a distance of four thousand five hundred yards. The Ping-Yuen and Chen-Yuen keeping together, followed the enemies' movements in a smaller circle, the whole evolution taking a spiral form. Occasionally the distance between the opposing ships was reduced to two thousand yards, and once to one thousand two hundred yards. The Japanese aimed at keeping a long distance away, so as to avail themselves of their superior speed, and make the most of their quick firing guns, in which armament they vastly excelled the Chinese. The object of the Chinese was to come into close quarters, so as to use their slow firing guns of large caliber with full effect.

Other Chinese vessels endangered were the King-Yuen, which was badly injured by fire, the Chao Yung, which foundered in shallow water, and the Yang Wei, which was partially burned., and afterwards destroyed by a torpedo.

On the Japanese side, in addition to the vessel which was rammed by the Chih-Yuen, the Yoshino and the Matsusima were badly injured by fire. The former of these two, after receiving a series of volleys from two Chinese vessels, was enveloped in a cloud of white smoke which lay heavily on the water and completely covered the ship. The Chinese vessels waited for the cloud to clear away and got their port guns ready, but before the

Yoshino became visible their fire was diverted by a Japanese ship of the Matsusima type which came on the port quarter. The guns which had been laid for the Yoshino were fired at this newcomer with the result that she too began to burn.

In the latter part of the battle the Chinese ironclads ran short of common shell, and continued the action with steel shot, which proved ineffective.

An officer of the Japanese navy who was on one of the vessels in the engagement, was sent to make a verbal report to the mikado, and related some interesting details of the battle. He says that the fleet consisted of eleven war ships and a steam packet, Saikio Maru, which had been fitted up with guns as a cruiser, conveying Admiral Kabayama, the head of the

THE YOSAINO

naval command bureau, on a tour of inspection. Here is what he says about the latter boat: "It was our own turn next to suffer. The Saikio Maru had worked her deck guns to the best of her ability, but she was scarcely adapted for fighting in line against ironclads. Frequently she was in imminent danger, the Chinese quickly perceiving that she was a weak ship. A well placed shell from the Ting-Yuen pierced her side, and exploding made a complete wreck of the steering gear as well as doing other damage. She was put out of action, and pointed the best course she could by means of her screws. But this was a poor makeshift, and in trying to get away, she ran to within eighty metres distance of the Ting-Yuen and Chen-Yuen, both these ships having starred in pursuit of her at full speed. The two Chinese commanders evidently thought that the Saikio Maru intended to ram them, for they sheered off and thus left her room to escape.

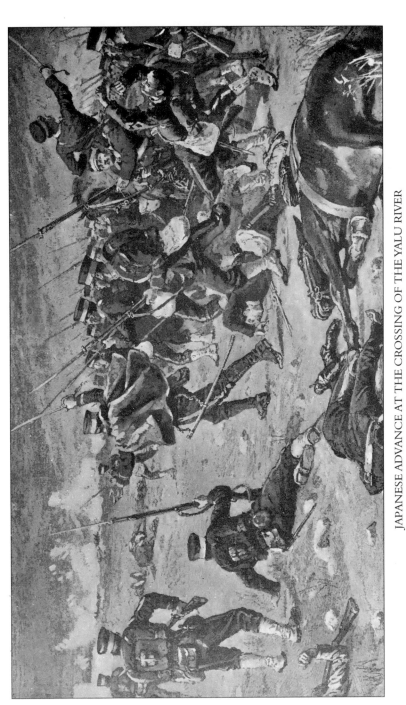

JAPANESE ADVANCE AT THE CROSSING OF THE YALU RIVER

She went away southward at her best speed. The Chinese discharged two fish torpedoes after her, but the projectiles either passed underneath the ship's keel or missed their direction. The fire which had slackened during this incident, recommenced with redoubled energy, but we still made better practice with our guns. The Chao Yung was partially disabled, though she still fought on against two of our cruisers who were closing upon her. The doomed vessel went astern and settled down in shallow water. She was covered, but two-thirds of her masts were visible, and the rigging was soon crowded with scores of Chinese crying loudly to be

THE MATSUSIMA

saved. It was a pitiful sight, but the fighting was too hot to allow us to help them. At the same moment the Yang Wei was reported disabled. She retired slowly from the fighting line rolling heavily, masses of dense smoke emerging from her. We had suffered on our side, but not nearly to such an extent. A shell had burst upon the flagship Matsusima, dismounting the forward quickfiring gun, and killing a number of men. The gun too was flung violently against the ship, doing considerable damage. The Matsusima had received a great part of the Chinese fire throughout and this last disaster had rendered her useless for further fighting. Her commander and first lieutenant had been killed. One hundred and twenty of her men had been killed or wounded; but the ship still floated.

Admiral Ito and his staff were transferred to the Hasidate and in a few minutes they were again in the thick of the fight.

"The Hiyei in the mean time had been receiving the fire of two powerful Chinese vessels. She was manoeuvered skillfully and returned their fire, until a shell bursting within her set the woodwork in flames. A second shell exploded in the sick-bay, killing a surgeon and his assistant, and some of those who had been wounded earlier. The captain was compelled to run her out of action, to extinguish the flames, and this having been

H. SAKOMOTO, Commander of the Akagi

accomplished his wounded men were transferred to another ship, and he steamed once more into line. The Yoshino had been fought throughout in a magnificent manner. She steamed in advance of the Hiyei when the latter was disabled and was backing out of line. She took the enemy's fire, and replied with the greatest spirit. She was hit frequently, and her forward barbette was damaged, but her injuries can soon be repaired. The Chinese used

their torpedo boats at times and incessant care was necessary to avoid their projectiles. On our war ship, the Akagi, the captain was aloft in the tops watching especially for torpedo movements and signalling by flags directly they were detected. He was in this position when the mast was shot away, and the tophamper fell with a crash upon the deck. The captain and two lookout men were killed. The first lieutenant took command and fought the ship till darkness stopped the action. Towards the close of the day dense smoke was seen issuing from the war ships Ting-Yuen, King-Yuen, and Ping-Yuen, and it was believed by us that all were on fire. Great confusion prevailed on board them, but they did not retire from action. Firing was still kept up intermittently on the Chinese side, though the guns of many of their ships were silenced. At sundown the Chinese squadron was in full retreat. We took a parallel course intending to renew the battle in the morning. The night was dark, the speed was only equal to that of our slowest damaged ship, and we were compelled to keep at some distance from their course on account of their torpedo flotilla, which might have attempted a night attack. We lost sight of the enemy during the night. At dawn we endeavored to discover their position, but failed. The Chinese squadron must have reached protected shelter. Then we returned to the scene of the action, and found that the war ship Yang Wei, which had been disabled when the battle was half over, had been run ashore. Her crew had abandoned her. We fired one fish torpedo and completed her destruction. This was the only torpedo fired by the Japanese either in the action or after it."

From a concensns of the opinions of eye witnesses, it appears that the Chinese were at least as anxious to continue the fight as were the Japanese. Before five o'clock the Japanese ceased firing. It was observed that the distance between the fleets was rapidly increasing and the Chinese failed to diminish it. The Chinese then saw the Japanese change course in a westerly direction towards the islands of Yang-tao and Hai-yung-tao. The Celestials followed them for an hour, and saw the course changed again to a southerly direction, while some of the ships of the second Japanese division that had vanished earlier in the fight now joined those of the first. By this time nothing but the smoke of the withdrawing fleet was visible and the Chinese returned. They were joined by the ships which had been partially disabled but were still in condition to proceed, and altogether withdrew towards Port Arthur. A message was sent to the transports from which the troops had disembarked on the banks of the Yalu river, ordering them to weigh anchor and follow the fleet.

It is evident that there remained room for each side to claim the victory in this naval battle. The Chinese succeeded in disembarking the troops, which was the avowed object of their expedition. They fought brilliantly, inflicting considerable damage upon their opponents, and assert that the battle was terminated against their will by the withdrawal of the Japanese vessels.

The Mikado's men on the other hand, destroyed several of the best battle ships in the Chinese navy with great loss of life to the crews, and plead that the Chinese withdrew from them. The truth probably is that each fleet was so damaged and the men so exhausted with the long contest that they were mutually willing to quit. Inasmuch as casual spectators of impartial mind are not in a position to observe the details of a battle royal of this sort, it seems that the decision must be left unsettled except as the destruction of so many Chinese vessels may be certainly credited as a victory for the Japanese. The withdrawal of the Chinese fleet towards Port Arthur, and its previous inactivity seem to be partially responsible for the handing over of Corea to the Japanese, giving them first the advantage of possession in the invaded country.

The peculiar constitution of the Chinese navy is partially an explanation of the discipline prevailing. The navy is not properly an imperial or even a national force. The four fleets are provincial squadrons raised, equipped, and maintained by the viceroys or governors of the maritime provinces to which they are attached. No arrangement could possibly be more unsuited for the purpose of naval war, and to it may be partially attributed the previous inaction of the Chinese fleet while their numerically inferior antagonists were using the sea at will. Stirred up at length, doubtless by peremptory orders from Peking, the Chinese admiral, in place of throwing his whole strength into a decisive operation, seems to have committed himself to a subsidiary objective. Naval history teems with examples of the drawbacks that inevitably result from being thus led away. To have attacked the Japanese when convoying troops to Chemulpo, or to have fought a naval battle at Chemulpo or Ping-Yang inlet might have led to important results. In place of adopting such a course, the Chinese utilized their fleet for the first time in convoying troops to the mouth of the Yalu river in the north-east corner of the bay of Corea. The great difficulty experienced in advancing overland from Manchooria doubtless suggested this plan, but the object at best was purely secondary. And with the fleet scattered and partially destroyed it would seem that the troops, both artillery and infantry, with their stores lauded at the mouth of the Yalu river, would be practically helpless so far from support or a base of supplies.

The Japanese fleet which met that of China in the battle of the Yalu river was composed as follows: The Matsusima, Itsukusima and the Hasidate, each of four thousand two hundred and seventy-seven tons displacement and seventeen and one-half knots; The Takachiho and the Naniwa, each of three thousand six hundred and fifty tons, and eighteen and seven-tenths knots; the Akitsushima, of three thousand one hundred and fifty tons, and Chiyoda, of two thousand four hundred and fifty tons, and each nineteen knots; the Yoshino, of four thousand one hundred and fifty tons and twenty-three knots; the Fuso, three thousand seven hundred and eighteen tons, and the Hiyei, two thousand two hundred tons, each thirteen knots; the Akagi six hundred and fifteen tons, and twelve knots; beside the Saikio Maru, a steam packet fitted as a cruiser and four torpedo boats. It will be seen that in numbers the fleets were about equal. But in tonnage the Chinese fleet was superior, having several vessels larger than any of the Japanese, while on the other hand the speed of the Japanese vessels averaged very much above that of the Chinese. The armament too of the Japanese fleet was superior to that of the Chinese, being composed more largely of quickfiring guns. In type the vessels of the opposing squadrons differed considerably. While six of the Chinese ships had side armor, only one Japanese vessel was thus protected; and while ten Chinese ships had protection of some form, only eight Japanese carried any armor.

The Japanese had the advantage of their opponents in speed, but to a less extent than might be expected. The number of knots shown for each ship in the lists was of course the best possible, and is equally delusive for both sides. Notwithstanding, the Japanese had so much the greater speed that they were able to steam around their opponents to some extent. There are some lessons to be drawn from this battle by those who have wondered what the result of a contest between the modern war ships would be. The Chinese made one attempt to ram, and discharged one torpedo from a ship and three from a boat. The attempt to ram resulted in desperate damage, though not in destruction to the ship attacked. The rammer herself was afterwards sunk, it was believed by gun fire. All the torpedoes discharged were ineffective. The Japanese tried to use neither the ram nor the torpedo. Beside the Chih-Yuen, the Lai-Yuen and Chao Yung were sunk by shot and the Yang Wei was run aground to avoid foundering in deep water. The Japanese flag ship Matsusima was so severely injured that Admiral Ito had to shift his flag to the Hasidate. The Hiyei was forced out of action for a time, and the armed packet steamer Saikio Maru had to go out of action altogether. The mast of the Akagi was shot away, and by the fall killed the captain and two men, all of whom were on the top. Such being the variety of the ships engaged, important lessons are forthcoming from this first great modern naval battle. Many theories fondly beloved and eagerly proclaimed have had to be abandoned for their holders to fall back upon the old and well tested principles of naval war. The gun has maintained its position as a weapon to which all others are merely accessories. The best protection, as Farragut pointed out, is a powerful and well directed fire. Stupendous losses, unimaginable destruction, have been confidently predicted as a necessary result of a naval battle fought with modern weapons. This did not prove to be the case, and the damage inflicted in the five or six hours' fighting at the mouth of the Yalu might have occurred in the days of the '74s. Allowance must be made for the probable defects in the Chinese gunnery practice, but their seamen fought like heroes, and greater endurance than was shown on either side can never be expected. The accuracy of naval fire is always over-estimated in time of peace. The disablement of the heavy guns of the Chen-Yuen and her continued fighting with her light armament are a useful object lesson. This vessel like many others was built solely with a view to carry her four thirty-seven ton guns. The remaining armament was doubtless distributed promiscuously as space offered. Both barbettes were quickly disabled, and machinery gave place to man power. On board ship, as on land, it is the man who ultimately counts, even though in time of peace he is often forgotten.

From this survey of the characteristics of the two fleets, it may be perceived that each fairly represented a different principle.

The principle represented by the Chinese was that advocated by the school which puts matter above mind, for their fleet contained the biggest ships, the less numerous but heaviest guns, and the most extensive torpedo armament. The principle of which the Japanese may be taken as the representative is that of a school which appeals to history and experience, and not to theories evolved out of the inner consciousness of people without practical knowledge of the sea, and which maintains that the human factor is both the most important and the unchanging factor in war, which must in its broader features remain much what it has always been.

Whatever the claims of victory made by the opposing forces, the fact remains that Admiral Ito stayed at sea with the Japanese fleet and that the damages were repaired as fast as possible on board the ships; while the Chinese went into port, where their repairs could be made in safety and at leisure. Japan unquestionably had command of the sea. The menace which operated successfully in the early stages of the war was changed for the prestige of a greal moral and material victory.

JAPANESE INFANTRY ATTACKING A CHINESE POSITION

Effects of the Battles of Ping-Yang and the Yalu River—How the two Nations Received the News—Withdrawal of the Chinese Fleet—Armies Moving North to the Boundary—Li Hung Chang Losing His Rank and Influence—Possible Destination of the New Japanese Army—Prince Kung—Chinese Driven out of Several Positions in the North of Corea—Abandoning the Peninsula—Danger to Foreigners in china—Captain Vou Hannecken—The Japanese advance into Manchooria.

The effects of the battles of Ping-Pang and the Yalu River upon the governments and peoples of the two belligerent nations were characteristic. Japan was the scene of rejoicings most hearty in every city and village of the empire. Congratulations were sent from the emperor to the commanders of the military and naval forces, and memorials complimentary to them were voted by the Japanese parliament. Additional levies of troops were made and hurried into Corea, with the intention that the war should be prosecuted with renewed vigor.

In China on the other hand, the dazed government was scarcely able to realize what had happened. Reports were made to the emperor which caused him to declare that the defeat was merely the result of the cowardice of his commanders, and that they must be punished for the losses. The emperor once began to contemplate a change of counsellors, and the dismissal of all mandarins and others who had been concerned in the conduct of the war. Li Hung Chang's position in imperial favor began to waver. The captain of the cruiser Kwaog Kai was beheaded for cowardice. At the battle of the Yalu River he saw one of the enemy's ships approaching to attack him, and immediately turned and fled with his vessel as rapidly as possible. He intended to escape to Port Arthur, but as he was endeavoring to shape a course thither which would keep him out of range of the enemy' guns, he ran the vessel ashore and she became a total wreck.

The Coreans, except those under the immediate influence of the home government, were not yet willing to accept the Japanese indulgence for that of China, which had been so strong throughout their lives. A body of two thousand Japanese left Fusan just before the battle of Ping-Yang to march to Seoul. Their advance was, however, opposed by the Coreans, who harassed them continually by guerilla warfare. The Japanese lost heavily, and were compelled to return to Fusan having lost nearly half of their number. Two thousand fresh troops were immediately sent to that port from Japan to guard the neighboring settlements, where some three thousand Japanese permanently resided. Another uprising of the armed Tonghaks, whose rebellion had been one of the first features of the war, was apprehended.

The remnant of the Chinese fleet sought refuge after the battle of the Yalu river under the protection of the Port Arthur forts, where they were soon locked up by Japanese ships which patrolled the neighboring waters, preventing the exit of Chinese vessels the Chinese army defeated at Ping-Yang fled to Wi-ju, at the apex of the most northerly angle of the Bay of Corea, on the Corean side of the mouth of the Yalu River. About seven thousand Chinese troops had been landed there from the transports which were escorted by the Chinese squadron engaged in the battle at the mouth of the river. The governor of Manchooria began to concentrate all the troops raised in that province upon Mukden and the route between that city and Wi-ju, and extensive earthworks were thrown up along the road.

It was believed by the Chinese that Mukden would be the scene of the next great battle of the war. This famous Manchoo city possessed a political and dynastic importance, which might easily render its downfall decisive for the war, irrespective of all strategic considerations. It was the sacred city of the royal house, the ancestral home of the reigning family of China. It contained the tomb of many of the emperor's august ancestors, d accordingly was invested in the eyes of all good Chinamen with a halo of sanctity reflected on the Lord of the Dragon Throne himself. The capture of the city in which so many sons of heaven had found sepulchers would be accepted throughout the empire as an omen that the present occupant of the royal seat was not worthy of divine protection, and such omens, in days of disastrous wars, are often fulfilled with remarkable celerity. As the politicians about the court were perfectly aware of what the consequence of the fall of Mukden would be it was natural that they should take every precaution to prevent such a catastrophe. Furthermore, in Mukden the Chinese emperor was supposed to have gold and silver accumulated in the course of two centuries, to the amount of 81,200,000,000.

Mukden is only one hundred and fifty miles from Wi-ju, with which place the Manchoo city was connected by a road, comparatively good for

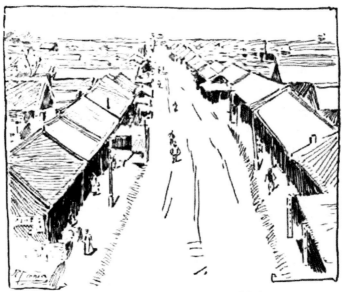

PRINCIPAL STREET OF MUKDEN

China, as it had been the main route to Peking, and even the Chinese recognized its strategic importance by running telegraph wires along it. It is easy to see why the Chinese began to increase the fortifications of the sacred city, and why they made a stand at Wi-ju in the hope of interrupting the Japanese advance.

The levies of troops concentrating on Wi-ju, Mukden, and the intervening territory were hardy men from the north, of excellent material to be worked into soldiers, but they were badly armed. Only about four thousand and good rifles, but further supplies were being hurried up from the southern arsenals. The Chinese force intrenched upon the Yalu River was about thirty-eight thousand, including the troops that had escaped from the Ping-Yaug defeat to fall back upon Wi-ju. Many of the forces which they found there were also raw levies, badly armed. The loss of field guns, rifles, and ammunition at Ping-Yang greatly embarrassed the Chinese war department. It was recognized that a battle must be fought at the river, and it was earnestly desired to retrieve the disaster of Ping-Yang.

It was immediately after the series of defeats in Corea that the effort began to be made by the enemies of Li Hung Chang to find a means for his degradation. Even two weeks before the battle of Ping-Yang, the government at Peking appointed two officers to act as censors of his proceedings, and especially of his conduct of the war. One of these officials was a notorious enemy of the viceroy. The censors at first contented themselves with taking note of Li Hung Chang's actions and movements. Immediately after the news of the disaster at Ping-Yang reached Peking, the emperor was persuaded that the defeat of his army was due to the mismanagement of the viceroy. The intrigue was completely successful, and on the morning of September 18, an imperial edict was issued depriving Li Hung Chang of his three-eyed peacock feather, the reason assigned for the disgrace being incapacity and negligence in making preparations for the war. Much sympathy was expressed for the viceroy, who was thus made the scapegoat for the disasters. The real responsibility rested with the Tsung-li Yamen, which had been making war with an inadequate force inefficiently organized and hampered by tradition. Li was not a member of the Grand Council, but it was sought to make him responsible for its blunders.

Within a few days after the Corean engagements, another Japanese army was mobilized at Hiroshima for service in the field. The destination of this fresh expeditionary force of thirty thousand men was kept a secret, nothing being known except that another effective blow was contemplated by General Kawakami, the Von Moltke of Japan. The sea-going fleet of China was practically paralyzed for the time, and the Japanese were free to transport a force in any direction. The island of Haiyung-tao, in Corea Bay, had been made a coaling station for the Japanese fleet, thus enabling the Japanese torpedo boats to keep a constant watch at the mouth of the Gulf of Pechili and secure advance warning of offensive or defensive operations. It was believed

CHINESE TROOPS TRYING TO SAVE THEIR ARTILLERY

that Count Yamagata favored an attack upon Niuchwang from the sea. This city in the possession of the Japanese would form a base for a movement upon Mukden or upon Peking itself, and the forces landed there could cooperate with the army advancing from Corea. A second possible destination for the new force was Peking itself. It was believed that an army of that size could

TRANSPORTING CHINESE TROOPS

reach the capital by disembarking at a point on the coast about half way between Taku, the city at the mouth of the Peiho River, on which Peking is situated, and Niu-chwang.

The third alternative was an expedition to Formosa. The island had hitherto remained outside the sphere of operations, and

Chinese troops from the southern provinces had been transported there in considerable number. This movement of forces had been interrupted only by the wreck of one steamer, and the necessary caution required to avoid a collision with Japanese cruisers, which at times patrolled that portion of the China sea. There were probably fifteen thousand men in the island, drawn in part from the Black Flags, and excellent in quality, but lacking in military training and even arms and equipment. The natural wealth of Formosa was known to be considerable, and its geographical position from a commercial point of view immensely important, so that there were good reasons to believe this a possible destination for the forces.

It is interesting to note the general order issued by the Japanese minister of war September 22, to the troops which were about to take the field, and to the others which were already in active service. It went far to prove to the civilized world, whose eyes were upon the operations of the war, that it was the desire of the Japanese authorities to conduct their hostilities with as much consideration for the humanities as is ever possible in war. The order was as follows:

"Belligerent operations being properly confined to the military and naval forces actually engaged, and there being no reason whatever for enmity between individuals because their countries are at war, the common principles of humanity dictate that succor and rescue should be extended, even to those of the enemy's forces who are disabled either by wounds or disease. In obedience to these principles, civilized nations in time of peace enter into conventions to mutually assist disabled persons in time of war, without distinction of friend or foe. This human union is called the Geneva convention, or more commonly the Red Cross association. Japan became a party to it in June, 1886, and her soldiers have already been instructed that they are bound to treat with kindness and helpfulness such of their enemies as may be disabled by wounds or disease. China not having joined any such convention, it is possible that her soldiers, ignorant of these enlightened principles, may subject diseased or wounded Japanese to merciless treatment. Against such contingencies, the Japanese troops must be on their guard. But at the same time they must never forget that however cruel and vindictive the foe may show himself, he must nevertheless be treated in accordance with the acknowledged rules of civilization, his disabled succored, his captured kindly and considerately protected. It is not alone to those disabled by wounds or sickness that merciful and gentle treatment should be extended. Similar treatment is also due to those who offer no resistance to our arms; even the body of a dead enemy should be treated with respect. We cannot too much admire the course pursued by a certain western nation which in handing over the body of an enemy's general, complied with all the rites and ceremonies

JAPANESE MILITARY HOSPITAL

suitable to the rank of the dead man. Japanese soldiers should always bear in mind the gracious benevolence of their august sovereign, and should not be more anxious to display courage than to exercise charity. They have now an opportunity to afford practical proof of the value they attach to these principles."

At the very time that these actions were occurring in Japan, measures of increased severity were being taken in China to punish those who were supposed to be responsible for the defeat. The emperor and his counsellors were in a state of alternate terror and indignation, at the break, down of the war arrangements and the possibility of a Japanese invasion. The emperor declared that the recent defeats could only have been caused by incompetence, or corruption, or both, among those charged with the conduct of the war, and the enemies of Li Hung Chang sedulously encouraged this mood. The viceroy himself remained to all appearances entirely unmoved. He made no preparation to proceed to the headquarters of the army in the field as it had been reported he would do, and it was believed that he would not leave Tien-tsin as long as his enemy had the ear of the emperor.

As Chinese fortunes went down, and admirals and generals and princes lost their high standing in the good graces of the emperor, other officials rose in favor to take their place. The personality of some of these men is peculiarly interesting because of the intimate connection and high authority they had from this time in the conduct of the war.

On the 30th of September an imperial decree was issued, appointing Prince Kung, the emperor's uncle, and the presidents of the Tsung-li Yamen and the Admiralty, as a special committee to conduct the war operations in co-operation with Li Hung Chang.

Prince Kung, whose proper title was Kung-tsin-wang, or the Reverend Kindred Prince, whom the emperor of China brought back to honor from retirement and disgrace by appointing him co-director with Li Hung Chang of the war arrangements, was a man who in the past had played a very important part in the history of China. At the outbreak of the war he was some sixty-three years of age, having been born about 1831. He was a man of great vigor and determination of character, and was possessed of abilities of a very high order. Prince Kung was the sixth son of Emperor Tankwang, who died in 1850. His personal name, which was used only by his family, was Yih-hu, while the people called him Wu-ako, or the Fifth Elder Brother. Prince Kung came to the front first in 1860, when Emperor Hien Feng the son of Tankwang fled from Peking, on the advance of the allied armies of Great Britain and France. At this critical moment the former returned to the capital, assumed the reins of government, and entered into negotiations with the allies. Having accepted their ultimatum, he surrendered the northeast

REVIEW OF CHINESE TROOPS AT PORT ARTHUR

gate, which commanded the city, on October 13, and eleven days later the treaty of Peking was signed by him and Lord Elgin.

The following year Emperor Hien Feng died, leaving a son as heir, whose age was only five years. Four of Prince Kung's elder bruthers were already dead, and the fifth had lost his position in Emperor Tankwang's household by being adopted into the family of another emperor. There was thus no one to claim precedence of him as the first prince of blood royal, during the minority of Tung-chi, the new emperor. A conspiracy had, however, been formed against him, with which he found it necessary to grapple immediately. The late emperor had left the administration of affairs practically in the hands of a council of eight, of whom Prince I was at the head. This council had decided upon a plan of action for seizing the reins of power. They proposed to obtain possession of the emperor's person, to put the empress-regents out of the way, and to kill Prince Kung and his two surviving brothers. Prince Kung, however, was not to be found napping. Having received news of the plot, he at once took measures to prevent its successful accomplishment, by carrying off the young emperor to Peking. The conspirators were then arrested and brought to trial. The Princes I and Chin, being of the blood royal, were permitted to take the "happy dispatch." The rest of the conspirators were either beheaded or banished. Thus did Prince Kung save from destruction the reigning dynasty of China.

For his great services he, was at once proclaimed "Regent Prince," and in conjunction with the two empress-regents assumed the government of China. He immediately adopted a vigorous policy in dealing with the Tai-Ping rebels, which was crowned with success. After Colonel Gordon's capture of Sachow, at the head of his ever victorious army, Prime Kung bestowed upon him a medal and ten thousand taels, which were refused. Prince Kung also successfully put down the Mohammedan rising in Yun-nan and Ran-pu, and opened up diplomatic intercourse with European powers. Prince Kung's determination not to accept the gunboats purchased in 1861 nearly led to serious results, and cost England $5,000,000. This crucial period was followed by another in 1870 when the Tien-bin massacre occurred. In all these events

Prince Kung showed that he possessed the gifts of a great statesman. When Emperor Tung-chi died childless in 1875, the choice of a successor to the dragon throne lay between Tsai-ching, the son of Prince Kung, and Tsai-tien, the son of Prince Chun, his younger brother. As the election of the former would have compelled the retirement of Prince Kung from active participation in the government of China, and as a continuance of his services was a matter of absolute necessity for his country, Tsai-ching was passed over in favor of Tsai-tien, a child of only four years of age, who adopted the name of Kwang-Su, or illustrious successor. Prince Kung, however, continued to act as regent of the country. The present emperor assumed the reigns of power in 1887, and subsequently he dismissed with disgrace the man whom he was afterwards pleased to honor, and who had rendered to China and the reigning dynasty such services as ought never to be forgotten.

When the Chinese fled from Ping-Yang towards Wi-ju they left behind them nearly a million dollars in treasure, thirty-six guns, two thousand tents, one thousand three hundred horses, and a considerable quantity of rice and other stores. Hard pressed by the pursuing Japanese, they abandoned their remaining four guns at An-ju, a town some seventy-five miles north of Ping-Yang. Thirty miles farther on, at Chong-ju, an important provincial town, they made a temporary halt, having received orders to hold the place pending the arrival of large reinforcements from the north. But the pursuit was too hot, and Chong-ju was evacuated without fighting. The next stand attempted to be made was at Ngan, where the troops were reinforced by orders from Shin-King, the province in which Mukden is situated. For a few days it was prophesied that the decisive battle of the war would be fought there, but the Chinese again abandoned their position and fell back upon Kaichan.

The Japanese army, while pushing forward towards Manchooria, showed the greatest consideration in their dealings with the Coreans, and any attempt at robbery or outrage on the part of the soldiery was most severely punished. The private soldiers were under the strictest orders to pay cash for everything that they obtained from the natives, and pains were taken to see that they should carry out their instructions. The result was that the Coreans began to appreciate that the Japanese were Letter friends to them than were the Chinese. The latter had been very severe in their exactions of supplies from the populace, and even though the Corean sympathies had been with

JAPANESE SOLDIERS DIGGING A WELL

the Chinese, the common people objected to the expense of quartering the army without recompense.

On the 4th of October the main portion of the advance

Japanese column reached Yong-chon, a little to the south of Wiju, after the difficult march from Ping-Yang, retarded by an extensive commissariat department and many guns. No sign of the enemy was reported at this place. Four days later, scouts reported that a small Chinese force still occupied Wi-ju, and a detachment of Japanese infantry and cavalry was thrown forward, supported by light artillery, to dislodge them. The Chinese offered but a slight resistance and fled precipitately before the smart attack, finally succeeding in getting across the Yalu. The larger body of Chinese troops had withdrawn across the river before this time, so that the forces remaining in Corea numbered not more than two thousand. Their loss in killed and wounded probably did not exceed one hundred. Wi-ju was occupied by the Japanese on the same day, and on the day after they began a reconnaissance which revealed the fact that the Chinese were still in force in the northern bank of the river. Eight intrenched batteries were discovered, and the enemy were rapidly throwing up fresh earthworks and building new batteries. Obviously the next fight was to be expected at this place, and if the Chinese held their grounds it would be a sanguinary one.

Marshal Yamagata still maintained his base at Ping-Yang, as being more convenient for securing his supplies by sea, while General Nodzu remained in advance with the forces. The Japanese line of communication was now complete throughout Corea, a sufficient number of troops being scattered through the peninsula at Fusan, Asan, Chemulpo, Seoul, Gensan, and Ping-Yang to guard against any hostilities on the part of the natives, and to make reinforcement by land safe. The government of Wi-ju was placed in the hands of a Japanese officer acting as special commissioner. The field telegraph was established in working order within two days after the capture of the place, and a regular courier service to the rear was inaugurated at once.

At the same time two or three detached revolts were in progress, the most important one being that of the Togakuto rebels in the province of Kiung-sang. These rebels were still in arms and in the mountain fastnesses it was hard to get near them. They had with them fifty Chinese soldiers who escaped when the Chinese were defeated at Asan and then joined the rebels. Those who had taken up arms against the corrupt Corean officials in the Province of Chung-chong had been dispersed, however, and the more formidable ones were now being gradually hemmed in.

When the middle of October came, the two armies were still facing each other on the banks of the Yalu. The Chinese had not yet fired a shot but kept at work night and day improving the natural advantages of their position. On the Japanese side there was no desire unduly to hurry the fighting, Marshal Yamagata choosing to wait for his heavier artillery and supplies before attacking. Spies kept him admirably informed as to the movements of the enemy, their defenses, and their artillery. They estimated the total strength of the Chinese massed along the north bank of the Yalu as between twenty-five and thirty thousand.

While the two armies are thus facing one another across the Yalu River, the Chinese having been driven from their last foothold in Corea, let us turn to the condition of affairs in the capitals of the two nations. The enemies of Li Hung Chang in Peking were busy in their efforts to cast disgrace upon him. Sheng, the taotai or chief magistrate of Tien-tsin, fell into disgrace and it was immediately alleged that he was a nephew of Li Hung Chang's and that the latter was probably a sharer in the results of his dishonesty. Just before the war broke out Sheng was commissioned to purchase arms and ammunition for the imperial troops, to be distributed to them as they arrived from the interior on the way to Corea. Rifles and cartridges were duly purchased, and nearly all were served out to the troops. As soon as they were put to the test of actual service they were found to be almost worthless, and strong complaints were sent to Peking and Tien-tsin. Li Hung Chang himself conducted an inquiry, and learned therefrom that Sheng bought from German agents three hundred thousand rifles of obsolete pattern, part of the discarded weapons, in fact, of more than one European army. The contract price of these rifles as between Sheng and the German sellers was two taels each, but the price charged by Sheng to the imperial treasury was nine taels each. The cartridges were of very inferior quality and of various pattern, and Sheng made a large profit on them also. After Sheng's guilt was proven upon him by the viceroy, he retired to his palace and for a time was seen no more in public. It was stated semi-officially that he applied for and was granted leave of absence on the ground of ill health. But a few days later it was reported that he was again enjoying the authority of his office, having been sustained against Li's wishes by some of the viceroy's enemies. Li's enemies became bolder and bolder. Placards denouncing him as the cause of China's troubles were posted on the walls of Tien-tsin and children in the streets sang doggerel songs ridiculing and insulting the great viceroy.

The foreigners resident in Peking and Tien-tsin became very restless under the impending invasion of China by the Japanese. Assaults on foreigners in Peking and its environs, which have been of constant occurrence during the last ten years, increased in frequency and gravity. Several English and American families withdrew to Shanghai because of the prevalence of street rowdyism. Tien-tsin was full of troops from the interior, but nearly all of them were the merest rabble, wretchedly clad, mutinous through lack of pay and insufficient rations, and useless for real war because of their antiquated weapons. Their continued presence in Tien-tsin was a distinct danger alike to Chinese and Europeans. An imperial edict published in Peking assumed full responsibility for the protection of foreign residents, denounced rowdyism, and ordered the punishment of certain culprits who had assaulted travelers. It assured the strangers the protection of their persons and their property, and was especially favorable to missionaries. The whole tone of the edict was considered highly satisfactory, and yet the government had failed to punish those who were responsible for the assaults and had taken no cognizance of the murder of a missionary, except to permit the governor of the province where the crime was committed to retain his high position.

A rebellion broke out in the district of Jeho, in the province of Chihli early in October, consequent on the rumored invasion of the Japanese. The imperial summer residence was in this city. Another Chinese rebellion broke out in the province of Hoopih about one hundred miles from Hankow. The local authorities attempted to quell the first rising but failed. Some of their soldiers were killed and others joined the rebels. Two mandarins lost their lives. In consequence of the urgent demands of the imperial authorities the province had been quite denuded of troops and there was practically no means at the command of the authorities to keep them in check. The Europeans at Hankow were seriously alarmed and many of them withdrew to Shanghai.

The emperor of China, early in October, began to take the initiative, attempting to infuse new energy into the national defense. It was indeed reported that he had disguised himself, and in person visited Tien-tsin, accompanied only by a few trusted servants, in order to see for himself what was going on, and particularly to learn the truth as to the alleged incapacity of Li Hung Chang to carry on the arrangements for the war. It was not, however, the emperor who made the journey in disguise, but his former tutor and trusted adviser Weng Toung Ho, the President of the Board of Revenue, or Finance Department. He also went to Port Arthur, Wei-hai-wei, and other places, and thoroughly informed himself of the state of affairs, civil, naval, and military. On returning to Peking he made an exhaustive report to the emperor, upon which the latter immediately began to take more interest in public affairs. He declined to sign documents until they had been previously read and explained to him, and called for special reports from the naval and military commanders. His next act was to summon to Peking the viceroys and governors of provinces, to receive from them accounts of the steps taken to comply with the demands of the imperial government, and to obtain from them their views as to the state of affairs. It was believed however by foreigners most able to judge that throughout all these actions the dowager empress of China was the active power in control. It was also believed that she was really a friend to Li Hung Chang, and that he would not suffer ultimate destruction unless she turned against him.

Another important action taken by the emperor was to confer the highest grade of the Order of the Double Dragon upon Captain Von Hannecken for his services at the naval battle of the Yalu River and to place him under practically sole control of the naval forces of China.

Constantine von Hannecken, the German officer who was put

in supreme control of what was left of the Chinese navy, had already seen a great deal of service in the war with Japan before his promotion to that post. He was on board the Kow-shing when she was overhauled and sunk by the Japanese cruiser Naniwa-Kan, with a loss of more than a thousand Chinese soldiers. Von Hannecken was left struggling in the water when the Kow-shing sank, but had the rare good fortune to be picked up by a boat. Still more recently he was high in command of the Chinese fleet at the disastrous battle of the Yalu River. He was slightly wounded but was soon ready for action again. This brave man was born in Wiesbaden, Germany,

in 1854, and was a son of the late Lieutenant-General von Hannecken. He served the usual term in the German army, and in 1879 went to China, where he was soon high in favor with Li Hung Chang. He mastered the Chinese language in a single year. His technical military knowledge, amiability, and tact, gained for him the position of personal adjutant to Li Hung Chang, with a large salary. He devoted much of his time to the construction of bridges and forts, and the fortifications at Port Arthur and Wei-hai-wei

CONSTANTINE VON HANNECKEN

were built under his personal direction. He was rapidly promoted to the highest military places within the gift of Li Hung Chang and the government, and received buttons, feathers, and jackets galore.

About a year before the outbreak of the war, having grown rich in the service of the dragon throne, he resigned from the Chinese army and returned to his home in Germany. After a stay of a few months he sailed again for China with the intention of settling his affairs there and retiring to Germany. The war with Japan changed this plan, and he promptly reentered the service of China

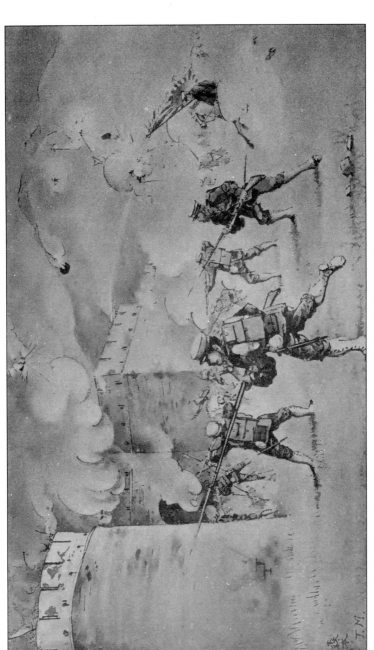

THE ATTACK ON PORT ARTHUR
Japanese Drawing

Admiral Ting and Captain Von Hannecken visited Wei-hai-wei to examine its defenses, and satisfied themselves that the harbor was practically impregnable from the sea. Japanese war vessels continually patrolled all pa its of the Gulf of Pechili, and were frequently seen from Port Arthur, Chefoo and Wei-hai-wei. The Japanese fleet was also sighted several times ten miles off Shanhai-kwan, less than two hundred miles from Peking.

The main body of the Chinese army was now entrenched in a strong position protected by a line of rectangular forts newly constructed across the northeast border of the province of Chihli. The Manchoos were held in reserve nearer Tien-tsin than Peking. Sung Kwei, the emperor's father-in-law, was in command of five thousand picked Manchoo soldiers at Shan-hai-kwan, which was a city of great strategic importance., the starting point of a great highroad to Peking from the coast.

General Sung, formerly commander of Port Arthur, was appointed to be Generalissimo of the Pei-Yang army corps in manchooria and Chief Commander of the Manchoo levies, with the exception of the Kirin division, which remained under the command of the Tartar general. The Chinese headquarters were established at Chiu-lien-tcheng. Generals Yeh and Wei were degraded by imperial edict.

On the 15th of October the newly-elected Japanese Diet met for a short preliminary session at Hiroshima, where the mikado had established his headquarters. The election of officers was immediately proceeded with, Mr. Kusumoto being chosen president, and Mr. Shimada vice-president. The formal opening of the Parliament took place two days later. The mikado in his speech announced that he had decided to convene an extraordinary session, and had given direction to his ministers to submit for the deliberation of the Diet a bill providing for increased expenditure for the army and navy, which was an important matter. His Majesty declared that he was greatly pained that China should have forgotten her duties in regard to the maintenance of peace in the east in conjunction with Japan, she having brought about the present state of affairs. "However," proceeded the emperor, "as hostilities have begun we shall not stop until we have obtained our utmost objects." In conclusion, His Majesty expressed the hope that all subjects of the empire would co-operate with the government, in order to promote the restoration of peace by means of the great triumph of the Japanese arms.

The president of the two chambers of the Diet presented an address in reply to the speech from the throne, thanking the mikado for advancing the imperial standard and for personally assuming the direction of the war. The victories which had been secured by the Japanese arms by land and sea were the natural result. The address in conclusion said: "His Majesty rightly considers China the enemy of civilization. We will comply with the imperial desire to destroy the barbarous obstinacy of that power."

In the House of Peers, on October 19, Count Ito, the premier, made an elaborate speech in support of the government measures for meeting the expenses of the war, and defended Japan against the charge of having precipitated the hostilities. He narrated in detail the circumstances which had led up to the war, and read the correspondence which had passed between the mikado's government and the authorities at Peking, before the rupture of diplomatic relations. The premier's statement made a great impression, and intensified the keenly patriotic feeling manifested by the members of the Diet, not a dissenting voice being raised against the ministerial bills. The following day the war budget of 150,000,000 yen passed both houses unanimously. This was the most important part of the proceedings of Parliament. The two houses fully demonstrated that they desired to hold up the hands of the government, and grant everything which might be asked to insure the success of the Japanese arms.

Simultaneously with the opening of Parliament an important diplomatic move was made by the Japanese. Now that Japan was practically in undisputed possession of Corea, the moment was considered opportune for the carrying out of those thorough reforms in the internal government of the country, to which Japanese statesmen looked forward as the best guarantee against foreign influence in the future. In order to strengthen the hands of Mr. Otori, the Japanese minister at Seoul, the emperor selected Count Inouye, minister of the interior, to proceed to the Corean capital to act as special adviser to Mr. Otori.

The Japanese Parliament had occasion to welcome an important

Corean messenger. The second son of the peninsular monarch left Chemulpo on the day the session began, as a special envoy to the mikado, returning the visit made to the king by the Marquis Sainonji. The young prince and his embassy, consisting of eight leading nobles, were received by the mikado and his principal ministers, being welcomed most cordially.

Just prior to the opening of the session, the British government addressed a circular note to the ministers of the great powers, suggesting intervention in the affairs of the east. The Chinese were in readiness to make terms of peace, conscious of the enormous sacrifices and risks which would have to be incurred before she could bring her immense reserves of strength into action, and being devoid of military ambition. The British cabinet council which decided upon this letter met on October 4, and three days later it was generally known, in spite of government denials, that the action had been taken. The reception of it was not cordial. In reply to the proposals put forward by England, the German government formally intimated that it was not prepared to join in any measures for circumscribing the political results of the conflict between China and Japan. The French government shared the same view, and the United States was earnest in the same expression. Russia, too, decided to avoid interference in connection with other nations, preferring to retain the opportunity of individual interference. On the part of Russia, the military commanders in the Amoor province were ordered to hold troops in readiness, in view of the fact that the situation in China might make intervention necessary. There seems to be good ground for believing true the rumor, oft repeated after the battle of the Yalu, that China had made to Japan overtures for peace, on the basis of an acknowledgment of Corea's independence, and payment of an indemnity for the losses and expenses of the war. The proposal was rejected by Japan as inadequate. Altogether it seemed that the initiative taken by the British foreign office was premature to say the least.

The mikado, in his address to Parliament, made no allusion to the proposals for peace, but seemed rather to look on the prosecution of the war to the end as the sole means of insuring lasting tranquility. With England's effort for European intervention in mind, Parliament adopted a resolution that, "No foreign interference will be suffered to obstruct the great object of the national policy, to secure a guarantee of permanent peace in the orient. 5; A renewed offer of mediation in the interest of peace was made to China and Japan in the name of some of the European powers, after the adjournment of Parliament. China declared her willingness to conclude an armistice or a peace on any reasonable terms; Japan refused to consider the proposal until it should be made directly at Hiroshima "From a quarter formally accredited and empowered to offer it."

The movements of troops, both Japanese and Chinese, were now multiplying to such an extent, that except for one familiar with the geography of eastern Asia, they were very confusing. Almost every day it was reported that some Japanese force had made a landing on the Chinese coast, rumor after rumor of this sort being circulated and denied. Chinese troops massed in the vicinities already named, their numbers constantly increasing. An army of five thousand Japanese was taken by transports along the east coast of Corea to Possiet harbor, near the boundary of Siberia, and five thousand Russian troops were posted on the other side, facing them, to guard the Siberian frontier. Corea was being steadily cleared of Chinese stragglers, deserters from the late army and others, who if allowed to be at large might develop into bandits or spies. The restlessness of the natives in the province of Chulla was difficult to restrain, and a combined force of Japanese and Corean troops was despatched to the district to quell the outbreak. Rumors of land battles in the north of Corea, on the lower Yalu, were circulated every day, but for a time were foundationless. Towards the end of October, troops began to pour into Tien-tsin in large numbers daily, and were disposed for the defense of the capital. Most of the new arrivals were infantry, the bulk of the cavalry being sent to the Manchoorian provinces to the northeast.

The fleets of the two nations were now again in fighting condition, although the loss of many vessels suffered by the Chinese at the Yalu had left them in strength far inferior to the Japanese. The Chinese fleet was concentrated at Port Arthur and Wei-haiwei, where it was believed to be safe from attack or favorably situated

SURRENDER OF CHINESE GENERAL AND STAFF

for offensive operations. The Japanese squadron under Admiral Ito was concentrated at Ping-Yang. On October 18 the last of the transports carrying the second Japanese army steamed out of the harbor of Ujina on their way to Hiroshima, where they were held in readiness for active operations.

The extraordinary session of the Japanese diet at Hiroshima was closed October 22, all the bills submitted by the government having passed unanimously. Before separating, the Diet voted a memorial urgently

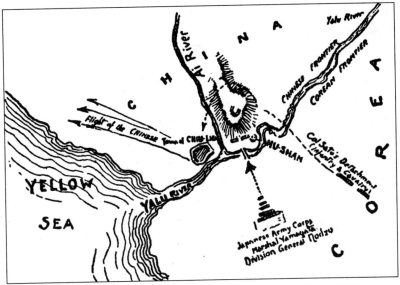

MAP OF TERRITORY ADJACENT TO THE MOUTH OF THE YALU

requesting the officers of the government to execute the desires of the Mikado, in order that Japan might achieve a complete victory over the Chinese, whereby peace would be restored in the east and the glory of the Japanese nation increased. A resolution was passed unanimously, placing upon record the thanks of the nation to the army and navy, for the gallantry and patriotism displayed by all ranks, and for the splendid success which had attended the Japanese arms.

On October 24 Count Yamagata, commander-in-chief of the Japanese forces in Corea, threw a small force across the Yalu, thus invading Chinese territory. In order to understand the subsequent operations, a brief topographical explanation is here necessary.

At a little distance below Wi-ju, the Yalu, flowing west, receives a tributary, the Ai, coming from the northeast. Chiulien lies in the western, or obtuse-angled corner formed by the junction of the two rivers, some distance back from their banks. Within the eastern, or acute -angled corner the land rises to an eminence called Hu-shan. A traveler by the main road from Wi-ju to Chiu-lien, having crossed the Yalu, must pass on the left or to the west of Hu-shan, which overlooks the highway, and thus reaching the Ai must cross it also to Chiu-lien. The Chinese had intrenched Hu-shan, and posted there a force estimated by the Japanese at three thousand five hundred, but subsequently alleged by prisoners to have aggregated seven or eight thousand.

The plan pursued by Field-Marshal Count Yamagata was to occupy a long stretch of the Yalu River, so that his point of passage would remain to the last uncertain, and any flanking movement on the east by the cavalry, of which the enemy possessed a large force, was rendered impossible. Having rested his troops and completed his arrangement for a final advance, he threw a battalion across the river under Colonel Sato, at Shai-ken-chau, a place ten miles up stream from Wi-ju. The passage was made by wading and was unopposed. The detachment was composed entirely of riflemen, no calvary or artillery accompanying them. A Chinese earthwork had been thrown up at this point to oppose a landing, but a slight deviation enabled the detachment to cross without interference. An attack was immediately opened on the Chinese position, which was garrisoned only by a few artillerymen and infantry. They fled after the first two or three rounds had been fired, and the Japanese captured the works with a rush. A regiment of Manchoorian cavalry arrived as the little garrison fled, and covered their retreat. The Chinese made for the batteries constructed lower down the river, the infantry throwing away their arms in their flight. The Chinese loss was about twenty killed and wounded, while on the Japanese side not a man was hit. The Japanese force now moved down the river and captured the Chinese fortifications at the Suckochi feny, where they passed the night. The Japanese engineers had pontoons in readiness for passage across the river.

During the night of the 24th, the Japanese pontoon men threw a bridge across the Yalu at the ferry, and at dawn the main body of the army, having passed over unopposed, commenced an attack against Hu-shan, Colonel Sato's brigade coming into action simultaneously from the other side. The battle began at 6:30 A.M., and lasted until a fewtminutes past 10. At first the Chinese held their ground with tolerable firmness, but presently, finding their position swept by rifle and artillery fire from a hill on their right flank, of which possession had been taken by a brigade under Major-General Osako, they broke and fled across the Ai to Chiu-lien. The reserves, however, did not join the rout. Posted advantageously, they preserved their formation and maintained a resolute fire, until thrown into confusion by a flanking movement, which placed a large force under Major-General Tachimi to the rear of their left. Then they too gave way, and retreated in confusion across the Ai, so hotly pursued that they had to abandon ten pieces of artillery. The Japanese had lost twenty killed and eighty-three wounded; the Chinese two hundred and fifty killed and a somewhat large number of wounded. Two divisions of the army then crossed the Ai and encamped on the east of Chiu-lien, the brigades of Major-General Tachimi and Colonel Sato posting themselves on the

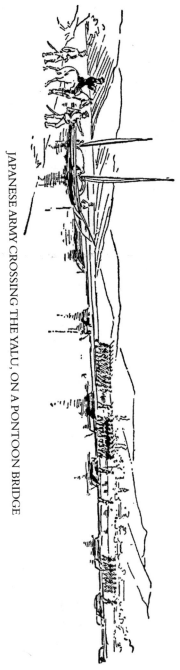

JAPANESE ARMY CROSSING THE YALU, ON A PONTOON BRIDGE

same side of the Ai, but further north, so as to menace the same road from Chiu-lien northward to Feng-hwang. Field Marshal Yamagata and Lieutenant-General Nodzu took up their quarters in a farmer's house to the northeast of Hu-shan. Thus with all the advantages of elevated ground, a position fortified at leisure, and a force ample for defensive purposes, the feebleness and faulty strategy of the Chinese converted into a mere skirmish what ought to have been a sanguinary battle.

The following morning, October, 26, before dawn, a general advance was commenced against Chiu-lien. It was supposed that the enemy would make an obstinate stand there, since after Feng-hwang the fortified town of Chiu-lien ranks as a position of eminent importance in the defense of southwestern Manchooria. Moreover, throughout the night a cannonade had been kept up from the town against the Japanese camp, and though the invading columns were posted so that the enemy's missiles passed harmlessly over them, this resolute service of guns seemed to promise stout fighting on the following day. But in truth the artillery was employed merely in the vain hope of intimidating the assailants, or in order to cover the flight of the garrison. The Japanese encountered no resistance whatever. At eight o'clock in the morning they entered Chiu-lien. The enemy had decamped in the direction of Feng-hwang before dawn, leaving behind him almost everything, twenty-two guns, three hundred tents, large stores of ammunition and quantities of grain and forage.

The series of defeats following the crossing of the Yulu River by the Japanese seemed to complete the Chinese demoralization in that vicinity. The defeated forces probably numbered more than twenty thousand men, the victorious army was considerably inferior in numbers, the batteries were well built, and the position was a strong one. The continuous loss of artillery, and throwing away of muskets and rifles wherever the Chinese made retreat, was gradually depleting the stores of arms possessed by the forces in Manchooria, leaving them unable to fight even if they had desired to. A little fighting evidently went a long way with them. Did they carry away their artillery and stores, these precipitate retreats might possess some strategical character, but they simply saved their own lives, leaving all their material of war behind

JAPANESE AT PORT ARTHUR

them. The troops at Chiu-lien were not ill-disciplined or badly armed from a Chinese point of view. Coming from Port Arthur, from Taku, and from Lu-tai, they ranked among the best soldiers China could put into the field. If such men proved themselves so conspicuously invertebrate, it was to be questioned whether or not the addition to their number of a few thousand Tartars would make them stand more stiffly in a subsequent conflict. It seemed even to the friends of China that her capacity for resisting the invasion of Manchooria in the face of well-organized and resolute attack, was simply contemptible.

The second invasion of Chinese territory was made by the second Japanese army corps, twenty-two thousand strong, under the command of General Count Oyama. These forces sailed in transports from Hiroshima, and on October 24 commenced landing in a little cove northeast of Talien-wan Bay and protected by the Elliot islands from the open sea. Talien-wan Bay was avoided because the Chinese were known to have made some preparations to resist a landing there. The peninsula which juts out southwestward between the Gulf of Liao-Tung and Corea Bay is known variously as the Liao-Tung peninsula and the Kwang Tung peninsula. Every yard of it was familiar to the Japanese military staff, and had been included in their system of minute cartography, so that whatever point they selected was well chosen. Up to the last moment it had been supposed by the general public that Port Adams, on the west of the peninsula, would be the port of debarkation, but as that would have involved the passing of a great flotilla of transports into Pechili Gulf, it was considered too hazardous an operation. The last of the flotilla of fifty transports left Hiroshima October 18, and the fleet having assembled at Shimonoseki, steamed westward on the morning of the 19th. A distance of eight hundred miles had to be traversed, and in this case as in all previous operations everything worked with smoothness and success. On the evening of the 23rd the great flotilla reached its destination, and on the following morning the landing was commenced.

There was no resistance. The Pei-yang squadron did not show. Had there been any ordinary exercise of vigilance on the part of Admiral Ting's war ships they must have sighted the

Japanese flotilla in ample time to strike at it. That they would have effected nothing in the face of the convoying squadron may be taken for granted, but if the prospect of failure deterred them from making any effort to protect their own headquarters, China's only dockyard and really important naval station in the north, they certainly deserved the indifference with which the Japanese treated them. From the time of the naval battle of September 17, the Pei-yang squadron played no part in the war. Many attempts were made to prove that it had not been vitally hurt in the encounter, and that a few days would suffice to put it in a thorough state of repair. But whether repaired or not it disappeared from the scene, and the Japanese cruisers thenceforth roamed at will along the Chinese coasts.

With the move towards the investment of Port Arthur, and the crossing of the Yalu, the war entered upon a new phase. In selecting Port Arthur as an objective point, the Japanese were well advised. By such an attack a dockyard of the first importance was threatened, and full advantage of naval superiority could be taken. The Kwang Tung peninsula, or "Regent's Sword," was peculiarly inaccessible by land, while a power in command of the sea could land men at pleasure at several points within a short distance of Port Arthur, and with a small force only could isolate it from the mainland.

Two days after the landing of troops on the peninsula, the collection of a third army at Hiroshima commenced. This force was to number twenty-four thousand, and be under the command of Lieutenant-General Viscount Takashima. At the same time another revolt of some little magnitude arose in the south of Corea, and two thousand rebels attacked the quarters of the Japanese commissary at Anpo. The malcontents were afterwards dispersed by a military force though not without difficulty.

We have now reached the end of October. The first Japanese army is safely installed on the north bank of the Yalu River in Manchoorian territory, threatening the road to Mukden, Niuchwang and the intervening cities. The second army is safe on shore on the Kwang Tung peninsula, threatening China's proudest naval station. The next month will see the fall of Port Arthur and the practical destruction of all Chinese hopes of ultimate success.

REVIEW OF THE PROGRESS OF THE WAR
TO THE FIRST OF NOVEMBER

Characteristics of the two Nations in War—China's Ignorance of the Coast of Corea—Japan's Knowledge of Chinese Topography and Climate—Patriotism In the Two Countries—Bad Judgement of China in Methods of Conducting the War—The Governmental Weather-vane and Its Revolutions—No Commander-in-Chief for the Chinese Army—Official Corruption in Civil as well as Military Officials—The Battles of Ping-Yang and the Yalu River—Handling the Forces of the Enemies.

At this period in the war, occurs a lull which makes it possible and wise to take a glance at the whole course of affairs during the hostilities, since the declaration three months earlier. The war has advanced far enough to prove the mettle of both combatants, and to furnish data for judging of the probable issue of the struggle, at least from a purely military point of view. At the beginning of November, prophets were quite well equipped with material for predictions that were surely not to be disappointed, and it is from the aspect at this date that the present chapter takes its view. On the one side there is little but praise to be offered. The Japanese have proved themselves assiduous students of all modern armaments, and have in many points bettered their European instruction. They have made good their claim to he the rising power of the Orient.

Of the Chinese a diametrically opposite account must be given. From a military standpoint nothing favorable can be said of: them, and the only palliation of their failure is that they were wholly unprepared for an unexpected aggression. The course of the war has brought out in strong relief what has not always been clearly recognized, the essential differences between the two belligerent nations. A stronger contrast is scarcely imaginable than that between China and Japan, though they, are so near and have been nursed on a common literature. With passionate effort the Japanese have ransacked the western world for, its treasures of knowledge, and have vigorously applied what they have learned. The Chinese, on the other hand, have set their faces against the science of other nations with an unhappy mixture of apathy and contempt have rejected the teaching which has pressed upon them. In the same spirit they have spurned the knowledge of their own country and of their own forces, while the Japanese have been for years making a minute study of both, and possess maps and details which the Chinese themselves have not and do not care for. The Chinese have carried on a large trade with the Yalu river, but the government knew nothing of the coast. Captain Calder of Port Arthur made a holiday expedition to the Manchoo-Corean coast, found the country beautiful, and recommended the naval authorities to let the cadets go and improve themselves by surveying it. Nothing was done, the sole reason being that the incidental expenses of the ships would be increased by being at sea, and the captains would not save so much of their monthly allowance. Now the only survey the Chinese admiral possesses even of the scene of the late naval battle, is the outline made by Captain Calder himself. The Japanese navy has complete clarts both of the Corean and the Chinese coasts. In the sumlmer of 1893 a small expedition of Japanese disguised as Chinese, in a native boat surveyed the islands and coasts of the Gulf of Pechili, spending eight days in the immediate neighborhood of Port Arthur. The topography and physiography of North China have been their study for years.

A Japanese physician even devoted a whole year to the climate and pathology. With his headquarters in Tien-tsin, where he plied the foreign doctors incessantly with queries, this Japanese investigator thoroughly explored the province of Chihli, and probably knows more of the climatic conditions of North China than any other living man. He pretended he had the intention of practicing among the Chinese, as possibly he may in the not distant future. The Chinese have started exotic medical schools, but they have not overcome the elementary difficulty about dissection, and the enterprise is but half hearted. As for employing competent men to gather knowledge, the whole idea is foreign to the Chinese official mind, and they only accept ungraciously as a gift the results of the explorations of enthusiasts for science. It is not, therefore, the accident of being a little earlier in the field, or quicker in movement to seize the benefit of an opportunity, that gives the Japanese such crushing advantages over the Chinese, but rather a deep-seated, congenital love of improvement on one side and hatred of it on the other.

Another essential difference between the people is their exhibition of patriotism. The Japanese are saturated with it, while the Chinese have none. The instinct of loyalty is there, and it can be called out by any man, native or foreign, who is worthy of it, but in the sense of nationality the Chinese have no capacity for enthusiasm, and the people as a whole are indifferent as to who rules them, so long as they are left to cultivate their gardens. For want of a patriotic focus, what would elsewhere be treachery is in China a commonplace of official practices; every man to the limit of his small ability selling his country for his private benefit, and no one able to cast a stone at his neighbor. In Japan it would be impossible to get a man to betray his fatherland; in China where is the man who would not? From the same root springs the incredible difference between the peoples in their treatment of soldiers and sailors. In the one country they are made heroes of, the people at home send delicacies to the troops abroad, honor the dead, and nurse the wounded. In the other the men are treated worse than dogs, robbed of their small pay, deserted, discarded, or grossly neglected by their leaders whenever they can be dispensed with and their monthly pay saved. Attachment between men and officers in China is a rare, though not an unknown thing, for the Chinese are, after all, human at heart, if one can but penetrate the pile of hereditary corruption which has covered up the divine spark.

The foregoing are but examples which might be multiplied indefinitely, of the antitheses of Chinese and Japanese character and mode of action. If to all this is added the fact that the Japanese are a people who delight in war, while the Chinese abominate it, no further search is needed for explanation of the actual result. It is simply ignorance overcome by science, indifference by energy.

The Chinese have conducted the campaign in the manner those best acquainted with them would have predicted, doing on most occasions the utterly wrong thing, or stumbling on the right thing at the wrong time in the wrong way. But the most pessimistic prophet could hardly have predicted the utter inaptitude of the Chinese military movements. It is not only that they have failed to learn the modern art of war, but that they have forgotten the old methods. It was thought that Chinese troops, though deficient in enterprise, might at least make a respectable defense. They were advised never to risk a pitched battle, but to retreat slowly, giving trouble to the enemy by night attacks on his baggage, and compelling him to use up an army corps to keep open his line of communication. They failed in every point, and allowed themselves to be chased and caught like sheep, losing stores, guns, and munitions. When all else failed, it was said that winter would come to their assistance, as the Japanese could never stand the cold, while the Chinese and Manchoos were inured to it. But when the cold came it was found that it was not the Japanese but the Chinese who suffered, having abandoned their warm clothing in precipitate flight. Their heart was never in the business, and nothing therefore could go right with the Chinese conduct of the war.

While the war was incubating, China had to make up her mind how she was to meet the aggression of the Japanese in Corea. Candid friends, who knew well that her inchoate forces could never be a match for any organized army whatsoever, commended strictly defensive strategy. She was caught in the false position—in a military sense, though it was politically correct—of having a small force isolated in southern Corea, while the Japanese were occupying the capital in strength. The fighting value of the respective fleets was as yet an unknown quantity, but on the Japanese side there was confidence in their own superiority, and on the part of the Chinese a tacit acquiescence in that estimate. Under such circumstances an over-sea campaign was an absurdity for China, and the commonest prudence dictated that the small garrison at Asan be withdrawn before the outbreak of war.

This crisis in affairs was met, as crises usually are in China, by divided counsels; moral cowardice on the part of those who knew, blind rage on the part of those who did not know, and the submission of the judgment of the informed to the arbitrary decrees and even the insidious advice of the uninformed. To speak plainly, Li Hung Chang on, a whom the burden of the war would in all oases rest, and who knew something, though very little, of the power of discipline organization, and who from the first was strongly opposed to the intervention in Corea, which was forced on him by pressure applied from Peking, was for withdrawing the garrison from Asan. In answer to his memorials to the throne, he had obtained the imperial authority and had hired transports to bring the troops over into Chinese territory. But other

SINKING OF THE KOW-SHING. *(Drawn by a Chinese Artist.)*

counsels supervened, and Li Hung Chang refrained from giving effect to his own views. As the Japanese were by imperial fiat to be driven out of Corea, it followed that the garrison at Asan must be strengthened, and China committed herself to the conditions of war dictated by the enemy, an offensive war oversea, which was entirely beyond China's capacity.

There were still discussions and hesitations up to the moment of dispatching troops by sea to Corea. When the expedition of troop was seen to be inevitable, the Chinese were advised to take at least the precaution of having the transports escorted by a strong naval squadron. This was decided to be done, and the illfated Kaw-shing left Taku on the clear understanding that an escort of warships would join her outside Wei-hai-wei, which was two hundred and twenty miles distant, and roughly

NAVAL SKIRMISH, JULY 25TH. *(Drawn by a Chinese Artist)*

half way to Asan. But before the transport had got so far on her voyage, the official weathercock had set in another direction. The diplomatic Yuan-ei-Kai, former resident in Corea, where he had done so much to irritate the Japanese, now advised that the appearance of warships with the transports, might give umbrage to the Japanese, and in deference to this opinion, before the pendulum had time to swing back, the Kawshing with twelve hundred men on board, was sent unprotected to the bay of Asan. The Japanese consular establishment, with its wonderfully organized intelligence department, was still in Tien-tsin, perfectly informed

ROUTED CHINESE FLYING BEFORE THE VICTORIOUS ENEMY

of everything that was being said and done in the most secret places, and making free use of the telegraph wires.

With the tragic destruction of the Kow-shing, the war was begun most disadvantageously to the Chinese. Being by one and the same stroke deprived of the expected re-enforcements and cut off from the sea, the small force at Asan had either to fight to the death, surrender, or make

SKIRMISH ON JULY, 27TH. *(Drawn by a Chinese Artist)*

good their retreat by a long and dangerous flank march. This last course was adopted, and after making sufficient stand to cover their retreat, not without inflicting loss on the enemy, they succeeded in joining the Chinese army which had entered Corea from the north-west. The numbers of the retreating force were given as four thousand, but they were certainly less.

The simultaneous engagements by land and sea on the same day, July 25, proved that the Japanese had determined to begin the war in earnest. The naval action in which two Chinese ships were waylaid as they were leaving the Corean coast, served to prove that the Chinese ships could both fight and run away, and that the Japanese ships were very ably manoeuvred, but the affair had little other significance.

Enraged by the sinking of the transport in time of nominal peace, the emperor of China ordered the fleet, over the head of Li Hung Chang, to pursue the enemy to destruction. In obedience to the imperial mandate,

BEFORE THE WALL OF SEOUL (Drawn by a Chinese Artist)

the Pei-yang squadron, in the early days of August, steamed for the Corean coast, but before sighting it steamed back again. The viceroy Li then interested himself to obtain a modification of the decree, and the fleet was commanded to remain on the defensive for the special protection of the Gulf of Pechili, which instruction held good until the middle of September, when the fleet was forced to accept battle off the Yalu river.

August 1st, troops were ordered to enter Corean territory from the Manchoorian side, and in the course of the month a considerable force had filtered its way to the city of Ping-Yang, the strongest strategical point in western Corea, and even to a considerable distance beyond. The massing of these troops was conducted in the old rough-and-tumble, half-hearted Chinese fashion. There was no head, but separate and rival commands, each general looking only to the viceroy, Li Hung Chang for orders and supplies, and receiving more of the former than of the latter.

These Chinese generals are an old world curiosity, scarcely conceivable in our age. They might be described as army contractors rather than fighting agents, for like the civil mandarins they buy their posts as an investment. The battalion or camp is farmed, as regards its expenses, by the general, who draws from government a lump sum for the maintenance of the force, and makes his economies according to his conscience, by falsifying his muster roll and defrauding his men. At the battle or rout of Ping-Yang there were soldiers who were three, four, and even five months in arrears of pay, some generals deliberately calculating on the casualties of war to reduce the number of eventual claimants on the pay fund. The most notorious offender, General Wei of Ping-Yang notoriety, who had less than half the troops he drew pay for, and these mostly untrained coollies, hustled into the ranks to take the place of unpaid deserters, and in whose program fighting had no place, had paid certain influential persons liberally for his command. Desertion, it may be observed in passing, is not regarded as a calamity by an avaricious Chinese general.

Chinese officers are however by no means all abandoned to money making. Some are liberal with their funds, just as some are brave and loyal, and are backed by equally brave and loyal soldiers. The efficiency of a force depends altogether on the personality of the general, and as in feudal times in Europe, it is to their chief rather than to any government or country that the troops feel the ties of allegiance. As the leader is, therefore, so are the men. General Tso-pao-kwei for example, who bore to his grave the honors of the fight at Ping-Yang, was a man well known to many foreigners of different classes, missionary and others, and the unanimity of good opinion of him is quite remarkable. He was not only brave, but a courteous and kindly gentleman who gained the affections of all around. A Mohammedan himself, all his soldiers were of the same faith, and they stood shoulder to shoulder like heroes in the face of overpowering odds.

During the month of August, while the Japanese forces were advancing upon Ping-Yang in three columns, there were outpost skirmishes in which the Japanese were frequently worsted. These affairs were naturally enough reported by the Chinese commanders concerned, according to their lights, as victories, and when it is remembered how the view of each is bounded by the horizon of his own camp, it is easy to see how they could deceive themselves as to the significance of such apparent success. The truth seems to be that the Chinese commanders in and about Ping-Yang did not realize that they were surrounded, each perhaps thinking it was the other's business. They had sent out no scouts, nor posted videttes to watch the mountain passes to the north of them. These elementary military precautions had been pressed on Li Hung Chang, who sent repeated orders to the front to have them seen to; but nothing was done, for according to the vicious tradition of the Chinese service, the word is taken for the deed, and orders which are either impracticable or inconvenient are simply ignored or forgotten, without the delinquent being ever called to account. Spacious but wholly fictitious excuses would in any case serve the turn in a system whose fetich is universal sham. Perhaps, as there was no commander-in-chief, but a number of independent commands, duties which concerned the army at large fell within the sphere of no one in particular. But in whatever manner it came about, the result was that the Chinese remained in comatose ignorance of the intentions of the enemy, until the only thing left was precipitate retreat.

The affair of Ping-Yang was observed by one military expert, a Russian, who speaks in high terms of the precision and completeness of the Japanese equipment and organization, but the opposition had been so contemptible throughout the war that the military qualities of the Japanese have not been seriously put to the proof. They remain a theoretical quantity. So far as the campaign had gone, to November 1, the chief obstacles encountered had been bad roads, standing crops, and sickness.

The second day after the flight from Ping-Yang, September 17, the naval battle off the Yalu River was fought. The collision of the fleets seems to have been somewhat unpremeditated. The Chinese were engaged in disembarking troops for the re-enforcement of the army at Ping-Yang, and it is a characteristically haphazard proceeding that they should have been landing troops one hundred and twenty miles from the front, to strengthen a position already abandoned. The battle which ensued, and which raged for five hours, has been described with as much fullness as the limits of this volume permit, but the ultimate truth about it will perhaps never be fully known except of course to the Japanese government. From the Chinese side it will be impossible to obtain a consistent account, not because of intentional concealment, but because of the simple reason that no one in the Chinese fleet was able to observe accurately what was going on, except near his own vessel. Nevertheless the salient points of the battle stand out clear enough. The sea fight was but a repetition of the land fight, with two important differences. The first of these was that as the nature of the cause rendered it impossible to sail modern ships of war at all by two-thousand-year-old tactics, the mere possession of a fleet required a European organization. But the organization was imperfect, and would have been unable to sustain itself in action, but for the presence of another element in which the Chinese land forces were entirely lacking, competent foreign direction. This factor also was most imperfect. The foreign officers had been extemporized hastily, the leader of them being not even a seaman. They were of various nationalities and were enlisted about the middle of August. Three engineers, two German, one English; two gunnery officers, one English, one German; had been for some years in the fleet, and volunteered for war service. One American engaged for many years in the Chinese naval college also volunteered for active service during the war. Captain Von Hannecken, bearing now the rank of Chinese general, commissioned as Inspector General of Fortifications, was entrusted with the anomalous office of adviser of the admiral, thus giving him the real command of the fleet. An English civilian with naval training also joined.

On entering on their duties, these officers found the fleet honey combed with abuses requiring patient reform, but they set themselves to make the best of things as they were, and to get the ships as quickly as possible into action, as the thing most needful in order to brace up officers and men. Von Hannecken urged unceasingly an offensive policy. He would seek out the Japanese and attack them wherever found, fall on their convoys, and generally assert the supremacy of China in Corean waters, from the Yalu eastward. In particular he urged the occupation of Ping-Yang inlet, so important for the support of the army which held the city of that name, and, if necessary, to fight to the death for the possession of a harbor at once so valuable and so easily defended. His prescience was indicated in the sequel, but to all such suggestions Admiral Ting replied with the imperial edict which forbade him to move out of Chinese waters. The convoying service for which the fleet was eventually told off in the middle of September was a sort of compromise, which, without transgressing too flagrantly the imperial restrictions, yet committed the fleet to an engagement on conditions not of its own choosing.

The handling of the respective fleets showed the great superiority of the Japanese professional training, and critics have commented on the weakness of the Chinese manoeuvring, but the first consideration was to get the Chinese to fight at all. The government had satisfied itself that without foreigners to lead them, the Chinese commanders would rather lose their ships in trying to escape than stand up to the enemy. The man, the only man available, who possessed the requisite qualities, personal and professional, including a competent knowledge of Chinese, happened to be a soldier, but he at least made the fleet fight, not as a trained admiral would have done with a trained fleet, but in a manner to inspire the Chinese with some confidence in themselves, in which till then they were greatly lacking. That is perhaps the most important result of the baptism of fire of the Chinese navy.

As regards the technical bearings of the action off the Yalu, the Chinese admiral and captains adopted the formation which they said had been taught them by Captain Lang as the most advantageous for attack. But obviously a plan communicated four years ago by an officer whom these same men had intrigued out of their navy, when he had taken it through only half its course of training, could not be considered an infallible weapon with which to meet the thoroughly efficient navy of Japan.

The fight brought out several of the weak points of the Chinese naval organization, and taught the officers many lessons. Most conspicuously was the fatuous economy of ammunition exposed. The most formidable ships for offense and defense were of course the two iron clads Ting-Yuen and Chen-Yuen, with their twelve and one-half inch guns. These guns throw a shell three and one-half calibres long, charged with forty pounds of powder. It is a projectile of low initial velocity, but a most destructive explosive, as the Japanese have testified. There were but four of these shells in the fleet, all being on board the Chen-Yuen. Of a smaller, and of course cheaper shell for the same guns two and one-half calibres long, used for target practice, there were in all fourteen in the two iron clads, and they were fired off in the first hour and a half of the engagement, after which only steel shot was left with which to continue the fight. From the condition of the flag ship and her consort, may be inferred that of the other vessels in the fleet. They were at once however, after the battle, well supplied with shell except of the larger size.

The Chinese fleet was at a disadvantage in manoeuvring from inferior speed, but a greater difficulty even than that was the perversity of the personnel. Even on board the flag ship orders were not carried out, but varied or suppressed at the discretion of the officers. In telegraphing from the conning tower to the engine room, the plans of the admiral were frustrated, by the officer who moved the telegraph signalling a low speed when the admiral was ordering a high speed, in order to close with the enemy. This trick was only discovered after the battle, by comparing notes with the German engineer who was below. How many other ways of cheating the commanding officer were resorted to during those critical hours, no one can tell. As for the other ships of the fleet, it is acknowledged that after the first round they kept no formation, each ship fighting her own battle, except the two ironclads with the foreign officers on board, which kept moving in concert till the close. The flagship lost all her signal halyards and a number of signal men in the beginning of the action, and thereby lost touch with the rest of the squadron.

From the capture of Ping-Yang, to the first of November, the progress of the war attested the circumspection of the Japanese, who from first to last resolved to risk nothing by land or sea. There was practically no resistance, and the Chinese government was tolerably aware that there would be none, either at the Yalu or at Feng-hwang-tcheng. What the government reckoned on, if they can be said to have made any reckoning at all, was that the forces assembled at Chiu-lien-tcheng would delay the advance of the enemy till something turned up, or till the winter should come to the aid of the invaded. Well, winter came, and lo it was the Chinese and not the Japanese who were its first victims. Poor General Sung, driven out of Kiu-lien-tcheng, and falling back on Feng-hwangtcheng, was followed up so sharp

JAPANESE CAVALRYMAN

that, with the remnant of his force, he had to retreat to the mountains, without extra clothing or baggage. The cold set in, and snow was falling on these shivering wretches, while the enemy was enjoying the comparative luxury of the towns and villages.

By this time in the history of the war, it seemed certain that in such a conflict as was to be anticipated, China would not entrust the ultimate defense of the empire to such loose levies as had been in the field. From the time of their organization, these

PORT ARTHUR—TRANSPORTS ENTERING THE INNER HARBOR

troops under arms have constituted a danger to the peace of China, whether in victory or defeat, and perhaps there was a certain cynical calculation in the release by the Japanese of prisoners, that they might swell the ranks of brigands. It was believed by many friends of China that the dispersion of these troops would make room for an army built up on a different system, should the government be at last aroused to a sense of the necessity for military reform.

Until this time, the government of China properly so called, had not been able to bring its intelligence to bear on the question of imperial defense. That had been left in the hands of the imperial viceroy Li Hung Chang, who has for many years conducted the foreign as well as the naval and military affairs of the empire. But during the fall the Peking government was gradually gathering the reins into its own hands. The return of Prince Kung to the counsels of the emperor was a marked expression of the new resolution. The summoning of Von Hannecken by imperial edict to Peking was another indication of the suspension of Li Hung Chang's function of general middleman between the empire and the world. Whether this new born energy for affairs was to have staying power sufficient to launch the government on the unknown sea of foreign science, and save the empire from disruption was problematical, but the war still raged on, and out of its immediate issues, it was predicted by many, was to arise a state of thing which would mock the slow progress of mere evolutionary reform, by a cataclysm which might do in one day what a century of deliberation could not accomplish.

LIEUT. GEN. VISCOUNT NODZU

THE ADVANCE UPON PORT ARTHUR

Landing of the Second Japanese Army at Kwa-yuen-ken—Capture of Kincho—Taking of Tailen-wan—Flight of the Chinese to Port Arthur—General Nodzu's force and its action—Pekin Authorities Despondent—Prince Kung Asks Foreign Intervention—Propositions of Peace Fail—Contractors Want to Destroy Japanese Fleet—Foreigners in Chinese Service—The Emperor Receives Visitors—Drawing Near to Port Arthur—People of the Peninsula—Skirmishes on the Way—The Night Before the Battle.

The troops of the second Japanese army landed at a place called Kwa-yuen-ken near the mouth of the Pili River, northeast of Talien-wan Bay. From the mouth of the Pili to Kinchow, the principal town in the peninsula, the distance is fifty-four miles. The debarkation was completed without interruption, and the march southwestward began. The capture of Kinchow, at the narrowest point in the Adams Isthmus, was made without difficulty, and the victorious forces continued on their way. November 7 the Japanese occupied Talien-wan. The more the captured Chinese position here was examined, the greater became the astonishment at the poor defense made. The defensive works were excellent in design. Six large and strongly constructed forts commanded Talien-wan bay, mounting all together eighty guns of various sizes and patterns. Many of them were comparatively modern and excellent of their kind. All of these guns, as well as large stores of ammunition, fell into the hands of the Japanese.

Beside the forts on the bay, the Chinese had constructed across the narrow neck of the peninsula, which was here about seven miles wide, a series of earthworks of an elaborate kind. The whole system had evidently been planned by an engineer of high skill. It was completely fitted with telephones and other modern appliances for communication. The works had been designed to facilitate a concentration of troops at any threatened point in the shortest possible time. The batteries were powerfully constructed and well armed. The greatest strength of the forts on the bay was on the side facing the sea. Some successful reconnoitering revealed weakness upon the land side. An intimation was conveyed to Count Ito that the seaward forts were of such strength that a bombardment from the Japanese fleet would assuredly result in serious damage to some of the ships. Marshal Olyama informed his colleague that he believed a land attack would be attended with success, and that idea was therefore put into effect.

The Japanese fleet took a station off the bay, and opened a tremendous bombardment of the forts on the 6th of November. For many hours the firing scarcely ceased, and on the following day it was resumed. On the 7th, covered by the bombardment, the land force attacked Talien-wan at

CHINESE EARTHWORKS

daybreak by a general assault, and the success was complete. The Chinese, taken by surprise, fled panic-stricken towards Port Arthur.

The losses in the capture of these two fortifications, Kinchow and Talien-wan, were not great on either side. The Chinese garrison at the former place consisted of one thousand infantry and one hundred cavalry. They fled to Talien-wan, which was defended by three thousand infantry and one hundred and eighty cavalry, and all together retreated thence towards Port Arthur. On the Japanese side the losses were only ten killed and wounded, and the losses of the Chinese, who offered practically no resistance, were not much greater. As in previous retreats, the Chinese threw away their arms in their flight, and reached Port Arthur with nothing but the clothes they wore.

During these days of action by the force under Oyama, General Nodzu's troops had not been idle, Immediately after the capture of Chiu-lien, the Japanese headquarters' staff moved there from Wi-ju. Two columns were sent after the fleeing Chinese, Colonel Sato moved upon An-tung, which was taken without fighting. General Tachimi, with the first division, moved upon Feng-hwang on October 27, and on the 31st the town surrendered.

VIEW OF TALIEN-WAN BAY

· No prisoners were taken by the Japanese. The orders were to disarm and scatter the enemy wherever found, and this was done with vigor. By Marshal Yamagata's orders, the peaceable inhabitants were treated with the utmost consideration. All food purchased was paid for and laborers were paid for any extra help required. As a result the Japanese camp was thronged with Chinese peasants offering produce, and more Chinese laborers asked for work than could be engaged.

The enemy divided in flight from Feng-hwang, some going to Mukden, others to Hai-tcheng, and others to Taku-shan. Most of the generals fled to Mukden. As the last fugitives left Fenghwang it was set on fire, and the flames wrecked the village before the Japanese could extinguish them. Cold had set in among the Manchoorian hills by this time and some snow had fallerr. The victorious army therefore took pains to make itself as comfortable as possible, advancing slowly, living off the county, and driving all enemies before it.

In Peking at this time the authorities were busy attempting to devise means of safety for their armies, and to provide for their own escape from threatening danger. Li Hung Chang was deprived of all his decorative honors. Liu Kunyi, viceroy of Nanking, was made viceroy of Tien-tsin. Chang Chi Stung, Viceroy of Wu-chang, was appointed viceroy of Nanking. Hu Yuff, a judge of Kwang-hsi, and Captain Von Hannecken were ordered to enlist and equip a force of troops after the German model, as the nucleus of a new grand army of China. Finally Prince Kung was appointed Chief Controller of Military Affairs, with Prince Chung to assist him, thus further centralizing the power.

Another imperial edict gave executive effect to the sentence passed by the military courts upon General Wei. It declared that by his withdrawal from the battle of Ping-Yang he caused the defeat of the entire army. Furthermore, he was adjudged guilty of embezzling public funds entrusted to him for the specific purpose of paying his soldiers, and of gross incompetence and violation of duty in that he permitted the troops with whom he retreated to maltreat and rob the people along the line of route, thereby lowering the national character. For these offenses General Wei was degraded from military rank and deprived of all his honors. It was also announced that Admiral Ting kept from the knowledge of the throne many important matters connected with the naval battle of the Yalu, and that while losing some ships and getting others crippled he inflicted scarcely any damage upon the enemy. The admiral was therefore deprived of all the honors recently bestowed upon him under a misapprehension of the facts.

How despondent was the view of the situation held by the Chinese authorities may be judged by the first action taken by Prince Kung after his promotion. On Sunday, November 4, before the news of the Japanese success at Talien-wan had reached the Chinese, owing to the cutting of the telegraph wires, he invited the representatives all the powers to assemble at the Tsungli Yamen to hear what the Chinese government had to say respecting the critical situation. At this audience Prince Kung calmly avowed the complete impotence of his country to withstand the Japanese attack, and appealed to the powers to intervene. He made an appeal for their assistance in bringing about some agreement for the termination of the war, indicating as a basis of negotiation a willingness of China to abandon her claim to the suzerainty of Corea, and to pay a war indemnity to Japan. This appeal was made formally and officially, and marked for the first time the fact that China recognized her utter defeat.

Having concluded his speech, Prince Kung handed to each minister a note embodying his remarks. The ministers were favorably impressed, and they applauded the frankness of China's confession. They promised to support her appeal to their respective governments, with a view to the restoration of peace, and in order to avert the dangers threatening all interested. Simultaneously with this action of Prince Kung, the Chinese minister to Great Britain and France endeavored to enlist the assistance of the foreign offices of those countries, but again the effort to secure peace for China by the intervention of western nations met with little encouragement.

A diplomatic complication arose between Japan and France early in November which had an element of comedy in it and is of interest here. Two American citizens, John Brown and George Howie, of British extraction, offered their services to the Chinese government in the capacity of torpedo experts. They claimed to be in possession of an invention capable of most destructive effects in naval warfare, and having succeeded in convincing a Chinese agent of the validity of their claim, they were engaged to employ the invention against the Japanese navy, in consideration of a payment of 1100,000 down, $1,000,000 for each naval squadron destroyed, and a proportion of the value of each merchantman sent to the bottom. With their contract in their pocket, they sailed from San Francisco, and at Yokahama transferred themselves to the French steamer Sydney. Meanwhile the Japanese authorities, having obtained intelligence of the two men's proceedings, telegraphed instructions to Kobe, and in that port the alleged inventors were taken off the ship, together with their Chinese companions. The French minister inclined to push the case in their favor, but diplomacy and international law was so clearly on the side of the Japanese that he withdrew his efforts. After their arrest however, the two men signed a stringent guarantee binding themselves not to assist the Chinese during the present war, and this with the representation of the American minister secured their release.

The Japanese forces occupying Talien-wan used their time to advantage in strengthening their positions, completing the telegraph line along the north shore of Corea Bay, to a junction with the line which had already been built across the Yalu River from Corea, and in preparing for their investment of Port Arthur. Admiral Ito's sailors and marines destroyed all the torpedoes placed by the enemy in the bay and its approaches. They also captured several torpedo boats and apparatus. The fleet and the transports all entered the bay, and there remained to act in harmony with the land forces. A few days after the occupation of Talien-wan, the advance column of the first Japanese army, pursuing from Feng-hwang that portion of the divided fugitive Chinese who were seeking Port Arthur, met the outposts of the second invading army, and communication was thereby established, both by telegraph and by messenger service, through Japanese garrisons, in a chain extending the full length of the Corean peninsula and around Corea Bay to Talien-wan.

Consternation was caused in Peking by the discovery, which one would have supposed not difficult, that the Pei-yang squadron was caught in a trap at Port Arthur. Li Hung Chang had made efforts to bring all the damaged war ships out of that harbor, ordering the squadron to keep within range of the guns of Weihai-wei. But on account of somebody's violation of orders, a dozen Chinese vessels of war were now within the Port Arthur harbor, hemmed in by the neighboring Japanese fleet. The responsible Chinese officials appeared to be callous to the fate of the empire, giving their chief attention to matters of personal interest and gain.

Port Arthur was now effectively invested and threatened, and to provide for their personal safety, Kung, the taotai of the

PORT ARTHUR—JAPANESE COLLIES REMOVING CHINESE DEAD

place, together with several military leaders, abandoned Port Arthur as hastily as possible. The effort made by one Englishman, anxious to preserve some Chinese dignity, to save Port Arthur, was received with considerable surprise and not by any means appreciated.

The position of foreigners in the employ of the Chinese government has always been anomalous, but the exigencies of the war have shown up the relationship between Chinese and foreigners in a vivid and highly instructive light. Their rooted aversion to foreigners, which springs from fear, does not withhold the Chinese from flying to seek foreign aid in their extremity. On these occasions they betray a superstitious feeling towards the foreigners, regarding him as a sort of medicine man who can see through a millstone or work any other miracle. Their idea is to hire him by the job, and when the job is done cast him off as any other laborer. When war came upon them, the Chinese fleet was in a quandary, scuttling about from one snug harbor to another, the officers knowing nothing of their enemy, his movements, or his capacities. Though they were told they had the strongest fleet, they would have preferred not to put its presumed superiority to too severe a test, yet they had the imperial order to destroy the enemy unconditionally. In this extremity, the authorities cast about for extemporized foreigners to help them.

A hardy Scandinavian came first to the rescue, offering to scout, pilot, or fight for them, run a torpedo boat, or do anything that youthful daring might legitimately venture. Only he stipulated for a twenty-knot steamer, performing, however, in the meantime, the emergency service in a common tugboat of less than half that speed. The promise of a fast steamer was broken, as every promise of every Chinese official, with few exceptions, from the beginning of time has been broken, and until the end of the war the hardy Norseman had to content himself on the deck of that same wet and lively tugboat. Comical indeed were the adventures he had with his convoys of troops, munitions, and stores, which never would follow the program laid down for them, sometimes bolting from the smoke of their own escort, and and he chasing them back into their own ports whose forts would open fire on him. This was the uniform experience of Europeans who served the Chinese. The zeal and loyalty were all on the side of the aliens, whose hearts were broken in hopeless efforts to make the Chinese do their duty to their own country. Every foreigner who served China, no matter in what capacity, unless he belonged to the class which is content to draw pay and say nothing, had the same strenuous battle with his employers to compel them to interest themselves in their own service. The Chinese, on their part, failed to comprehend the folly of the foreigner who was not content to draw his pay and keep quiet.

At Port Arthur there were some half dozen rival generals, but no one in command, each caring only for his own camp, and all at loggerheads with the others. The head of the port, the poor taotai, of the literary graduate order, was a brother of the present minister to England. There was also the admiral of the Pei-yang squadron, the most likely man to assume the responsibility of a general command; but for fear of getting himself disliked by Taotai Kung or the generals, he kept his hands out of mischief. Finally, the English harbor master at Port Arthur went to Tien-tsin, and showed the condition of affairs to the viceroy. The result was that the viceroy sent instructions to Kung, which the latter ignored, flying from Port Arthur at the first chance. The collapse of Chinese resistance was proceeding at a rate which more than astonished the Japanese themselves. With Kinchow and Talien-wan captured almost without a blow, although amply supplied with the means of making a vigorous and protracted defense, and all the soldiers joining in an ignominious rush for Port Arthur, it seemed that the Chinese were exhibiting all that reluctance to make trouble which characterized Crockett's famous 'coon, demonstrating their willingness to come down to any required extent if Marshal Oyama would only consent not to shoot.

The force under Yamagata, advancing from Feng-hwang in two divisions, one towards Port Arthur and one on the road to Mukden, met no resistance that was strong enough to intercept their advance, although there was some fighting at two or three stands. The right division advanced northwestward and entered the Manchoorian highlands by the Mo-thien-ling pass where a force was gathered to oppose it. The left division marched towards Siu-Yen where another Chinese force was encamped. It was the outpost of this division, pursuing the Chinese fugitives through Taku-shan, which made junction with the second army and completed the chain of communication.

On the 9th of November the Japanese advanced and attacked Namquan pass, a strongly fortified neck between Society Bay and Talien-wan. There was no concerted defense, and each Chinese detachment was separately routed. Some thousands of refugees from Kinchow, who were flying towards villages in the vicinity, were mistaken for the enemy and were fired upon from the rear of the defenses, many being killed.

Again the Chinese authorities in Peking decided to seek peace through the influence and intervention of western powers between herself and Japan. On the morning of November 15 the emperor gave an audience to the diplomatic representatives in Peking, and all the ministers were present. His Majesty's action in thus receiving the diplomatists caused considerable stir in high Chinese circles, such a violation was it of imperial Chinese etiquette. This audience was granted on the occasion of the presentation of letters of congratulation by the ministers, on the sixtieth birthday of the dowager empress. For the first time in Chinese history the audience was held in the imperial palace itself. As an especial mark of courtesy the foreign ministers entered by the central gate, the gate through which the emperor only is usually allowed to pass.

The ministers had audience with the emperor separately, and the reception was of a distinctly formal character, lasting but a few minutes. The audience took place in the hall where His Majesty was accustomed to hear the Confucian classics expounded. He was seated cross-legged on the Dragon Throne, surrounded by a numerous body of princes and officials. In front of His Majesty was placed a small table covered with yellow satin, which concealed the lower half of his person. In the short interviews with each minister, who stood some ten feet from His Majesty, Prince Kung and Prince Ching acted alternately as masters of the ceremonies, and interpreted the speeches. The emperor spoke entirely in the Manchoo tongue. He appeared small and delicate, possessing a fine forehead, with expressive brown eyes, and an intellectual countenance. The emperor's position, surrounded as he was by the dignitaries of his court, gave him an imposing appearance, although to a close observer he looked and spoke like a lad of sixteen or seventeen years. His Majesty did not indulge in any social conversation with the visitors, but spoke formally to all. The interview was granted in the hope that western sympathy would be secured for the threatened orientals.

Now that the approach to Port Arthur has brought the Japanese army almost to the walls, let us take a brief retrospect of the operations of the month. On the 24th of October the debarkation of the second army on the Liao Tung peninsula began, to the northwest of the Elliot islands, at Kwa-yuen. No opposition of any kind was encountered, but natural difficulties such as shallow beaches and great range of tides impeded the operation, so that all the stores were not landed until the evening of the 30th. The troops however were put in motion at once, and on October 28th the advance guard reached Pitszwo, a place of some importance at the junction of the Niuchwang, Port Arthur, and Taku-shan road. This place was twenty-five miles from the port of debarkation. Forty-five miles farther southwest, the troops came upon Kinchow, at the point where the two post roads of the peninsula met. On November 6 the Japanese captured this town without difficulty, and the next day Field Marshal Oyama's troops, pressing close on the heels of the flying enemy, reached the formidable isthmus a couple of hours after them, and to the accompaniment of a thunderous bombardment from the fleet, seized the defenses without a struggle. After such a singular display of blundering and cowardice on the part of the Chinese, what followed was not astonishing. The troops passing the isthmus, found themselves on the shore of Talien-wan Bay, one of the best harbors in North China. Ample preparations for defense had indeed been made, but they were not utilized by the cowardly soldiers. The Japanese themselves were taken by surprise. They had not contemplated such a fiasco.

Meanwhile the army had continued its march towards Port Arthur. Their line of communication to the rear, both by land and sea, was perfect. The commissariat was in the best condition for service. The hospital corps was active and modern in its manner of work. Nurses of the Red Cross Society, both men and women, accompanied the army and were provided with everything in the power of the commander to grant, being shown every courtesy. On the other hand, efforts made by hospital corps to reach the Chinese wounded from the Chinese side of the lines, met with utter failure. Two Red Cross nurses were turned back by the Chinese authorities at Tien-tsin, they declining to be responsible for the safety of non-combatants. The Taotai Sheng said, "We do not want to save our wounded. A Chinaman cheerfully accepts the fates that befall him."

More than a fortnight had Marshal Oyama's army been marching in two divisions, eastern and western, down the peninsula to Port Arthur. The distance was less than fifty miles, but the country was a difficult one, there being practically no roads available except in the cultivated valleys. As the army approached the objective point, there were occasional brushes with the enemy. At Ye-jo-shu on November 18, the army was more than half way from Kinchow to Port Arthur, and almost within sight of the goal. The next day's march was expected to bring the forces to camp on the safe side of the hills, within an hour's ride of Port Arthur, unless the Chinese should prevent. The next day was to be devoted to rest and to making sure that everything was properly arranged and ready for the fray; and it was confidently asserted that on the evening of the day after, November 21, the Japanese army would sleep peacefully in Port Arthur with Dragon Flags for bed quilts.

On the morning of the 18th the Chinese made a reconnaissance in force, but retired without discovering much except a Japanese scouting party, which had a narrow escape. The army was moving along steadily with General Nishi leading the vanguard, General Yamaji, his staff, and the war correspondents all with the main body, and General Nogi bringing up the rear. The field marshal and his staff were also behind, and General Hasegawa was on the left wing, with his forces practically covering the country down to the south coast. In front and on the right as far as the not very distant north coast, small bodies of cavalry and infantry were thrown out along the valleys. The country was magnificent for defensive purposes, studded with moderately steep hills, ranging from low undulations up to huge crags two thousand feet high, with hundreds of rocky ravines and gulleys; broad fertile valleys never very level, intersected by winding water courses, like a labyrinth, almost dry at this season.

Every two or three miles there were small villages roughly built of stone, nestling in hollows, with a few trees here and there. In and about the villages scores of natives crowded, curious to see the foreigners they feared; on the hilltops were the more timorous ones, watching awhile and then hurrying away perhaps to tell the Chinese army what they had seen, but no attempt was ever made to stop them, except occasionally to ask a question or two. The road was the military road connecting Port Arthur with Kinchow, Niuchwang and Peking. There was not the least sign of anything having been done to keep it in repair since it was first cut a quarter of a century ago, the soft parts were deep rutted, and would be well-nigh impassable after heavy rain, while the rocky parts were jagged and strewn with stones of all sizes and shapes. Over the plains dust drove in black clouds which enveloped the column, suggesting the great dust storms of North China. There was bright sunny weather, but the nights were cold during the march down the peninsula.

The day's march which had begun at seven in the morning, was to end at Ye-jo-shu, a big village near the sea, about ten miles northeast of Port Arthur. Before entering the village General Yamaji was met by an aid-de-camp with news of fighting ahead, half way to Port Arthur. After a little hesitation the general granted the request of two of the correspondents to permit them to go forward, and they galloped off to the left in a southwesterly direction. Five miles away, among the hilltops, they caught a glimpse of a small, square, stone building, like a fort or watchtower, and all around it could be discerned figures moving amidst clouds of smoke. The road was lined many yards on either side with men and animals, all racing in the same direction, spurting to be first at a ford or a narrow defile, urging and helping each other, and only afraid the enemy might retire too soon.

It was an hour after midday, and Nishi's force had just begun to pitch camp south of Ye-jo-shu, when a courier arrived and announced that the outer pickets were being forced and cut off. Firing had begun at eleven o'clock, but did not become serious until an hour later. Cavalry were rushed to the front, then infantry, then artillery and ammunition trains as they could be mustered and got away. The correspondents galloped hard where the land allowed, past soldiers looking to their rifles and pouches as they ran, past lumbering guns and kicking mules, past panting coolies and Red Cross men, threading their way through the throng, cheering the wounded as they were taken to the rear, smiling bravely in spite of pain. Progress was delayed in the narrow lanes of a picturesque village, in

JAPANESE SKIRMISHERS BEFORE PORT ARTHUR

a little wooded hollow where the artillery stuck in a broad, shallow stream. But by eager efforts it was got clear, and went on scrambling up the bank, splashing and stumbling through half dried ditches plunging in the soft sand, and bumping over boulders, sparing neither man nor beast in the rush up the glen to the top of the hill. There stood Brigadier-General Nishi, watching a "strategic rearward" movement of the Chinese in the plain beyond, and directing operations intended to cut them off if possible. Two strong columns were pushed out right and left, like the horns of a crescent among the hills encircling the valley, towards the sea northwest and Port Arthur southwest. The artillery was already on the spot, but was not used yet; there was no need to let the Chinese know how much strength was massing before Port Arthur.

The engagement originated simply in a surprise meeting of opposing scouts. The Chinese had been creeping all over the valley and surrounding hills, along the ravines and behind the ridges; Japanese had been striking out in twos and threes, reconnoitering many miles into the enemy's country. Suddenly shots were heard, and a general move was made on both sides for the main road in the center. The Japanese seeing no great force in front, and knowing how quickly help could be brought from behind them, stood their ground at first. About noon however three stong columns of Chinese with cavalry and artillery, probably three thousand in all, filed out through the hills from main roads and by-paths leading from Port Arthur. The Japanese were in great danger of being surrounded before the advance guard could arrive. Only a score of cavalry and about two hundred infantry, they had to fight their way back at pretty close quarters, hand to hand at one point. The Chinese advanced with an immense display of banners almost to the foot of the hill where Nishi stood; but the small force of three hundred Japanese cavalry sent out to draw them on, seemed to scare them off, for by half past one they were in full retreat, in good order, over the same paths by which they had come, only just in time to escape the consummation of the Japanese flank movements. It was no use trying to pursue them into the hills about Port Arthur; for as the full force of Nishi's brigade was collecting about the old stone monument the Chinese army was disappearing through the passes six miles away.

A cavalry patrol of seven went forward and followed cautiously along the main road until dusk, turning back at a village just under the hills. They saw the bodies of the seven Japanese who had been left dead on the field, hacked, stripped, beheaded, and in two cases minus the right hand; they saw the cavalryman's horse lying partly flayed with the skin turned back where two large pieces of flesh had been carved out and carried away. They saw traces of the Chinese every few yards, but no bodies; they must have been removed, for the men of Satsuma had not died

RETREAT OF CHINESE SOLDIERS AFTER THE FALL OF PORT ARTHUR

for nothing. They saw no signs of life except the patrols and men with stretchers for the dead, as they rode back slowly into camp at Ye-jo-shu, over ten miles of wretched roads, the horses nearly dead with the fatigue of a long day's work, stumbling at every step, and finally having to be left with the coolies while the riders walked most of the way. These coolies were simply wonderful in their endurance; after the helter-skelter race for

JAPANESE SOLDIERS REMOVING DEAD BODIES

the monument they came up smiling only a few minutes behind, in spite of their forty pound pack on their shoulders.

The advance was slow during the 19th and 20th, the desire being to give the soldiers as much rest as possible before the hard work of the assault. On arriving at Dojoshu, a village at the foot of the hills near Port Arthur, about noon on the 20th, the troops were halted. Oyama had gone around to survey the field, and was expected back every minute, so the time of waiting was passed in a hurried midday meal. Suddenly the boom of heavy guns was heard, and the Chinese were seen advancing in two columns, the right one by Suishiyeh, under the eyes of the troops who held the hill where the army had halted, and the left by way of the west side of the valley, out of sight behind the foot hills. They had at last learned that the invading armies had almost surrounded them, and must be dislodged if possible. But it was not possible now. It was too late.

As soon as the advancing left column got within a mile, a portion of the Japanese artillery opened with shrapnel. The forts replied as soon as the positions were revealed. About 3:00 o'clock the Chinese column got within short range of the Japanese batteries, and was struck fairly in the center by the first two shells. The foolish banners dropped at once, and the column lay down. Bravely the line was reformed twice, but the shelling was too hot and too accurate. The Chinese got their field guns into position but could do nothing for practically none of the Japanese were exposed to them or to the forts. There was a little musketry fire on both sides, but of no importance. The artillery settled the affair, and by 5:00 o'clock the whole of the Chinese army had marched back into camp. The forts away on the sea-front got into action before dusk, and dropped a few 12-inch shells uselessly on the hilltops a mile beyond the Japanese; but when the last streak of daylight had disappeared, all was quiet. During the rest of the night there was no sound nor sign on either side.

THE CAPTURE OF PORT ARTHUR AND THE MASSACRE

Description of the Great Chinese Naval Station—Strength of its Position—The Defences—Arrangement of Japanese Troops, and Plan of Attack—The first Assault—Attack and Counter-Attack—Fall of the Chinese Forts—Action of the Fleet—The Japanese in the Streets of Port Arthur—Massacre of Fugitives—Japanese Red Cross Society and its Previous Good Work—Shocking Details of the Atrocities Committed After the Taking of the Town—Four Days of Violence and Cruelty—Stories of Eyewitnesses—Japanese Explanations and Excuses—Effects of the Capture of Port Arthur on the War.

Port Arthur, or to give it its native name, Lu-shun-kou, was the largest naval station possessed by the Chinese. Situated at the extreme southern end of the Liao-Tung peninsula, Port Arthur in its earlier days afforded convenient shelter for winter-bound junks employed in carrying timber from the Yalu River to the ports westward. At that period it was merely a small village consisting of less than one hundred mud houses, an occasional shop, and three or four inns. The prosperity of the town began with the determination of the authorities in 1881 to establish a naval dockyard at the port. At first the work was entrusted to native contractors, who however proved to be quite incapable of carrying out so extended an undertaking, and in 1887 a French company took up the contract, completing the work in three years. The port then boasted of a large basin with a depth of twenty-five feet at low water. Spacious wharves and quays bordered this brain, and were connected with the workshops by a railroad. Two drydocks were built ready for repairing ships of all sizes, from iron-clads to torpedo vessels. Foundries and workshops were constructed on the most improved models, and containing the best modern machinery. The fact that the harbor was always free from ice, even in the coldest of winter, added to its value. By the time of the beginning of the war, the number of houses had multiplied until they were able to contain a population of about six thousand, exclusive of the garrison. There were also two large temples, two theatres, and several banks, besides the necessary stores and warehouses.

Such land defences as this important dockyard possessed when the war broke out, were limited to nine small redoubts connected by mud walls in some cases, on the north and northeast, and three redoubts on the southwest. On the north side a range of hills from three hundred and fifty to six hundred and fifty feet high, running from the sea to a shallow inlet of the harbor, enclosed the position. The top of these hills were not more than two thousand five hundred yards from the dockyard and town. The original line of defenses was still closer to the town, and on the northern side was only about one thousand yards in advance of the vital point. The strongest part of the position was a group of three coast batteries surrounded by a continuous mud wall, and crowning a hill on the right of the entrance to the harbor. The works all appeared to be designed for the protection of the narrow harbor mouth, which at the entrance was only a few hundred yards wide.

Upon the outbreak of the war, much additional fortification was carried out. The normal garrison of four thousand was greatly increased, and the troops who were drilled on the European model garrisoned the fortifications, and were to be further assisted in the defense of the port by submarine mines and a fleet of torpedo boats. The forts were armed with heavy Krupp guns, and the artillery men were especially trained by a German officer. Within the defenses there were all of the most recent scientific appliances, electric search lights, torpedo factories, etc., and the forts were connected by telephone.

The Japanese army broke camp at Dojoshu village before Port Arthur at 1:00 A.M. on November 21, and marching by circuitous and very difficult routes over the outlying hills, sometimes quite close to the sea at Pigeon Bay, got into line of battle before daylight. The moon was in the last quarter, and gave very little light; the sky was quite clear, and the weather dry and cool. The positions were as heretofore described.

The key of the position was the northwest triple fort on Table Mountain, and there the whole weight of the opening attack was concentrated. The field marshal and his staff were mostly near the center of the line, and the heavy siege artillery was planted on the best position available near the center, and north to northeast of Port Arthur, five or six miles away, with Suishiyeh and the forts right opposite and well in range. The first division under General Yamaji occupied the right wing, and had the roughest and most broken country to traverse. Nine batteries of field and maintain guns were got into fine positions, on lofty ridges, nearly on the same level and almost within rifle shot of the forts; while behind the artillery lay large bodies of infantry ready for a rush. Brigadier-General Nishi had charge of the extreme right, and Brigadier-General Nogi the right center, near the field marshal. On the left, Brigadier-General Hasegawa had his mixed brigade rather wider apart, as the hills were not near enough to aid greatly in an assault on the forts; nor were the hills very good as artillery positions. Hasegawa had only two batteries, but the flying column under Lieutenant-Colonel Masamitsu, that had moved from San-ju-li Ho on the south shore road was with him, and had a mountain battery beside two battalions of infantry and a thousand cavalry.

The first shot was fired within two or three minutes of seven o'clock, from a battery of thirty guns, just as the day was becoming light enough for gun practice. Then for an hour the Japanese guns blazed into the Table-Top forts, which with their guns of all sizes kept up a spirited reply. In the forts, and in the rifle pits on the hillside under the walls, were about one thousand infantry; near the Japanese batteries trenches had been dug in the stony ground during the night, and sneltered ravines had been carefully selected, where practically the whole of the first division, at least ten thousand men, lay in wait. The Chinese shells came close by their ears in dozens, bursting or burying themselves on the other side of the little ravine behind. Many of the boulders about were struck, but strange to say not a man was killed. In the first half hour there must have been three hundred shells over an area of as many yards, but the average elevation was slightly too high, and no damage was done.

Meantime the Japanese were getting to work all along the line. Each battery had a telescope fixed to bear on the desired target, though the dense morning mist and the thick clouds of smoke frequently made it quite impossible to see for a time. It was easy enough to tell that the Japanese had got the reins from the very first. The opening shot of the day, which all watched with intense interest, had struck within five yards short of a Krupp gun in the nearest of the three forts. The closeness of this shot, in semidarkness, at an unknown range estimated to be one thousand yards, was a fair indication of what followed. One by one the Chinese guns ceased fire towards eight o'clock, and suddenly a great shouting came across the valley from the fort. The Japanese infantry were singing a march song as they charged the forts, and in a few minutes a huge cheer ran all along the line over the hilltops and In the valleys where the rest of the Japanese were, and great cries of "Kot-ta-Victory" "The Chinese emptied their guns and small arms as the Japanese swarmed up on three sides, firing every few yards and then rushing forward the enemy, not numerous enough for hand-to-hand combat, waited no longer but fled over the edge of the hill, down to the fortified camps before the town; and the Table Mountain forts displayed the flag of the Rising Sun.

After this first success, the rest of the battle was practically little more than a question of time, although there was still a great deal of hard fighting to follow. Neither side had yet lost more than fifty or sixty in killed and wounded, and there were still many thousand Chinese soldiers to be considered. Had the forts been fully manned with plenty of picked marksmen, they should have cost the invaders several hundreds if not thousands and should have held out longer. And if the Chinese artillery had been as accurate and steady as the Japanese, the vast difference in position and shelter should have more than compensated for the disparity in numbers. Careful planning, rapidity of attack, and individual bravery were all on the Japanese side. The Chinese did not, indeed, run at the sound of shooting, as has been said. They stood their ground manfully and tried their best to shoot straight up to the last minute; but they never attempted to face the foe hand to hand to "Die in the last ditch."

Only one definite counter-attack was made; a large force, probably near two thousand of Chinese infantry with a few cavalry, marched out around the hills westward, north of the Port Arthur lagoon, to turn the Japanese right flank. General Yamaji, who never showed fatigue all day but kept near the front calmly and resolutely at every move, detected the attempt at once, and dispatched Brigadier-General Nishi with the third regiment and the mountain battery to meet it. The extremely rough, broken country rendered movement slow, and this part of the battle dragged on until the afternoon.

The second' regiment had occupied the Isusen forts shortly after eight o'clock, and the artillery was then ordered forward. The guns had come on late from Talien-wan, by forced marches night and day,

JAPANESE ATTACK ON PORT ARTHUR

over a very difficult route, and only arrived at Dojoshu on the night of the 20th, after the enemy's attempt to dislodge the field and mountain guns. The same night twenty of these large guns had been taken into position for the fight north and west of Suishiyeh, and from one to three kilometers from the nearest forts. They were supported by the whole of the first division, fifteen thousand men less twenty-four hundred men detailed to garrison Kinchow and Talien-man. Deducting also the regiment of twenty-four hundred sent to head off the flank movement in the west, there were ten thousand left before the Table

Mountain forts. Not more than a third actually took part in the storming. The rest were waiting ready for use if needed, all along the line from the advance guard under Nishi, near the lagoon, to the center under Nogi, about Peh-ka-shu village, where the skirmish was on the 19th. Here, midway between the camp at Dojoshu and the large village of Suishiyeh, Field Marshal Oyama and his staff remained during the first part of the day, communicating his orders by aides-de-camp, never by flag, or flash signal, or bugle, to Yemaji and Hasegawa on the left.

Peh-ka-shu was about a kilometer north of Suishiyeh, and Suishiyeh about five kilometers north of Port Arthur town, and one kilometer from Table Mountain fort on the east, and Pine Tree fort on the west. About half way between Peh-ka-shu and the sea, southeastward, was So-tai-shu where Hasegawa faced the line of eight forts along a wall of five or six kilometers. Of course this brigade did not cover all the country; he had about five thousand men near the center and two thousand near the sea. The five thousand were about equally divided between Shoju and Niryo, each one regiment of two thousand four hundred with artillery. In attacking, two battalions of eight hundred each formed the front, and one was held behind until within range. Then the whole opened out in skirmishing order and charged, and the Chinese exploded several mines, but without effect, as the fuses were not well timed. Some electric mines were also used but wrongly timed.

While Yamaji was attacking the northwest forts, Hasegawa engaged the attention of the northeast forts, in order to prevent them from concentrating fire on the Japanese right. No serious attack was made by the mixed brigade until the first division had made the winning move. Thus the Chinese right wasted their energy on almost bare country, while the weight of the Japanese attack fell on the almost entirely isolated Chinese left. The strategy succeeded completely, for by the time the Chinese discovered their mistake it was too late. The Shoju, or Pine Tree Hill forts opened a heavy fire across Suishiyeh plain, on the hills occupied by the Japanese; but Isu was already finished and the whole weight of Japanese artillery was centered on the largest Shoju fort. Thus the Japanese right wing, which had been briefly

THE ATTACK ON KINCHOW
JAPANESE DRAWING

threatened by the forts on its left and the Chinese column on its right, was never really in any danger, for while the third regiment under Nishi was storming Isu, the second regiment with its back to the third beat off the enemy's infantry, and the mountain, field, and siege batteries gave Shoju far more than it could face.

It was surprising how the Chinese stood to their guns; they worked like heroes and aimed their guns well. But what could a fort or a half-dozen of forts do, against fifty guns hidden in the mountains, moving to get better positions when possible, and firing systematically and simultaneously at one point.

A furious fusillade was maintained by both sides for nearly two hours; but the Chinese shots got wilder and wilder as the Japanese improved, until finally the Shoju magazine blew up and set fire to the sheds inside of the forts. Then shortly after eleven o'clock, Hasegawa charged all along the line, and took all the eight forts one by one. The big Shoju fort, which had done such determined work was, of course, evacuated as soon as it caught fire, and for two hours afterward the ruined wood-work burned and the piles of ammunition continued to explode. The second largest fort, Liang Leong, or Double Dragon, held out longest. Twice the Japanese advancing along a ravine tried to break cover and rush up the hill, but were met by bombs from the mortars, and had to get back into shelter and try musketry again. Again they came up magnificently at their officers' call, and scrambled up the mountain side in the teeth of a galling cross fire. At the ramparts, not a Chinaman remained. They fled from fort to fort along the high wall, firing as they went, and making a stand at every point till too close for rifles. All over the hills they were chased and for many miles around hardly a hundred yards could be passed without sight of a Chinese corpse. Those who escaped got down into the town with the main body of the Chinese army.

Meanwhile there had been heavy firing, chiefly infantry, between Suishiyeh, Isu and Port Arthur. There was a flat tract about three miles square, with low ridges of mud and stones across, behind which the Chines riflemen lay. They had tried to make a stand about the walled camps below Isu, but shells and shrapnel soon cleared them out. The Japanese then mustered in the same place about two thousand men from the right wing and right center, increasing in number every minute, and ready to force the town itself. Between these camps and the big drill ground at the entrance to Port Arthur were some three thousand Chinese in skirmishing order, making the most of every bit of cover and firing desperately. Behind them the Chinese field guns, some dozen in number, tried to locate the enemy and occasionally succeeded; one shell shattered the corner of the largest camp, where a dense body of Japanese stood behind the wall waiting for orders, and killed several of them. Still farther back, a big hill which threatened the town swarmed with riflemen, who were sheltered by piles of stones and abundantly supplied with ammunition. Last of all the shore forts were firing a little, but could not aid much in the melee.

Steadily the Japanese crept forward from cover to cover, assisted by artillery from Suishiyeh, until the parade ground and the general's pavilion overlooking it had been mastered and cleared, and nothing remained but the trenches of Boulder hill, or Hakugoku, the town itself, and the shore forts. Along the south of the parade ground ran a broad, shallow stream that came down the Suishiyeh valley, flowing into a creek west of Hakugoku. Three times the Japanese came out from behind the parade ground wall, to cross the bridge, but were driven back by a withering hail of bullets. At last they forced it and rushed across with a cheer, and spread out over the face of the hill pursuing the Chinese up to the town itself. The Second Regiment fired volleys as it advanced to the town. Not a shot was fired in reply. The battle was over as far as Port Arthur was concerned.

The Japanese fleet was not inactive during the assault by the land forces. At 10:30 A.M. the Japanese vessels, comprising the Matsusima, Chiyoda, Itsukusima, Hasidate, Yoshino, Naniwa, Akitsushima, Takachiho, Fuso, Hiyei, and Kongo steamed past Port Arthur, rounding the promontory. The Chiyoda here began to fire shells over the forts at a very long range. A tugboat from Taku was searched by the Japanese, but was allowed to proceed. At 4:00 o'clock the fleet returned, passing Port Arthur again, at a distance of about six miles, and one of the big forts fired at the Chiyoda but failed to hit her. The admiral did not respond to the fire nor alter his course but steamed slowly on. A few minutes later, as the Chinese troops were hurrying down to the harbor, ten torpedo boats dashed from the fleet, separating in pairs and firing three-pounder Hotchkiss guns at the exposed soldiers. The fire was briskly responded to by one fort to the left of the harbor, but not a single shot told. A steamer which had towed a junk out of Port Arthur with Taotai Kung in it, making his escape, was cut off on her return and ran ashore, where the crew deserted her and took to the hills.

As the Japanese troops reached the edge of the town, driving the Chinese before them, a halt was called before the army marched in,

PORT ARTHUR FROM THE BAY

as the force was not yet assembled in strength. This delay enabled the Chinese to take to boats, and scores of sampans and junks were soon moving off, some over the lagoon to the mountain fastnesses of Lao-tieh-shan promontory in the southwest, and some out to sea, in full view of the Japanese fleet. When the first division was all assembled before the town, with the left wing to the northeast in case the enemy should rally and try to dash out, the order was given to enter the town and storm the inner fort, Golden Hill. The Second Regiment led, firing volleys file by file through the streets, past the docks, and the burning army stores, up the hill, and into Ogunsan, which was practically abandoned without an effort at defense.

During the evening Hasegawa's brigade went over the hills, and occupied the two eastern shore forts called the "Mule's Jaws." The following morning Yamaji's first regiment marched around the lagoon and occupied the peninsula forts, which had been deserted during the night. Where the Chinese all vanished to, appeared rather a mystery to the victors. It was found that most of them got away along the beach past Hasegawa, and the rest westward in small parties under cover of darkness. In such a wide stretch of hilly country, it was easy for them to conceal themselves if they once escaped the vicinity of their foes. Port Arthur was in full possession of Marshal Oyama, with the fleet under Admiral Ito safe in the harbor.

Now comes the most painful recital of the war. It is difficult to reconcile in any one's mind the pretensions to enlightened civilization which the Japanese had claimed, with the horrible atrocities committed by the victorious army during the days following the capture of Port Arthur. Let us glance at what had been the history of Japanese treatment of the wounded in previous battles.

It will be remembered that in a foregoing chapter of this work, the proclamation of the Japanese minister of war enjoining humanity upon all his soldiers was quoted, and that it was stipulated that the ignorance of the Chinese as to the true meaning of humanity would cause them to commit atrocities no doubt, which must not be imitated in retaliation by Japanese troops. At Hiroshima, the military headquarters of Japan during the war, was the principal military hospital and the establishment of the Red Cross society, which to investigators were a remarkable revelation after all that had been said about Japanese inhumanity and indifference to suffering. As long ago as 1877, when the Satsuma clan raised the standard of rebellion, a benevolent society was founded to aid and care for the sick and wounded, enemies as well as friends, after the manner of the European Red Cross societies. Subscriptions at once began to pour in, the emperor and empress helping greatly, and throughout the Satsuma war the young organization distinguished itself admirably. From that time special efforts were made to bring the society up to the high standard of its western models in every way; and when the government of Japan in 1886 declared its adhesion to the Geneva convention, the "Hakuaisha" was reorganized and formally enrolled on the international list of Red Cross societies. Since then it had made rapid progress, its membership reaching nearly thirty thousand in 1893, with funds liberally augmented by the emperor, and an annual income before the war with China of $70,000. Since 1887, a large number of women, including members of the royal family and of the nobility, have become qualified nurses of the order and have taken instruction in the making of articles for use in its work. The objects of the society, as set forth in the rules, are to help the sick and wounded in time of war, and to prepare for the same by organizing a trained staff in time of peace. The last activity of the Red Cross society prior to the war in 1891, when the central provinces of Japan were devastated by an earthquake which caused the loss of more than seven thousand lives, besides untold suffering.

With the object of training a staff properly, the society in 1886 established a hospital of its own in Tokio, and three years later, when this one was outgrown, a new one was erected on a splendid site provided by the emperor and empress. The hospital itself covers some two acres, and the grounds about ten. After the war began, the membership funds and operations of the society were all multiplied about three times above normal. All the working staff was under the control of the army medical staff, and operated in conjunction with the army corps. At Hiroshima in the permanent military hospital, Chinese wounded by the scores and hundreds were received and treated with the same care that was given to the Japanese. For order, cleanliness, and convenience these institutions would reflect credit on any country. Just prior to the battle of Port Arthur, the female nurses of the Red Cross societies in Hiroshima numbered eighty-eight and more were soon to come from Tokio. Like the men they had uniforms of European pattern, and all wore the badge of membership. Many had other badges representing special qualifications or services.

In Corea there were two hospitals managed by the Red Cross society, one near Chemulpo and the other near Ping-Yang. At the seat of war the society had a staff of forty, consisting of a chief manager, a secretary, a treasurer, five doctors, two pharmacists in charge of the drug supplies and thirty male nurses.

To those who love contrasts, it will be startling to note the difference between the spirit of the Japanese Red Cross society, which was doing everything that humanity and science could suggest for wounded Chinamen, and that of the victorious army at Port Arthur in its atrocious butchery of unarmed fugitives.

The execrable deeds which followed the taking of the place pushed into the background the question of how many hundreds on one side or the other fell in the battle. The massacre of the whole remaining population of Port Arthur, between two and three thousand, without distinction of age or sex, and that by the soldiers of Marshal Oyama's army, for a time passed practically without mention in the newspapers of England and the United States. Three of the famous correspondents who entered the town with the Japanese army were Creelman of the New York World, Villiers of the London Standard, and Cowan of the London Times. The first detailed description of the atrocities witnessed by these correspondents was that made by Creelman, and for a time after his story was published, other leading American journals denounced it as false. One month later it was found that Creelman's shocking story was true in every essential particular. No words except those from the lips of men who saw the acts of inhuman barbarity can justly describe the scenes. Said Cowan, in a letter dated at Kobe twelve days after the taking of Port Arthur:

"What happened after Port Arthur fell into Japanese hands, it would have been impossible and even dangerous to report while on the spot. At the earliest possible moment, every foreign correspondent escaped from the horrifying scene to a place where freedom of speech would be safe; and as we sailed away from Port Arthur on the Nagoto Mam eight days ago, almost astonished to find ourselves escaping alive from the awful epidemic of incredible brutality, the last sounds we heard were those of shooting, of wanton murder, continued the fifth day after the great battle. When the Japanese army entered Port Arthur on the 21st, beginning a little after two o'clock in the afternoon, the Chinese had resisted desperately till the last, retreating slowly from cover to cover, until they got back among the buildings on the outskirts of the town. Then at last all resistance ceased; they were thoroughly defeated, and made a stampede through the streets trying to hide or to escape, east or west as best they might. I was on the brow of a steep hill called "White Boulders," in Japanese Hakugoku, commanding a close view of the whole town at my feet. When I saw the Japanese march in, firing up the streets and into the houses, chasing and killing every live thing that crossed their path, I looked hard for the cause. I saw practically every shot fired, and I swear positively that not one came from any but Japanese. I saw scores of Chinese hunted out of cover, shot down, and hacked to pieces, and never a man made any attempt to fight. All were in plain clothes, but that meant nothing for the soldiers flying from death got rid of their uniforms how they might. Many went down on their knees, supplicating with head bent to the ground in kowtow, and in that attitude were butchered mercilessly by the conquering army. Those who fled were pursued and sooner or later were done to death. Never a shot came from a house as far as I could see, and I could hardly believe my eyes, for, as my letters have shown, the indisputable evidence of previous proceedings had filled me with admiration of the gentle Japanese. So I watched intensely for the slightest sign of cause, confident that there must be some, but I saw none whatever. If my eyes deceived me, others were in the same plight; the military attaches of England and America were also on Boulder Hill and were equally amazed and horrified. It was a gratuitous ebullition of barbarism they declared, a revolting repudiation of pretended humanity.

"Gun shots behind us turned our attention to the north creek leading into the broad lagoon. Here swarms of boats were moving away to the west, loaded to twice their normal limit with panic-stricken fugitives, men, women, and children, who had stayed too late in the beleaguered town. A troop of Japanese cavalry with an officer, was at the head of the creek, firing seaward, slaughtering all within range. An old man and two children of ten and twelve years had started to wade across the creek; a horseman rode into the water and slashed them a dozen times with his sword. The sight was more than mortal man could stand. Another poor wretch rushed out at the back of a house as the invaders entered the frontdoor, firing promiscuously. He got into a back lane, and a moment later found himself cornered between two fires. We could hear his cry for quarter as he bowed his head in the dust three times; the third time he rose no more, but fell on his side, bent double in the posture of petition for the greatly vaunted mercy of the Japanese, who stood ten paces off and exultantly emptied their guns into him.

"More of these piteous deaths we saw, unable to stay the hands of the murderers; more and more, far more than one can relate, until sick and saddened beyond the power of words to tell, we slowly made our way in the gathering gloom down the hill, picking a path through rifle-pits thick with Chinese cartridge cases, and back to headquarters. There at the Chinese general's pavilion, facing a spacious parade ground, Field Marshal Oyama and all his officers assembled, amid the strains of strange music from the military band, now a wierd, characteristic Japanese march, now a lively French waltz, and ending with the impressive national anthem, "Kaminoga," and a huge roar from twenty thousand throats, "Banzai Nippon!" All were overflowing with enthusiastic patriotism and the delight of a day's work done, a splendid triumph after a hard fought fight; none of the Japanese dreamed that their guests from the west were filled with horror, indignation, and disgust. It was a relief to get away from that flood of fiendish exultation, to escape from the effusive glee of our former friends, who would overwhelm us with their attention which we loathed like caresses from the ghouls of hell. To have to remain among men who could do what we had seen was little short of torture.

"Robbed of our sleep on the eve of the battle, and utterly exhausted, we lay long next morning until the sound of shooting roused us. To our surprise and dismay, we found that the mas sacre of Wednesday, which might have been explained though certainly not excused on the ground of excitement in the heat of battle, the flush of victory, and the knowledge of dead comrades mutilated, was being continued in cold blood now. Thursday, Friday, Saturday, and Sunday were spent by the soldiery in murder and pillage from dawn to dark, in mutilation, in every conceivable kind of nameless atrocity, until the town became a ghastly Inferno to be remembered with a fearsome shudder until one's dying day. I saw corpses of women and children, three or four in the streets, more in the water; I stooped to pick some of them out to make sure that there could be no possibility of mistake. Bodies of men strewed the

JAPANESE SOLDIERS MUTILATING BODIES

streets in hundreds, perhaps thousands, for we could not count—some with not a limb unsevered, some with heads hacked, cross-cut, and split lengthwise, some ripped open, not by chance but with careful precision, down and across, disemboweled and dismembered, with occasionally a dagger or bayonet thrust in private parts. I saw groups of prisoners tied together in a bunch with their hands behind their backs, riddled with bullets for five minutes, and then hewn in pieces. I saw a junk stranded on the beach, filled with fugitives of either sex and of all ages, struck by volley after volley until—I can say no more.

"Meanwhile every building in the town was thoroughly ransacked, every door burst open, every box and closet, every nook and cranny looted. What was worth taking was taken, and the rest destroyed or thrown into the gutter. Even Mr. Hart, Renter's war correspondent on the Chinese side, whom we found when we entered Port Arthur, was robbed of everything but the clothes he had on, while his cook and two scully boys in the same house were shot at their kitchen stove, while doing nothing but their regular work: Mr. Hart himself had told the Chinese hotel keeper before the battle not to leave the town, because the Japanese would certainly do no harm to citizens or property. So thoroughly had been the discipline maintained, and so perfect the show of civilized methods in warfare, that the present outburst of cold-blooded brutality was the very last thing to have been thought possible.

"The Japanese alleged that the populace of the town had been armed with guns and express ammunition, and that the army when entering the town had been attacked from the houses. I did afterward find cartridges such as these lying about; but I never saw one fired. I never saw any attack from the houses. I saw the Japanese firing before they entered, and as they entered, without intermission.

"The Japanese who had been wounded and killed or captured in several skirmishes before the day of the battle, had been horribly mutilated by the Chinese. We saw several bodies along the line of march, and it is said others were found in the town, with hands and heads cut off, stomachs opened, etc. And some were burnt at Kinchow, and one said to be burnt in Port Arthur. Moreover, placards have been found offering rewards and stating prices, for heads, hands, or prisoners. So the Japanese soldiers swore revenge, and they carried out their vow thoroughly in barbarous eastern style. All that can be said is that the Chinese committed nameless atrocities which the Japanese repaid a hundred fold.

"It is unavoidable that innocent persons must be killed in war. I do not blame the Japanese for that alone; Chinese soldiers dress as peasants and retain their weapons, and attack when they can under cover of disguise. It therefore becomes excusable to some extent to regard all Chinese as enemies, with or without uniform; in that the Japanese are plainly justified. But regarding them as enemies, it is not humanity to kill them; they should be taken alive. I saw hundreds killed after being captured and tied. Perhaps that is not barbarity; at any rate it is the truth. On the day of the battle, soldiers fresh from the excitement of a hard struggle cannot help being somewhat bloodthirsty, perhaps. At any rate their nerves are tense, their blood is up, they are violently excited. Not that it is right to be so, but it is usual. But the battle was on the 21st, and still on the 25th, after four nights' sleep, the slaughter was continued. Some allowance must be made for the intense indignation of the soldiers whose comrades had been mutilated by the Chinese. Indignation is perfectly justifiable; the Japanese were quite right to feel incensed. But why should they express themselves in the very same barbarous manner? Is it because they are also barbarous at heart like the Chinese? Of course they say 'No.' Then they will have to prove it, for the fact remains that a dozen white men saw these Japanese commit these savageries for four clear days after the day of the fight."

Creelman's story was as graphic and as shocking in its details, and included many of the same sights which were related by Cowan. He says in part: "The story of the taking of Port Arthur will be one of the blackest pages in history. An easy victory over a Chinese mob, and the possession of one of the most powerful strongholds in the world, was too great a strain upon the Japanese character, which relapsed in a few hours back to the state from which it awakened a generation ago. Almost the entire population found in Port Arthur have been massacred, and the work of butchering unarmed and unresisting inhabitants has continued day after day until the streets are choked with corpses. The march upon helpless Peking or a surrender of China to her foe is a small matter in its vital significance compared with this appalling crime against the nineteenth century, at a moment when Japan asks to be admitted as an equal into the family of civilized nations. The Japanese lost about fifty dead and two hundred and fifty wounded in carrying a fortress that would have cost them ten thousand men had it been occupied by European or American troops, and yet the sense of uncontrolled power which let loose the savagery which had been pent up in the Japanese under the external forms of civilization, has proved the utter incapability of the nation to stand the one sure test. Japan stands disgraced before the world. She has violated the Geneva convention, dishonored and profaned the Red Cross, and banished humanity and mercy from her councils. Victory and a new lust for dominion have set her mad.

"All attempts to justify the massacre of the wretched people of Port Arthur and the mutilation of their bodies, are mere afterthoughts. The evidence is clear and overwhelming that it was the sudden breaking down of Japanese civilization under the stress of conscious power. The tremendous facts revealed by the war so far are, that there is practically no Chinese army in existence; that Japan has been arraying herself in the outward garb of civilization, without having gone through the process of moral and intellectual development necessary to grasp the ideas upon which modern civilization is founded; that Japan at heart is a barbarous nation, not yet to be trusted with sovereign power over the lives and property of civilized men. Up to the moment Port Arthur was entered I can bear witness that both of her armies now in the field were chivalrous and generous to the enemy. There was not a stain on her flag. But it was all blind sentiment. The Japanese were playing with the Red Cross as with a new toy and their leaders were never weary of calling the attention of other nations to the spectacle.

"When Port Arthur fell, not even the presence of the horrified British and American military attaches and of foreign newspaper correspondents served to check the carnival of murder. I have again and again tried to save helpless men from slaughter by protest and entreaty, but in vain. The sign of the Red Cross was jeered at, and in the midst of the orgies of blood and rapine, with troops tramping over the bodies of unarmed victims who lost their homes, the fat field marshal and his generals paced smiling, content at the sound of rifle shots mingling with the music of the national hymn and the clink of wine glasses. I am satisfied that not more than one hundred Chinamen were killed in fair battle at Port Arthur and that at least two thousand unarmed men were put to death. It may be called the natural result of the fury of troops who have seen the mutilated corpses of their comrades, or it may be called retaliation, but no civilized nation could be capable of the atrocities I have witnessed in Port Arthur. Every scene I have described I have looked upon myself, either in the presence of the American and British military attaches, or in the company of Mr. Cowan or Mr. Villiers. The field marshal and all his generals were aware that the massacre was being continued day after day.

"We watched the Second regiment as it marched into town, firing volleys as it advanced. Not a shot was fired in reply. The soldiers had made their escape, and the frightened inhabitants were cowering in the streets.

As the troops moved on they saw the heads of their slain comrades hanging by cords with the noses and ears gone. There was a rude arch in the main street decorated with bloody Japanese heads. A great slaughter followed. The infuriated soldiers killed every one they saw. I can say as an eyewitness that the wretched people of Port Arthur made no attempt to resist the invaders. Just below me was a hospital flying the Red Cross flag, but the Japanese fired upon the unarmed men who came out

MARSHAL OYAMA

of the doorway. A merchant in fur cap knelt down and raised his hands in entreaty. As the soldiers shot him he put his hands over his face. I saw his corpse the next day, slashed beyond recognition. Women and children were hunted and shot at as they fled to the hills with their protectors. All along the streets I could see the bleeding store keepers shot and sabered. A junk was discovered in the harbor crowded with fugitives. A platoon was stretched across the end of a wharf, and fired into the boat until every man, woman and child was killed. The torpedo boats outside had already sunk ten junks filled with terror stricken people.

"The Japanese had tasted blood, and the work went on the second day. I saw four men walking peaceably along the edge of the town, one man in the street carried a naked infant in his arms. As he ran he dropped the baby. I found it an hour later, dead. The third, the father of the baby tripped and fell. In an instant a soldier had pounced upon his back with a naked bayonet in his hand. I ran forward and made the sign of the Red Cross on the white non-combatant's bandage around my arm, but the appeal was useless. The bayonet was plunged three or four times into the neck of the prostrate man, and then he was left to gasp his life out on the ground. I hurried back to my quarters and awakened Frederick Villiers, who went with me to the spot where I left the dying man. He was dead, but his wounds were still smoking.

"While we were bending over the corpse we heard shooting a few yards around a road, and went forward to see what it was. We saw an old man standing with his hands tied behind his back. On the ground beside him were the writhing bodies of three other pinioned men who had just been shot. As we advanced a soldier shot the old man down. This was the third day after the battle. Next day I went in company with Mr. Villiers to see a courtyard filled with mutilated corpses. As we entered we surprised two soldiers bending over one of the bodies. They had ripped open the corpse. When they saw us they cowered and tried to hide their faces.

"It is but fair to the Japanese to relate what they had to offer in contravention of these shocking reports so well substantiated. The Japanese minister to Great Britain, Mr. Takaki Kato, while passing through New York some weeks after the taking of Port Arthur, offered these explanations.

"Port Arthur, while vastly important as a stragetic point, was scarcely more than a village as far as the number of its inhabitants was concerned. These, which at the outside could not have numbered more than two or three thousand, consisted of a few petty merchants, laborers, and workmen in the docks, their families, and the wives and children of some of the soldiers. This was all that Port Arthur consisted of, as far as population was concerned in times of peace, except the military forces that manned the forts. Second, it had long been known that the Japanese forces were advancing on the fort. All the non-combatants, women and children, were removed to places of safety long before the battle began; indeed the exodus was begun fully a month beforehand. Third, in the face of these reports of wholesale slaughter, how do you account for the fact that between three and four hundred Chinese soldiers were taken prisoners in and about the town of Port Arthur immediately after its occupation?

"The victorious army was compelled before entering the town to pass through a narrow defile which was strewn with the mutilated bodies of their advance troops. There lay their comrades in arms, not only dead, but with every evidence that they had been tortured to death by the most revolting and brutal methods. Picture such a scene of horror, and you will have a faint conception of the sight that greeted our victorious soldiers as they marched through that narrow pass. These were their comrades, their companions, that lay before them as ghastly evidences of inhuman brutality. Can you appreciate the low murmur of horror that passed along the line? Can you understand how each man then and there in his heart determined to avenge such fiendishness, and then can you blame our men for killing every Chinese soldier found hidden in the town when they first entered? Yes, there were excesses, regrettable but surely exhonorable excesses, after the battle of Port Arthur. But these wild tales of the wholesale slaughter of innocent women are fiction pure and simple. A few women may have been killed in the general melee that followed the first entrance into the town, but that was accident, not intention, if it occurred at all. With a very few exceptions all the men killed proved to be Chinese soldiers who had discarded their arms and uniforms.

"What our troops saw of Chinese barbarity did not begin with Port Arthur nor did it end there. The most atrocious cruelties were the rule at Ping-Yang, Kinchow, and indeed every engagement. Before accepting this reported wantonness of our troops at Port Arthur we must take into consideration what the Japanese troops did before and what they have done since. Nowhere has there been butchery or cruelty, but kindness, moderation and nobility. This in spite of all that our soldiers saw of the fate of their unhappy companions; this in the face of new barbarities that were revealed almost daily. Is this not a credit to our soldiers worthy of national pride and international appreciations?

"The variety of explanations offered to excuse the atrocities was considerable. It was reported from Port Arthur a few days after the charges had been made, that the capture of the place was indeed marked by regrettable excesses, but the offenders were not regular soldiers. It was said that the night after the capture of the stronghold, a number of coolies attached to the army as laborers came into the town from the camps. These men carried swords, in order to obviate the necessity of always having regular troops told off for their protection. Unfortunately they obtained access to some Chinese stores of liquor, and became intoxicated. While in this condition they were reminded of the atrocious cruelties committed by the Chinese upon defenseless Japanese prisoners, and became frenzied. All the coolies practically ran amock, and no Chinamen whom they met was spared. It was declared that some of the coolies were at once arrested, and that Marshal Oyama was already investigating the affair, when he received instructions from imperial headquarters at Hiroshima to institute a rigorous inquiry.

The barbarities practised by the Chinese against the Japanese, which resulted in the atrocious retaliation, were fully corroborated from many sources. A correspondent of the American Bible Society wrote thus from Shanghai:

"The reported inhuman atrocities of the Chinese are fully confirmed. They were guilty of barbarities too revolting to mention. A scouting party of Japanese, including an interpreter, were captured by the Chinese near Port Arthur just before the attack on the fortress. They were fastened to stakes by nails through their shoulders, burned alive, and then quartered and their ghastly remains stuck up on poles by the roadside. Some Japanese members of the Red Cross society were captured by the Chinese soldiers and flayed alive. During the attack on Port Arthur the defenders used explosive bullets. Is it any wonder that the Japanese generals issued the order that no quarter should be shown? The track of the retreating army has been marked by pillage, rapine, wanton destruction and outrage, so that the people welcome the Japanese."

Japanese diplomats in Washington did not take kindly to the civilized censure of Japanese atrocities. They had read up on Andersonville, Libby Prison, Fort Pillow, Wounded Knee, the British cruelties in India and Africa, the Russian record, and they were ready to compare notes with civilized armies on the subject of cruelty in war. They also brought forward native Japanese papers which described the taking of Port Arthur, and declared that those who were killed after the assault suffered only because of the frenzy of a few Japanese, shocked by what they had seen of the cruelties to their own comrades. It was declared that the Japanese officers and the body of the troops did all in their power to stop the bloodshed. Furthermore, the Japanese government asked for a suspension of judgment until the merits of the case could be investigated.

The savage massacres which marked the capture of Port Arthur were not the first, nor will they be the last which will disgrace the conduct of troops calling themselves civilized. English troops were guilty of similar massacre in the Peninsular campaign, at least one time in the Crimea, and repeatedly in suppressing- rebellion in India. Our own troops in the west have been stung to ruthless massacre by the discovery of their tortured dead in Indian villages. Fort Pillow gave ghastly proof of the readiness to butcher in our war. French troops in Algeria, New Zealand colonists in suppressing a Maori rising, and Boers in South Africa have slaughtered without mercy. These occasions neither palliate nor excuse barbarity. It is wrong in all races, and in all races from time to time it will come to the surface. The amazing fact about Japan is that it is the first Asiatic nation in all history which has fought any battles and conducted any military operations without massacre. The slaughter or slavery of surrendered troops has been the unbroken rule of Asiatic warfare for centuries. Japan has actually been able to reverse the practice and habit of generations, to school its soldiers to mercy, and even in the present instance it has been followed, as Wellington's massacres in the Peninsula never were, by investigation and an attempt at repressing like disorder in the future.

As an indication of the trend of thought of Chinese newspapers, and of ignorance of the Chinese people concerning the truth of the war, it is amusing to note the report of one of the vernacular papers on the fall of Port Arthur. This paper editorially says:—"In allowing the Japanese to take Port Arthur, General Tso was actuated by motives of the deepest strategy, and the able manner in which he attained his end, without allowing his opponents to penetrate his designs, stamps him as one of the greatest military commanders China has ever seen. Knowing Peking to be the ultimate goal of the Japanese, General Tso was satisfied that should a too obstinate resistance be offered at any point, the Japanese would leave the Chinese unconquered in his rear, and would push on to the capital; whereas, if an important place like Port Arthur should fall into their hands, the little men would enjoy the sensation as they would a new toy, and it would delay them in their march while the road to Peking was rendered impregnable.

General Tso, therefore, inflicted all the loss possible upon the Japanese, without allowing them to be absolutely discouraged, and then when defeat was staring his opponents in the face, gave the signal to his troops to retreat, which they did in good order. So great was the loss of the Japanese, that it was not until some hours after the last Chinese soldier had departed, that they ventured to enter the forts. "General Tso displayed marked military skill in his defensive tactics, and by ordering half-charges of powder to be used in the big guns, and filling the shell and torpedoes with sand, deluded the innocent commander of the Japanese fleet into the belief that the defenses and sea forts of Port Arthur were innocuous. As a result the Japanese fleet boldly ventured close to the forts and within the line of the torpedo defenses, and before they discovered their mistake three men-of-war, seven transports, and twenty-one torpedo boats were sunk by the Chinese fire and submarine mines. The result of General Tso's actions prove, as we have always maintained, that it is inadvisable for China to employ other than native commanders in the present war. In hand-to-hand combats the savage and flesh-eating Fanquoi is physically superior to our men, but no man other than one conversant with the military wisdom of our enlightened race could have planned and brought to a successful conclusion the train of events which ended in the offering of Port Arthur as a bait to our diminutive opponents."

From a military point of view, the capture of Port Arthur by the Japanese was an event of the first importance, while its moral effect and its consequent influence upon the diplomatic situation was very great. It transferred from one side to the other all the advantages of a fully equipped arsenal and dockyard, occupying a commanding strategical position, and therefore modified all the conditions, naval as well as military, of the campaign. It made the defense more hopeless than ever, and extended the chain of Chinese disaster.

CHANG YEN HONG

ENVOY SENT BY CHINA TO JAPAN TO NEGOTIATE TERMS OF PEACE BEFORE THE DESPATCH OF
Li Hung Chang.—See pages 623 and 655.

China Makes Another Attempt Towards Peace—The Envoy Rejected Because of Lack of Credentials and Rank—President Cleveland Offers to Help Create Peace—Chinese and Manchoos at War—Japanese Victories Immediately after the Taking of Port Arthur—More Corean Politics—The Third Japanese Army—Preparing for a Descent on the Chinese Mainland—Wei-hai-wei and Ire Capture.

Even before Port Arthur had fallen, China was making another attempt to secure peace through the intervention of foreign nations. As this seemed slow in coming, however, it was decided that an informal effort to stop hostilities would be made, one indeed of such a sort that it might be disavowed if criticism seemed to demand. Consequently, Mr. Gustav Detring, the Chinese Commissioner of Customs under Sir Robert Hart, was sent to Japan to feel the way in preliminary negotiations. In its perplexity and distress, the Chinese government took the step which only extremity could have driven it to take. It swallowed the pill which was of all things most bitter. The emperor, on the advice of his council and at the instigation of Prince Kung and Li Hung Chang, appointed a foreigner as envoy to Japan. The office was not one which timid Chinamen would envy, because none of them were ambitious to hand down their names to posterity in connection with the humiliation of their country. The wisest man in office was Prince Kung, but he was not the dictator which he was supposed to be. He was thwarted by other influences, among them the Grand Council, of which he was not but ought to have been a member.

In this confusion, the grand imperial effort towards centralization of authority had partially at least failed, and the failure had the effect of rehabilitating for the moment the Viceroy Li Hung Chang, who once more stood out as the only possible practical man. This aged statesman had many faults, which those who were nearest to him saw most clearly, but if we compare even his faults with the wisdom of his compeers, he was still the one-eyed man among the blind, the only man at the time in the empire who was capable of anything, and whose removal from the scene would have been regarded with grave apprehension by all who were interested in the maintenance of order against chaos.

Mr. Detring, with his suite, left Tien-tsin November 22 by rail to Tung-ku, embarked there on a steamer, under the German flag, called the Li-yu, and steamed down the Gulf of Pechili past Chefoo and Wei-hai-wei. Not until the vessel reached Japan did they know of the fall of Port Arthur. The vessel proceeded to Kobe, where no one was permitted to land at first. The envoy at once sought communication with Count Ito, and applied to the local authorities to inform His Excellency thereof. The result was not an invitation to Mr. Detring to visit Hiroshima, but the dispatch of the Secretary-General of the cabinet, Mr. Ito Moiji, to confer with him at Kobe. From this point there is a difference of statement as to what occurred. The Chinese declare that before the arrival of the secretary, Mr. Detring had been recalled by his government, and having taken leave of the governor he left at daylight on the 29th without waiting to see Mr. Ito, who had arrived the previous night. The Japanese, on the contrary, assert that they refused to entertain any proposals from Mr. Detring, as he was not properly accredited and had no authority whatever to make peace negotiations. However that may be, it is certain that he returned to China without having an audience with any Japanese officials, and that the peace negotiations were never even begun.

The next surprise was that whereas the United States had declined to entertain England's proposal for a coalition of powers to restore peace to the orient, President Cleveland subsequently tendered to Japan his good offices as mediator. He hoped that by his aid peace might be restored, and restored in such a manner as to secure to Japan the just fruits of her victories. A reply declining his proposal, couched in duly grateful terms, was conveyed to the president by Japan, and he having learned in the interval that the European powers would not agree to intervene conjointly, ceased his own activity. It was still hoped however that Minister Denby at Peking and Minister Dun at Tokio would be able to use their good offices in advancing peace. Japan was holding out the insistence that China must speak for herself if she wanted peace. Japan however did go so far as to say that if China had any propositions of peace to make, they might be transmitted in the beginning through the United States ministers in Japan and China. It was still evident however, that China would hold off as long as possible, in the hope that something would turn up to relieve her of the necessity of suing for peace.

The Manchoo princes feared and mistrusted the Chinese, who seemed to be indifferent to the issue of the war and intent only on obtaining individual advantage. It was reiterated again and again, that the Chinese secret societies desired Japanese success in order that the Manchoo dynasty be overthrown and the Chinese restored to power. Captain Von Hannecken, at the request of the Tsung-li Yamen, submitted a comprehensive scheme of military reorganization. This was approved by the emperor and the Manchoo statesmen, but was frustrated by the strategem of certain wealthy taotais, on the alleged ground of economy. The question was then referred from Peking to Tien-tsin. Thus the central and provincial governments reduced each other to impotence. Genuine reform in China appeared to be hopeless, owing to the invincible ignorance of the rulers. There was much popular discontent at the imbecility of the government.

Let us now return to the other forces of Chinese and Japanese, whose movements, comparatively unimportant, have been neglected for the advance on Port Arthur. A considerable portion of the Chinese fleet was still in the harbor at Wei-hai-wei, sometimes cruising out for a little while, but usually safe at anchor. Several of the Chinese vessels had slipped out of Port Arthur harbor when Japanese backs were turned, and steamed across to supposed safety at Wei-hai-wei. On November 22 the Chen-Yuen, the largest and most formidable battle ship remaining to the Chinese, ran ashore while entering Wei-hai-wei harbor, and trying to avoid the torpedoes placed in the channel. She was somewhat damaged by a torpedo, and was finally beached and rendered useless for the time. Commodore Liu Taitsan, who was in command of the vessel, anticipated official condemnation by committing suicide.

The fall of Port Arthur was followed immediately by a succession of victories for the Japanese arms in Manchooria, the first

Japanese army continuing its success. The advance of this army towards Mukden terrorized the people of Manchooria, and the abandonment of the sacred city by its inhabitants began. The country around was in a state of desolation. The wounded mostly remained in villages between Niuchwang and Mukden, the state of the country preventing the Chinese medical staff and foreign volunteers from proceeding thither. Mukden was evacuated in the beginning of November by the foreign residents, who remained at Niuchwang. The Roman Catholic fathers remained at their station in Manchooria, but the Protestant missionaries returned to safer regions.

At Jeh-ho the Mongols rose in rebellion, in revenge for the assassination of six Mongolian princes. Troops had to be called to put down the insurrection, as had so often occurred before during the war.

On the day of the taking of Port Arthur, a large body of Chinese troops under General Sung attacked Talien-wan and Kinchow, where Japanese had been left to guard baggage trains and provisions. The conflicts were sharp, and a number was killed on both sides, but the Chinese were finally forced to retire. The day after Port Arthur's fall, the greater portion of Count Oyama's army turned and marched northward through the Laio. Tung promontoiy, in the direction of Niuchwang. Ten thousand troops were left behind to guard Japanese interests at Port Arthur.

November 25, sharp fighting took place near the Mo-thien-ling pass, between a portion of General Sung's army and the Japanese under Count Yamagata. After the Chinese troops had retired from Chiu-lien, they concentrated north of Mo-thien-ling, and the engagement was an attempt to turn the Japanese right flank at Tsokow. The conflict opened with a sharp fusillade, and the Chinese fought with considerable stubbornness for a time, losing heavily before they finally retired. The attack was the most determined effort that the Chinese had made since Ping-Yang. The alarm which existed among the residents of Manchooria, causing their exodus to Niuchwang, was caused quite as much by Chinese soldiery retreating or disbanded, as by the Japanese army's advance. Many deserters had joined the bands of robbers and brigands to raid the country in every direction.

The first army, under Field Marshal Yamagata, finding the country in the direction of Mukden wasted and deserted, while guerrilla troops harassed them continually, now abandoned the march to Mukden and joined the second army, which had turned north, near Niuchwang, Field Marshal Oyama had sent his transports and a portion of his fleet around the Liao-Tung peninsula, to move towards Niuchwang, paralled with his army. General Techimi's division met the enemy December 10, and after a pitched battle defeated them with heavy loss. It being reported that a large force of Chinese under General I was encamped near Kinkua-hu, General Techimi was ordered to advance upon that place. His scouts reported the Chinese to be in considerable force, and to consist of cavalry as well as infantry. General Techimi separated his division into two columns, and delivered a simultaneous attack early in the morning. The Chinese offered a stout resistance, and severe fighting ensued. The superior shooting and discipline of the Japanese soon told. The enemy were gradually driven back, and finally they broke and fled in disorder, the Japanese pursuing them for several miles. The majority of the Chinese escaped in the direction of Tso-hun-kou. The Japanese lost about forty killed and wounded, and their opponents one hundred.

Field Marshal Yamagata, who had been in command of the first army since its organization, at last broke down in health under the strain of his responsibility and labor, and was compelled to return home in the hope of restoring his health. He was succeeded by Lieutenant-General Nodzu, his friend and adviser with the troops. The news of Yamagata's illness caused much distress in Japan, and he was welcomed with the highest honors, both from the government and the people.

In China the position of the government seemed to be precarious. Dissatisfaction was rife in Peking and Tien-tsin over the conduct of the war, and every one in turn was accused of responsibility in the matter. The Manchoo and Chinese elements were bitterly opposed, and an anti-war which advocated peace at any price was increasing rapidly. The court of inquiry which sat at Peking to inquire into the circumstances connected with the loss of Kinchow and Talien-wan, held that Kinchow was strong and well-garrisoned and ought never to have been surrendered. The commandant was therefore sentenced to degradation from military ranks for allowing the Japanese to take the place. The foreign residents in Peking, Tien-tsin, and Chefoo were by this time getting nervous over their own prospects for safety, owing to the disorder and rioting that prevailed, enhanced by the threatened invasion of the Japanese army. Marines were sent to Peking from the war ships of all western nations in Japanese waters, and attached to the legation for the protection of their countrymen in China. Anti foreign feeling in the capital was on the increase, and the blue jackets were welcomed most heartily when they landed.

Early in December Corea suffered another political crisis, owing to the duplicity of the government. All the Corean ministers professed gratitude to Japan, for giving them the opportunity of undertaking the administrative and social regeneration of their country. They promised Count Inouye, the Japanese resident, faithfully to follow his advice and to carry out with the least possible delay the program of reforms recommended by him. Count Inouye however discovered, that while making these professions, the ministers were plotting to obstruct his policy of reform, and had even gone so far as to send messengers to various parts of the country to incite the people to rise against the Japanese. He therefore informed the Corean government that Japan would give no further assistance to the king in suppressing the Tonghak rebellion. The minister of the interior at once resigned, and the king promised to make inquiry and punish those guilty of treachery. In a private audience, Count Inouye sharply remonstrated with His Majesty, explained that reforms were necessary to save the country from barbarism, complained of the encouragement given to the plotters and repeated his threat to recall the Japanese troops sent out against the Tonghaks. The king promised that matters would be put right. The following day the ministers called in a body upon Count Inouye. They admitted that they had behaved in a deceitful manner, begged that he would pardon their duplicity, and assured him that they would in future give faithful consideration to his suggestions and his schemes of internal reform.

There is a little confusion in the names of towns around the Gulf of Liao-Tung, owing to the duplication of names. Kinchow is a village to the north of Talien-wan Bay and was one of the first points of attack by the Japanese when they landed on the promontory. At the extreme northern point of the gulf is a city of the same name, and several reports that were made as to the capture of Kinchow were discredited because of this confusion. The first Kinchow was indeed occupied by Japanese troops from the time of its capture. The other one, however, was not threatened at all. Unless mention is made here to the contrary, references to troop movements around Kinchow refer to the village at the head of the promontory.

The bulk of the second Japanese army moved to Kinchow, on its way northward after the capture of Port Arthur, and the Chinese force which attacked the Japanese garrison at Kinchow on November 22, fell back to Foochow, a little to the northward of Port Arthur, on the road to Niuchwang. About the 1st of December General Nogi's brigade left Kinchow, with orders from Marshal Oyama to attack Foochow. The garrison of the city was reported to number five thousand, and the position was favorable for defense. The brigade moved forward very rapidly, as there was no organized opposition to its advance. On the 4th, General Nogi heard that the Chinese were retreating, and on the following day the Japanese entered Foochow without firing a shot. The Chinese had evacuated the city and had retreated northward towards Niuchwang.

The first Japanese army continued clearing the country north of the Yalu. Large bodies of Chinese were in the triangle formed by lines drawn between Chiu-lien, Niuchwang, and Mukden. The mountains around about Feng-hwang, which constituted a strong strategic position, had been in the hands of the Japanese since October, and now General Tatsumi attacked the highest pass, Lien-shan-kuan, from the east. On December 12 a strong Japanese scouting party from Feng-hwang sighted a large force of Chinese advancing from the west. The Japanese, who consisted entirely of cavalry, sent word back to Feng-hwang, and keeping the Chinese in sight fell back upon the main body. The Chinese pushed on as far as Yih-man-shan, where they encamped for the night. The Japanese force set out to attack the Chinese position, and at dawn the next morning the fight began. The Chinese were fully four thousand strong, and while the fight was in progress two more regiments joined them. The Japanese fell back to a stronger position, and adopted defensive tactics. The Chinese forces, emboldened by their temporary success, made repeated efforts to break through the Japanese lines, but each attack was repulsed. Seeing that the Chinese were in such force, General Nodzu ordered one battalion of the fifth division to reinforce the garrison of Feng-hwang. This reinforced garrison then started on Thursday night, December 13, to strengthen the Japanese advance posts at Yih-man-shan. Colonel Tomayasu was in command of the Japanese force, which numbered one thousand four hundred men with six field guns.

At daybreak an attack was made upon the Chinese left flank. The enemy was well posted, and fought better than any troops heretofore encountered by the Japanese in Manchooria. The struggle was a severe one, but the Chinese left wing gave way before the Japanese charge, and threw the center into confusion. A hot and continuous fire prevented the Chinese from recovering their formation, and a second charge drove them into a disorderly retreat. The contents of the camp and thirty prisoners fell into the hands of the Japanese. The Chinese lost some two hundred and fifty killed and wounded and the Japanese about one hundred.

It is difficult to convey a clear idea of the various operations in Manchooria, for no map accessible to general readers is sufficiently accurate to afford trustworthy indications, and the field of fighting extended over a considerable area among places too small in many instances to be recorded on a map. There were in fact, at this time, December, three Japanese and three Chinese armies operating in Manchooria. The Japanese forces consisted of the second army under Oyama, in the Liao-Tung peninsula, and the right and left wings of Yamagata's force, who had been succeeded by Nodzu. The first army, Yamagata's, after passing the Yalu and capturing Chiu-lien, separated into two parts, the right wing nominally twelve thousand five hundred strong, moving northward along the Mukden road under the command of Nodzu, and the left wing of equal strength, under the command of

Katsura, moving westward down the Yalu, its object being ultimately to establish communication with Oyama's forces, twenty-two thousand strong, when the capture of Port Arthur should have freed the latter to advance northeastward up the peninsula.

The Chinese armies were also three. One of these armies was massed at the north, defending the approaches to Mukden. It aggregated about twenty-five thousand men so far as could be ascertained, but its fragmentary fashion of fighting rendered a total estimate difficult. The second army was grouped in the southwest, guarding the coast roads to China proper, via Niuchwang. This army, according to the accounts, aggregated about thirty thousand. Its headquarters were at Kai phing, where a junction would naturally be effected between Oyama's forces and the left wing of Yamagata's army. The easiest method of obtaining a clear idea of the situation, is to follow in outline, the operations of the various armies.

The southeastern Chinese army was composed of the Amoor frontier forces, under General I. It was moved down under direct orders from the throne, the strategical idea being to strike swiftly and secretly at Marshal Yamagata's weak point, namely, his long line of communications between the Yalu River and his outposts, fifty miles north of Feng-hwang. Thus General I's operations ultimately resolved themselves into an attempt to recover Feng-hwang. He marched against it from three directions, the main northerly road, and two easterly roads. The Japanese did not wait to receive his attack. On December 10, Major-General Techimi, who commanded the van of the Japanese right wing, launched his battalion at I's van of three thousand men on the main road, and by consecutive onsets cut the enemy in two, driving a part of his force into the mountains eastward, and a part along the main road northward. Two days later a reconnaissance sent eastward from Feng-hwang found the main body of I's forces on the Aiyang-pien road, and the following morning a battalion moved out to attack him. But it having been seen that he mustered fully six thousand, and that advancing along two roads his front extended over a distance of more than three miles, the Japanese plan was modified so as to deliver the chief assault against his left wing, orders being also forwarded to Techimi, then operating north of Feng-hwang to move east and south with the object of taking I's right wing in the rear. December 14 saw the attack on the Tartar general's left wing. It was completely rolled back and broken, the Japanese pursuing its remnants far into the mountains. The Chinese lost one hundred and fifty killed and sixteen prisoners, and abandoned four Krupp guns, a number of horses, and a quantity of war material. The Japanese had twelve killed and sixty-three wounded. I's right wing made no attempt to hold its ground after the defeat of the left. It retired in a northeasterly direction and its retreat was subsequently changed into a route by collision with a Japanese pursuing column sent out from Techimi's position.

The northerly army of China consisted of that portion of General Sung's troops that retreated along the main road towards Mukden after the fall of Chiu-lien and Feng-hwang, together with the Mukden garrison. They held the pass of Mo-thien-ling against several attacks of the Japanese, and remained there in force after severe winter set in. They had several collisions with Techimi's outposts, but none of importance to the general conduct of the war.

The western Chinese army consisted partly of troops originally engaged in the defense of Chiu-lien and Feng-hwang, partly of the Niuchwang garrison, and partly of a Mongolian force that had come down to join them from the northwest. This was the largest force and aggregated nearly sixty thousand. After the battles around the lower Yalu, these troops had been driven inland by the Japanese, taking Hai-tcheng as their objective point, but halting on the way at Siu-Yen. They were driven out of here by the Japanese, and moved westward to Simu-tcheng, a town eighteen miles southeast of Hai-tcheng. On December 11, the Japanese troops under Osako, moving northward from Siu-Yan, reached the advance posts of the enemy and made an attack. The Chinese force consisting of three thousand infantry and four hundred calvary, with eight guns, was driven back after a brief resistance, and the next day another body four thousand five hundred strong, with six guns, was dislodged from a position three or four miles further on. The Japanese, following up their advantage, took possession of the Simu-tcheng the same afternoon. This division and the co-operating division which had taken another road, entered the place almost simultaneously after two days of unbroken success. They advanced together on the following day, and at 11:00 A.M. Hai-tcheng was in their possession. Its garrison was found to consist of only one thousand five hundred men, who after a show of resistance retired northeastward in the direction of Liao-Yang. The occupation of Haitcheng placed the Japanese on the high road from Niuchwang to Mukden, some twenty miles from Niuchwang and eighty from Mukden. This was a position of considerable strategical importance. For the moment however, Japanese troops turned southward a few miles in the direction of Kao-Khan, a fortified town not far from the mouth of the Liao River. This movement was connected with the march of the second army up the Laio-Tung peninsula, to which reference must now be made.

After the capture of Port Arthur and the completion of arrangements relating to the occupation of that place, Marshal Oyama returned to Kinchow and made preparations to advance northward against Foochow, an important walled town of twenty-five thousand inhabitants fifty-three miles to the northward. General Sung, with some six thousand men held Foochow, and a vigorous resistance was anticipated. But on December 5, the Japanese van entered the town unopposed. The advance was then resumed to Kai-phing, a city of still greater importance sixty-three miles distant. And as this army moved northward, the left wing of the first army moved southward from Hai-tcheng, as has just been said, threatening Kai-phing from the other side and cutting off the garrison's direct line of retreat. It is interesting to note that wherever Japanese troops took possession of a city or district, an officer was immediately appointed to be military governor, the inhabitants were kindly treated, and every effort was made to preserve peace and free the natives from annoyance or oppression.

On the 17th and 18th of December the scouts of General Katsura's division brought word to him of important movements of the enemy, who appeared to be advancing in strong force. All this proved to be nothing more formidable than the flight of General Sung's army northward. On the night of the 18th the Chinese army was ascertained to be passing within a few miles of the Japanese camp, and Katsura therefore moved against them with his full strength. The Chinese were overtaken on the following morning. Osako's brigade was the first to be engaged. The enemy made a stand at the village of Kungwasai and severe fighting ensued. While this was proceeding Oshima's brigade coming from Hai-tcheng entered the field and joined hands with Osako. The combined force consisted of four complete regiments, five batteries of artillery, besides other troops. The Japanese artillery, which was well placed, played havoc with the Chinese, who stubbornly stood their ground. The Japanese infantry charged splendidly and cut their way through the Chinese army, but the enemy rallied and fired steadily. A desperate hand-to-hand struggle took place. After five hours' fighting, the Chinese began to falter and soon they were in full and disorderly flight, some to the westward and others north. The Chinese lost probably five hundred killed and wounded and the Japanese loss, too, was very severe. This was probably the most obstinate engagement yet fought by the armies in Manchooria. The Chinese had strongly entrenched themselves at the little village of Kungwasai, near Hai-tcheng, and they defended their position most vigorously. The ground was thick with snow, and the battle was a desperate one. Charge after charge made by the Japanese was faced and the assaulting troops driven back. But with a fourth charge the battle ended, the Japanese rushing into the Chinese works and carrying everything before them.

The constant succession of defeats of the Chinese forces, made imperial circles in Peking a nest of nervous uncertainty. Factional fights existed among the officials, and no one knew when his position or his head was safe. The empress dowager remained firm in her confidence in Li Hung Chang, and this fact served to retain him the title of viceroy. All of his decorative honors had however by this time been stripped from him, and only the queen's favor and the fact that it was not wise to make of him an open enemy saved him from losing his last title. Early in December Prince Kung was appointed president of the Grand Council. He lost no time in moving towards severe punishment the military and naval officers who for being defeated were adjudged traitors. An imperial decree imperatively ordered the arrest of Taotai Kung the civil commandant and the four generals who commanded at Port Arthur in order that they should be sent to Peking to be tried and punished for the loss of the fortress. Admiral Ting was also arrested for failing to defend the dockyard. Generals Yeh and Wei of Ping-Yang fame were handed over to the same board of punishment. The foreign officers serving in the Chinese fleet sent to Prince Kung a unanimous protest against the infliction of punishment upon Admiral Ting, declaring that the charges made against him were unjust and that they would resign if he was punished. In response to this protest therefore an edict was issued continuing the admiral in command of the fleet.

The late viceroy of Nanking, Liu-kun-yi, was now appointed to the chief command of all the Chinese forces in the field, thus superseding Li Hung Chang and Prince Kung so far as military command was concerned. He had made an impression at the palace by his energy and by his plans for resisting invaders. Immediately upon his appointment Liu petitioned to be relieved from the office, pleading indisposition, but his request was refused at the palace. His desire was taken as an indication that he felt himself incapable of successfully carrying out the arduous task imposed upon him. In the face of the emperor's imperative orders Liu could not avoid accepting the command, and he therefore began making appointments to his staff and preparing for his immediate departure to the front.

At last on December 21, it was given out to the world that peace negotiations with Japan were to be begun in earnest, in the hope that the crowning humiliation of a Japanese occupation of Peking might be averted. The emperor selected Chang Yen Hoon, vice-president of the Tsung-li Yamen as his peace envoy and, it was said, invested him with the fullest powers to treat. It was announced that he would proceed immediately to Japan with an adequate suite and ample credentials. He was a man of great ability, and great confidence was expressed in the success of his mission. Mr. Dun, United States minister at Tokio, learned that the Japanese government would receive the Chinese envoy with every consideration due to his rank, and with an honest desire to help him to bring his mission to a successful conclusion. But from the very beginning there was strong evidence to indicate that China was not acting in the best of faith, for no authoritative statement was made by the government at Peking of the appointment of such a plenipotentiary. This suspicion was only too well corroborated a few weeks later.

The Chinese government, after deciding to send an envoy to Japan, addressed a formal request to President Cleveland for the assistance of a recognized statesman in connection with the forthcoming peace negotiations in Tokio. The president lost no time in replying. It was officially announced in Washington December 27, that the Hon. John W. Foster, Secretary of State in the cabinet of President Harrison, after the death of secretary Blaine, had been appointed legal adviser to the Chinese peace plenipotentiary who was about to be sent to the government of Japan. Before entering President Harrison's cabinet Mr. Foster had represented the United States as minister at Madrid and he acted as agent of the United States in the court of arbitration of the Bering Sea question at Paris. He was one of the foremost among international lawyers in the United States, with large experience in Chinese affairs. His selection by President Cleveland was not an official one, but was merely in response to a request from China for friendly assistance. Mr. Foster had no official standing from the United States, but acted simply as an adviser to the Chinese envoy.

A curious incident comes well substantiated regarding Mr. Foster's preparations for his trip. Shortly before he sailed for China, it is said, a party of Wall street men went to see him on the subject of the Chinese indemnity. This indemnity was destined to have an important bearing upon American politics. Should the indemnity be paid in gold, our own treasury reserve would be drawn upon rather seriously. Should it be paid in silver the demand for the white metal would undoubtedly create an enormous demand for the product of western mines to the great advantage of the silver producing states. The Wall street men visited Mr. Foster in a body and urged him to favor a gold settlement. The diplomat became very much incensed at this. He declared that the representations of the bankers were a gross violation of diplomatic ethics, and that he would act as he thought best in the interests of China. From that time forward the prospective treaty was anticipated with great interest by American bankers.

The eighth session of the Japanese parliament was opened at Tokio, December 24. In the absence of the emperor at Hiroshima his speech was read by one of the ministers. It took occasion to congratulate the country for the success of the Japanese arms and declared the need of further persistence towards the successful conclusion of the war. Political sentiment, so far as party spirit was concerned, did not run high in Japan, for nearly all parties were united in support of the war. The session of parliament therefore awakened no marked interest.

The collossal nature of the task that devolved upon Japan when she undertook to reform the Corean administration was becoming daily more apparent. The first difficulty presenting itself was the fact that all the high offices of state were occupied by proteges of the queen, members of the Ming family. The queen was a woman of considerable and large ambition. She exercised great influence over the king and employed it to secure preferment and appointment for her own relatives. But the queen and her friends were indefatigable supporters of China. The Chinese resident always worked in their interests; they firmly believed that Chinese supremacy would be re-established sooner or later; and they were wedded to Chinese systems as affording the widest scope for self-aggrandizement. Thus they stood in the very forefront of the opponents of reform. That was recognized from the outset, and the device was adopted of entrusting the chief powers to the Tai-wen Kun, an inveterate enemy of the Ming family. But the old prince whose political record was written in blood cared not one jot for reform. His one idea was the Tai-men Kun. Moreover he too believed in the restoration of Chinese influence and wishing to enlist it in his own behalf he opened secret correspondence with the Chinese generals, promising them that the appearance of their troops before Seoul should be the signal for a widespread insurrection of the Tonghaks to attack the Japanese simultaneously. These letters were discovered and placed in the hands of Count Inouye. He invited the Taimen Kun to the Japanese legation and quietly showed him the incriminating documents. Of course there was no imperative reason why any Corean subject should prefer Japan to China. The Tai-wen Kun had a right to choose between the two, but he had no right to hold the regency under pretex of furthering reforms which he was secretly working to defeat. It was not difficult to induce him to resign the regency. He saw that the game was lost and consented to efface himself from the political arena. At the demand of the Japanese minister, the Corean king formed a new cabinet more satisfactory to Japanese influence and the crisis was passed. The revolts of the Tonghaks, however, seemed to be almost continuous and every day brought news of a riot engendered by them.

The Japanese armies which we left in Manchooria near Kaiphing, were posted on a curve extending from that city near the sea, to Hai-tcheng, which was strongly fortified, and posts also extended from there to the Mo-thien-ling hills. They thus occupied a strong position for defensive and offensive purposes. Very severe weather had set in early in January and hundreds of Japanese soldiers were suffering from frostbite. The Chinese forces had withdrawn to Kao-khan near Niuchwang, although the force occupying Liao-Yang had advanced some distance towards Hai-tcheng, which the Japanese were occupying.

Early on the morning of January 10, a brigade under General Nogi marched against a Chinese force encamped in the vicinity of Kai-phing. The attack was made at dawn, but the deep snow rendered military movements, especially the bringing up of guns, a matter of great difficulty. The Chinese had twelve fieldpieces and two gatlings which were well handled. Their force numbered about three thousand. The fight lasted four hours, and consisted mainly of an exchange of shot and shell until the Japanese were in position on the Chinese flank, when an infantry charge was ordered and the Chinese fell back before the heavy fire. The final attack upon the center was splendidly made and by 9:00 o'clock the Chinese were well beaten. There was some stiff fighting at the last, but by 10:00 o'clock the Japanese were in full possession of the town. Two hundred Chinese were found dead in the positions which they had held, and one hundred and fifty were taken prisoners. The Chinese force was commanded by General Seh, who expected to be strongly reinforced before the Japanese attack could be made. On learning this, General Nogi sent out scouting parties towards Yo-chow. They reported that a

Chinese army estimated to number ten thousand men had been marching upon Kai-phing but having heard of the defeat of General Seh this large force had immediately retired towards Yingtsu, the port of Niuchwang.

Either confidence or desperation of the Chinese was exemplified in the vicinity of Niuchwang a few days later when two Chinese corps marched against the Japanese advanced lines, and opened an attack. One of these corps advanced from Liao-Yang, whilst the other marched from the direction of Niuchwang. They were estimated at from twelve to fourteen thousand men and they had with them several fieldpieces and gatling guns. They came in sight of the Japanese lines before noon and continued their advance until within less than two miles. Then they halted and a consultation was held amongst their staff. They made no further advance, much to Japanese disappointment, but simply began a heavy fire from their artillery. At 2:00 o'clock in the afternoon, General Katsura ordered the Japanese to reply, and a concentrated fire was opened upon the Chinese ranks. The total Japanese force concentrated to receive the Chinese attack consisted of four battalions of infantry and one battalion of artillery with twelve guns. The artillery fire continued for an hour, when seeing that the Chinese were being thrown into confusion by the bursting shells, General Katsura ordered a charge upon the enemy's right wing. It proved to be entirely successful. Five guns which protected the enemy's right were captured at once, and the whole force immediately retreated. Another charge upon the center scattered the Chinese. The majority fled to the north, whilst a portion retreated in the direction of Niuchwang. The Chinese losses were roughly estimated at nine hundred, and the Japanese scarcely one-tenth of that number.

The first army, finding the country in the direction of Mukden wasted and deserted while guerilla troops harassed them continually, now virtually abandoned the march to Mukden and formed a junction with the second army drawing together at the acute angle to which they had been so long converging. Oyama and Nodzu met and from that time worked with their forces conjointly. The Chinese were becoming bolder in the vicinity of Hai-tcheng which made the necessity greater for a union of forces. At the same time Mukden itself was in a state of riotous disorder, the Manchoo and Chinese troops continually at conflict with one another and therefore scarcely needing the attention of the Japanese to attack either side. Military operations in Manchooria were now exceedingly difficult owing to the depth of snow and the bitter cold weather. Both armies were suffering from the rigors of the season, and neither regretted the opportunity for a cessation of active hostilities. General Nogi moved forward his headquarters to Huntsai. Cavalry skirmishes between scouting parties between Niuchwang and Kai-phing, and between Niuchwang and Hai-tcheng were of daily occurrence and with them we will consider the season's campaign of the armies in Manchooria closed.

The raising of Li Hung Chang's enemy, Liu-kun-yi, to the chief military command in China stirred up more and more trouble for military and naval officers as the time went by. Half of the generals of the army and the admirals and commanders of the navy were arrested, charged with various degrees of guilt, and many of them were sentenced to death. As a matter of fact, however, not many of these sentences were carried out, although General Wei was beheaded in Peking, January 16. The influence of Li Hung Chang could not, however, be destroyed, even though he had been relieved of all his functions except that of governor general of his province. His connections with prominent officials in China had been too intimate and his strength too great that all could be taken away from him even by imperial edict. The old viceroy, the Bismarck of Asia quietly bided his time and waited the results that he felt sure would come. The Chinese envoy and his suite of fifty-six lingered at Shanghai day after day delaying their start to Japan with the avowed explanation that further instructions were expected, but with the understanding frankly held by every one except themselves that they were really detained in the hope that something would turn up, that some special providence would interfere to relieve them of the necessity of presenting China's suit for peace to her ancient enemy.

And now the third Japanese army was ready for its descent upon the Chinese coasts and another invasion of the Celestial Empire was impending.

THE EXPEDITION TO CAPTURE WEI-HAI-WEI AND ITS SUCCESS

Plans for the Third Japanese Army—Description of Wei-hai-wei and its Defences—Arrival of the Japanese Troops—Landing of the Forces at Yung-tcheng Bay—Bombardment or Tengchow—Capture of Ning-Hai—Wei-hai-wei Fort Taken—Severity of the Weather—Action of the Fleets—The Torpedo Boats—Continuing the Bombardment—A White Flag From the Chinese—Surrender—Admiral Ting's Suicide—After the Surrender.

The command of the sea definitely gained by the Japanese at the battle of the Yalu, now enabled another expeditionary force to be landed on the shores of China, this time on the Shantung peninsula, which juts out between the Gulf of Pechili and the Yellow Sea on the south, as the Liao-Tung peninsula does between the Gulf of Laio-Tung and Corea Bay on the north. Since that eventful action, the Chinese fleet had remained in port, and the Japanese had been free to use the water-ways of the east, as if no enemy's ships existed. To undertake a new enterprise was merely a question of men and means. The transports employed at Port Arthur were available, and a third army twenty-five thousand strong was mobilized at Hiroshima in December. These troops were embarked for an expeditionary force to threaten Wei-hai-wei. There were fifty Japanese transports in the squadron, convoyed by a few war ships, and the fleet sailed away from Japan just before the middle of January.

Wei-hai-wei is about twenty-five miles west of the extreme northeastern point of the Shantung promontory, and fifty miles east of Chefoo, which was the nearest treaty port. Wei-hai-wei consists of an island some two miles long, and the adjacent mainland, running in a semi-circle around the bay. Between the island and the shore is a large and safe harbor, with an entrance at either end. At both entrances, two rows of submarine torpedo mines furnished protection against invading squadrons, and on the island stood the naval and gunnery school of China, and the houses of the foreign instructors. The island was defended by three forts, one at the east end, one at the west, and the third on a little island connected with it. On the hills which rise from the island also six small batteries with quick firing guns. In one of the forts were four heavy Krupp guns, in another three, while in the third were two Armstrong disappearing guns of twenty-five tons, on revolving planes. On the mainland was a small village, while three forts commanded the eastern entrance to the harbor, and three the western, armed in the same way as the forts on the island. Seven men-of-war remaining to the Chinese fleet were at anchor in the harbor, and would be useful in defense of the place,

DISTANT VIEW OF WEI-HAI-WEI AND ITS SURROUNDINGS

though not enough for battle at sea against a fleet. The fortifications were built under the direction of Captain Von Hannecken, and several foreigners in the Chinese service had remained there throughout the war as artillerists and in other capacities. The Chinese Admiral Ting was also there, against whom the Chinese censors had been speaking so bitterly. There were strongly equipped forts, a beautiful harbor, a good naval school, and all was ready to be captured by the Japanese.

The Japanese transports touched at Talien-wan Bay on the way to the Shantung promontory, and took on board some of the officers who had been with the army around Port Arthur. Except for these however, the troops moving on Weihai-wei were all new in the field. On the 18th of January a small reconnoitering party of Japanese naval officers landed from a boat in Yung-tcheng Bay, having left their ship out of sight around the eastern headland. They arrived in the night, cut the telegraph lines connecting Shantung promontory lighthouse with Wei-hai-wei, and afterward, being of course in disguise and familiar with the Chinese language, made inquiries of the peasantry. They discovered that the commander of Wei-hai-wei, having heard of warships off the promontory, had sent some five hundred troops to defend Yung-tcheng. The Japanese then decided to land at dawn on the 20th. Yung-tcheng Bay is about four miles southwest of the northeast promontory lighthouse, and faces nearly due south. On the east is a bold headland connected by low hills with a chain of abrupt heights running west. The west headland, enclosing the bay, is not so high and ends in a spit of sand and rocks, beyond which are two smaller shallow bays, and Yung-tcheng town about seven miles away due west. Nestling close under the west slope of the strip is a small village. Yungtcheng Bay is about a mile wide, and hemispherical. The anchorage is good for large vessels to within one hundred yards of the beach, and the large fleet assembled there for hostile purposes was well protected.

The Japanese flotilla was led by five war ships which were two or three hours ahead of the rest—twenty transports carrying one division of infantry, with an escort of four war ships. Other war ships were on patrol duty, with torpedo boats blockading "Wei-hai-wei completely. The transports which came on the 22nd contained another brigade of infantry, a strong force of artillery, some cavalry, and the large and important commissariat and transport sections.

The Chinese troops first took up a position on the sand spit and opened fire on the ships with four fieldpieces, without effect. Meantime some two hundred Japanese marines were being landed on the beach under the eastern bluff. As the boats drew near the shore a few shots came in their direction, but the Chinese marksmanship was utterly useless. The Japanese succeeded in getting ashore without any mishaps whatever by 7:00 A.M., while daylight was still faint. The ground was covered with snow a few inches deep. A shell from one of the war ships set fire to a small cottage where the Chinese were, and they were forced to retire to the village behind the knoll. Here planting their guns, four Krupp fieldpieces, on rising ground, with infantry in the broken ground about the village, they tried their best to make a stand; but the guns of the war ship were making the position untenable, and a bayonet charge of marines put an end to their resistance. They fled to Yung-tcheng, leaving their cannon. The losses on either side were slight. By eight o'clock the transports had arrived, and the landing of troops began, finishing before dusk. The disembarkation of the rear guard, which came on the second fleet of transports, was also carried on expeditiously on the 23rd.

During the afternoon of the 20th a battalion of the newly landed soldiers pushed on without delay or rest to Yung-tcheng. The Chinese force of about five hundred made slight resistance; there was a little firing, but no casualty on either side, and the place was taken. A detachment of Japanese followed westward in pursuit of the enemy. A quantity of arms, ammunition, and stores fell into the victor's hands at Yung-tcheng.

The first thing done by the Japanese on landing was to make a small floating jetty of sampans and planks, from the sandy beach to water deep enough for launches. Rough sheds were also erected rapidly, so as to make the place a convenient depot as a subsidiary base of operations. Here the troops were sheltered as they landed, moving over to Yung-tcheng as rapidly as possible, so that within a few days they were almost all quartered in the town and surrounding villages. The inhabitants went about their business as usual, evincing only a little timid curiosity towards the invaders.

Japanese strategy was to be credited, to considerable extent, with the easy landing granted to their troops in Yung-tcheng Bay. War ships had been cruising back and forth along the north shore of the promontory, keeping the commanders of various posts nervously expectant of an attack. Finally on Saturday, January 19, war vessels drew near to Tengdhow, some thirty miles northwest of Chefoo, and began a bombardment which lasted throughout the day. The Chinese worked their guns well, but were not equal to the Japanese gunners either in rapidity or precision of fire. Many of the Chinese guns were dismounted by the Japanese fire, and others were rendered useless through absence of sufficient ammunition. By nightfall all the forts were silenced and the city was at the mercy of the invaders. Two thousand Japanese landed and kept up an incessant fire from fieldpieces upon the land side, while the ships were bombarding the water front. This demonstration was only for the purpose of creating a diversion, and attracting Chinese attention to Tengchow, while averting it from Yung-tcheng.

On January 23, a Japanese force landed at Ning-Hai, midway between Wei-hai-wei and Chefoo, and the former city was therefore surrounded. The landing was covered by the guns of a dozen war ships, but there was no opposition. The troops at once marched upon the city of Ning-Hai, situated near the point of landing, and the place fell into their hands after a very feeble resistance. The occupation of Ning-Hai isolated Wei-hai-wei from Chefoo. The Chinese arsenal was almost exactly half way between the two Japanese landing places, and the coast road being in occupation of the Japanese, news from the threatened garrison had to be carried over mountain paths with considerable difficulty.

The strong Japanese fleet of war ships, transports, and torpedo boats was now assured of safety from any possible attack in Yung-tcheng Bay, and the war ships patrolled back and forth between the two landing places in constant threat of Wei-haiwei, and forbidding the exit of the Chinese vessels which were penned in that harbor. The expeditionary force had landed all the necessary heavy guns and ammunition, beside forage, food, and other necessaries. The British and German flagships were in Yung-tcheng Bay, besides several American war vessels. The two land forces now moved upon Wei-hai wei, one from the east and one from the west.

The forts on the mainland at Wei-hai-wei were captured by the Japanese on January 30. The taking of the Chinese stronghold was due to skillful combined movements on the part of the Japanese land and naval forces, the main attack, however, being made by the troops on shore. The resistance, considering the strength of the place, was feeble. Some of the forts, however, were stubbornly defended, and the loss was heavy on both sides.

The Japanese troops of the sixth division were under arms at two o'clock in the morning, and the advance was at once ordered. As soon as it was daylight the assault on the enemy's defensive lines began, and by nine o'clock the outlying batteries and intrenchments were almost all in the hands of the Japanese.

Meanwhile the second division was delivering a direct assault from the southwest on the Pai-chih-yaiso line of forts, a position of great strength, with precipitous sides about one hundred feet in height. The attack was made under cover of a furious bombardment from the Japanese men-of-war. The main point of Chinese resistance was here. After the fighting on this side had been going on for some hours, the sixth division, having driven in the enemy before it, made a detour, and advancing behind Mount Ku which concealed the movement, made a strong attack from that side on the Pai-chih-yaiso forts. By half past twelve these forts were in possession of the Japanese. By preconcerted arrangement the signal was at once given to the Japanese fleet, which proceeded without delay to take possession of the eastern entrance of the harbor.

The Japanese fleet had been keeping well off the shore, throwing a few shots occasionally into the batteries upon Leu-kung-tau island, but the main attack was upon the eastern forts. The ironclads dropped their long distance shots into the Chinese position with fair accuracy, but eight of the smaller Japanese vessels steamed along the shore within easy range and worked their guns steadily and well. One well placed shell caused a terrific explosion in Fort Number One, pointing to the eastward, and that fort took no further part in the fighting. A few minutes later Japanese troops rushed in and their flag went up. At half past twelve another deafening roar proclaimed that an explosion had taken place in Fort Number Two. Whether this was due to Japanese fire, or whether the Chinese deliberately blew it up, was not known, but the fort was destroyed. The Chinese firing flagged after this. At last only one gun in Fort Number Three could be worked, the Chinese fled, and the Japanese swarmed in. This action evidently discouraged the men in Fort Number Four for the garrison abandoned the place and joined their retreating countrymen, while the fort fell into the hands of the Japanese intact.

The Chinese fleet had been busy throughout the fight, but kept well under shelter of the island. Their shell fire was mainly directed upon the masses of Japanese infantry, advancing against the land forts, and the batteries upon the island were similarly employed. With the capture of Number Four fort the Japanese were in a position to turn the guns upon their enemies, a fact of which they were not slow to take advantage. They opened fire upon the Chinese fleet and upon the land batteries, doing more damage in a short time than their fleet had been able to accomplish during the day. This was too much for the Chinamen, and abandoning their former tactics, the battleship Ting-Yuen steamed out from her island shelter, and coming in close to Fort Number Four, hammered away vigorously for a full half hour. By that time every gun in the fort had been silenced, and the Japanese were fairly shelled out of it.

The resumption of the fight on Thursday, January 31, by the Japanese fleet was rendered impossible by a severe northerly gale accompanied by a blinding snowstorm. The decks of the ships, and also the guns were covered with ice. Seeing that the position was becoming dangerous for his ships, Admiral Ito ran to Yungtcheng Bay for shelter and safe anchorage, leaving a small squadron to keep watch at the entrance to Wei-hai-wei harbor. On shore the Japanese made great efforts to strengthen their position, and for the next few days there was desultory firing, but no continuous bombardment.

The hardest day's fighting for the Japanese fleet was Sunday, February 3. The tempestuous weather which prevailed during Friday and Saturday kept the main squadron in shelter, and while the other ships were watching the two entrances to the harbor, their work gave greater opportunities for seamanship than for gunnery. They engaged the island forts occasionally and exchanged shots with the Chinese war ships, but the land batteries did most of the firing. Sunday, however, was the navy's day although the land batteries were not idle. Almost with daybreak the fleet opened fire upon the forts of Leu-kung-tau island which replied vigorously. The bombardment soon became terrific. The flagship and several other large vessels were in possession outside the bay, and concentrated their fire upon the eastern island batteries.

The second division rained shell upon Fort Zhih. The bombardment had scarcely begun when the Chinese fleet joined in very gallantly. The Ting-Yuen used her thirty-seven ton guns without effect, but succeeded in drawing some of the Japanese tire to herself. The Lai-Yuen, the smaller ship, stood towards the Japanese and fought well, suffering considerable damage and many casualties. Two of the Chinese gunboats also took an active part in the defense and were not badly damaged. These four vessels fought with great determination until darkness set in when the firing ceased on both sides. The bombardment had caused great damage to the Chinese works, particularly at Zhih, where many men had been killed and wounded. Several guns were dismounted and towards the close of the fight the fire from the Chinese batteries slackened in a marked manner.

The sea was still rough on Sunday night, but the Japanese ships did not seek shelter. It was confidently expected that some of the Chinese ships would endeavor to escape during the night, and the harbor exits were therefore blocked by the Japanese fleet. Admiral Ting however made no move, and when morning broke his squadron was seen in its old positon, under the shelter of the island. It was learned from a prisoner taken on shore that Admiral Ting had issued a general order to his captains that even if the defenses on the mainland should fall into the enemy's hands, the war ships must remain inside the harbor and help the island forts to destroy the Japanese fleet. Every officer was ordered to remain at his post until the last, under pain of dishonor and death.

Monday morning the bombardment was resumed. The Japanese fleet engaged both forts and ships, and the land batteries bombarded the Chinese squadron. The fire from Fort Zhih continued weak, and the Chinese battleships were so repeatedly and so seriously hit that their guns were handled with difficulty and with less spirit. Finally, towards the close of the fight, the Ting-Yuen was disabled. It gradually settled down, and at length foundered amid loud shouts of triumph from the Japanese on land and sea. The Chen-Yuen, too, was badly damaged.

When the remaining vessels of the Chinese fleet were captured, they were in serviceable condition, but badly damaged. The torpedo boats of the fleet made a rush through the western entrance, of the harbor, to escape capture. The Japanese flying squadron immediately gave chase, and for hours maintained a most exciting pursuit. Some of the torpedo boats were sunk almost before they cleared the harbor, but others managed to get past the Japanese squadron. They were not however in a condition to make their best speed, and one by one they were overtaken and either sunk, driven ashore or captured. The Japanese fleet, on the other hand did not escape unscathed. The torpedo boat which sank the Ting-Yuen was destroyed by a hail of shot, eight of her crew being drowned. Another Japanese torpedo boat had her engineer and all her stokers killed by a shell bursting in the engineroom, and indeed it was a much damaged flotilla that returned to Admiral Ito. Only one boat escaped entirely uninjured. So severe was the cold that on one of the torpedo boats during the stealthy approach to the bay, a lieutenant and his two lookout men were frozen to death at their posts.

Monday on shore was as busy as on sea and the fighting continued without cessation throughout the day. The guns in the eastern and western forts that could be brought to bear upon the Chinese fleet and the forts on the island were worked all day by Japanese gunners and the Chinese artillery men fought their guns well in reply. On the land side the infantry of the sixth division moved against some minor lines to the west still held by the Chinese. The latter did not wait for the Japanese onslaught, but fled away westward leaving arms and stores behind them. By noon there was not a single fortress or battery on the mainland around Wei-hai-wei that the Japanese had not captured.

Marshal Oyama meantime had ordered the fourth division to attack the town of Wei-hai-wei itself. The place however surrendered without a shot being fired. The Chinese garrison had fled in the early morning, and the citizens opened the gates to the Japanese forces. No injury was sustained by the town or inhabitants. As fast as was practicable, fresh guns were mounted in place of the disabled ones in the captured forts, and every hour added to the weight of metal thrown against the Chinese fleet and island forts. But night, set in, and the Chinese fleet fought with as much determination as ever. Search-lights were kept playing by both belligerents throughout the night. An occasional shot was fired by one or the other, but the fierce cannonade of Sunday was not resumed until dawn. Then the large Chinese war ships, sheltering themselves as much as possible under the island, shelled the various forts in turn. The smaller Chinese vessels were scattered about the bay, taking little part in the fighting, and escaping the attention of the Japanese gunners. The Chinese had burnt or sunk every junk and boat in the harbor in order to prevent their being used by any large body of Japanese to make an effectual landing upon the island. The roar of the big guns during Monday was incessant. Shells were dropped repeatedly into the island forts, and the Chinese battleships were hit again and again, but there was no sign of the fleet giving in or of their ammunition giving out. At night the firing ceased, and again the search-lights illuminated land and sea.

On the night of Monday, February 4, the Japanese after many hours' exertions succeeded in clearing the entrance to the harbor of Wei-hai-wei of all the torpedoes and submarine mines that had been laid. And under cover of the darkness torpedo boats stole in and launched their projectiles at one of the great Chinese ironclads. The torpedoes took effect, and the vessel sank.

Day after day the shore forts at Wei-hai-wei, aided by the Japanese fleet, continued their bombardment of the Chinese war ships and the forts on the island, getting a reply which gradually diminished in strength. The fleet could not escape from the harbor, owing to the presence of the Japanese flotilla just outside, so they fought on bravely, doing much damage indeed to the Japanese, but accomplishing no final results. The timber obstructions at the eastern entrance to the bay were destroyed by the Japanese to admit their torpedo boats to that side, as they had already been admitted to the other entrance. With the Chinese torpedo fleet escaped and destroyed, there was no adequate defense against this threat. Finally it seemed that there was no use in further resistance.

On February 12, a Chinese gunboat flying a white flag came to the Japanese fleet with a message from Admiral Ting. He proposed to the Japanese commander-in-chief to surrender all his ships remaining afloat and all arms and ammunition, and to give possession of the forts still holding out, upon the sole condition that Admiral Ito would guarantee the lives of the Chinese sailors and soldiers, and of the European officers serving under the Chinese flag in the fleet and in the island forts. Admiral Ito, in reply to the offer, acceded to the terms and demanded that the naval station should be thrown open. On the morning

of the 13th however, the Chinese messenger returned and informed the Japanese Admiral that Admiral Ting had committed suicide on the previous evening, and that his responsibility was transferred to Admiral McClure. The news was even more startling than that of a single suicide, for Admiral Ting's commodore, the general in command of the island forts, and Captains Liu and Chang had all taken their own lives through grief and shame at having to surrender. Admiral

ADMIRAL MCCLURE

Ting before committing suicide wrote a politely worded letter addressed to the Japanese commander-in-chief explaining his reasons for taking his life and enclosing letters which he requested might be forwarded to their destination.

The only officer of high rank left on the Chinese war ships was Admiral McClure, the Scotchman who had been recently appointed to act as second in command to Admiral Ting. Admiral McClure sent word by the staff officer that having succeeded to the command by the death of Admiral Ting, he was prepared to carry out the surrender and to consult Admiral Ito's convenience in the matter. He suggested that Admiral Ito should give his guarantee to the British Admiral or to some other neutral naval officer, that as soon as the Chinese war ships and island forts had been handed over, the soldiers and sailors and the Chinese, and foreign officers should be set free. Admiral Ito replied that no guarantee was necessary beyond the Japanese word and he peremptorily declined to furnish one. This decision was accepted without further demur, the Chinese flags were everywhere lowered and the transfer of ships and forts was at once proceeded with.

The soldiers who had held the island first gave up their arms, and then were put on board Chinese and Japanese boats and taken on shore. Escorted by Japanese troops, they were marched through the Japanese lines, out into the open country and there set free. They were treated with every

JAPANESE SOLDIERS ESCORTING CHINESE PRISONERS

respect and seemed surprised that their lives were spared. On the morning of February 15, the officers and sailors of the Chinese ships were disposed of in similar fashion. The foreign officers, about a dozen all together waited for a neutral ship to take them away.

During the progress of Chinese reverses at Wei-hai-wei, the excitement in other Chinese cities was intense, increasing as the distance from Wei-hai-wei decreased. Chefoo, the nearest treaty port and the home of many foreigners, was in a tremor of fear. A bombardment or an invasion of the city was dreaded from the victorious troops to the eastward, and not the least danger was that from the Chinese troops who had been disarmed and turned loose to make their way to Chefoo after the surrender. The emperor was so incensed at the loss of Wei-hai-wei that he took the unusual course of authorizing the governor of the Shantung province to behead all fugitives without previously reporting to the throne.

Wei-hai-wei will be remembered in the history of this war as the only spot at which the progress of the Japanese was interrupted by serious and prolonged resistance on the part of the enemy. Admiral Ting's bravery could scarcely be questioned, though his strategy might be. His action in surrendering property was gravely censured, the general opinion being that if he could no longer hold out he should have found means to destroy the valuable stores in his control, instead of giving them up to the conqueror. As a material result of the surrender other than the strategic and moral effect, the Japanese acquired four large ships left in serviceable condition, several gunboats and torpedo crafts, fort artillery, and great stores of ammunition, food and coal.

The work of taking over the arsenal, island forts, and war ships was completed by the Japanese without the least confusion. The ships which needed repairs, including the ironclad Chen-Yuen, were temporarily repaired at Wei-hai-wei, and then sailed for Japan with Japanese crews, to go into dockyards for refitting. Marshal Oyama and his staff occupied the Chinese government building. All of the foreigners who took part in the defense of Wei-hai-wei, except the American Howie, were paroled and sent to Chefoo in the steamship Kang Chi. This vessel also carried the bodies of Admiral Ting and his fellow officers who committed suicide. The Japanese fleet paid a touching tribute to the memory of their brave opponents. As the Kang Chi steamed out of the harbor all the vessels had their flags at half mast, and from Count Ito's flag ship minute guns were fired for some time after the vessel sailed. The European war ships at Wei-hai-wei also lowered their flags, as a testimony to the bravery exhibited by the late admiral.

Several junks arrived at Chefoo bringing soldiers from Weihai- wei. The men all expressed astonishment at the consideration which the Japanese had shown for them, and the tribute which their enemies paid to Admiral Ting's body had created a great impression on them.

It will be remembered that Howie was one of the Americans arrested early in the war by the Japanese officials at Kobe. He was on his way to China, under contract to destroy Japanese ships by means of a new explosive whose secret he possessed. He was released at Kobe at the intercession of the American minister to Japan, under the promise that he would not assist the Chinese in the present war. He was detained at Wei-hai-wei for a trial by court-martial, and it was believed that unless his government interfered his punishment might be a severe one.

After the capture of Wei-hai-wei all efforts were directed by the Japanese towards strengthening the land defenses and those on the island. Fresh guns were mounted in many places. The island forts were still manned by marines, while the mainland forts were each held by a battalion of infantry, as well as by artillery men. The amount of stores seized was so great that the troops had a superabundance of supplies. The roads were patrolled for miles around. A civil commissioner was appointed, and Marshal Oyama issued a proclamation assuring the inhabitants of kind treatment and of his protection so long as they followed peaceful pursuits. Inasmuch as no atrocities had been committed and the Japanese did little looting, the confidence of the people was retained and they continued their usual vocations. The Japanese withdrew from the advanced positions east and west of Wei-hai-wei, evacuating the town of Ning-Hai. A large part of the army then left for Talien-wan Bay.

THE END OF HOSTILE OPERATIONS

The Armies in Manchooria and their Aottons in the Cold of January—Skirmish and Battle—Assault on Niuchwang and Capture of the City—Desperate Fighting in the Streets—Taking of Ying-Kow—A Threat Towards Formosa—Attack on the Pescadore Islands—Capture of Hai-chow—The Island of Thao-hua—Peking thought to be in Danger from the Japanese.

We left the Chinese and Japanese troops in Manchooria centered about the region around Niuchwang, trying to pass the cold weather with the least suffering possible. There was no considerable interruption of time between hostile encounters, possibly on the supposition that they could keep warmer by fighting than by remaining idle. On the morning of the 17th of January the Chinese under General Chang and General Twi began aggressive movements. Some twelve thousand strong they attacked Hai-tcheng, but were repulsed after a short struggle. Five days later, on the morning of the 22nd, the Chinese again attacked the Japanese position, but were repulsed by two o'clock in the afternoon with heavy loss. This was rather a long distance battle, with a good deal of artillery practice in it. The Chinese worked their guns fairly well, but could not compete with the Japanese gunners, who were the better protected and suffered little. When the Chinese began the retreat, the Japanese guns were moved forward and played upon the retiring enemy. The Chinese then became demoralized, and made speedy retreat towards Niuchwang. The Japanese loss was very slight.

On the same day as the last battle, simultaneously with the attack on Hai-tcheng, General Seh with ten thousand men and a strong force of artillery advanced from the port of Niuchwang against Kai-phing. An artillery engagement ensued on the 24th of January, which ended in a precipitate retreat of the Chinese.

General Nogi now moved forward his headquarters to Huntsai. The Chinese army under General Seh was considerably reinforced, chiefly by Tartar troops with large bodies of cavalry, and skirmishes with the Japanese scouts were of daily occurrence. The strength of the enemy in the immediate vicinity of Niuchwang was more than twenty thousand men. On the 30th of January it was found that the Chinese had occupied Liao-Yang in force, and that the western contingents were gradually advancing southward. General Hoi-Pang-Tao was on his way to Ying-kow with a large force. On the 1st of February the Viceroy Liu arrived at Niuchwang and assumed the supreme command of the operations in Manchooria. He brought with him an army said to number nearly twenty thousand, so that his whole force numbered probably twice that many. It seemed certain that the viceroy intended to advance against Hai-tcheng in full force. The Japanese armies were also united, or in close touch with one another, at Kai-ping and Hai-tcheng, ready for a decisive battle. February 16 a Chinese army of fifteen thousand men attacked Haitcheng from Liao-Yang and the Niuchwang road. The fighting lasted three hours, and extended over a considerable tract of country. The attack was successfully repulsed, one hundred and fifty Chinese being killed and wounded, and the Japanese loss considerably less than that number.

The news of the capture of Wei-hai-wei reached the Japanese and Chinese forces in Manchooria, and the Viceroy Liu was evidently disheartened, for there was an entire absence of activity during the next ten days. The incessant drilling in the neighborhood of Niuchwang was stopped, and the forces were steadily dwindling through desertion. On the last day of February, after a period of comparative inaction, the Japanese troops began an advance on Niuchwang and its port Ying-kow. On that day General Noclzu attacked the Chinese positions between the Liao-Yang and the Niuchwang roads. The Japanese artillery first opened a heavy fire upon the Chinese. This lasted over an hour, and then the fifth Japanese brigade threw itself upon the Chinese right wing with such impetuosity that the enemy scarcely made a stand in that part of the field, but broke and fled in disorder. While this was going on, the main Japanese column under General Nodzu marched against the Chinese center, which rested on the village of Chang-ho-tai. Position after position was carried by the Japanese infantry, and the enemy was finally driven in disorderly retreat northwestward towards Kinchow city, at the northern extremity of the Gulf of Liao-Tung.

The sixth brigade had been told off to clear the Chinese out of the villages along the Laio-Yang road. This it accomplished without loss, and then by pre-arrangement it joined hands with the main column, the

CHINESE SOLDIERS ON THE MARCH

combined forces thereafter occupying Tung-yeng-tai and all the villages and heights near that place, in the direction of Liao-Yang. General Nodzu's division extended its line southwestward from Hai-tcheng, so that the army extended through a very wide front. The Chinese forces engaged numbered about eighteen thousand men with twenty guns. General Yih was in command. They lost one hundred and fifty men killed, and about two hundred wounded. The Japanese losses amounted to about half as many.

Early the next morning the Japanese resumed their advance, this time without opposition of any sort. The Chinese retired before them, and when night fell the Japanese limit extended nearly to Maitzu. Throughout the advance upon Niuchwang there was no opposition offered worthy the name, and the annals of the march bring little fame to the Japanese defense.

The reconnaissances eastward and northward made by General Nodzu's scouts on Friday, March 1st, brought the information that the main body of the Chinese forces had fled by the northern road, with the evident intention of rallying and making another stand at Liao-Yang, the only place of importance between Hai-tcheng and Mukden. Lieutenant-General Katsura's brigade was ordered to pursue the enemy. By that evening the troops had covered about eight miles of difficult ground, and had got within a mile of Kan-thouan-phu, where several thousand Chinese were known to be ready to give battle. The Japanese advanced against the town at daybreak, only to find that the enemy had fled during the night. After resting his troops Katsura resumed the pursuit. It was thought that the Chinese would make a stand at Sha-ho-phu, a small town situated on the river Sha and commanding the high road to Liao-Yang, but the place was occupied by the Japanese on Sunday, March 3, without serious opposition. The next morning Katsura moved on until within five miles of Liao-Yang, which brought him within forty miles of Mukden.

While Katsura was driving the routed Chinese before him along the Mukden road, General Nodzu with all the remaining forces at his disposal was moving towards Niuchwang Old Town. The troops were under arms at dawn on Monday. The fifth division moved against the town from the southeast, while the third division came from the north. The movement was admirably timed, despite the difficulties of the ground. In three hours the men of both divisions were in position, and at ten o'clock a heavy shell fire was opened upon the Chinese fortifications. The Chinese appeared to be confused; their artillery fire was bad, and they kept massing troops at points which were never threatened. Many of their guns were dismounted, and after a two hours bombardment the Chinese abandoned the walls and retreated into the town. The Japanese infantry then poured into the place, both divisions forcing their way into the gates and over the walls almost simultaneously.

So far the Japanese had suffered very little loss. The leading brigade of the first division charged several Chinese regiments still standing their ground, and they at once fled precipitately towards Ying-kow, followed by the Japanese cavalry. Meantime, in the town the Japanese infantry were warmly engaged. The main body of the Chinese, when driven from the batteries and walls, had taken refuge in the narrow streets and houses. Every window and every housetop was occupied by sharpshooters. The fighting was of a desperate character. The Chinese seeing all hopes of escape cut off, fought until they were shot or cut down. The headway made by the Japanese was painfully slow. Each street had to be effectually cleared before an advance could be made to the next. Each house had to be assaulted and taken.

Throughout the day the fighting continued, but slowly the Japanese cordon was brought more closely around the center of the city, and by eleven o'clock at night all opposition had ceased. Many of the Chinese, after nightfall broke through the Japanese lines, and made their escape into the open country, but a large number accepted quarter and remained in the hands of the Japanese. The Chinese fought with desperate valor. Repeatedly they charged the Japanese troops in the streets, and hand-to-hand fighting was frequent. The officers too, encouraged the men by their own example, and the defense of the streets was conducted with some military skill. Nearly two thousand Chinese killed and wounded were found in the houses and streets, and six hundred prisoners were taken. The Japanese losses exceeded five hundred in killed and wounded. A large quantity of stores and provisions fell into the hands of the victors, beside eighteen cannon, and a large quantity of rifles and ammunition.

After the engagement of the 4th, Lieutenant-General Yamaji's division of the second Japanese army advanced upon Peh-miatotsu, where it had been reported that the main body of General Sung's defeated forces had halted. The enemy, however, did not wait for the Japanese troops, but fell back upon Ying-kow. General Nogi, following close along the coast road, came up with the Chinese and attacked them. During the fighting which ensued the Chinese were reinforced from Ying-kow, but they were soon driven back under the protection of the town batteries, leaving many dead upon the field. Most of the Chinese retreated in a northeasterly direction, but General Sung and troops immediately under his command made another stand at Ying-kow. The Japanese artillery was well handled, and the infantry fought with great spirit, driving the Chinese before them. By the time the town was entered General Sung and his troops had fled towards Chen-sho-tai. Meanwhile the Japanese artillery had concentrated their fire upon the shore forts, which protected the estuary. The Chinese brought their heavy guns to bear upon the assailants, and held their own for some time, but finally the Japanese infantry under cover of the fire of their artillery, carried the forts one after the other, and by nightfall Ying-kow was in undisputed possession of the invaders.

As soon as the fort had been captured, guards were placed for the protection of the foreign settlement, and the streets were strongly patrolled. Scouts were sent out along the Niuchwang road to meet General Nodzu's patrol. On the morning of the 6th, General Noclzu sent a brigade towards Ying-kow, which the second army was to attack that day. Tung-kia-thun was found destitute of Chinese troops, and the Japanese advanced nearly to Kao-khan without seeing anything of the enemy. Here they camped for the night, and before morning the outposts of the two forces had met and had exchanged the good news of the success of each. The retreating Chinese, under Generals Sung and Ma, were reported to have halted at Chen-sho-tai.

The occupation of Niuchwang and its port by the Japanese marked a distinct phase in the interesting campaign in Manchooria. For many weeks Niuchwang and Ying-kow had sheltered the Chinese army. From them a succession of feeble attacks upon the Chinese positions had been delivered. General Sung's unwieldy forces were now broken up; the Japanese front was advanced to the river Liao; and the first and second armies had joined hands. The third important fortified harbor had fallen into the hands of the Japanese. The defense of Niuchwang was maintained with vigor, the Chinese fighting most bitterly to the very end, but uselessly. This coast defenses too at Ying-kow made some show of resistance, but being attacked in the rear had quickly fallen in accordance with all established precedents.

The general situation in Manchooria was now entirely changed. The Japanese encouraged by the half-hearted attacks to which they had been subjected, had broken up the forces in their vicinity. The difficulties of movement in large bodies, combined with the incapacity of commanders, and general disorganization, had effectually prevented the Chinese from gaining any advantage from their superior numbers. Niuchwang, a city of sixty thousand people, a town with an immense annual trade, had fallen into Japanese hands, and its capture was unquestionably an important stroke.

On the Japanese right Katsura had pushed forward until he was near Liao-Yang, and after the occupation of Niuchwang relieved some of the troops there, another brigade moved northward to his support. The country centering at Niuchwang was practically in undisputed possession of the Japanese. Thus, after a march of about four hundred miles, the troops of the first army which landed at Chemulpo were once again on the seaboard, and in possession of an important port.

CHINESE SOLDIER LADEN WITH PROVISIONS, SHOWING WINTER DRESS

On the 9th of March the first division of the first Japanese army attacked Thien-chuang-thai, on the western side of the river Liao, to which place General Sung fled after the capture of Yingkow. A fierce engagement ensued, lasting three hours and a half. The main body of the Chinese force numbered seven thousand men with thirty guns, and the Japanese forces were but few less than that number. General Katsura commanded the Japanese center, and General Oku the right wing. The left wing was composed of Yamaji's troops from Kai-phing. The Chinese fled towards Kinchow, leaving fourteen hundred dead on the field. For strategic reasons the village was burned, and the Japanese returned across the river.

A proclamation was issued by the Japanese commander at Ying-kow urging the inhabitants to continue their peaceful pursuits, promising all law-abiding inhabitants justice and protection, and warning them of the consequences should they commit any belligerent acts or create any disorders. The commanders of the foreign war ships in the river called on the Japanese general, and asked him to telegraph to their respective admirals that all the foreigners in the town were safe. The general complied with this request, as well as with that of the consuls who asked him to telegraph in the same way to their governments. All Chinese were strictly prohibited from entering the European quarter, unless employed by or having business with the foreign residents. Six hundred troops were told off to carry this order into effect and to patrol the streets. English and American officers united to express their thanks to the commanding general, for the elaborate precautions taken to insure the safety of foreigners.

It will be remembered that from the very beginning of the war a Japanese descent upon Formosa was one of the operations expected and frequently reported. To provide against this threatened danger, a large body of the famous troops from the south of China known as the Black Flags, were sent to the island to intrench themselves and arrange for its defense. They were scarcely settled in comfort when they began a series of outrages on the native population that made them feared and hated by every one, and justified their name. Early in February they extended their outrages from the native population to the British residents. Disturbances on the island increased, and affairs became so bad that foreign residents became alarmed and left in haste. The British consul at the chief treaty-port of the island, sent to Hong Kong an urgent call for assistance, which was furnished without delay. The war ship Mercury left for the island in haste, and its presence acted strongly to quell the disturbances and insure safety for the people. A Japanese squadron too, which was seen patroling the island on several occasions, acted as a damper upon the spirits of the rioters, and the Chinese authorities themselves were able to quell the disturbance. Twenty-five of the ring leaders were arrested and punished, and peace was restored.

After this time, operations in the south were abandoned until early in the spring, when a fleet of Japanese transports moved down the west side of the island of Formosa, to the group of small islands known as the Pescadores, between Formosa and the mainland. The Chinese feared that an attack upon Canton was contemplated, but in reality there was at no time any considerable danger of this. The Japanese desired to be exceedingly careful of the interest of all foreign nations in the treaty ports, and so naturally avoided an attack on any city where they might be endangered. The real point of attack intended by this course, was the town of Makung, in the southwest of the island of Pong-hu, the largest of the group. Makung had a large and absolutely safe harbor, capable of affording accommodations for vessels of large draft, and was protected by its citadel and a line of defensive works. Admiral Ito was in command of the squadron, which numbered nine cruisers and two gunboats. Bombardment was begun March 23, from all the vessels of the fleet, the fire centering on the east fort, which dominated the others. A thousand troops from five transports landed simultaneously and attacked the same fort. The Chinese evacuated the place during the night, and the Japanese entered at 6:00 o'clock on the morning of the 24th, and turned the guns upon the other forts. One of the western forts blew up before it was evacuated. One thousand Chinese prisoners were taken, the rest of the garrison escaping in junks. Three thousand Japanese troops now garrisoned Pong-hu, securing a southern base of operations for the Japanese fleet. Within a few days the Japanese were in entire possession of the Pescadore Islands.

South of Yung-tcheng Bay, the Chinese coast line had remained inviolate up to this period of the war, in spite of frequent rumors from startled Chinese sources, of the appearance of Japanese squadrons and their threatened attack. The Japanese fleet had been profitably used to foster a continual state of nervous terror in all the Chinese coast cities, but attention was now turned suddenly in a very different direction, and actively developed towards the southward. Simultaneously with the attack on Pong-hu, the

Japanese on the 24th of March made a descent upon Hai-chow, on the sea-board of the province of Chiang-su, some two hundred miles north of Shanghai. It was early in the morning when the Japanese squadron appeared off Hai-chow and at once opened fire upon the small forts there. Under cover of the bombardment a force of several thousand Japanese troops, landed and attacked the Chinese positions. After a few hours' fighting, the stout resistance of the Chinese proved unavailing, and they abandoned their works, having lost some three hundred killed. The island of Yuchow, which lies off Hai-chow had already been occupied by the invaders. At Hai-chow the Japanese were less than fifty miles in a direct line from the Grand Canal connecting Nanking with Peking, which at this point approaches nearest to the coast. The canal had been the chief route by which supplies were conveyed to Peking, and had been of invaluable service for the movement of troops to the capital and to the front by way of Tientsin. The threatened dash of the Japanese upon this main artery of travel startled those who realized it. This sudden and unexpected descent upon the Chinese coast served to bring home the realities of war to a section of the population which probably had never heard of the Japanese successes. The Viceroy of Nanking awakened to his danger, and hastily ordered troops to the front to oppose the Japanese advance and recapture Hai-chow.

A third portion of the Japanese fleet, with war ships and transports, appeared simultaneously with these other operations, sailing past Taku into the neighborhood of Shan-hai-kwan. Passing the latter city, which marks the end of the Great Wall of China where it comes down to the coast, the fleet left terror behind, and moved upon the island of Thao-hua. This island lies but a few miles off the mainland, and fifty-five miles northeast of Shanhai-kwan, at a point where the main highway from Manchooria to Peking lies close to the coast line. It was therefore about half way between Niuchwang and Taku, the port of Peking, and an excellent base for offensive operations against the capital.

The armies in Manchooria were practically idle during the latter part of March. The Chinese had nearly all withdrawn to Kinchow, in the north, while the Japanese contented themselves with restoring order in Niuchwang and Ying-kow, and in completing the military arrangements consequent on the junction of the armies. Snowstorms prevented an intended advanced towards Kinchow.

The first of April therefore found the Japanese ready to act on the offensive at several points, spread over a distance of one thousand two hundred miles, and extending from the Pescadore Islands in the south to Niuchwang in the north. On the Liao River the combined forces numbered nearly forty thousand men, with a further strength of some ten thousand

GAP IN THE GREAT WALL AT SHAN-HAI-KWAN

men on the Laio-Tung peninsula at Kinchow, Talien-wan and Port Arthur. The whole of these troops could be transported to Shan-hai-kwan in twenty-four hours, as soon as the port of Ying-kow was free from ice. There were no troops to be spared from the garrisons at Port Arthur or Wei-hai-wei, but further levies would undoubtedly be brought from Hiroshima to these places to await transport. The distance to Shan-hai-kwan from all these ports were short so that the troops could be closely packed for the short voyage. In a few days therefore, at least seventy-five thousand men could be concentrated at Shan-hai-kwan and the transports would be available for maintaining a supply service. At the same time the possession of the island of Chao-hua would facilitate the cutting of the line of Chinese communications between Manchooria and Peking. With Hai-chow held by the Japanese and threatening the line of communication from south to north by the Grand Canal and Japanese forces threatening Formosa and the south, the possibility of the repulse of an advance in force on Peking seemed very slight. It was the approach of these dangers and the final certainty that nothing else could be done to avert them that brought the Chinese at last to humiliate themselves and sue for peace at the hands of the Japanese.

John W. Foster in Japan—Failure of Peace Embassy—Diplomatic Discussions—Foolish Pride—Li Hung Chang again in Favor—His Journey—The Viceroy Knew China—The Envoy in Japan—Attempted Murder—The Mikado's Appeal—What the Assault Indicated—Declaration of the Armistice—Provisions of the Armistice—Continuing Negotiations—Signing the Treaty—Its Terms—No Alliance of China and Japan—The Mikado Proclaims—Peacefulness Enjoined—What of the Future?—Ultimate Effect of the War.

While the war operations during the first three months of 1895 were in progress, peace negotiations too were actively under way. The annals of the hostilities which have occupied the last few chapters might have been interrupted by paragraphs telling of the progress and defeat of different efforts to secure peace; but it seemed more intelligible to the prospective reader to place him in full possession of the particulars of the military affairs as they developed, without interruption. Not until the end had nearly come did the peace negotiations for one moment interrupt hostilities, and there was consequently no need to interrupt the consecutive record. It now remains a final task to outline the various peace negotiations after those that have already been described, and follow oriental diplomacy to its conclusion.

We left the Chinese peace envoys lingering at Shanghai in January, after several weeks of idleness resulting from continual postponement of their departure. At last the imperial government abandoned its hope that something would intervene to destroy the necessity of a suit for peace, and the embassy was ordered to start. The Chinese peace envoys arrived at Kobe January 30, and were received by the Secretary of the Foreign. Department. When the envoys came ashore, a mob greeted them with hostile demonstrations and they had to be protected by a large force of police. After consulting with Mr. Foster, their American adviser who had reached Kobe several days before, the envoys left in a special steamer for Ujina. The general tenor of Japanese opinion was that the negotiation would prove fruitless, as China was scarcely ready to accede to the Japanese demand.

It was acknowledged however, that the present embassy showed a much more sincere desire for peace on the part of China than did the Detring mission which resulted in such a fiasco.

Ex-Secretary Foster was treated with especial courtesy during his stay at Tokio and Kobe. Mr. Foster exchanged many telegrams with the Chinese government in reference to the power and authority of Chang and Shao, the Chinese peace commissioners, regarding which the Japanese were all along very doubtful. The diplomatic contest promised to be stubborn. China did not seem to realize that Japan would demand a cession of territory, and it was anticipated that the humiliation of losing any of her continental domain would be more than she was willing to endure. Mr. Foster was frankly given to understand that unless ample' powers were guaranteed by their credentials the envoys would not even be admitted to a hearing.

Count Ito and Viscount Mutsu who were appointed to treat with the Chinese peace envoys, received the credentials which were presented to them as coming from the emperor of China, and found them to read as follows: "By decree we appoint you our plenipotentiaries, to meet and negotiate the matter with the plenipotentiaries appointed by Japan. You will, however, telegraph to the Tsung-li Yamen for the purpose of obtaining our commands, by which you will abide. The members of your mission are placed under your control. You will conduct the mission in a faithful and diligent manner, and fulfill the trust reposed in you. Respect this."

It was immediately officially announced that the plenary powers with which the mikado's government demanded that the Chinese envoys should be invested, were found to be utterly defective. The envoys were therefore refused further negotiations, and were requested to leave Japan without delay. It was believed by many that the Chinese envoys were quite ignorant of the trick that had been played upon them by their government. They supposed that they had been given full powers to treat for peace, but they found that not only had they no power either to conclude or sign a treaty, but that their credentials did not even contain an intimation of the purpose of the mission which they had to Japan. The ministers, however, told them that Japan was willing to reopen negotiations with a properly empowered embassy. The envoys therefore left Hiroshima after two days in the Japanese city, and returned home via Nagasaki.

The rebuff sustained by the Chinese envoys created some astonishment among the highest officials in Peking, but not much apparent concern. Just at this time, early in February, they were having glowing reports from General Sung in Manchooria. He claimed to have already beaten the Japanese on many occasions, and promised if well supplied with men and stores to drive every invader from Chinese soil. Japan's excuse for refusing to treat with the envoys, scarcely satisfied some export diplomats. It was insisted that it would have been very unusual for any government to endow its agents with final powers as long as it was able to communicate with them daily and hourly if necessary by cable. The Chinese government once gave final powers to one of its ambassadors who went over to Russia to negotiate a boundary treaty, and his head mould have been amputated when he returned Peking, had it not been for the intercession of the Russian ambassador, who suggested that his government would resent such punishment inflicted upon a person so recently honored by the Czar. He offered at the same time to consider the treaty suspended, until the Chinese authorities might have an opportunity to examine it and suggest any changes they might like to have made. After this experience it was not likely that the emperor of China would confer final powers upon any ambassador. It was asserted that since modern forms of communication had been introduced, it has not been the custom to give final powers to agents who visit civilized nations. Therefore it was assumed that the objection raised in Japan to the credentials of the Chinese envoys was a diplomatic ruse for the purpose of gaining time for the Japanese generals to reach Peking. This was disproven by the cessation of efforts, which Japan might have made to reach Peking, but it may have been true that Japan wished to bring China into still further distress, so that her demands would be more surely granted.

The very important action was now taken by the Chinese emperor of restoring to Li Hung Chang an his honors which had been taken away, because of the succession of defeats in the early weeks of the war, and appointing him imperial commissioner to negotiate for peace with Japan.

China then requested that the Japanese peace commissioners might meet Li Hung Chang at Port Arthur to conduct the negotiations at that place. A prompt reply was received from Hiroshima, in which the Japanese government absolutely declined to treat anywhere but upon Japanese soil. The Grand Council of the Chinese empire met on Sunday. February 24, and deliberated for several hours upon the question, "Shall the war with Japan be prolonged or shall we treat for peace?" It was resolved that before the council took a final decision, the same question should be put to all the provincial authorities, from the first to the third rank inclusive. Their opinion was urgently demanded by telegraph. The replies received were nearly all to the effect, that although the war was unjustly provoked by Japan, it was very desirable that peace should be concluded. Some of the replies, however, declared that the terms of peace should not be too exacting. China had learned something by her failures of two peace missions, Detring's and the last embassy.

One of the ancient Chinese methods of waging battle was to play "Soft, voluptuous airs to melt the heart of the enemy." How far China had advanced in practical wisdom might be gathered from her latest diplomatic manoeuvre which seemed to indicate that the Chinese diplomacy of the present followed the military usages of antiquity. Ever since the eventual triumph of the Japanese became a moral certainty, China had been given vague intimations of a desire to secure peace. These intimations unaccompanied by any definite terms were steadfastly ignored by Japan, until the Chinese government gave notice that it had sent a peace commission to the mikado. When the useless credentials of these commissioners were examined in Japan, they were turned back without consideration, and the Chinese pretended surprise at the treatment, asserting that Japan was simply seeking to further humiliate the empire. To unbiased observers it seemed quite as reasonable to believe that the Chinese were playing to gain time, meanwhile assailing the enemy with the "soft, voluptuous music of peace." This policy of antiquated diplomacy wee terminated abruptly.

Li Hung Chang's star was again in the ascendant. Even as he journeyed towards Peking his calumniators continued their attacks. In Shanghai it was positively asserted that he was now given a chance to accomplish what he had long awaited, the overthrow of the Manchoorian dynasty in China. It was also declared that Kung, the disgraced Ex-Taotai of Port Arthur, had made a confession showing the traitorous designs of Li. It was said that Li had been leagued with the officials of the palace at Peking for the overthrow of the dynasty, ever since he was deprived of his yellow jacket, his peacock feather, and his various offices. All this now had no weight. The privy council heartily supported Li's mission to Japan. Prince Kung silenced all opposition to it by presenting papers showing that the previous failure was due to a backward policy, for which the council were themselves to blnme, and exonerating the viceroy. The emperor completely vindicated Li Hung Chang, confessing that he had tried others and found him alone trustworthy. He therefore granted him the fullest powers to deal with the Japanese. The central government publicly assumed the entire responsibility for the condition of the national defense, explaining it as the result of blindness to the progress of other nations. This placed future reforms in the hands of Li.

The American minister at Peking assumed a personal interest in the matter at this point, and telegraphed to Japan the text of Li Hung Chang's proposed credentials. At last, after a tedious exchange of messages, the credentials were accepted by Japan and arrangements were made for the journey of the envoy. Li Hung Chang was received in audience by the emperor and the dowager empress five times within as many days, and in his conversations with them spoke frankly of the condition of the empire. His powers to negotiate were made complete, his commission bore the emperor's signature, and on the fifth day of March he left Peking for Japan.

There were signs at last that the Chinese were beginning to recognize the imperative necessity of concluding peace with, Japan. With their strongholds in Japanese hands and their flect practically annihilated, the sooner they made submission the more easy would be the terms which they could obtain. It was therefore gratifying to all friends of the empire to learn that the viceroy had been appointed as envoy to proceed to Japan to discuss terms of peace. Holding a position second only to that of the emperor himself, it was impossible that the Japanese should refuse to treat with him on account of his inferior station, or his insufficient credentials. His mission was the first genuine attempt that China had made to open negotiations. It was a proof that Chinese pride and obstinacy had at length been overcome, and that there was a real willingness to take steps calculated to bring the disastrous war to a close.

But for the messenger himself! Surely history, which delights in setting at naught the hopes and filling the fears of men, never saw a sadder faring forth than the journey of Li Hung Chang to Japan. He was old now, paralytic, his side and arm half useless, his eyesight dim, his family long since gone, and all the fabric of empire to which his life had been given in ruins about him. He saved it once before in straits as great. He of Honan, Honan men about him, all come down from the central hills of China, sturdy and tall above the men of the plains whom they swept aside, Gordon and Ward aiding, leading and winning the early battles, but the work in the end done, and the rich harvest reaped by those sons of Honan whom Li Hung Chang found poor among their fields of tea and millet, and rained to half the posts of honor in China. That was thirty years ago. The great work spread and grew. The old boundaries of the empire were regained. The Russian advance in Asia retired for the first time in two centuries. On the Amoor it was halted. France retired discomfited. England treated Chinese frontiers with a new respect. In Burmah, in Siam, in Nepaul, Chinese aid was sought. The big empire was never so big, never looked so strong, never had more deference or outer respect since the days of the great Tai-Tsung, when China ruled from the Pacific to the boundary of the Roman empire, and the Roman empire extended to the Atlantic-two realms between the two oceans.

Through it all one man knew how hollow it was, Li Hung Chag He pleaded for railroads and telegraphs. He bought war ships and ironclads. He urged that the old policy be reversed and the military and naval forces of the empire duly or ganized. For years he had seen the cloud gathering, and in the great quagmire of Chinese corruption and conservatism sought to make ready for it. It had been in vain. Army, fleet, and court had collapsed. Corea and Manchooria were conquered. If Peking was not occupied it was because Japan wished to leave some semblance of central authority with which to treat. Any war-fine could be levied by the victors; any vassalage exacted of the vanquished. Port Arthur could be made a Gibraltar. The policy of Peking could be controlled by Japan. Japan would dominate the Asiatic seacoast. The Japanese ambassador at Peking would be supreme whenever his government chose to speak.

All this was in the mind of the paralytic old man as he journeyed by land and sea. For forty years he had greatly ruled, a great empire was the greater for his work, and it had all come to this. Were the French tri-color to be near Berlin, and Bismarck wearily seeking peace at Paris, the tragedy were no less than that, with Li Hung Chang as its central figure in the east. Li Hung Chang spent a few days at Tien-tsin, and then passed on down the river to Taku, whence he sailed with his suite on March 15 for Shimonoseki. The viceroy sailed in royal state, with a suite of one hundred and thirty persons in two veesels. On the morning of the 19th they reached their destination in Japan. Shimoneseki ie on the extreme southwestern coast of Japan and it was here that in the early '60s the foreign powers forced Japan to assent to certain indemnities demanded of the empire. Upon arriving, the envoy was immediately visited by the representatives of the Japanese foreign office, and later Li Hung Chang accompanied by his American adviser, John W. Foster, visited the Japanese minister of foreign affairs. This was the first time in his life that the venerable statesman of China had ever set his foot on other than Chinese soil.

The viceroy and his party were escorted to the foreign office by Mr. Inouye, who cordially greeted the statesman, and placed his services at his disposal. The party was received on landing by a guard of honor, and was taken to the foreign office in carriages under escort. The following day was spent by the peace envoys in examining each other's credentials and powers. Both aides devoted much time and thought to this matter and were assisted by experts in matters of diplomacy and etiquette.

The Chinese letter of credential proved to be precisely what might have been expected from Chinese character. The phraseology had been repeatedly discussed through the ministers of the United Stah in Tokio and Peking and a form satisfactory to Japan agreed upon. Whether intentionally or not the Chinese had given more than one indication of waywardness in preparing the document. They were very particular in honoring their emperor with his proper title but they did not insert that of the emperor of Japan. Moreover they used an expression signifying that it was in consequence of Japan's desire for peace that an ambassador was sent. This was not allowed to pass uncorrected. As finally amended the paper was virtually in accordance with Japan's dictation.

In the end all the documents were found to be in due form, and polite notes to this effect were exchanged. Subsequently Li Hung Chang and his suite went ashore.

The viceroy was received with a military salute, and all the honors due to his exalted rank. He proceeded to the chief hotel, where accommodation h d been prepared for him and part of his suite. Further communications passed on the morning of March 21, and at half past two in the afternoon the first business conference ference in connection with the peace negotiations began, Li Hung Chang, Count Ito, Viscount Mutsu, and their secretaries, together with the sworn interpreters being present. The deliberations which were conducted secret, lasted for an hour and a half. There was much diplomatic fencing, Li Hung Chang being evidently anxious to ascertain at the earliest possible moment the terms upon which an armistice might be granted. Nothing occurred to suggest the possibility of a break down of the negotiations, and some gratifying progress was made towards a general understanding.

It must be remembered that during all this time there was no cessation in the war operations which were going on in Manchooria and on the Chinese coast. Fresh troops were being hurried forward from Japan for active service, and the war spirit gave no sign of subsidence. In Yokohama the success of the peace negotiations was regarded as doubtful. The military element, which was all in favor of the continuance of the war until the victory of the Japanese was made complete by the capture of Peking, had at that time a predominant voice in Japanese politics, and this feeling was reflected in parliament. Notice was given in the house of representatives of a resolution declaring that the time for peace negotiations had not arrived.

While negotiations were thus progressing, they were interrupted by an incident that amazed and shocked the civilized world. As Li Hung Chang was returning to his lodgings on March 24, after having attended a conference with the Japanese peace plenipotentiaries, he was attacked by a young Japanese who sought to murder him. The young man's name was Koyama Rokunosuki, and he was but twenty-one years of age. The bullet struck the Chinese envoy in the cheek, and it was believed that the result would not be serious. The news of the attempt at assassination created much excitement in Japan, in China, and in the western world. The ministers of state and other officials visited Li Hung Chang without delay, to express their deep sorrow at the occurrence. Every precaution was taken by the police and military to prevent any trouble. The mikado was deeply grieved at the affair, and sent his two chief court physicians, Surgeons Sato and Ishiguro, to attend the Chinese envoy. The bullet entered the cheek half an inch under the left eye, and penetrated to a depth of nearly an inch and a half. The Chinese plenipotentiary strongly objected to undergoing an operation for its removal. The empress of Japan, to show her own regret, sent two nurses to assume the care of the old man, and from every side letters and telegrams of regret and sympathy arrived in great quantities.

Beside the physicians, the mikado sent the imperial chamberlain to convey his condolences to the viceroy, and to the public he issued the following proclamation:

"A state of war exists between our country and China, but she with due regard of international forms and usages sent an ambassador to sue for peace. We therefore appointed plenipotentiaries, instructing them to meet and negotiate at Shimonoseki. It was consequently incumbent upon us, in pursuance of international etiquette, to extend to the Chinese ambassador treatment consistent with the national honor, providing him ample escort and protection. Hence we issued special commands to our officials to exercise the utmost vigilance in all respects. It is therefore a source of profound grief and regret to us, that a ruffian should have been found base enough to inflict personal injury on the Chinese ambassador. Our officials will sentence the culprit to the utmost punishment provided by the law. We hereby command our officials and subjects to respect our wish, and to preserve our country's fair fame from impairment by strictly guarding against a recurrence of such deeds of violence and lawlessness."

The would-be assassin belonged to the class known as the Soshis, or political bravos, who are always ripe for any acts of riot or violence. When the attack was made, Li Hung Chang was in a palanquin being conveyed to his hotel from conference with the Japanese negotiators. He had nearly reached the house, when a young man rushed out of the crowd, and seizing the hand of one of the carriers in order to stop the palanquin fired his pistol almost point blank at the Chinese plenipotentiary. There was little room for hesitation as to his motives. He was a fanatic who thought to serve his country by murdering the Chinese statesman. No delusion, it is hardly necessary to say, could be more gross than such a one. The criminal had done a grievous injury to his country and its government. Japan had striven long, earnestly, and successfully, to earn the reputation of a civilized state. Nobody of course should be unjust enough to upbraid her with the conduct of an irresponsible and apparently an isolated malefactor. Individuals with ferocious passions and ill-balanced minds are to be found in all countries, and such a crime as this, deplorable and unusual though it was, might have occurred in any European capital or our own capital city under similar conditions. Nevertheless, there were those who chose to take it as an index of national feeling condemning the country for the act of one. The manner of the expressions of regret that came so universally from every Japanese voice seemed to offer sufficient disclaimer against the existence of any such a cruel sentiment. Resolutions were presented in the Japanese diet expressing deep regret at the attempt upon the life of the Chinese plenipotentiary, and the native newspapers were unanimous and sincere in the same expressions. It had to be recognized, however, that an element existed among such people as the Soshis, inclined to violence under such circumstances, and precautions were doubled. No government is adequate to control fanaticism of the extremer sort, and the attempt upon the life of Li Hung Chang was a symptom of the frenzy which had been engendered in a large element of the Japanese people by the war. It was now learned for the first time that Mr. Detring was attacked by a Soshi in November, but was defended by the police. He kept silence in order to avoid embittering the situation.

The immediate effect on the negotiations of the attempted assassination of Li Hung Chang was that the emperor of Japan on March 29, declared an unconditional armistice. This was avowedly done because of the attack on the Chinese plenipotentiary and was so declared in notifications which were sent to all countries and to all Japanese legations. The language of the notification thus sent out was as follows: "On the opening of the negotiations the Japanese plenipotentiary proposed armistice, which Japan was willing to accept on certain conditions. While this negotiation was going on, the untoward event happened on the person of the Chinese plenipotentiary. His majesty, the emperor, in view of this unhappy occurrence, commanded the Japanese plenipotentiaries to consent to a temporary armistice without conditions. This was communicated to the Chinese plenipotentiary."

It was now felt that the power of the Japanese government to execute the armistice would be put a critical test. The military power of Japan, in the judgment of many intelligent observers, had almost outstripped the civil power during the war. This had caused serious concern as it was feared that the military element backed by the war spirit among the people would not submit to ah armistice even if the civil authorities ordered one. To meet this emergency a change of army commanders was made early in March. There had been three army corps operating in different campaigns and each under a general of supreme authority over his particular campaign. Prince Komatsu was created commander-in-chief over all armies in anticipation of an armistice. The purpose of this step was to concentrate authority in one man in close touch with the imperial household who could thus execute an armistice by a simultaneous cessation of hostilities by the three armies. It now remained to be seen whether Prince Komatsu could execute the important commission given to him. The splendid discipline shown by the army during the war gave assurance that there would be immediate acquiescence by the military, and yet Prince Komatsu had to contend against a war spirit inflamed by many victories. It had been said that an armistice would be so unpopular among the people and soldiery that it would insure the political retirement of Japan's two chief statesmen, Count Ito and Viscount Matsu, who had served as peace envoys.

On the opening of the negotiations, after the arrival of Li Hung Chang at

Shimonoseki, the Japanese plenipotentiaries at first proposed the following conditions for the conclusion of an armistice:— The occupation of Shan-hai-kwan, Taku, and Tien-tsin by Japanese troops; Japanese control of the uncompleted railroad from Shan-hai-kwan to Tien-tsin and custody of the various forts and fortifications, together with the arms and ammunition; the payment by China of the war contributions required for such occupation.

Li Hung Chang sought to obtain more moderate conditions, but the Japanese plenipotentiaries refused, and it was then proposed to continue the negotiations without a suspension of hostilities. This was the stage which the negotiations had reached at the third conference, when the attempt was made on the life of Viceroy Li. In view of this circumstance the emperor of Japan waiving the conditions previously made ordered the Japanese plenipotentiaries to consent to an armistice until the 20th of April. The armistice was to apply to the forces in Manchooria and in the circuit around the Gulf of Pechili, including the two great promontories, but did not include any operations to the south of that region. Neither government was to be prevented from making any new distribution or disposition of their troops not intended to augment the armies in the field. The movement of troops and the transport of goods contraband of war by sea were, however, prohibited and if attempted would be made at the risk of capture. The armistice was to terminate should the peace negotiation be broken off in the meantime, and a, convention embodying these terms was signed.

The news of the armistice was received excitedly by the Japanese and Chinese living in the United States, but only the former found it possible to concede the truth. A characteristic crowd of excited Chinamen gathered in front of a Chinese temple in their own quarter of New York City discussing a flaming red poster, the translation of which read: "The war between China and Japan has ended and it is time for every one to rejoice. Our fathers and brothers have fought the old enemy and those who have not been butchered will be honored at home. China is a greater country than Japan, and if the war had been allowed to go on the Japanese would have been whipped out of their boots and China would have annexed Japan as a colony. It is well for Japan that her people have been called off by the emperor, but the time will not be long before the war will be opened again, for it is written in the mystic language of the shrine that China and Japan cannot dwell forever on the same earth."

During the time of Li Hung Chang's illness resulting from his wound, his son, Li Ching Fung, acted as his representative in Japan and continued the negotiations. On April 7th the wound in Li's face had completely healed and the bandages were removed. The young man who had committed the assault was sentenced to imprisonment for life at hard labor, while the chief of police and the prefect of Shimonoseki, together will all their staff, were dismissed in disgrace.

After three days of obstinate silence the assassin dropped his air of bravado and made a full confession to Judge Toyama, who conducted a private examination at the Bakan court. The prisoner declared that he had long brooded over the causes leading to the disturbance of peace in the east, and had reached the conclusion that the evil practices of Li Hung Chang were accountable for all of them, beginning with the mismanagement of affairs in Corea. He believed that as long as Li lived peace could not be restored and resolved at one time to go to China and kill the viceroy. This purpose was defeated by his inability to raise the necessary money, but when he learned that Li was coming to Japan as peace ambassador he felt that his opportunity had arrived. He bought a revolver in Yokohama, March 11, and the next day started for Tokio, reaching Bakan, March 24. At 4:15 o'clock that afternoon he approached the sedan chair in which the ambassador was returning from the conference hall to his lodgings in Shimonoseki and discharged his weapon, aiming it at the victim's breast. Although he endeavored to study his right arm by clasping it with the left, lie missed his aim inflicting only a slight wound.

The conditions of the peace which was to be concluded by treaty now began to interest the civilized world almost as closely as the two contending nations. The conditions which were demanded by the Japanese were guessed at by every one who thought himself competent to form an opinion, and the varying opinions were sent out for discussion in the press of the world. At one time it was asserted to be arranged that Japan would conclude on offensive and defensive alliance with China, the object being to oppose European interests in the far east. This prospect occasioned considerable excitement among European diplomates. It was recognized that should China's numbers and enormous resources be united to Japanese progression, activity, and administrative ability, the coalition would be almost impregnable to any assault that might be delivered upon it, and that it might enjoy excellent success in any Asiatic aggressions which it cared to attempt.

It will be unprofitable here to discuss the various conditions of peace that were supposed to be proposed when we have at our command the settlement that was actually made. Nor is it worth while to consider the threatened intervention of Great Britain and Russia and France and Germany, each to protect her own interests in the east, for as a matter of fact no such interventions were made unless through the most secret diplomacy. Inasmuch as Japan's demands did not encroach upon any rights possessed by those countries in the east, there was no proper reason why they should intervene.

Finally on Monday, April 15th, a peace convention was actually signed at Shirnonoseki by the plenipotentiaries of China and Japan. The independence of Corea was recognized. It was conceded that Japan should retain temporarily the important places that she had conquered. Port Arthur, Wei-hai-wei, and Niuchwaug, including all the territory east of the Liao River. The island of Formosa was ceded permanently to Japan. An indemnity was provided for, to be paid by China to Japan, of 200,000,000 taels in silver, which is equivalent to about $150,000,000 in American gold. China agreed to no longer impose upon foreigners the odious tax known as Likin, levied upon all goods and" sales, and a uniform standard tael was required to be adopted by China for her currency. All foreigners were to be permitted to introduce into China factories and machinery, and to lease warehouses in the interior. The important commercial concessions given to Japan were thus extended to all other treaty nations. The occupation of Port Arthur and Wei-hai-wei and of the conquered Manchoorian territory were to be temporary, lasting only enough to guarantee the payment of the war indemnity by China. The terms of this payment provided that it should be made in silver in six annual installments. Japan retained extra-territorial jurisdiction in China, that is the right to try her own subjects arrested in

China on charges of crime, and on the other hand China gave up the right to extra-territoriality in Japan.

The Chinese customs were not placed under Japanese control by the terms of the treaty as had been alleged, and the stipulations provided that on the payment of the first two installments of the indemnity to be paid by China, Wei-hai-wei might be evacuated, provided China pledge her customs revenue in order to insure the payment of the balance due. This it was officially announced was optional, and might never take effect, while at the present time there was no intention of touching the customs revenue of China. It was understood that china conceded practically everything required by Japan, except making Peking an open port, and this was strenuously resisted. At the solicitation of the Chinese envoy too, the indemnity demanded was reduced from there hundred million to two hundred million taels.

So frequently were reports circulated, that Japan and China had concluded an offensive and defensive alliance, and that the commercial advantages secured by Japan were to be exclusive, that the government felt it desirable to deny those statements and issue the following announcement regarding the matter:

"Misapprehensions are reported to be current in Europe in regard to the terms of the Japan-China treaty. It has been represented that Japan has secured a two per cent and volorem duty on imports instead of specific duty and has also formed an offensive and defensive alliance with China. The commercial concessions obtained by Japan beyond those already secured by the treaty powers under the favored nation clause comprise the right to navigate the Yang-tse-Kiang to Chung King, and also the Woon Sung River and the canals leading to Soo Chow and Hank Chow and the right to import machinery and certain goods duty free and to establish factories. These concessions are not exclusive to Japan. They naturally extended to European, powers, in virtue of the favored nation clause. In securing these privileges for all Japan expects the approval of all the powers. The reported offensive and defensive alliance does not exist."

Li Hung Chang and his suite started home to China escorted to their vessels by a guard of honor, and Count Ito and Viscount Matsu, the officers who negotiated the treaty of peace were received in audience by the emperor on their return to Hiroshima. He expressed himself as entirely satisfied with the principal points of the treaty which added much to the glory of the empire, and highly pleased at the signal service rendered by them. On the afternoon of April 22 the following proclamation was issued by the Japanese mikado:

"Through peace, national prosperity is best promoted. Unfortunately, the rupture of relations with China forced upon us a war which, after a lapse of ten months, is not yet ended. During this period our ministers, in concert with the army, navy and diet, have done all in their power to further our aims in obedience to our instructions. Our ardent desire, with the assistance of bur subjects, in loyalty and sincerity, is to restore peace and thereby attain our object—the promotion of national prosperity. Now that peace is negotiated and armistice proclaimed, a permanent cessation of hostilities is near at hand. The terms of peace fixed by our minister of state give us complete satisfaction. The peace and glory thus secured renders the present a fitting time to enlighten you as to the course of our future policy.

"We are rejoiced at the recent victories which have enhanced the glory of our empire. At the same time we are aware that the end of the road which must be traversed by the empire in the march of civilization is still far distant and remains yet to be attained. We therefore hope, in common with our loyal subjects, that we shall always guard against self-contentedness, but in a spirit of modesty and humility strive to perfect out military defense without falling into extremes. In short, it is our wish that the government and the people alike shall work to a common end and that our subjects of all classes strive each in his sphere for the purpose of laying the foundation of permanent prosperity.

"It is hereby definitely made known that no countenance will be given by us to such as, through conceit at the recent victories, may offer insult to another state or injure our relations with friendly powers, especially as regards China. After the exchange of the ratifications of the treaty of peace, frendship should be restored and endeavors made to increase more than ever before the relations of good neighborhood. It is our pleasure that our subjects pay due respect to these expressed wishes."

Let us now take a hasty glance in conclusion at the condition in which the three countries with which we have dealt are left at the close of the war, and the prospects for their future. The Japanese government is in the hands of a progressive and able emperor, supported by a cabinet composed of the foremost statesmen of the east, and reigning under constitutional forms. Naturally elated by the wonderful success of their arms, it is to be fairly expected that they will continue in the progressiveness which has marked the island empire's history since Perry opened the door for western light to shine in. In the east they should become by virtue of the abilities the dominant power, unless by chance the Chinese have learned a lesson which they will put into effect. With the constant impression of western civilization upon them, it is to be hoped that the Japanese will acquire a firm moral and intellectual basis for the manners of life that their intelligence and activity have adopted, and become in the best sense a civilized nation. What they lack now to reach this point, are the things that can only come by a succession of generations of civilization. Wonderful record as the last forty years have made for the island empire, they have not given to that realm yet a complete and rounded civilization. The best friends of Japan hope and believe that she will not permit her splendid successes of the war to make her over lordly and conceited.

China is the enigma of the east. It is certain that the influences of their defeat will open the Chinese empire very rapidly to modern civilization and investment. But whether or not China retain her conservatism and refuse to adopt the things that are interspersed among her people can scarcely be predicted. The established system has received a severe shock from the Japanese victory, and surely a new or civilized and more vigorous one will take its place. It is an actual fact that so far as can be said by those most familiar with the country, the knowledge that the war has even been in progress has probably not yet penetrated to the confines of the empire, so poor are the means of communication and so indifferent are the people of one region to the things that are happening to those of another province. An experienced traveler in China relates that he penetrated from Shanghai southwestward through China towards India immediately after the destruction of the summer palace of the emperor by French and English troops, and the investiture of Peking thirty-five years ago. The expedition was considered dangerous, as the antagonism of the whole country, smarting under humiliation and defeat was to be feared. On arriving at Ichang, eleven hundred miles from the coast, the war news had just come to the knowledge of the government officials; three hundred miles farther west there was absolute ignorance that any war had occurred. At the city of Pingshan, two thousand miles west of the coast, the party heard of a Mohammedan insurrection of some years standing, ranging in the province of Yun-nan, but the bare fact of such an important disturbance had not yet reached the coast. Certain it is however, that if China does assimilate the lesson that she has had a chance to learn, a new power will exist in the east that will need to be watched by western nations.

As to Corea it is difficult again to prophesy. Should Japan take stringent pains to provide for civilizing that hermit kingdom, it is possible that the work may be done, but so difficult are the political conditions in that peninsula, and so unsympathetic are the Corean rulers and chief men with all western ideas of progress, that the task will be a bitter one. If Japan maintains the independence of Corea in its purity, that must mean that she will keep her own hands out of Corean affairs. This is scarcely to be expected, for the energetic empire has imposed upon herself the task of reforming Corea, and it is sure that she will make strenuous efforts to do it.

As one result of the war between China and Japan must be to increase the points of contact between the eastern and western worlds, the fortune of parties and the evolution of domestic politics in those countries must, in future, command to a greater degree than in the past, the attention of American and European observers. Political evolution has been rapid in Japan. Changes which in Anglo-Saxon countries have been the slow product of centuries, are, in this portion of what has been called "the unchanging east," crowded into little more than a single generation. What may be done in Corea and China cannot be told. But the fairest prophecy would be that the horrors of war will be utilized, by the influence of time and a better understanding, to improve and modernize the Orient.

THE END